Indian Agriculture

T0293591

This volume examines the transitions in Indian agriculture since the 1980s and emphasizes the role of neoliberal policies and their impact. The essays presented here deal with a range of pertinent and contemporary issues, including global food security, livelihoods of agricultural labourers, and public and private investment. These weave together glimpses of the impasse faced by petty commodity producers (marginal and small farmers) and their subsequent economic distress and social exclusion. Comprehensive in analysis, this book will be useful to scholars and researchers of agricultural economics, political economy, political science and public policy.

Parmod Kumar is Professor and Head, Agricultural Development and Rural Transformation Centre, Institute for Social and Economic Change, Bengaluru, Karnataka, India. He has authored many research volumes and articles in national and international journals. He leads several research projects sponsored by the Government of India and international organizations. He is the editor of the *Journal of Social and Economic Development* and part of the editorial board of *Indian Journal of Agricultural Marketing* and *Agricultural Situation in India*. He was conferred the IDRC India Social Science Research Award for his work on the public distribution system.

S. Mohanakumar is Associate Professor at the Institute of Development Studies, Jaipur (IDSJ), Rajasthan, India. Previously he worked as Scientist in the Economics Research Division of the Rubber Research Institute of India, Kottayam, Kerala, under the Ministry of Commerce & Industry, Government of India. He has taught decentralized planning and development at the Kerala Institute of Local Administration (KILA) in Thrissur, Kerala. He is also a social activist and is currently active in the environmental movement against granite quarrying at Mookkunnimala, Thiruvananthapuram, Kerala. He writes extensively on the political economy of agriculture, development, wage labour and related issues.

Indian Agriculture

Performance, growth and challenges

Essays in honour of
Ramesh Kumar Sharma

Edited by Parmod Kumar and S. Mohanakumar

Routledge
Taylor & Francis Group

LONDON AND NEW YORK

First published 2016
by Routledge
2 Park Square, Milton Park, Abingdon, Oxon OX14 4RN

and by Routledge
711 Third Avenue, New York, NY 10017

First issued in paperback 2017

Routledge is an imprint of the Taylor & Francis Group, an informa business

British Library Cataloguing-in-Publication Data
A catalogue record for this book is available from the British Library

Library of Congress Cataloging-in-Publication Data
A catalog record has been requested for this book.

ISBN 13: 978-1-138-48846-5 (pbk)
ISBN 13: 978-1-138-96203-3 (hbk)

Typeset in Galliard
by Apex CoVantage, LLC

Contents

Figures

Tables

Contributors

Vinoj Abraham is Associate Professor at the Centre for Development Studies, Thiruvananthapuram, Kerala.

Mondira Bhattacharya is Associate Fellow at the National Council of Applied Economic Research (NCAER), New Delhi.

Elumalai Kannan is Associate Professor at the Agricultural Development and Rural Transformation Centre, Institute for Social and Economic Change, Bengaluru, Karnataka.

Shakti Kumar is Assistant Professor in the Department of Economics and Rural Development, Dr. R.M.L. Avadh University, Faizabad, Uttar Pradesh.

Rajendra P. Mamgain is Professor at Giri Institute of Development Studies, Lucknow, Uttar Pradesh.

S. Manasi is Associate Professor at the Centre for Research in Urban Affairs, Institute for Social and Economic Change, Bengaluru, Karnataka.

Surendra Meher is a faculty member at the Department of Economics, Babasaheb Bhimrao Ambedkar University, Lucknow, Uttar Pradesh.

Bibhu Prasad Nayak is Fellow at the Energy and Resource Institute (TERI), New Delhi.

Srinivasulu Rajendran works at AVRDC – The World Vegetable Centre, Eastern and Southern Africa, Tanzania.

Promodita Sathish is Additional Economic Adviser, Ministry of Information and Broadcasting, New Delhi, and belongs to the Indian Economic Services (IES).

Sachin Kumar Sharma is Assistant Professor at the Centre for WTO Studies, Indian Institute of Foreign Trade, New Delhi.

Jitender Singh is currently Deputy Director in Office of the Economic Adviser, DIPP, Ministry of Commerce & Industry, Government of India, and belongs to Indian Economic Service (IES).

Foreword

As a friend and admirer of Professor R. K. Sharma, it is with much happiness that I welcome this collection of essays prepared in his honour by his younger colleagues and others as a token of their respect and affection for him. The development strategy and policy issues highlighted in these essays are currently at the top of the policy agenda in India and several developing countries. More worrisome is the fact that the developing countries have not been able to get a firm policy grip over them. In fact, in India the situation is so critical that the observers who until yesterday were describing India along with China as the two fastest growing economies in the world, are almost overnight compelled to describe India as a case of policy paralysis with an economy drifting towards stagnation.

In terms of what is observable with the help of data and indicators, the policy paralysis has three dimensions. Efforts by the Government of India (GoI) to accelerate growth and make it inclusive remain infructuous; the latest assessment by the IMF (September, 2013) shows the likely growth rate in 2013–14 to be only 3.5 per cent; second, the measures taken by the Reserve Bank of India (RBI) to combat inflation are not having any impact at all; and third, the NAC (National Advisory Council) programmes based on the criteria of rights, entitlements and empowerment are now being viewed by growing numbers as purveyors of doles rather than contributors to human development. The common citizen must indeed be alarmed when he finds the three top-level policymakers – GoI, RBI and NAC – more like adversaries than a cohesive team. A little reflection would show that the three face a common barrier of exclusiveness in Indian society. Whether it is protection against inflation or fruits of growth or improvements in human development, they bypass many, if not most, of those desperately in need of these benefits.

A theme which runs through the essays in this collection is the theme of exclusiveness in Indian society. The essays provide glimpses of growth and consequences of exclusiveness in the agricultural sector and rural areas, which are the principal victims of social inequities and injustice rampant in our society. How did exclusiveness originate, and how did it grow to become the monster it is now? Let me present a layman's view. When processes of growth and development were initiated in independent India, the emerging patterns and trends resembled those predicted by conventional economics and were also observed in the currently developed countries during their development and change processes. Diversification of the economy, shifting of focus from the primary sectors to the secondary and tertiary sectors, migration from rural areas to towns and cities, breakdown of traditional institutions and relations were all observed as described in the textbooks. However, there were also effects which conventional economics assumed would be eliminated with economic growth and development in the larger economy but were not in India and in most of the developing countries. Exclusiveness had its roots and was nourished right from day one by these outcomes consisting of inequities in traditional societies, inability of the masses to share the fruits of development and concentration of resources and power in the hands of the few who dominated and scaled the heights of affluence. Those at the top knew what was going on but kept mum and supported the processes. Those who suffered, the vast masses, were too weak to protest and remained mute spectators. As a result, exclusiveness seeped and continues to seep into the very structure of the society. Today, what we all condemn as exclusive growth is merely a symptom of the exclusiveness assimilated by the societal structure.

The essays in this volume present rigorous and detailed analyses of the sector/programme on which they focus. Taken together they provide a comprehensive perspective on what the volume title aptly calls, 'Indian agriculture: performance, growth and challenges'. The essays cover in their analyses the exclusiveness encountered in their sector/programme. At the sector/programme level, exclusiveness could appear only as one among the numerous implementation problems faced in the field. It is when we put together the glimpses scattered over the essays that we can begin to see exclusiveness as a monster threatening the very stability and development of Indian society. Viewed across essays, two messages stand out loud and clear. First, Indian agriculture is fighting a losing battle on the critical front of raising productivity which is now the principal source for growth and development. This comes out well in studies on total factor productivity (TFP) as also in sectors like horticulture with substantial potential for the future. A key finding is that agriculture is unlikely to achieve a 4 per cent per annum growth rate, which the policymaker considers essential for sustained growth in the economy. Second, equally unlikely are any substantial improvements in the welfare of the poor and the excluded. Considering the factors at both national and global levels, the prospects for food security are described as 'grim'. The non-farm activities are not developing adequately to absorb the millions who are being pushed out of agriculture. There is proliferation of low productivity activities in the informal sector, which generate poverty rather than eradicate it. Even new institutional forms like contract farming and retailer chains reaching out directly to farmers are seen to prefer dealing with only the better-off sections among the farmers. I am convinced that whether the changing face of India eventually wears a smile or a scowl depends on our readiness to confront the monster of exclusiveness at the societal level. I consider this perspective as a valuable contribution made by this volume. I commend the editors and contributors for doing a fine job. My dear friend Professor R. K. Sharma has every reason to feel fulfilled, as those whom he trained to walk are now ready for marathons!

Professor V. M. Rao
Former Member, Commission for Agriculture Costs
and Prices and Honorary Professor, Institute for Social
and Economic Change, Bangalore

Preface

This volume is written in honour of our great guru Professor Ramesh Kumar Sharma. Professor Sharma, popularly known among the students of the Centre for the Study of Regional Development (CSRD) at Jawaharlal Nehru University (JNU) as R. K. Sharma Sir has been a great source of inspiration for his students. One can imagine his popularity and the keen interest he bestows on his students from the fact that he has guided and aptly supervised 26 Doctor of Philosophy (Ph.D.) students who have successfully been awarded doctorate degrees. He also ably supervised not less than 50 Master of Philosophy (M.Phil.) students. Besides, there were several students who successfully completed their M. Phil. and registered for Ph.D. but left their doctorate programme in the middle due to having obtained a good job or quit due to other reasons. In other words, he has almost succeeded in scoring a century of research students.

Therefore, this volume speaks about the honour and respect he has earned among his students as he always gave preference to his students over his family as well as his personal obligations. He has always been available to his students, and we the students never had to seek an appointment for meeting with him during the course of our research work. He helped the students not only academically but also in other ways by taking a great personal interest. We the students of Professor Sharma are indebted not only to him but also to a great extent to his family as well. By writing this volume in his honour, we (his students) have tried to record our gratitude to Professor Sharma and his family members.

This volume is a collection of 14 chapters written by scholars who have all completed their doctorate degree with Professor Ramesh Kumar Sharma. There are others who have completed their Ph.D.s with Professor Sharma but due to some reason could not contribute to this volume.

This collection was initiated by the editors, and all the authors took a keen interest in sparing time to write a chapter each. After receiving all the chapters, a one-day workshop was organized in CSRD, JNU on 13 August 2011. The chapters were circulated to the discussants in advance. The chapters were divided into three themes, and for each theme two discussants were invited with advance draft of the chapters. The workshop was successfully completed along with the presentation by the authors, the inputs from the discussants and two hours of open discussion for each theme. After the workshop, authors were asked to revise their chapters in the light of comments by the discussants and the open discussion. The chapters so obtained were then sent for an anonymous referee's comments. The final chapters contributed by the authors were then audited by Dr Parmod Kumar, one of the editors of this volume. After incorporating all the changes in this long process, the chapters were finalized for publication.

The editors thank the discussants, Dr Seema Bathla, Dr Deepak Mishra, Professor Amresh Dubey (all JNU), Dr Anjani Kumar (NCAP), Dr C.S.C. Shekhar (IEG) and Dr Rakhee Bhattacharya (Rajiv Gandhi Foundation), for their hard work of going through the chapters and providing their discussants' notes on the chapters, which proved very useful in improving the quality of this volume. The editors also express their gratitude to the anonymous referees for their able referee comments that helped the editors in bringing the volume to order. The editors also express gratitude to the Chairperson, Faculty and Administrative Staff of CSRD, JNU, for providing their space and other facilities for organizing the workshop in the CSRD. Professor Sharma not only contributed to the discussion but also made arrangements for tea and dinner after the workshop. The editors thank all who helped directly or indirectly in the compilation of this volume.

Finally we (the editors) convey our approbation to Professor V. M. Rao for accepting our request for drafting an apt Foreword for this volume within a short span of time.

We expect that the findings of this study will be useful to policymakers as well as academicians interested in issues related to agriculture. The book will be helpful to planners, policymakers, researchers, students and the academy.

Parmod Kumar
S. Mohanakumar

Chapter I

Introduction

Parmod Kumar and S. Mohanakumar

A transformation is taking place in the basic structure of Indian agriculture during the recent period, especially in the post liberalization period whereby the crop sector is losing out to horticulture, husbandry and other allied activities. There has been a fast decline in the contribution overall of the agriculture and allied sectors to the gross domestic product (GDP), but the relative share of the economically active population eking out a living from farming remains unjustifiably high. The contribution of agriculture comprising primarily crop production and livestock sectors to GDP has declined to 12 per cent during the eleventh plan period, while the contribution of sub-sectors in agriculture and allied activities, namely forestry and logging (1.7 per cent) and fishing (0.7 per cent) have been relatively stable. Capital formation in agriculture has been static, around 7 per cent of the gross capital formation in the economy for many years. Although the quinquennial rate of growth in agriculture during the eleventh plan period was (3.3 per cent) higher than the rate of growth of the tenth plan period (2.2 per cent), it lagged behind the targeted growth rate of 4 per cent for agriculture during the eleventh plan period. In the twelfth plan period, agriculture is poised to grow by 4 per cent to back up the 9 per cent growth in the overall economy. Further, food grain production is envisaged to grow by 2 per cent and non-food grain production by 6 per cent.

On an average, a household in India spends half of its income on food items in which cereals alone account for 15 per cent of the total consumption (Chengappa 2013). Under a situation of trailing growth in agriculture, sectoral imbalance would drive the price of farm produce up. A higher price for farm produce would deprive a vast chunk of the rural population from their entitlement to daily provision. Further, the disparity in the growth performance between farm and non-farm sectors has deterred capital from agriculture, which brought the productivity growth to a standstill by the close of the eighth plan period. Around 200 million hectares of land (62 per cent of the total cropped area) in the country is rain-fed. The area under irrigation still remains around 48 per cent of the gross cropped area, and the potential of bringing more cultivated area under irrigation is limited, which may further deplete the ground water level in arid and semi-arid zones.

Further, cropwise distribution of area under irrigation varies markedly from 91.70 per cent for wheat to 14.4 per cent for coarse cereals (Government of India 2012). The yield growth of food grain production in rain-fed areas has either stagnated or even turned negative in certain cases (Government of India 2012). The rain-fed area comprising semi-arid and arid zones accounts for 56 per cent of the total cropped area and 48 per cent of the food-growing region in the country. The importance of perspective planning for agriculture becomes more relevant given the fact that 77 per cent of pulses, 66 per cent of oils seeds and 45 per cent of cereals are produced in the rain-fed areas. Poor soil management system, inadequate availability of seeds, water, and partial or near-total withdrawal of the market support system and a further squeeze on the spending on research and development (R&D) in agriculture have played havoc with farming in the arid and semi-arid zones. The economic implications of the relative backwardness of farming in arid and semi-arid zones stem from the fact that the farm-dependent population and the proportion of rural poor in the primary production sector are higher in these areas compared to irrigated zones. The observed variation in the median agricultural income across states is a reflection of the regional differences in the material conditions of farming and animal husbandry. A farmer earned Rs. 3,535 per annum from crop production and livestock in Andhra Pradesh while a farmer in Punjab earned Rs. 52,129 during 2004–5 (Desai *et al.* 2010). Moreover, 11 per cent of farms have been making losses in crop production resulting in a negative net income from agriculture and allied sectors (Desai *et al.* 2010). The observation that educated households tend to rent-out their patch of land and less educated households rent-in reveals that farming has ceased to be a vocation worth engaging in for people who have alternative avenues of livelihood.

The dismal performance of agriculture and allied sectors for the past few decades has caused resource outflow from the farm sector, particularly in the crop production segment. The resource outflow from the crop production sector took several turns such as: (1) land transfer to non-farm activities. In areas where the state directly mediated the market transfer, it attracted resistance from the farming community, resulting in direct and forced evacuation of the farm-dependent population by the state; (2) income-induced shift in the consumption pattern has changed the cropping pattern from coarse cereals, cereals and pulses to commercial crops for the market, (3) cattle rearing has almost ceased to be a complementary economic activity to the farm sector, and the surge in the demand for milk products has separated cattle rearing from the farm fold to a commercial activity on a large scale; (4) international demand for oil and other non-food crops has resulted in large-scale cultivation of crops such as natural rubber, Bt cotton, oil seeds and other crops meant for the production of oil substitutes; (5) for marginal and small farmers and cattle rearers, their vocation has ceased to be the primary source of livelihood; (6) wage labourers have migrated to the construction sector or are engaged in petty trading in urban slums with little qualitative improvement in their living standards; (7) the stagnant segment in the labour force who cannot find alternative avenues of livelihood outside the rural area are forced to be contented with engaging in different vocations or work under the Mahatma Gandhi National Rural Employment Guarantee Act (MGNREGA) and thereby lose their identities as farm workers. This has resulted in the weakening of collective bargaining, decline in unionization and building up of political consciousness; (8) the government mediates the transfer of farm land to non-farm activities by tagging peasants and small farmers, as part of the process, as neither wage labourers nor petty producers.

The slow growth in agriculture and allied sectors has affected the rural labour market too. There has been severe shortage of farm workers for agricultural operations. The crop production sector attracts less labour from the rural market. Wage labourers in the younger age group from rural labour households have migrated to the non-farm sector in urban areas in search of livelihood. Farmers have been struggling to retain their land for cultivation and assets for livelihood. Private capital involvement in (R&D) of technology in agriculture has been lukewarm since the 1980s (Ramasamy 2013). It is an outcome of a complex set of factors playing upon one another as cause and effect, including non-remunerative returns from agriculture, price volatility and uncertainty in farm income and lack of complementary investment from the public sector.

Research in agriculture as an area of study shot into prominence in the first half of the twentieth century. Mainstream research in agricultural economics in India is focused on the supply side. The demand-side constraints are assumed either non-existent or trivial. The supply side-centred paradigm draws heavily on the American tradition of research in agricultural economics, which originated between 1900 and 1922. The technical competence of agricultural economists is mostly confined to modelling. The analysis is primarily driven by the objective of establishing the association between agriculture and commerce (Fox 1987: 55). To a great extent, the tradition of research in agricultural economics in India is closer to the American tradition. For a comprehensive and contemporary understanding of developments in the primary commodity production sector, the purview of analysis of agricultural economics has to be extended to social sciences, with emphasis on policies of the state and their consequences on different social classes of the farm population and the economy at large. The analysis of the agricultural production process from the perspective of different social classes and the state is imperative to contextualize the stress in the farm front since the introduction of the new economic regime since 1991. The present volume is an attempt to weave together different facets of agriculture in a liberalized market economy in India.

An overview

This volume provides a comprehensive analysis of the different aspects of agriculture and allied sectors from the perspective of different competing paradigms during the past two to three decades. Analysis of the primary commodity production sector has been extended from its tradition of focussing on production relations and agrarian transformations to incorporate ecological, environmental, gender and livelihood concerns in the present day. Different facets of change in the primary agricultural sector have been justifiably handled in the book from a mix of competing paradigms. The thrust on wage rate and labour issues lies in the fact that the regional differences in the daily wage rate of rural labour are an act purposely calibrated by different apparatuses of the state. Real wage is directly related to the reproduction cost of labour, and reproduction cost is largely influenced by the interventions of the state. The part on crop diversification addresses the crucial question of state-mediated shift in cropping patterns. Crop diversification, particularly in Asia and Latin America, has assumed immense importance from the perspective of food security, employment and livelihood of socially and economically vulnerable sections of society. The last part on agriculture market, trade and institutions, covers the viewpoint of neoliberal institutions' entry into agriculture and their impact on peasants and labourers in the agricultural sector.

In summary, the essays presented in the book are organized as chapters whereby each essay enters as a chapter in the book. The book is compiled into three main themes in three parts, namely (1) Farm Production, Subsidy and Investment; (2) Farm Labour, Livelihood Diversification and Nonfarm Employment; (3) Agriculture Market, Trade and Institutions.

The part 'Farm Production, Subsidy and Investment' includes six chapters. The first chapter written by the editors introduces the book and presents its overview. The second chapter written by Parmod Kumar is titled 'Global food security: issues and challenges'. The part on production in the book solemnly starts with the issue of food security. Food security has become important not only for a developing country like India but also in the global context. The chapter presents existing trends in food production and area under various crops and their yield level in the leading countries across the globe along with their trends in five continents. Growth in world food production, since the 1950s, has kept ahead of population growth, despite the addition of some 3.5 billion extra mouths. The average per capita cereal production peaked at 371 kilograms in the early 1980s and again fell to around 350 kilograms in the mid-1990s. Since 1984, the world's population has been growing faster than cereal production. Looking at the period 1980–2010, against the rising cereal production in the 1980s with some fluctuations in the 1990s, the area under cereals has moved in the opposite direction since the 1980s and with higher velocity in the 1990s. On the one hand, the world production of cereals increased from 1.5 billion tonnes in 1980 to 2.4 billion tonnes in 2010. The area under cereals, on the other hand, decreased from 717 million hectares in 1980 to 673 million hectares in 2000, and since then there has been slight increase in the area after 2006 up to 683 million hectares in 2010. During this three-decade period, world production of cereals increased at a significant rate of 1.3 per cent per annum, while area decelerated at –0.2 per cent per annum. In the case of pulses, the total world production increased from 41 million tonnes in 1980 to 68 million tonnes in 2010 with wide fluctuations in the 1990s. Similarly, world area under pulses increased from 61 million hectares in 1980 to 76 million hectares in 2010 with similar fluctuations in area during the 1990s. Oilseeds production saw the most spectacular increase during the past three decades. The world production (nine major oilseeds) increased by threefold from 130 million tonnes in 1980 to 400 million tonnes in 2010. The area under oilseeds also increased during this period but by a lesser extent, only less than twofold from 109 million hectares to 196 million hectares.

This chapter also looks into the trends in demand for food for human consumption as well as other uses among major countries and regions of the world. It further highlights the existing estimates on demand and supply in the medium-term future available from various sources. The world human consumption of cereals increased from 630 million tonnes in 1980 to 966 million tonnes in 2007. The aggregate consumption increased from 1.4 billion tonnes in the 1980 to more than 1.8 billion tonnes in 2000 and further to almost 2 billion tonnes in 2007. During this almost three-decade period, world aggregate consumption of cereals increased at a significant rate of 1.2 per cent per annum while human consumption increased at an even higher rate of 1.5 per cent per annum. It is interesting to note that whereas human demand constituted only 49 per cent of aggregate demand of total cereals, the proportion of human demand to total demand for rice and wheat was much higher, around 85 and 72 per cent, respectively. In other words, a much higher proportion of course grains like millets, maize and barley are used either as feed for animals or for industrial processing including their use in manufacturing alcoholic beverages as well as biofuel. The proportion of coarse grains used for human consumption directly (without processing) turns out to be only around one per cent.

In the case of pulses, the total world human consumption increased from 28 million tonnes in 1980 to 43 million tonnes in 2007. The aggregate consumption of pulses increased from 40 million tonnes in 1980 to 56 million tonnes in 1990. It came down to 55 million tonnes in 2000 but increased to 60 million tonnes in 2007. World human consumption of edible oils increased from 21 million tonnes in 1980 to 45.5 million tonnes in 2007. However, human consumption was only a minuscule proportion of total consumption of edible oils. The aggregate demand for edible oils was 202 million tonnes in 1980 that increased more than twice to 470 million tonnes in 2007. Thus human demand for edible oils was less than 10 per cent of total demand.

For the whole period, the aggregate demand for cereals increased at the rate of 1.2 per cent per annum. On the supply side, world production of cereals increased at a significant rate of 1.3 per cent per annum from 1980 to 2010. Thus, although production increased slightly more than increase in aggregate demand, demand for human consumption increased slightly more than that of production during the whole period. Thus, overall production has barely been sufficient to meet the aggregate demand for cereals. For pulses, the aggregate demand increased at 1.04 per cent per annum compared to the 1.08 per cent per annum increase in world production during the whole period of the study. The human demand for the same time period increased at the slightly higher rate of 1.21 per cent per annum. In consonance with world production, world consumption of edible oils increased consistently throughout the period since the 1980s. The growth in human as well as aggregate demand for edible oils was positive across all the continents, and the aggregate demand increased at around 3 per cent per annum during the whole period of the study in consonance with the growth rate of production of oilseeds.

The chapter concludes that although increase in oilseeds production was quite impressive, the recent stagnation and possible fall in world grain production would be of serious concern, as factors other than population growth would continue to push grain demand upwards. The demand for grain as feed increases rapidly once income increases beyond a certain level. Whereas projected growth in cereal consumption for food was very close to population growth, expected growth in feed grain demand was more than twice the expected population growth. The future of world food security looks grim given the adverse effect of the impending climate change which is already visible in some way or the other.

The issue of public and private investment is raised in the third chapter titled 'Public and private investment in Indian agriculture' authored by Surendra Meher. This chapter examines the state level trends and magnitude of household components of investment in agriculture using the 'All India Debt and Investment Survey' data compiled by the RBI. It also examines the factors that influence private investment and output in agriculture at the state level. The author finds that there has been a clear decline of public investment in Indian agriculture based on the Central Statistical Organization (CSO) series particularly during the 1980s. Even after broadening the concept of public investment by including several items that are essential for agricultural growth and development, the trend showed a clear decline. It was observed that the proportion of households reporting capital formation in farm business declined from 19.3 per cent in 1971 to 10.3 per cent in 2002–3. Non-farm business, on the other hand, had an impressive growth rate of average value for both cultivator and non-cultivator households in rural sectors of the country. There was a broad diversification of rural households towards non-farm business among both cultivators and non-cultivators.

There was a large variation in the value of fixed capital formation per cultivator household as in the states of Gujarat, Haryana, Maharashtra, Punjab, Tamil Nadu and Rajasthan, the average value per cultivator household being much higher than the national average in 2002–3. In contrast, in the Eastern states, namely Orissa, West Bengal and Bihar, the average value of capital formation in farm business among the cultivator households was remarkably lower than the national average. The regression analysis revealed that cultivators in states having better agricultural infrastructure including canal irrigation, better roads, level of literacy and institutional credit tend to have higher investment in their farm business and higher output in their agriculture. It was found that canal irrigation was the most important factor inducing private investment and enhancing agricultural production. The chapter concludes that the states in the Eastern region lag behind as far as rural and agricultural infrastructure is concerned, and so public investment should be undertaken to improve and make their agriculture more productive and remunerative. Reduction of wasteful expenditure in the name of subsidy may be subsequently phased out, which could help generate more resources for public investment.

As the consumption basket in India is diversifying towards high-value commodities, like fruits and vegetables, milk and meat products, there is consequential diversification on the supply side as well. On the one hand, foodgrains are being replaced by non-foodgrains and fruits and vegetables, and on the other, the crop sector is giving way to animal husbandry, fishery and non-farm activities. The fourth chapter looks into the supply-side diversification in the crops sector towards fruit and vegetable crops. Authored by Srinivasulu Rajendran, the chapter 'Growth in fruit and vegetable crops: emerging trends and patterns' looks into how diversification is taking place in different states. It examines the patterns and trends emerging in fruits and vegetables grown across the states in India. The chapter also looks into the factors that contribute to growth and thereby adds value to the existing knowledge base for policy implications.

The study shows that extensive area had been brought under fruit and vegetable cultivation in almost all the states, but the proportion of land under fruits and vegetables in total for horticulture crops varies across the states. In states like Himachal Pradesh, Maharashtra, Jammu and Kashmir, Andhra Pradesh and Tripura nearly half of the horticulture land was devoted to fruit cultivation by 2009–10. On the other hand, in Haryana, West Bengal, Bihar, Punjab, Uttar Pradesh, Assam and Orissa, vegetable crops dominated in horticultural areas. The findings of the study indicate that surge in the production of these crops, collectively and individually, was more an outcome of improvement in yield rather than area expansion during 1993–4 and 2000–1. Increased use of modern seeds, chemical fertilizers and electricity together contributed to increase in productivity. This scenario somewhat changed during the 2000s, as all horticulture crops experienced expansion in production due to both area and yield, where a higher contribution was made by area than yield. In contrast, a relatively lower contribution of yield indicates technological gaps and weak extension services during this period. It also points to the fact that the National Horticulture Mission which was introduced in 2005 for developing the horticulture sector largely remained lopsided in its outcomes. It has so far remained highly successful in expanding the area but failed to scale up the productivity levels which it was expected to promote.

The chapter argues that the horticulture sector has huge potential and can assume an important role in uplifting the socio-economic conditions of people living in rural areas in developing countries like India. In order to realize its full potential, it is imperative to address the issues of decline or stagnant fruits and vegetable yield, given that land will become a scarce resource in the years to come. Until now, government policies have remained overtly supportive to area expansion over technology improvement and its real-time use at the farm level. At present the challenge is not only to augment productivity through region-specific technological advancements, but also to improve soil fertility, establish strong extension services networks, assure irrigation and deal with the growing marginalization of land. The fast-shrinking agricultural land due to its diversion to non-farm activities and the fast-evolving occupational structure in the country where mass exodus is taking place from rural areas to urban areas in search of better jobs will further cause problems in the development of the horticulture sector in the country.

The fifth chapter, authored by Elumalai Kannan, presents 'Total factor productivity growth and its determinants in agriculture'. The contribution of technology in output growth is measured by the growth of total factor productivity (TFP). There is empirical evidence to suggest that TFP growth declined during the 1980s. However, with increase in public and private investment during the current decade, the present status of TFP growth is not well researched. Moreover, very few studies are available at present on TFP in Southern Indian states like Karnataka. This chapter is an attempt to fill the gap in the literature. The chapter estimates trends in the TFP of important crops in the State of Karnataka. From the policy perspective also, it is important to assess and understand the determinants of TFP so as to take appropriate initiatives for accelerating agricultural output growth. The TFP growth is estimated for ten major crops in Karnataka, and the factors affecting it are analysed at the state level. The widely used Tornqvist–Theil Index was utilized for constructing an aggregate output and aggregate input index of individual crops. Two outputs and nine inputs were used to construct the output and input index. The growth analysis revealed that the yield of most crops, in particular foodgrains, declined during 1980–1 to 1989–90 leading to stagnation in production. However, during 1990–1 to 2007–8 there was a reversal of growth in production and yield for some food and non-food crops. Among various growth promoting factors, public investment in agriculture played an important role in accelerating growth.

Although the TFP of most crops registered decline in productivity growth during the 1990s, there was a revival in terms of positive TFP growth recently. For Karnataka State as a whole, input and output indices registered a growth rate of 0.77 and 1.85 per cent, respectively, during 1980–1 to 2007–8. TFP increased at 1.09 per cent per annum contributing about 58.67 per cent to the total output growth. Further, the analysis of determinants of TFP indicates that the government expenditure on research, education and extension, canal irrigation, rainfall and the balanced use of fertilizers was the important driver of crop productivity in Karnataka. A low TFP growth implies that there is a huge scope for increasing agricultural production through new technological breakthrough by enhancing investment in research and technology and rural infrastructure. More public and private investment should be encouraged in underdeveloped regions of the state through providing incentives and a favourable policy environment.

Continuing the debate on raising TFP by raising the level of investment, the next chapter presents a discussion on agricultural subsidies and their relation to investment. The sixth chapter titled 'Agricultural input subsidy in Haryana: some critical aspects', is authored by Sachin Kumar Sharma. Given the context, this chapter analyses some of the issues and problems related to input subsidies to the agricultural sector with a case study of Haryana. The study focuses on the estimation of three input subsidies, namely electricity, canal irrigation and fertilizer. Haryana is an agriculturally developed state which also generates considerable amount of foodgrain surplus. However, intensive use of subsidized inputs has led to many problems like water logging, salinity, over exploitation of ground water and fiscal burden on the exchequer of Electricity Boards and Irrigation Departments. The results of this study show an upward trend of input subsidy in Haryana over the past three decades.

The subsidies have placed an unsustainable burden on the finances of the central and state governments, which has severely limited the public sector's capacity for financing investment in agriculture and irrigation. The pricing policy of various inputs has led to cultivation of water-intensive crops in Haryana leading to the problem of water logging and salinity in certain areas. Subsidies on irrigation through canal water and electricity have led to the distortion of the cropping pattern in favour of water-intensive crops. Similarly, underpricing of electricity has led to the depletion of ground water in some areas. The need of the hour is institutional reforms and replacement of subsidy by public investment that should be targeted at small and marginal farmers. However, before increasing user charges or rationalizing input subsidies, there is a need to improve the quality of services, as farmers are willing to pay if they are assured of reliable services. The present situation if not improved may lead to unsustainable agriculture with lots of problems like soil erosion, salinity, low productivity.

The second part of this book pertains to Farm Labour, Livelihood Diversification and Non-farm Employment and contains five chapters. Under this theme, the issues related to wage rate, farm employment and crop and enterprise diversification are discussed. The seventh chapter on 'Determinants of agricultural wages: a panel data analysis' is authored by Promodita Sathish. This chapter attempts to find out determinants of agricultural wages within the basic framework of demand and supply of labour. Panel data regression analysis has been adopted to identify the determinants of wages for the period 1960–1 to 2005–6. The chapter reveals that occupational diversification was the most important determinant of real wages in the agricultural sector. The responsiveness of real wages to demand-side variables declined during the pre-reform period and with much higher magnitude during the post-reform period. Consequently, major agricultural variables like labour productivity and irrigation had less impact on agricultural wages during the pre-reform period and even smaller impact during the post-reform period. Further, the effect of labour productivity in determining real wages decreased over time. The responsiveness of wages to irrigation, which was in the form of public investment, also declined over time. Thus, decline in public investment in the agricultural sector during the 1990s not only affected agricultural growth, but also dried up one of the main sources of growth of agricultural wages.

Diversification emerged as the most important determinant of real wages in the agricultural sector, and its responsiveness increased over time, especially during the pre- and post-reform periods. Occupational diversification and irrigation in terms of public investment boosted agricultural infrastructure and were also effective ways of enhancing agricultural wages. It further purports that only a small part of gains in labour productivity is translated into wage increase. Any land- or output-based strategy directed towards betterment of agricultural workers has significantly limited or smaller impact on real wages. Efforts should be focused on the promotion of non-farm opportunities which would siphon off excess workers from the agricultural sector, thus contracting the supply to the agricultural sector and thereby enhancing the wages of agricultural workers. The study also delineates the importance of public investment in irrigation to boost agricultural growth and also enhance wages in the agricultural sector.

The eighth chapter, authored by S. Mohanakumar, titled 'The state, labour and reproduction of low-wage space: experience from Kerala' addresses the question of why the daily wage rates for rural labour, particularly for those in the unorganized segment of the farm sector, differ significantly across districts in a relatively small geographical entity like Kerala. It is argued in the chapter that the state, in general, creates and maintains peripheries by keeping wage low in certain localities within the geographical boundaries of the state. The conventional wage determination model fails to capture the intervention of the state on behalf of capital in the rural labour market. Wage theories, in general, envisage that the value of labour power is cherished in terms of socially determined standard of living or the natural wage rate in the long run. Deviation from the natural wage or long run cost of reproduction of labour (value of labour power) is short-lived and is corrected by the supply-demand conditions in the market. Spatial or regional differences in the value of labour power or wage level within a geographical entity have not been, therefore, of much significance to both the classical and neo-classical framework of analysis. The conceptualization of Marx on the value of labour power gives the scope for an analysis of spatial differences in wages by bringing in the state as an active player in the process of wage determination.

To a great extent, the state, by its programmes and policies, geographically discriminates areas by denying basic infrastructure facilities for human development in order to keep the value of labour power to its minimum possible. Less investment in auxiliary means of production and the modern industrial sector in such backward areas would add on to the size of the relative surplus population, which in turn prevents the wage level from rising. The question why the state geographically discriminates is answered from its class bias that often socially and economically vulnerable sections live in backward areas within the jurisdiction of a local state. The intra-regional differences in wage in Kerala confirmed the hypothesis that the spatial difference in wage is an outcome of the state's bias against the class which is outside the mass base of the ruling class. Although, unionization, collective bargaining and past struggles of the working class are important to keep the wage level high, along with other demand-side variables in the wage determination process, the role of the state is one of the most influential actors in the determination of the value of labour power.

Conventional wage analysis ignores that dimension of the issue. A close perusal of infrastructure facilities for human development by districts in Kerala revealed that industrial establishments by government agencies are less in low-wage districts (backward areas) as compared to high-wage districts. A comparison made between high- and low-wage zones on consumption expenditure and its pattern, house type and other basic amenities of life showed that those indicators were significantly different for both farmer and labour households in high-wage and low-wage zones. The empirical observation that low-wage zones are created and nursed by the state on behalf of the capital for the supply of cheap labour confirms the hypothesis that regional wage differentials are an outcome of a state act compared to other factors influencing the wage levels.

The ninth chapter presents various aspects of child labour in the South Asian region. Titled 'Law, income and child labour in South Asia' the chapter is authored by Shakti Kumar. Child labour exists mostly in poor countries and among the people who are poorer. Poverty in South Asia is characterized by concentration of labour force in the primary sector along with declining share of agriculture in GDP despite having agriculture's dominance in employment provision. The findings of the study highlight that the child labour laws of South Asia pass on the responsibility of combating child labour from the society or nation to parents. However, due to poverty, parental income in South Asia is not sufficient to meet children's needs. Therefore, rather than pass on the responsibility from nation to parents, it should be collectively carried out by all the three because children are the assets of the parents, society and nation as a whole.

The tenth chapter on 'Diversification in rural livelihood in Uttarakhand' by Rajendra P. Mamgain examines the livelihood diversification among rural households in Uttarakhand in the context of both number of occupations and their relative contribution to household income. It measures the intensity of diversification in livelihoods, analyses the underlying factors for determining such diversification and examines the impact of diversification in livelihoods on income levels of households in rural areas of Uttarakhand. It also examines whether diversification in livelihoods is a risk mitigating strategy arising out of vulnerability in the nature of assets, which a household poses; or a profit maximization process wherein a household switches to more secure and high-income earning livelihoods.

Empirical analysis in the chapter clearly shows that highly diversified livelihoods do not result in any marked impact on improving income levels for rural households, and thus, much of the diversification in rural livelihoods is a coping mechanism. The factors that significantly contribute to income generation are availability of land, productive assets, number of principal workers and educational attainment. Diversification of traditional cereal-based agriculture into commercial crops, such as fruit and vegetable production, has significant potential for improving income levels provided it is supported by infrastructure. Thus, a viable and effective development strategy for the mountain areas of Uttarakhand should focus on bringing more land area under cultivation, providing infrastructure facilities like technology, transport, markets and input supply towards promoting large-scale commercial farming. This would also entail providing reasonable food security at subsidized rates to marginal farmers, so that they are encouraged to switch over to commercial farming. Also equally important would be to promote the growth of rural off-farm and non-farm enterprises, and at the same time these are to be supported by infrastructure and various tax incentives. Improving the education and skill levels of the labour force, particularly of women who dominate mountain agriculture, would be of utmost importance for enhancing their existing low levels of productivity and income levels. Particularly, training in adopting improved farm practices, post-harvest techniques, packaging and marketing will be very useful to promote the development of enterprises in the rural areas of Uttarakhand. Findings of the study are relevant for all states with hilly terrains.

The eleventh chapter emphasizes rural non-farm employment aspects under the wage, employment and diversification theme: 'Agrarian distress and rural non-farm sector employment in India' by Vinoj Abraham. This chapter argues for promotion of non-farm employment for raising the level of income of rural households. It looks into the employment effect of the agrarian crisis on the rural economy. In specific terms, it elicits the question of diversification into the rural non-farm sector (RNFS) employment under conditions of crisis. The findings of the chapter reveal that the rural labour market has shown signs of a deepening crisis, with underemployment increasing, participation rates of secondary workers rising, wage stagnation and rising self-employment. Further, owing to the crisis, there was a structural shift in employment towards non-farm work. In the crisis-affected regions, the push factors were largely in operation, while in normal regions, the pull factors were relatively more dynamic in generating RNFS employment. Some factors such as social group had significant effect on both distressed regions and normal regions. The multinomial logit model and marginal effects derived from the model also supported the argument. The analysis points to the fact that the effect of the agrarian crisis is not limited to the agricultural sector, rather it would spread to the input market. Moreover, given the muted effects of pull factors to the RNFS in crisis-affected distress regions, regular policy interventions may not generate the desired result. Rather, the specificities of RNFS in crisis-affected regions need to be understood within this context to stimulate productive employment both in the farm and in the non-farm sectors.

The third part of the book pertains to Agriculture Market, Trade and Institutions and contains three chapters. Institutions play a significant role in the development of any sector, and the same have huge significance in the advancement of technology and its dissemination among the farmers in agriculture. All crops have certain yield potentials. The potential yields of crops are the achievable or attainable yields that are derived through experiments conducted in research stations in various regions across the country by the Indian Council for Agricultural Research (ICAR) and its regional agencies. Crop potentials are derived based on improved technology and the recommended package of practices, which are supposed to be practical and functional in different farm locations. The All India Coordinated Research Projects (AICRP) and Frontline Demonstration surveys conducted by the ICAR have found evidences of large gaps in crop yield in the farmers' fields where improved technology has been adopted and what is obtained with existing practices followed by farmers. This yield gap is mainly caused by improper extension services, resulting in insufficient know-how of farmers and hence is called 'extension gap'. Due to stagnating crop yields in recent years, it is important to understand whether the genetic yield ceiling has been reached for principal crops and, if not, to identify factors that are not allowing yields to increase.

The twelfth chapter titled 'Nature and extent of yield gaps in principal crops in India', authored by Mondira Bhattacharya attempts to find the difference between achievable potential yields and the actual yields in both physical and value terms attained for 20 principal crops in various regions of India and also analyses the crop- and region-specific factors accounting for yield gaps. The study is based on data from both primary and secondary sources. The study found that yield gaps in physical terms exist for all the principal crops in the country, with potential yields being much higher than actual yields. Among cereals, the yield gap was highest for sorghum (212.04 per cent) and lowest for wheat (28.22 per cent).

Among pulses, it was highest for green gram (225.41 per cent) and lowest for bengal gram (115.39 per cent). For sugarcane, the yield gap was 31.66 per cent. Among fibre crops, it was high for cotton (150.09 per cent) and low for jute (20.88 per cent). Among oilseeds, it was highest for sunflower (180.84 per cent) and lowest for rapeseed and mustard (24.41 per cent). Among vegetables, the yield gap was highest for onion (172.92 per cent) and lower for potato (57.56 per cent). The yield gap for coconut was also quite high at 283.97 per cent. Second, yield gaps in value terms, that is the economic yield gap, is positive and high for all crops in all the states meaning that the actual net returns that farmers receive from crop cultivation are much lower than the potential net returns that they could receive if crop yields realized their true potentials. Third, from the field survey it was seen that underdeveloped regions showed higher yield gap for all crops compared to developed regions and the crop yield gaps of marginal and small farmers was found to be higher than that of medium and large farmers. This means that resource constraints restrain realization of higher yield in underdeveloped regions and lower farm size groups.

Further, a factor analysis identified several location-specific factors that kept the crop yields low in several regions. Significant among these were unbalanced use of fertilizers, lack of use of high-yielding quality seeds, inadequate use of manures and micronutrients, inefficient and poor water management, lack of proper marketing arrangements in the neighbourhood, lower access to electrified irrigation sources, inefficient extension services and lesser interest in agriculture. All these factors resulted in improper crop management and farming practices, which have to be addressed. Many of these lacunae would automatically be removed if extension services were revamped and supportive infrastructure services were strengthened and rendered more efficient. Research should properly incorporate farmers' constraints to high crop yields and productivity and provide farmers with appropriate technological packages for specific locations to bridge the yield gaps. Moreover, institutional and policy support to farmers is crucial for ensuring agricultural input supplies, farm credit, price incentives and adequate marketing systems in a holistic manner for increased crop productivity on a sustainable basis.

The thirteenth chapter on 'Performance of participatory irrigation management in Odisha: A study of Pani Panchayats in two irrigation projects' authored by Bibhu Prasad Nayak and S. Manasi makes an attempt to explore the status of participatory irrigation management (PIM) in Odisha and assess the performance of PIM institutions in two irrigation projects in the state based on some of the indicators like quality of O&M, participation of the users and impact on agricultural productivity. Though the state has initiated PIM by enacting legislations to facilitate the participation of farmers in irrigation management and launched several programmes to incentivize it, the implementation has not been very effective in terms of involvement of farmers in the management of irrigation. The constraining factors concerning this could be lack of adequate measures to engage the farmers in decision-making and focus on the formation of Pani Panchayats (PPs) rather than strengthening these institutions, and the responsibility shifting attitude of government officials with very little sharing of funds and power with users, etc. The PIM implementation does not seem to have invoked an interest among the farmers to take up the responsibility of managing their own systems. Inadequate and non-effective training didn't add to the capacity building of the PP leaders as well as members to understand the importance of various components of participatory institutions. So the PPs have emerged as mere paper institutions rather than having any effective impact on irrigation management at the ground level.

The last and fourteenth chapter by Jitender Singh on 'Impact of organized retail channels on revenue of farmers: a case study of Mother Dairy centres in Haryana' presents supply chain efficiency and inefficiency impact on agriculture. The chapter recognizes the fact that traditional marketing chains are characterized by the high margins of the middlemen, low prices to the farmers, low elasticity of derived demand, huge wastage of agricultural produce, and so on. The new marketing arrangements such as the farmers' market, for example Apani Mandi, contract farming and the emergence of direct procurement by organized retail chains are hopes for the emergence of efficient agriculture markets. However, there could be problems of exclusion of small farmers. Institutional reforms need to reduce the multiple layers of intermediaries. The direct procurement is still geographically restricted to the hot spots of the vegetable-producing regions, and not for all, and its impact on farmers depends on the terms and conditions of the procurement contract. The procurement system adopted by the agencies, namely Mother Diary (MD) and Reliance Fresh (RF), suggests that the approach adopted by RF was more informative in terms of price information, quality monitoring, mode of payments and other factors. On the practical side of the impact of MD it was observed that except green chilli, onion and musk melon, the prices of the local market were co-integrated with MD prices. The net revenue of the farmers for selected vegetables was found, on an average, to be 17 per cent higher for carrot, 134 per cent for lauki (bottle gourd), 17 per cent for green chilli, 45 per cent for onion, 50 per cent for bhindi (lady's finger) and 57 per cent for musk melon. There were positive spillover and other indirect impacts on the revenue of the farmers of the direct procurement by MD. The indirect benefits were not confined only to those supplying vegetables to MD; these rather were extended to all the farmers selling in the local mandi or terminal market. In short, the direct procurement of MD enhanced the farmers' revenue.

References

Chengappa, P.G. 2013. 'Secondary Agriculture: A Driver of Growth of Primary Agriculture in India', *Indian Journal of Agricultural Economics*, 68(1): 1–19.

Desai Sonalde, Amaresh Dubey, Joshi BL, Sen Mitali, Shariff Abusaleh and Vanneman Reeve. 2010. *Human Development in India: Challenges for a Society in Transition*. New Delhi: Oxford University Press.

Fox, J. 1987. 'Agricultural Economics', in John Eatwell, Murray Milgate and Peter Newman (eds), *The New Palgrave Dictionary of Economics*, Vol. 1, pp. 55–56, Macmillan Press Ltd: London.

Government of India. 2012. *Agricultural Statistics at a Glance 2012*. Directorate of Economics and Statistics, Department of Agriculture and Cooperation, Ministry of Agriculture, Government of India.

Ramasamy, C. 2013. 'Indian Agricultural Research and Development: An Introduction and Way Forward', *Agricultural Economics Research Review*, 26(1): 1–20.

Part I

Farm production, subsidy and investment

Chapter 2

Global food security
Issues and challenges

Parmod Kumar

The two commonly used definitions of food security come from FAO and USDA. The Food and Agriculture Organization (FAO) defines food security as a 'situation that exists when all people, at all times, have physical, social and economic access to sufficient, safe and nutritious food that meets their dietary needs and food preferences for an active and healthy life.' This definition comprises four key dimensions of food supplies: availability, stability, access and utilization. According to the United States Department of Agriculture (USDA), food security for a household means access by all members at all times to enough food for an active and healthy life. Food security includes: (1) ready availability of nutritionally adequate and safe food and (2) an assured ability to acquire nutritious food in socially acceptable ways.

All the four aspects of food security, namely availability, stability, access and use of food are influenced by income, production and what the producers offer as well as by the prices and price stability in food markets. Looking at the demand-side of food security, we expect the demand to grow considerably in the coming future. Owing to population growth and rampant urbanization, mainly in developing countries, not only demand but also the consumption pattern will be considerably affected. With urbanization, income is increasing and a lesser proportion of income will be spent on food. However, the absolute value will increase due to increasing population in those countries and so will the demand of quality, packaged food, standardized products, etc. Demand for renewable raw materials, specifically bioenergy, is starting to boom, which could cause agricultural prices to go up by 20 to 70 per cent and this problem will be exaggerated by high crude oil prices (Bruntrup 2008).

However, on the supply side, agricultural area is increasing only minimally worldwide. Large open areas are available only in Latin America and Sub-Saharan Africa, which haven't been used due to rain forests or political uncertainty (Bruntrup 2008). Productivity per unit area will be the most important driving force as there are vast regional differences in productivity. Depleting natural resources and climate change could constrain the agricultural sector with high oil and energy costs. Modern input and energy intensive agriculture, as a whole, is gradually losing competition vis-à-vis input-extensive and labour-intensive production modalities. This can be aggravated if agriculture is taxed for greenhouse gas emissions.

High energy prices increase the cost of shipping, trading and processing agricultural products, tending to make international markets less attractive than local and regional ones. With changing consumption patterns and increasing growth of supermarkets in developing countries, demand for higher quality and safety standards in foods is growing, leading to integration of markets that were hitherto running separately. International financial markets have discovered new incentives in agriculture and as a result agricultural finance and risk management is widely available, but speculative behaviour can also aggravate price fluctuations.

The issue of food security has become important not only for developing countries like India but also in a global context. This chapter presents existing trends in food production, including area under various crops and their yield level in the global scenario. The chapter also looks into trends in demand for food for human consumption as well as other uses among major countries and regions of the world. It further highlights the existing estimates on demand and supply in the medium term future available from various sources.

Global food supply trends

Before the price hikes in the recent past, the real price of food in the international arena had been falling since the 1950s. The green revolution that began in the mid-1960s saw the developing world farmers planting improved varieties of cereals, prompting extraordinary increases in yields and, consequently, falling food prices and reductions in poverty. But food prices have risen since the early 2000s, and particularly since 2006. The price of a tonne of wheat climbed from $105 in January 2000 to $167 in January 2006, which increased rapidly to $481 in March 2008 (IMF Primary Commodity Prices 2008). Forecasts for the next ten years predict continuing high prices because of structural changes in supply and demand. On the supply side, rising oil prices mean increased costs for fertilizers, machine operations and transport. Short-term supply shocks include poor harvests in some exporting countries, particularly Australia, where drought hit wheat production at a time of dwindling world cereal stocks. Speculation in commodity prices by investors may have contributed to price rises, and the falling value of the dollar made the situation even worse. Some exporting countries imposed taxes, minimum prices, quotas and outright bans on exports of rice and wheat. On the demand side, growing incomes in countries such as China and India mean rising demand for meat. Organisation for Economic Co-operation and Development (OECD) and FAO forecast that in non-OECD countries consumption of meat and dairy produce will rise by up to 2.4 per cent a year between 2007 and 2016 (von Braun 2007). Much of the additional meat and some of the dairy products will be produced by feeding grains to livestock. The increasing oil prices have further triggered the rise in food prices as rising oil prices has led to a major diversion of grains to biofuel production (FAO 2008). The United States and the European Union trying to enhance production of biofuel has led to an increase in the price of corn, which now poses a threat to the world's poor. OECD, FAO and USDA predict higher cereal prices over the next ten years than in the early 2000s but lower prices than in late 2007. The high prices are unlikely to last as farmers are expected to increase planting and yields. However, prices are unlikely to drop to former levels in the medium term.

The long-term prospects for global food security as we enter the twenty-first century often are portrayed in a daunting light. For example, it is portrayed that world population has been growing faster than cereal production since the early 1980s and, therefore, that global per-capita cereal output is now falling. The rate of growth of world cereal yield is also declining. The strong implication is that decline plausibly is caused by increasing environmental production constraints (FAO 2001). Large-scale hunger and starvation, especially in Africa and South Asia, is still prevalent. In addition to these problems, the human population is expected to rise from about 6 billion to 8 billion by the end of 2025. The Malthusian Principle seems to be reborn once again. With this as the backdrop, we try to analyse the broad trends of the global food situation in the medium term and its implications for India. The chief data source will remain that of FAO. The analysis is grossly divided into two sections, namely global food supply and global food demand trends. The section on global food supply trends presents share of major countries/regions in world area and production and their relative position in yield. This section also presents the trends in area, production and yield among the major countries/regions. The section on global food demand discusses trends in consumption across various countries and continents and also presents long run forecasts of world food situation.

Foodgrain production and productivity

To anticipate the future we must first consider the past. Historical trends show, generally, that world production growth, since the 1950s, has kept ahead of population growth, despite the addition of some 3.5 billion extra mouths. There were two periods of falling per capita cereal production. The first happened around 1960, which was mainly caused by the agricultural losses associated with Mao's disastrous Great Leap Forward in China. The second period appeared in the early 1980s. The average per capita cereal production peaked at 371 kilograms in the early 1980s and again fell to around 350 kilograms in the mid-1990s. Since 1984 the world's population has been growing faster than the cereal production. The falling per capita production might have been the result of increasing volatility in the global harvest that has increased in the recent years because of adverse climate effect (FAO 2003).

In this chapter we confine ourselves to the more recent period of the post-1980s. Before proceeding to analyse trends, the shares of major countries/regions in world area, production and yield are presented. Tables 2.1 to 2.5 present the area, production and the share of different countries/regions in world production during 1980, 1990 and 2000, and the most recent year of 2010. It is clearly indicated by the data that although cereal production has increased during this period (with some fluctuations in the 1990s), the area under cereals has moved in the opposite direction since the 1980s and with higher velocity in the 1990s (Figures 2.1 and 2.2). On the one hand, the world production of cereals increased from 1.5 billion tonnes in 1980 to 2.4 billion tonnes in 2010. The area under cereals on the other hand, decreased from 717 million hectares in 1980 to 673 million hectares in 2000, and since then there has been slight increase in the area after 2006 up to 683 million hectares in 2010. During this three-decade period, world production of cereals increased at a significant rate of 1.3 per cent per annum while area decelerated at –0.2 per cent per annum.

Among countries, China continued to dominate in production of cereals in the world, whereas India occupied first position in area. India occupied 14 per cent share of world area, whereas it produced 10 per cent share of world production of cereals. On the other hand, China occupied 13 per cent of world area and produced 20 per cent of world production because of its much higher productivity of cereals as compared to the world average. The United States was the third major country that occupied 8 per cent of world area, while its position in production was second in the world with 16 per cent share of world production. Among the five regions (where America includes both North and South America), Asia had the highest chunk of population, which

Table 2.1 Share of different countries/regions in world area and production – paddy

Countries/ regions	1980–1	1990–1	2000–1	2010– 11	1980–1	1990–1	2000–1	2010– 11
	Area				Production			
China	23.88	22.81	19.67	19.60	36.00	36.95	31.67	29.35
India	27.80	29.05	29.02	24.05	20.24	21.50	21.27	17.95
Indonesia	6.24	7.15	7.65	8.62	7.47	8.71	8.66	9.88
Bangladesh	7.14	7.10	7.01	7.68	5.25	5.16	6.28	7.34
Vietnam	3.88	4.11	4.98	4.89	2.93	3.71	5.43	5.95
Thailand	6.37	5.98	6.42	7.15	4.38	3.32	4.31	4.70
Myanmar	3.32	3.24	4.09	5.24	3.36	2.69	3.56	4.94
Philippines	2.40	2.26	2.62	2.83	1.93	1.91	2.07	2.35
Africa	3.26	4.11	4.91	5.89	2.17	2.45	2.92	3.40
America	6.61	4.98	4.94	4.76	5.81	4.37	5.34	5.53
Asia	89.32	90.11	89.67	88.87	90.74	92.12	91.02	90.37
Europe	0.72	0.72	0.39	0.47	1.12	0.88	0.53	0.66
Oceania	0.09	0.08	0.09	0.02	0.16	0.18	0.19	0.03
Developed countries	2.91	2.57	2.43		5.36	4.54	4.14	
Developing countries	97.09	97.43	97.57		94.64	95.46	95.86	
World	100.00	100.00	100.00	100.00	100.00	100.00	100.00	100.00
World*	144.41	146.96	154.06	153.65	396.87	518.57	599.36	672.02

Source: Author's calculations based on FAO data

Note: *Production is in million tonnes and area in million hectares

includes the world's two highest populated countries of China and India. Asia contributed almost half of the total cereal production as well as area. America was the next significant region, both in world cereal production and area. America contributed one-fourth of world production and one-fifth of world area under cereals. Europe's contribution towards area and production was almost same (one-sixth) while Africa and Oceania had the lowest share in both area as well as production. Oceania includes the two main countries of Australia and New Zealand, both being sparsely populated. Therefore, the consumption requirement of this region was also very small. Africa, on the other hand, was

Table 2.2 Share of different countries/regions in world area and production – wheat

Countries/ regions	1980–1	1990–1	2000–1	2010– 11	1980–1	1990–1	2000–1	2010– 11
	Area				Production			
China	12.30	13.30	12.37	11.18	12.54	16.58	17.01	17.70
India	9.35	10.16	12.76	13.14	7.23	8.42	13.04	12.40
United States	12.13	12.09	9.97	8.88	14.72	12.54	10.35	9.23
Russian Federation	–	–	9.91	9.97	–	–	5.88	6.38
France	1.93	2.23	2.44	2.50	5.40	5.63	6.38	5.87
Canada	4.72	6.10	5.04	3.81	4.38	5.42	4.53	3.56
Germany	1.00	1.05	1.38	1.52	2.56	2.57	3.69	3.70
Turkey	3.77	4.08	4.36	3.71	3.76	3.38	3.59	3.02
Asia	33.74	36.83	45.60	46.85	29.32	34.28	43.46	44.93
Africa	3.42	3.70	3.78	4.38	2.03	2.31	2.44	3.38
America	21.10	22.80	19.30	16.77	22.53	21.47	18.93	17.31
Europe	36.94	32.66	25.66	25.75	43.59	39.36	31.35	30.90
Oceania	4.79	4.00	5.66	6.25	2.53	2.58	3.83	3.47
Developed countries	32.76	34.13	46.41		44.33	42.85	50.19	
Developing countries	67.24	65.87	53.59		55.67	57.15	49.81	
World	100.00	100.00	100.00	100.00	100.00	100.00	100.00	100.00
World*	237.30	231.30	215.40	217.00	440.19	592.31	585.69	650.88

Source: Author's calculations based on FAO data

Note: *Production is in million tonnes and area in million hectares

mostly deficit in cereal production, and a majority of the countries in this region were dependent on food imports and, therefore, were more vulnerable to the fluctuating supply of foodgrains.

In the case of pulses, the total world production increased from 41 million tonnes in 1980 to 68 million tonnes in 2010 with wide fluctuations in the 1990s (Figure 2.3). Similarly, world area under pulses increased from 61 million hectares in 1980 to 76 million hectares in

Table 2.3 Share of different countries/regions in world area and production – total cereals

Countries/regions	Area				Production			
	1980–1	1990–1	2000–1	2010–11	1980–1	1990–1	2000–1	2010–11
China	13.25	13.21	12.73	13.21	18.08	20.73	19.77	20.46
United States	9.98	9.27	8.70	8.42	17.41	16.00	16.63	16.52
India	14.51	14.47	15.22	13.57	9.06	9.93	11.40	9.66
Indonesia	1.64	1.93	2.27	2.55	2.17	2.66	2.99	3.49
France	1.38	1.28	1.35	1.36	3.10	2.82	3.19	2.70
Brazil	2.94	2.61	2.56	2.74	2.14	1.66	2.23	3.11
Canada	2.69	3.04	2.71	1.91	2.67	2.91	2.48	1.87
Germany	1.08	0.98	1.04	0.97	2.11	1.92	2.20	1.83
Africa	8.95	11.21	13.07	15.26	4.68	4.78	5.42	6.43
America	19.52	19.01	18.58	17.66	25.79	23.99	25.82	26.44
Asia	42.50	43.84	47.61	48.07	40.78	44.71	48.36	49.03
Europe	26.82	24.02	18.10	16.14	27.64	25.29	18.68	16.68
Oceania	2.20	1.92	2.63	2.87	1.11	1.23	1.72	1.42
Developed countries	25.06	23.94	32.31		38.67	35.46	40.12	
Developing countries	74.94	76.06	67.69		61.33	64.54	59.88	
World	100	100	100	100	100	100	100	100
World*	717.20	708.47	672.72	682.54	1,549.91	1,952.38	2,060.20	2,432.24

Source: Author's calculations based on FAO data

Note: *Production is in million tonnes and area in million hectares

Table 2.4 Share of different countries/regions in world area and production – pulses

Countries/ regions	1980–1	1990–1	2000–1	2010– 11	1980–1	1990–1	2000–1	2010– 11
	Area				Production			
India	37.38	34.03	30.03	34.44	22.48	21.77	24.74	25.29
China	8.87	5.53	5.18	3.72	16.56	10.39	8.47	6.61
Canada	0.22	0.46	3.63	3.77	0.46	0.99	8.01	7.67
Brazil	7.79	6.95	6.75	4.61	4.92	3.85	5.52	4.77
Nigeria	2.58	2.82	5.76	3.45	1.38	2.38	4.04	3.38
Myanmar	0.87	0.98	3.61	4.97	0.87	0.72	2.99	6.49
France	0.17	1.06	0.73	0.56	0.88	6.31	3.73	2.41
Australia	0.31	2.02	3.43	2.30	0.43	2.29	3.92	2.81
Africa	15.42	18.91	24.39	27.51	13.10	12.18	15.70	19.94
America	15.16	14.80	17.11	15.33	15.14	12.91	21.62	21.34
Asia	57.21	52.14	49.70	50.53	50.31	44.01	45.73	46.15
Europe	11.85	12.08	5.32	4.29	20.84	28.50	12.91	9.67
Oceania	0.36	2.06	3.48	2.34	0.60	2.41	4.05	2.89
Developed countries	6.39	8.05	13.35		11.48	19.69	27.93	
Developing countries	93.61	91.95	86.65		88.52	80.31	72.07	
World	100	100	100	100	100	100	100	100
World*	61.28	68.80	64.84	75.98	40.79	59.05	55.44	67.65

Source: Author's calculations based on FAO data

Note: *Production is in million tonnes and area in million hectares

2010 with similar fluctuations in area during the 1990s (Figure 2.4). India occupied first position in the world area as well as production with 34 per cent share in area and 25 per cent share in production. China was the distant second with 4 per cent area and 7 per cent production share. Among the five regions, Asia occupied half of the area under pulses and produced a little less than half of the world production. Africa occupied second position in area under pulses, while America remained second in world production in 2010. Europe and Oceania lay at the fourth and fifth positions, respectively both in area as well as production.

Table 2.5 Share of different countries/regions in world area and production – nine major oilseeds

Countries/ regions	1980–1	1990–1	2000–1	2010–11	1980–1	1990–1	2000–1	2010–11
	Area				Production			
United States	27.50	19.35	20.00	16.85	40.09	29.41	29.31	23.81
India	15.59	18.40	15.26	12.53	6.39	9.39	7.45	6.18
Brazil	8.83	9.40	8.83	12.08	12.31	10.77	12.24	17.26
China	13.24	14.38	15.43	11.47	12.28	14.66	16.83	11.97
Argentina	4.77	6.63	7.82	10.18	4.79	8.17	9.85	13.91
Nigeria	0.89	1.22	1.64	1.65	0.45	0.76	1.25	0.79
Indonesia	1.14	1.57	0.95	0.66	1.15	1.40	0.85	0.42
Malaysia	0.09	0.06	0.07	0.07	0.09	0.05	0.05	0.04
Philippines	0.08	0.06	0.03	0.02	0.06	0.03	0.02	0.01
America	46.02	40.58	42.69	46.52	62.02	53.56	57.40	62.36
Asia	34.44	39.34	35.98	29.63	22.87	28.45	27.46	21.11
Europe	10.67	12.34	11.20	13.62	10.32	14.06	10.15	12.13
Africa	8.53	7.56	9.05	9.30	4.55	3.78	4.20	3.81
Oceania	0.34	0.18	1.08	0.93	0.23	0.16	0.78	0.58
World	100.00	100.00	100.00	100.00	100.00	100.00	100.00	100.00
World*	108.52	127.02	159.12	195.94	129.65	188.22	271.15	399.86

Source: Author's calculations based on FAO data

Note:*Production is in million tonnes and area in million hectares

The nine oilseeds include groundnut, castor seed, sesame, rapeseed-mustard, linseed, soybean, sunflower, nigerseed and safflower.

Oilseeds (nine major oilseeds as per Indian standards) production saw the most spectacular increase during the past three decades. The world production (of nine major oilseeds) increased by threefolds from 130 million tonnes in 1980 to 400 million tonnes in 2010 (Figure 2.5). Area under oilseeds also increased during this period but by a lesser extent, only less than twofold from 109 million hectares to 196 million hectares (Figure 2.6). The United States stood first in area as well

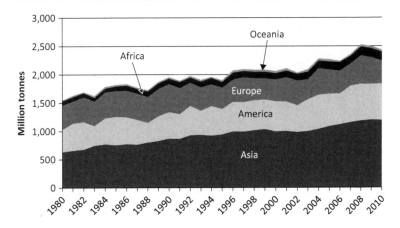

Figure 2.1 Cereal production: major blocks

Source: Author's calculations based on FAO Data

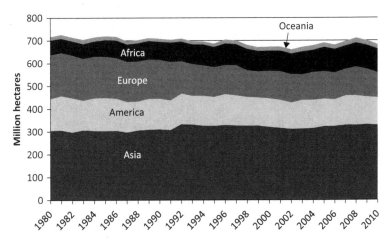

Figure 2.2 Cereal area: major blocks

Source: Author's calculations based on FAO Data

production of oilseeds in 2010. India, Brazil and China were closer in area, but Brazil having the highest productivity stood second in production followed by China. India contributed 12.5 per cent of world area and was second in area, but it contributed less than half of its share in world area in world production with only a 6 per cent share. Among the

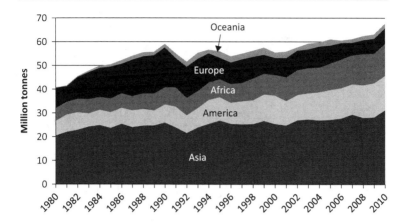

Figure 2.3: Pulses production: major blocks

Source: Author's calculations based on FAO Data

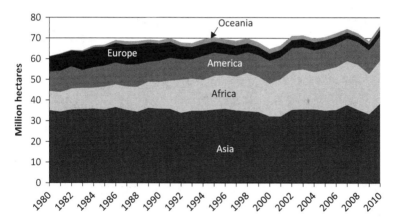

Figure 2.4 Pulses area: major blocks

Source: Author's calculations based on FAO Data

continents, America had the highest share in area as well as production in oilseeds. America was followed by Asia, Europe, Africa and Oceania, in descending order.

In our above discussion, we have seen that India's share in world area was much higher than her share in production in all the crops, namely cereal, pulses and oilseeds. This indicates that our yield per hectare is much lower compared to world average. Not only was India's yield less

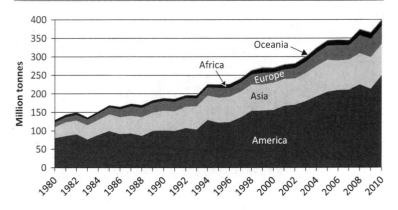

Figure 2.5 Oilseeds production (nine oilseeds): major blocks

Source: Author's calculations based on FAO Data

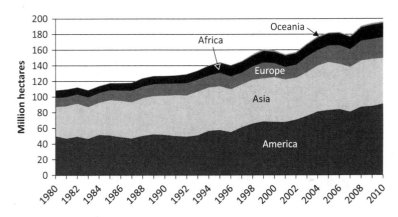

Figure 2.6 Oilseeds area (nine oilseeds): major blocks

Source: Author's calculations based on FAO Data

than the world average, but it was also less than most of the developed as well as developing countries as is seen from Tables 2.6 to 2.10. In rice/ paddy, India's yield was only 33 quintals per hectare, whereas, world average was 44 quintals in 2010. Even Asian countries like Bangladesh, Myanmar, Philippines and Vietnam had a higher yield rate as compared to India. Similarly in wheat, India's yield was less than that of the world average, although the difference in yield in wheat was much less than that of rice. India's average yield was 28 quintals while the world average

Table 2.6 Yield comparison among countries/regions – rice (quintals per hectare)

Countries/regions	1980–1	1990–1	2000–1	2010–11
China	41.4	57.2	62.6	65.5
India	20.0	26.1	28.5	32.6
Indonesia	32.9	43.0	44.0	50.1
Bangladesh	20.2	25.7	34.8	41.8
Vietnam	20.8	31.8	42.4	53.2
Thailand	18.9	19.6	26.1	28.8
Myanmar	27.7	29.4	33.8	41.2
Philippines	22.1	29.8	30.7	36.2
Africa	18.3	21.0	23.1	25.2
America	24.2	31.0	42.1	50.9
Asia	27.9	36.1	39.5	44.5
Europe	42.9	43.0	52.5	61.9
Oceania	49.9	80.8	80.0	93.4
Developed countries	50.6	62.4	66.3	67.1
Developing countries	26.8	34.6	38.2	40.5
World	27.5	35.3	38.9	43.7

Source: Author's calculations based on FAO data

was 30 quintals in 2010. Our yield in wheat was less than China, the United States and European countries, but it was higher than the Russian Federation, Canada and Turkey. Thus, compared to the rice yield, India was far better placed in the yield rate of wheat although still less than the world average. As in rice, India was badly placed in pulses and oilseeds. In pulses, although we were close to the world average, our average yield was 6.5 quintals per hectare compared to the world average of 9 quintals per hectare. However, our average was far less than China (16 quintals), Canada (18 quintals) and France (38.5 quintals). In nine major oilseeds, India's yield rate averaged at 10 quintals per hectare in 2010, whereas the world average was 24 quintals per hectare. Brazil, the United States, Argentina and China had two-to-three times higher productivity in oilseeds compared to India. Thus, despite having more area under cultivation, India was producing much less than Brazil and China. Given the above comparisons, India needs concerted

Table 2.7 Yield comparison among countries/regions – wheat (quintals per hectare)

Countries/regions	1980–1	1990–1	2000–1	2010–11
China	18.9	31.9	37.4	47.5
India	14.4	21.2	27.8	28.3
United States	22.5	26.6	28.2	31.2
Russian Federation	–	–	16.1	19.2
France	51.8	64.8	71.2	70.4
Canada	17.2	22.8	24.4	28.0
Germany	47.4	62.7	72.8	73.1
Turkey	18.5	21.2	22.3	24.4
Africa	11.0	16.0	17.5	23.2
America	19.8	24.1	26.7	31.0
Asia	16.1	23.8	25.9	28.8
Europe	21.9	30.9	33.2	36.0
Oceania	9.8	16.5	18.4	16.7
Developed countries	25.1	32.2	29.4	
Developing countries	15.4	22.2	25.3	
World	18.6	25.6	27.2	30.0

Source: Author's calculations based on FAO data

efforts in irrigation and use of other inputs to break the stalemate in productivity. Rising public investment in agriculture and increasing use of fertilizer and credit in the recent years is a positive move, but Indian agriculture needs a much bigger leap forward on a large scale to take off to achieve 4 per cent per annum growth rate in agriculture.

Trends in area, production and yield

In this section, we present the prevailing area, production and productivity trends in the major countries and regions of the world. We divide our period into the 1980s (1980 to 1990), 1990s (1990 to 2000), and 2000s (2000 to 2010). We also divide the whole period into two equal halves, that is 1980 to 1994 and 1995 to 2010. We can call it the pre- and post-liberalization period given the Indian scenario, although it does not hold true in the world scenario. The estimated trend growth rates

Table 2.8 Yield comparison among countries/regions – total cereals (quintals per hectare)

Countries/regions	1980–1	1990–1	2000–1	2010–11
France	48.5	60.8	72.4	70.9
Germany	42.3	54.1	64.5	67.2
United States	37.7	47.6	58.5	69.9
China	29.5	43.2	47.6	55.2
Indonesia	28.7	38.0	40.3	48.8
Canada	21.4	26.4	28.1	34.9
Brazil	15.8	17.6	26.6	40.6
India	13.5	18.9	22.9	25.4
Africa	11.3	11.8	12.7	15.0
America	28.5	34.8	42.6	53.4
Asia	20.7	28.1	31.1	36.3
Europe	22.3	29.0	31.6	36.8
Oceania	10.9	17.6	20.0	17.6
Developed countries	25.1	32.2	29.4	
Developing countries	15.4	22.2	25.3	
World	21.6	27.6	30.6	35.6

Source: Author's calculations based on FAO data

for cereals (wheat, rice and other coarse cereals), pulses and oilseeds are presented in Tables 2.11 to 2.18. We will focus our attention on pre-liberalization (1980 to 1994) and post-liberalization periods (1995 to 2010) as these two divide our analysis period into two halves and they also enable us to have a greater degree of freedom and higher level of confidence in the entailed growth rates. In the global context, this is also the period of pre-AOA (Agreement on Agriculture) and post-AOA.

It is seen from the trend growth rate of cereals that world production increased at a significant growth rate of 1.5 per cent per annum during the pre-liberalization period and 1.6 per cent in the post-liberalization period. The slight increase in production growth rate in the post-liberalization period was accounted by increase in area as well as yield level, especially during the second half of the 2000s. The yield growth rate declined slightly from 1.7 per cent in the pre-liberalization period to

Table 2.9 Yield comparison among countries/regions – pulses (quintals per hectare)

Countries/regions	1980–1	1990–1	2000–1	2010–11
India	4.0	5.5	7.0	6.5
China	12.4	16.1	14.0	15.8
Canada	14.2	18.7	18.9	18.1
Brazil	4.2	4.7	7.0	9.2
Nigeria	3.6	7.3	6.0	8.7
Myanmar	6.7	6.3	7.1	11.6
France	34.2	51.3	44.0	38.5
Australia	9.2	9.7	9.8	10.9
Africa	5.7	5.5	5.5	6.5
America	6.6	7.5	10.8	12.4
Asia	5.9	7.2	7.9	8.1
Europe	11.7	20.2	20.8	20.1
Oceania	11.3	10.0	10.0	11.0
Developed Countries	12.0	20.7	17.3	
Developing Countries	6.3	7.4	6.9	
World	6.7	8.6	8.5	8.9

Source: Author's calculations based on FAO data

1.5 per cent in the post-liberalization period, but it remained significant during both the periods. Area growth rate was significant and negative for cereals during the pre-liberalization period, but it turned positive but remained insignificant in the post-liberalization period. Throughout the 1980s and 1990s, cereals area declined and increase in production was wholly contributed by higher yield rate, but in the past decade cereals area increased slightly because of increase in cereal prices the world over in the post-2006 period. The major regions of America and Europe had a negative trend in growth rate in area under cereals during both the pre-and post-liberalization periods. Asia had significant positive growth in area in the pre-liberalization period, while growth rate turned insignificant in the post-liberalization period. Only Africa had positive significant growth in the pre- as well as post-liberalization periods although growth in the latter period was less than the former. Oceania, who had a miniscule share in area in cereals, saw positive and significant growth

Table 2.10 Yield comparison among countries/regions – nine major oilseeds (quintals per hectare)

Countries/regions	1980–1	1990–1	2000–1	2010–11
Brazil	16.65	16.98	23.62	29.16
United States	17.42	22.52	24.97	28.84
Argentina	12.01	18.27	21.47	27.88
China	11.08	15.11	18.58	21.29
Indonesia	12.02	13.21	15.24	13.11
Malaysia	10.95	10.45	13.66	12.16
India	4.90	7.56	8.32	10.06
Nigeria	6.06	9.24	13.08	9.75
Philippines	8.65	7.24	8.63	9.39
America	16.10	19.55	22.92	27.36
Europe	11.56	16.87	15.45	18.17
Asia	7.93	10.72	13.01	14.54
Oceania	8.25	12.59	12.24	12.77
Africa	6.38	7.42	7.91	8.36
World	11.95	14.82	17.04	20.41

Source: Author's calculations based on FAO data

Note: The nine oilseeds include groundnut, castor seed, sesame, rapeseed-mustard, linseed, soybean, sunflower, nigerseed and safflower

during the post-liberalization period. However, yield growth rate was significant and positive in all the regions except Oceania during the post-liberalization period. Yield growth rate was higher in the post-liberalization period compared to the pre-liberalization period in all the regions, except Asia, Europe and Oceania. The increase in trend growth in yield of cereals was quite impressive in America and Africa. Positive growth in yield of cereals in most regions was solely responsible for significant growth in world production during both the pre- and post-liberalization periods despite insignificant or negative growth in area in major regions during both the periods. Fall in area under cereals during the pre- and post-liberalization periods was mainly caused by decline in area under wheat and rice in Asia, America and Europe, decline in maize area in Europe, Oceania and Africa and barley area in America, Europe and Asia.

Table 2.11 Trend growth rate of wheat in major countries (per cent per annum)

Country	1980s	1990s	2000s	Pre-	Post-	Total
Area						
China	0.32	−0.60**	−0.55	0.42*	−2.11*	−0.93*
India	0.66***	1.65*	0.69***	0.62*	0.49**	0.77*
United States	−3.54*	−1.28***	0.35	−1.41**	−1.55*	−1.30*
Russian Federation	−	−2.66**	1.95**	−	1.25**	−
France	0.49	0.28	0.64**	0.09	0.48**	0.36*
Canada	1.59**	−3.45*	−1.01	0.16	−1.65*	−1.50*
Germany	1.07**	1.26*	0.97*	0.59*	1.59*	1.25*
Turkey	0.34***	−0.26	−2.02*	0.51*	−1.14*	−0.31*
Asia	0.50*	1.39***	0.45***	1.72*	−0.16	0.85*
Africa	0.43	0.96	1.41	0.27	0.58	0.67*
America	−1.42**	−1.61**	−0.47	−1.07*	-1.27*	−1.20*
Europe	−1.76*	−3.21*	0.84	−2.90*	0.54	−1.51*
Oceania	−3.54*	4.88*	1.49	−3.65*	1.94*	0.79**
World	−0.89*	−0.42	0.48***	−0.59*	−0.05	−0.29*
Yield						
China	4.78*	2.65*	3.13*	3.37*	1.96*	2.38*
India	3.91*	1.96*	0.31	3.25*	0.65*	1.92*
United States	−0.26	1.3	0.94	0.41	0.91***	0.77*
Russian Federation	−	−2.18	2.98**	−	3.30*	-
France	2.22**	1.43*	0.11	2.00*	0.04	1.02*
Canada	−1.80	0.88	3.34**	1.16	1.41***	1.41*
Germany	2.59*	2.05*	0.65	2.19*	0.46	1.41*
Turkey	0.83	−0.52	1.36***	0.72	1.36*	0.77*
Asia	3.64*	1.22**	1.53*	2.21*	1.27*	1.48*
Africa	4.47*	1.16	2.81*	3.92*	2.46*	2.52*
America	−0.18	1.37*	1.65***	0.89**	1.07***	1.08*
Europe	3.54*	1.31*	1.26	3.25*	1.09*	1.90*
Oceania	4.54***	2.78	−2.74	2.61***	−3.03***	0.66
World	2.74*	1.05*	1.34*	2.18*	1.18*	1.41*

Production						
China	5.10*	2.05*	2.58*	3.79*	−0.15	1.45*
India	4.58*	3.61*	1.00	3.86*	1.14*	2.68*
United State	−3.81*	0.02	1.29	−1.00	−0.64	−0.53**
Russian Federation	−	−4.84	4.93**	−	4.55*	−
France	2.72**	1.70	0.75	2.09*	0.51	1.39*
Canada	−0.21	−2.57**	2.33	1.32	−0.24	−0.10
Germany	3.66*	3.32*	1.62*	2.78*	2.05*	2.67*
Turkey	1.17	−0.77	−0.66	1.22**	0.23	0.45*
Asia	4.15*	2.61*	1.98*	3.94*	1.11*	2.33*
Africa	4.90*	2.12	4.21**	4.19*	3.04*	3.19*
America	−1.60	−0.24	1.17	−0.18	−0.20	−0.11
Europe	1.78*	−1.90***	2.10	0.36	1.63**	0.32
Oceania	1.90	0.36	−1.25	−1.04	−1.10	−1.10
World	1.85*	0.63	1.81*	1.59*	1.05*	1.05*

Source: Author's calculations based on FAO data

Note: Period 1980 implies (1980–9), 1990s (1990–9), 2000s (2000–9), Pre-(1980–94), Post-(1995–2009) and Total (1980–2009)

*Significant at 1%, **significant at 5% and ***significant at 10% level

World production of pulses was growing at a very impressive rate of around 4 per cent per annum in the 1980s, which came down to almost zero in the 1990s but found some momentum in the 2000s. The biggest decline in pulse production came from Europe, Oceania and Asia in the 1990s. The trend growth rate of production of pulses in Europe came down from 9 per cent per annum in the 1980s to −7 per cent in the 1990s. Similarly, in Oceania, production growth came down from 23 per cent per annum in the 1980s to 6 per cent per annum in the 1990s, while in Asia production growth was significant at 1.7 per cent per annum in the 1980s but became insignificant in the 1990s. The trends in production also declined in Africa from 2.7 per cent to 1.7 per cent per annum during the same time period. World production grew at 2.1 per cent per annum during the pre-liberalization period and came down to less than 1 per cent during the post-liberalization period. Decline in production of pulses was caused partly by a decline in area

Table 2.12 Trend growth rate of rice in major countries (per cent per annum)

Country	1980s	1990s	2000s	Pre-	Post-	Total
Area						
China	−0.56*	−0.47	0.21	−0.61*	−0.70**	−0.61*
India	0.41	0.67*	−0.22	0.52*	−0.16	0.19**
Indonesia	1.65*	1.41*	0.98*	1.45*	0.59*	1.10*
Bangladesh	0.08	0.17	0.45	−0.20	0.61*	0.26*
Vietnam	0.34**	2.36*	−0.38**	1.21*	0.30	1.23*
Thailand	0.75***	1.31*	1.19*	−0.32	1.07*	0.52*
Myanmar	−0.38	2.53*	3.43*	0.92**	2.91*	2.12*
Philippines	0.19	1.56	1.25*	0.21	1.33*	1.10*
Asia	0.23*	0.64*	0.51**	0.23*	0.23***	0.30*
Africa	2.71*	2.33*	2.41*	3.09*	2.00*	2.40*
America	−0.79	−0.40	−0.54	−1.29*	−0.40	−0.93*
Europe	0.97*	−6.10*	1.01***	−2.86*	0.37	−2.44*
Oceania	−1.04	4.31*	−29.61*	0.39	−17.73*	−4.78*
World	0.22	0.63*	0.55**	0.23*	0.29**	0.31*
Yield						
China	2.76*	1.46*	0.71*	2.04*	0.34**	1.15*
India	3.17*	1.33*	1.78**	2.92*	1.32*	1.71*
Indonesia	2.38*	−0.13	1.35*	1.79*	0.92*	0.95*
Bangladesh	2.22*	1.77*	2.51*	2.36*	3.32*	2.65*
Vietnam	3.97*	3.03*	2.35*	3.36*	2.64*	2.94*
Thailand	1.16*	2.03*	0.97**	1.14*	1.84*	1.68*
Myanmar	0.09	0.99*	2.28*	0.09	2.36*	1.12*
Philippines	2.01*	−0.29	2.19*	1.86*	2.45*	1.57*
Asia	2.36*	1.06*	1.38*	1.93*	1.07*	1.30*
Africa	1.21*	0.73***	1.64*	1.27*	1.19*	1.12*
America	2.47*	3.12*	2.23*	2.66*	2.55*	2.77*
Europe	0.14	3.21*	1.21*	0.42**	1.29*	1.52*
Oceania	1.82	0.58	−5.78**	2.80*	−2.56***	0.71***
World	2.28*	1.13*	1.37*	1.90*	1.11*	1.33*

Production						
China	2.19*	0.99**	0.92	1.43*	−0.36	0.53*
India	3.58*	2.00*	1.56	3.44*	1.16**	1.90*
Indonesia	4.03*	1.27*	2.33*	3.24*	1.51*	2.04*
Bangladesh	2.30*	1.94**	2.96*	2.17*	3.93*	2.91*
Vietnam	4.31*	5.39*	1.97*	4.58*	2.95*	4.17*
Thailand	1.90**	3.33*	2.16*	0.82***	2.91*	2.20*
Myanmar	−0.28	3.52*	5.71*	1.02**	5.26*	3.24*
Philippines	2.20*	1.28	3.44*	2.07*	3.78*	2.67*
Asia	2.54*	1.70*	1.89*	2.15*	1.30*	1.61*
Africa	3.93*	2.99*	4.05*	4.36*	3.19*	3.52*
America	1.69***	2.71**	1.69*	1.37**	2.15*	1.83*
Europe	1.10**	−2.89***	2.22*	−2.44**	1.66*	−0.93*
Oceania	0.78	4.89*	−35.39*	3.19*	−20.29*	−4.08*
World	2.50*	1.77*	1.93*	2.12*	1.39*	1.64*

Source: Author's calculations based on FAO data

Note: Period 1980 implies (1980–9), 1990s (1990–9), 2000s (2000–9), Pre-(1980–94), Post-(1995–2009) and Total (1980–2009)

*Significant at 1%, **significant at 5% and ***significant at 10% level

under pulses and partly by decline in the yield rate. World area increased with a significant growth rate of 0.8 per cent per annum during the pre-liberalization period but came down to 0.3 per cent during the post-liberalization period. Similarly, yield of pulses grew at a significant rate of 1.4 per cent per annum during the pre-liberalization period, which decelerated to (significant) 0.7 per cent per annum during the post-liberalization period. The decline in area was pertinent in Europe and Oceania from pre- to post-liberalization. Similarly, significant deceleration in yield occurred in Europe during that period.

World production of oilseeds increased most consistently throughout the period since the 1980s. World production of (nine major) oilseeds increased by 3.3 per cent per annum in the pre-liberalization period and further accelerated to 3.8 per cent per annum in the post-liberalization period. This acceleration came through growth in area as well as through growth in yield. The world area under oilseeds grew at 1.7 per cent per annum during the pre-liberalization period, which further increased to

Table 2.13 Trend growth rate of maize in major countries (per cent per annum)

Country	1980s	1990s	2000s	Pre-	Post-	Total
Area						
United States	−1.74	0.73	1.75**	−0.22	1.03*	0.56*
China	0.36	2.40*	3.39*	0.94*	1.83 *	1.71*
Mexico	−0.57	0.61	−1.06	0.71	−1.00*	0.19
France	2.06*	0.44	−1.72***	0.44	−0.75***	−0.24
India	−0.18	0.95*	2.93*	0.18	2.48*	1.17*
Indonesia	1.68	1.96***	2.27*	1.46***	0.45	1.26*
Italy	−2.64*	2.90*	−1.59***	−1.05**	0.26	0.65*
Romania	−1.78**	1.78***	−3.43*	−0.47	−2.30*	−0.60*
Asia	0.64	1.46*	2.95*	0.75*	1.68*	1.28*
Africa	3.99*	−0.19	2.24*	3.17*	1.28*	1.44*
America	−0.57	0.50	1.42*	0.12	0.72*	0.45*
Europe	0.67**	−0.36	0.36	−1.11*	0.76**	−0.30**
Oceania	−0.12	2.58**	−1.46	−2.15**	0.75	0.27
World	0.68***	0.58**	1.96*	0.68*	1.14*	0.79*
Yield						
United States	1.20	1.76	1.97*	1.55***	2.03*	1.65*
China	2.88*	1.09	1.79*	3.23*	0.77**	1.71*
Mexico	−0.99**	1.65**	3.24*	1.77*	2.89*	2.30*
France	2.74*	3.26*	0.91	2.37*	0.64	1.62*
India	2.08	2.28*	2.21**	2.28*	2.08*	2.18*
Indonesia	3.93*	2.86*	4.54*	3.13*	4.08*	3.40*
Italy	1.45*	2.90*	−0.32	1.59*	−0.33	1.17*
Romania	−2.08	2.22	2.77	−1.63	−0.01	0.06
Asia	2.77*	1.65*	2.54*	3.16*	1.57*	2.13*
Africa	−0.15	2.39***	0.98	−0.10	1.30*	1.05*
America	0.44	2.31**	2.30*	1.39***	2.37*	1.95*
Europe	0.87	2.92*	1.71	0.25	0.97	1.11*
Oceania	2.12	1.99**	1.62***	2.83*	0.56	1.82*
World	0.55	2.20*	2.03*	1.17**	1.81*	1.63*

Production						
United States	−0.54	2.48	3.71*	1.32	3.06*	2.21*
China	3.24*	3.50*	5.18*	4.17*	2.61*	3.42*
Mexico	−1.56	2.26**	2.18**	2.48**	1.89*	2.49*
France	4.81*	3.70**	−0.81	2.81*	−0.11	1.38*
India	1.90	3.23*	5.14*	2.46*	4.56*	3.35*
Indonesia	5.61*	4.82*	6.81*	4.60*	4.53*	4.66*
Italy	−1.20***	5.80*	−1.91***	0.54	−0.07	1.82*
Romania	−3.87***	4.00***	−0.66	−2.10***	−2.31	−0.54
Asia	3.41*	3.10*	5.49*	3.91*	3.24*	3.41*
Africa	3.85***	2.20	3.22*	3.07*	2.59*	2.49*
America	−0.13	2.81**	3.72*	1.51	3.09*	2.40*
Europe	1.54**	2.56***	2.08	−0.87	1.73**	0.81*
Oceania	2.00	4.57**	0.16	0.66	1.31	2.10*
World	1.22	2.79*	3.99*	1.86*	2.94*	2.43*

Source: Author's calculations based on FAO data

Note: Period 1980 implies (1980–9), 1990s (1990–9), 2000s (2000–9), Pre-(1980–94), Post-(1995–2009) and Total (1980–2009)

*Significant at 1%, **significant at 5% and ***significant at 10% level

2.2 per cent per annum during the post-liberalization period. Similar growth occurred in the yield of oilseeds. The trend growth rate in yield was observed at the rate of 1.3 per cent per annum during the pre- and post-liberalization periods. Highest area increase was observed in Europe and Asia during the pre-liberalization period and in America, Oceania and Europe in the post-liberalization period. Similarly, yield increase was very impressive in Asia and America in the pre-liberalization period and America, Asia and Europe in the post-liberalization period. Thus, almost all the regions in the world underwent increase in area as well as productivity in the post-1980s leading to more than three times increase in production of major oilseeds from 1980 to 2010 in the world.

To conclude, although increase in oilseeds production is quite impressive, the recent stagnation and possible fall in world grain production should be of serious concern because factors other than population growth will continue to push grain demand upwards. For example, the demand for foodgrains increases rapidly once incomes increase beyond

Table 2.14 Trend growth rate of barley in major countries (per cent per annum)

Country	1980s	1990s	2000s	Pre-	Post-	Total
Area						
Russian Federation	–	−11.71*	−1.00	–	−2.03***	−4.10*
Canada	−0.99	0.45	−3.10**	−1.58*	−2.62*	−1.46*
France	−3.92*	−1.46	1.35**	−3.74*	1.27*	−1.23*
Ukraine	–	−2.32	2.08***	–	1.90*	1.01***
Turkey	2.02*	1.25*	−2.41**	1.32*	−1.31*	0.25
Spain	2.74*	−3.10*	0.35	0.00	−0.82**	−1.05*
Australia	−1.94	1.71	3.22*	0.00	3.58*	2.22*
United Kingdom	−3.58*	−1.48	−1.75	−5.33*	−2.17*	−3.14*
Asia	1.12***	−1.91	−0.62***	4.10*	−2.39*	−0.11
Africa	1.43	−2.29	2.46***	0.22	0.86	−0.27
America	−0.17	−1.20	−2.57**	−1.67*	−2.63*	−1.96*
Europe	−1.36*	−5.54*	−0.14	−2.27*	−1.00**	−2.70*
Oceania	−1.76	1.56	3.18*	−0.03	3.51*	2.12*
World	−0.66**	−3.72*	−0.06	−0.70*	−1.06*	−1.69*
Yield						
Russian Federation	–	−3.01	2.41**	–	4.04*	1.92*
Canada	0.68	0.84	2.35***	1.41*	0.33	0.74*
France	3.27*	1.10***	0.73	2.52*	0.59	1.36*
Ukraine	–	−9.45*	0.92	–	1.42	−0.98
Turkey	−1.20	0.33	0.85	0.43	0.81***	0.84*
Spain	3.70	3.49	0.37	1.24	1.63	1.44*
Australia	4.96**	1.58	−2.13	2.86**	−1.89	0.96**
United Kingdom	0.96	0.62	0.60	1.19*	0.60	0.79*
Asia	−0.16	0.64	0.53	0.08	1.34**	0.79*
Africa	3.01	−1.16	6.47***	1.36	2.66	0.79
America	−0.26	0.53	1.88***	1.06**	0.54	0.75*
Europe	2.55*	1.17	1.13	2.06*	1.57*	1.48*
Oceania	4.86**	1.35	−2.14	2.74**	−1.87	0.81***
World	1.75*	0.60	0.92	1.17*	1.18*	0.94*

Production

Russian Federation	–	–14.72*	1.41	–	2.01	–2.18***
Canada	–0.31	1.30	–0.76	–0.17	–2.29**	–0.72**
France	–0.65	–0.37	2.07**	–1.22***	1.87*	0.13
Ukraine	–	–11.77*	3.00	–	3.32**	0.02
Turkey	0.82	1.58***	–1.55	1.75**	–0.50	1.09*
Spain	6.45***	0.38	0.72	1.79	0.81	0.38
Australia	3.02	3.28	1.09	2.86	1.69	3.18*
United Kingdom	–2.61*	–0.86	–1.16	–4.14*	–1.97*	–2.35*
Asia	0.96	–1.26	–0.10	4.18*	–1.05***	0.67***
Africa	4.44***	–3.47	8.93**	1.60	3.52	0.52
America	–0.42	–0.67	–0.69	–0.61	–2.08**	–1.21*
Europe	1.19***	–4.36*	1.00	–0.21	0.58	–1.21*
Oceania	3.10	2.91	1.04	2.71	1.64	2.93*
World	1.08***	–3.12*	0.86	0.47	0.12	–0.75*

Source: Author's calculations based on FAO data

Note: Period 1980 implies (1980–9), 1990s (1990–9), 2000s (2000–9), Pre-(1980–94), Post-(1995–2009) and Total (1980–2009)

*Significant at 1%, **significant at 5% and ***significant at 10% level

a certain level. Whereas, projected growth in cereal consumption for food is very close to population growth, expected growth in foodgrains demand is more than twice the expected population growth. The future of world food security looks grim even now, and it is very difficult to say with certainty how much this adverse effect of impending climate change will impact foodgrains supply. Its adverse impact is already visible in some way or the other.

Global food demand trends

The total quantity of foodgrains produced in a country added to the total quantity imported and adjusted to any changes in stocks that may have occurred since the beginning of the reference period gives the supply available in that country during that period. On the utilization

Table 2.15 Trend growth rate of cereals in major countries (per cent per annum)

Country	1980s	1990s	2000s	Pre-	Post-	Total
Area						
China	−0.46**	−0.09	0.72	−0.19	−0.62***	−0.35*
United States	−2.57**	−0.67	0.65	−1.27**	−0.52	−0.78*
India	−0.21	0.02	−0.10	−0.35*	−0.15	−0.25*
Indonesia	1.65*	1.54*	1.28*	1.44*	0.55**	1.13*
France	−0.59*	−0.07	0.41	−0.95*	0.48**	−0.16***
Brazil	1.46	−1.83**	1.51**	−0.25	1.07*	−0.37**
Canada	0.48	−1.72*	−1.36***	−0.57***	−1.65*	−1.35*
Germany	−1.00*	0.44	−0.29	−1.57*	0.08	−0.36*
Asia	0.05	0.42	0.58*	0.58*	0.01	0.27*
Africa	3.25*	1.41*	2.02*	2.84*	1.24*	1.71*
America	−1.10***	−0.55	0.22	−0.92*	−0.38	−0.61*
Europe	−1.13*	−4.02*	−0.02	−2.29*	−0.39	−1.97*
Oceania	−2.61**	3.74*	1.74*	−2.67*	2.08*	0.94*
World	−0.22	−0.47*	0.64*	−0.21*	0.09	−0.19*
Yield						
China	3.19*	1.85*	1.77*	2.63*	1.06*	1.72*
United States	1.16	2.18**	2.30*	1.67**	2.48*	1.99*
India	3.45*	2.13*	1.59*	3.38*	1.37*	2.17*
Indonesia	2.56*	0.25	1.87*	1.95*	1.49*	1.31*
France	2.81*	1.82*	0.25	2.40*	0.17	1.27*
Brazil	2.61*	4.51*	2.90*	2.67*	2.83*	3.17*
Canada	−0.87	1.48**	3.12*	1.08	1.41**	1.41*
Germany	2.55*	2.19*	0.77	2.31*	0.65	1.62*
Asia	2.70*	1.50*	1.84*	2.14*	1.44*	1.64*
Africa	0.50	1.03	1.80*	0.34	1.60*	0.98*
America	0.50	2.26*	2.54*	1.51*	2.32*	1.96*
Europe	2.77*	1.93*	1.58***	2.23*	1.54*	1.78*
Oceania	4.36**	2.39	−2.64	2.70**	−0.91	0.75***
World	1.86*	1.56*	1.73*	1.70*	1.48*	1.53*

Production						
China	2.74*	1.76*	2.49*	2.43*	0.44	1.37*
United States	−1.42	1.51	2.95*	0.40	1.96*	1.21*
India	3.24*	2.15*	1.50*	3.03*	1.22*	1.93*
Indonesia	4.21*	1.78*	3.14*	3.39*	2.04*	2.44*
France	2.22**	1.75***	0.66	1.45*	0.65	1.10*
Brazil	4.07*	2.69**	4.41*	2.42*	3.90*	2.80*
Canada	−0.40	−0.24	1.76	0.51	−0.23	0.06
Germany	1.55**	2.64*	0.48	0.74**	0.73	1.26*
Asia	2.75*	1.92*	2.43*	2.72*	1.45*	1.92*
Africa	3.75*	2.43**	3.82*	3.18*	2.84*	2.69*
America	−0.60	1.71***	2.76*	0.59	1.95*	1.35*
Europe	1.64*	−2.09**	1.55	−0.06	1.15**	−0.18
Oceania	1.75	6.12**	−0.90	0.03	−0.46	1.69*
World	1.64*	1.09*	2.37*	1.49*	1.58*	1.34*

Source: Author's calculations based on FAO data

Note: Period 1980 implies (1980–9), 1990s (1990–9), 2000s (2000–9), Pre-(1980–94), Post-(1995–2009) and Total (1980–2009)

*Significant at 1%, **significant at 5% and ***significant at 10% level

(demand) side, a distinction is made between the quantities exported, fed to livestock, used for seed, losses during storage and transportation and food supplies available for human consumption. Thus, the demand for food can be divided into direct demand for human consumption and indirect demand for other uses as mentioned above. Per capita demand for human consumption is obtained by dividing the respective quantity of human consumption by the population actually partaking in it. Following our supply analysis, this section presents trends in demand for foodgrains and edible oils across the major countries and regions. Before presenting trends in demand, a brief analysis has been done on share of different countries/regions in world consumption, share of direct and indirect demand in total demand and per capita consumption of different foodgrains and edible oils across countries and regions.

Tables 2.19 to 2.23 present the share of different countries/regions in world consumption of human demand and total demand during 1980, 1990 and 2000 and the most recent year of 2007. Cereal consumption

Table 2.16 Trend growth rate of millets in major countries (per cent per annum)

Country	1980s	1990s	2000s	Pre-	Post-	Total
Area						
India	−1.71**	−2.22*	−1.20	−2.04*	−1.00**	−1.64*
Nigeria	9.07*	2.62*	−1.25	7.93*	−1.61**	2.64*
Niger	1.46**	1.53**	2.83*	4.00*	2.15*	2.95*
China	−6.36*	−5.77*	−5.27*	−6.90*	−5.39*	−6.10*
Burkina Faso	5.87*	0.76	1.44*	3.70*	1.44**	1.44*
Mali	4.82*	−3.42***	2.88	4.78*	4.19*	2.50*
Uganda	2.49*	0.18	2.02*	2.43*	1.08*	1.25*
Sudan	5.51**	13.23*	0.16	2.28	−0.36	2.59*
Asia	−2.30*	−2.52*	−1.39***	−2.44*	−1.27*	−2.00*
Africa	4.11*	2.77*	1.25**	4.14*	0.78*	2.30*
America	−6.45*	1.62	−2.52	−4.01*	−0.18	−0.70
Europe	−0.63	−12.41*	−10.29**	−4.52**	−5.95*	−6.91*
Oceania	3.45	−0.71	−0.41	0.98	1.12	0.69***
World	0.05	−0.37	−0.12	0.05	−0.21	−0.21*
Yield						
India	1.41	2.05	1.90	2.40*	1.84**	2.18*
Nigeria	−1.67	1.06	3.52**	−2.87**	3.53*	0.48
Niger	−0.63	0.23	1.96	−0.62	2.32*	0.57***
China	1.05	0.24	−0.78	1.99*	−0.98	0.38
Burkina Faso	2.45***	2.83	1.97	2.45*	1.80**	2.09*
Mali	3.08	3.84***	3.96**	−1.22	1.16	0.23
Uganda	0.40	−0.57	2.49*	0.53	1.93*	0.59**
Sudan	−10.45**	1.50	3.35***	−1.42	3.17*	1.06***
Asia	0.47	1.08	1.20	1.22***	1.04	1.16*
Africa	0.43	0.29	2.32**	−0.57	2.08*	0.54*
America	2.29*	0.95	4.77***	2.21*	0.65	0.69**
Europe	8.53*	1.37	3.83**	1.70	3.89*	1.53*
Oceania	0.98	3.16	−5.04*	−0.38	−1.44	0.57
World	1.08	0.39	1.62	0.35	1.48*	0.69*

Production						
India	−0.30	−0.17	0.69	0.36	0.85	0.54
Nigeria	7.40*	3.69*	2.26	5.06*	1.92**	3.12*
Niger	0.82	1.76	4.79**	3.39**	4.48*	3.52*
China	−5.31**	−5.53*	−6.04*	−4.91*	−6.37*	−5.71*
Burkina Faso	8.32*	3.59	2.56	6.15*	3.24*	3.53*
Mali	7.90*	0.42	6.84*	3.56**	5.35*	2.73*
Uganda	2.89	−0.39	4.52*	2.96*	3.01*	1.83*
Sudan	−4.94	14.73**	3.52	0.86	2.81	3.65*
Asia	−1.83	−1.44	−0.19	−1.21	−0.23	−0.84*
Africa	4.54*	3.06*	3.56*	3.58*	2.86*	2.84*
America	−4.16*	2.57	2.26	−1.80**	0.48	−0.02
Europe	7.90*	−11.04***	−6.46	−2.82	−2.06	−5.39*
Oceania	4.43	2.45	−5.45**	0.60	−0.32	1.26***
World	1.13	0.02	1.50	0.40	1.27**	0.48*

Source: Author's calculations based on FAO data

Note: Period 1980 implies (1980–9), 1990s (1990–9), 2000s (2000–9), Pre-(1980–94), Post-(1995–2009) and Total (1980–2009)

*Significant at 1%, **significant at 5% and ***significant at 10% level

in terms of both human demand and aggregate demand including indirect demand, for feed, seed, wastage and processing has increased tremendously during this period. The world human consumption of cereals increased from 630 million tonnes in 1980 to 966 million tonnes in 2007. The aggregate consumption increased from 1.4 billion tonnes in 1980 to more than 1.8 billion tonnes in 2000 and further to almost 2 billion tonnes in 2007. During this almost three-decade period, world aggregate consumption of cereals increased at a significant rate of 1.2 per cent per annum while human consumption increased at an even higher rate of 1.5 per cent per annum. It is interesting to note that whereas human demand constituted only 49 per cent of aggregate demand of total cereals, the proportion of human demand to total demand for rice and wheat was much higher, around 85 and 72 per cent, respectively. In other words, much higher proportion of course grains like millets, maize and barley are used either for feed for animals or for industrial

Table 2.17 Trend growth rate of pulses in major countries (per cent per annum)

Country	1980s	1990s	2000s	Pre-	Post-	Total
Area						
India	0.01	−0.73**	1.76**	−0.07	0.16	−0.11
China	−2.96*	1.78	−3.14*	−5.39*	−0.29	−1.71*
Canada	13.58*	15.97*	1.55	14.01*	5.67*	10.91*
Brazil	1.32	−3.23***	−0.21	−0.20	−0.89	−1.39*
Nigeria	2.06	9.10*	−0.48	6.04*	−0.52	4.23*
Myanmar	−0.19	12.10*	5.53*	4.53*	6.56*	7.53*
France	21.47*	−3.48*	−10.99*	15.28*	−7.82*	1.45
Australia	24.38*	4.85*	−4.34*	16.02*	−3.17*	4.79*
Asia	0.21	−0.20	0.77	−0.06	0.11	0.01
Africa	3.17*	3.01*	2.46*	3.84*	1.93*	2.84*
America	0.72	−0.06	0.41	0.53	0.50**	0.43*
Europe	2.81*	−7.97*	−3.43**	−1.99***	−3.99*	−4.46*
Oceania	23.29*	4.76*	−4.33*	15.38*	−3.17*	4.59*
World	1.37*	0.03	0.84***	0.77*	0.34	0.39*
Yield						
India	0.99*	1.90**	−0.38	1.66*	−0.10	0.99*
China	0.08	1.00	1.22***	0.68	0.60***	0.91*
Canada	−1.53	1.82**	3.45***	1.13	0.42	0.92*
Brazil	−0.14	3.41*	2.64*	2.17*	3.06*	2.83*
Nigeria	4.81*	−3.61***	2.95**	2.87**	3.82*	1.82*
Myanmar	2.52	1.91*	5.44*	−0.72	4.31*	1.48*
France	3.34*	0.73	0.18	2.91*	−1.23**	0.35
Australia	1.96	1.61	0.68	0.57	−0.99	0.34
Asia	1.49*	1.20**	0.62***	0.71**	0.72*	0.81*
Africa	−0.50	−1.11	1.41*	−1.07**	2.04*	0.27
America	−0.53	3.63*	2.68*	1.77*	2.35*	2.51*
Europe	6.09*	0.83	−0.36	5.77*	0.69	2.17*
Oceania	0.17	1.41	0.62	−0.43	−1.01	−0.01
World	2.25*	0.05	0.58	1.37*	0.71*	0.69*

Production						
India	2.79**	1.18	1.38**	1.59*	0.06	0.88*
China	−2.88*	2.80	−1.91	−4.71*	0.31	−0.80***
Canada	12.05*	17.79*	4.99***	15.14*	6.09*	11.84*
Brazil	1.17	0.18	2.42**	1.97***	2.17*	1.44*
Nigeria	6.88*	5.47*	2.47**	8.91*	3.30*	6.05*
Myanmar	2.33	14.00*	10.97*	3.81**	10.87*	9.01*
France	24.81*	−2.75**	−10.81*	18.19*	−9.05*	1.80
Australia	26.35*	6.46**	−3.66	16.59*	−4.16**	5.13*
Asia	1.70*	1.00	1.38*	0.65***	0.83*	0.82*
Africa	2.67*	1.93**	3.87*	2.77*	3.97*	3.12*
America	0.19	3.58*	3.09*	2.30*	2.85*	2.94*
Europe	8.90*	−7.13*	−3.79**	3.78*	−3.30*	−2.29*
Oceania	23.46*	6.17*	−3.71	14.95*	−4.18*	4.58*
World	3.62*	0.08	1.42*	2.13*	1.05*	1.08*

Source: Author's calculations based on FAO data

Note: Period 1980 implies (1980–9), 1990s (1990–9), 2000s (2000–9), Pre-(1980–94), Post-(1995–2009) and Total (1980–2009)

*Significant at 1%, **significant at 5% and ***significant at 10% level

processing including their use for manufacturing alcoholic beverages as well as their use in biofuel. The proportion of coarse grains used for human consumption directly (without processing) turns out to be only around one per cent.

Among countries, China and India were the two major consumers of cereals, especially for human consumption. During the year 2007, China and India occupied 21 and 18 per cent share of world consumption of cereals for human purpose, respectively. No other countries had a share more than 4 per cent in world consumption for human purpose. Among the regions, Asia alone accounted for 64 per cent share of total human consumption of cereals, followed by Africa with a distant share of 14 per cent, America 11 per cent and Europe less than 10 per cent. However, in the aggregate consumption including that of indirect demand, the share of the United States was higher than India in the total cereal consumption, mainly because of high demand of cereals for feed for animals

Table 2.18 Trend growth rate of nine oilseeds in major countries (per cent per annum)

Country	1980s	1990s	2000s	Pre-	Post-	Total
Area						
United States	−2.37*	2.97*	0.09	−1.25*	0.72**	0.68*
India	2.46*	0.51	1.76**	3.24*	0.35	1.30*
China	2.64*	1.90*	−1.19**	2.03*	0.37	1.37*
Brazil	2.69**	2.39**	4.88*	1.55*	5.62*	3.37*
Argentina	5.58*	4.66*	5.02*	4.50*	5.48*	5.03*
Indonesia	5.65*	−2.15**	−0.80	5.07*	−3.51*	−0.48
Nigeria	3.78**	8.21*	3.35*	6.04*	1.38**	4.87*
Malaysia	−3.50*	5.50*	4.30*	−1.50***	1.78**	1.47*
Philippines	−1.59*	−4.78*	−0.86*	−1.71*	−2.03*	−2.82*
Africa	0.90	4.65*	2.49*	1.81*	2.07*	2.61*
America	0.46	3.53*	2.99*	0.63**	3.17*	2.35*
Asia	2.70*	0.93**	0.73**	2.68*	0.56*	1.35*
Europe	3.52*	2.05**	5.07*	2.47*	3.45*	2.50*
Oceania	2.49	22.05*	1.46	0.53	4.71*	6.83*
World	1.68*	2.56*	2.44*	1.72*	2.21*	2.06*
Production						
United States	−0.84	4.09*	1.69**	0.80	1.92*	2.08*
India	5.74*	2.59*	3.90*	6.18*	1.52***	3.28*
China	4.65*	4.80*	0.10	4.23*	1.59*	3.34*
Brazil	3.71**	6.45*	5.88*	3.16*	7.03*	5.46*
Argentina	8.45*	5.93*	5.61*	7.30*	7.30*	7.14*
Indonesia	6.85*	−1.09	−2.69**	6.00*	−3.25*	0.46
Nigeria	9.07*	10.63*	0.41	8.80*	2.76*	7.26*
Malaysia	−4.79*	6.57*	0.98*	−2.23**	2.06*	1.97*
Philippines	−3.65*	−3.55*	0.41***	−3.31*	−0.34	−2.19*
Africa	2.21	5.95*	2.83*	2.40*	3.36*	3.78*
America	1.62***	5.16*	4.14*	2.37*	4.44*	3.85*
Asia	5.20*	3.51*	1.68*	4.72*	1.72*	3.15*
Europe	8.47*	1.63	7.14*	4.51*	4.98*	3.58*
Oceania	6.12**	22.82*	1.08	3.44**	3.12	7.48*
World	3.43*	4.37*	3.81*	3.26*	3.75*	3.65*

Yield

United States	1.83**	1.36**	2.12*	2.18*	1.11*	1.37*
India	1.85	1.65**	2.12*	2.60*	0.91**	1.71*
China	2.83*	2.47**	1.48*	3.79*	1.04*	2.42*
Brazil	1.19***	1.68*	0.27	1.52*	1.73*	1.75*
Argentina	2.60*	−0.38	1.83**	1.74*	2.00*	1.22*
Indonesia	0.86**	0.30	−1.55**	0.63*	−0.29	0.22***
Nigeria	5.28*	2.16	−0.94	2.79*	1.92*	2.54*
Malaysia	−1.38	2.34**	−4.18*	−1.84**	−1.07	−0.27
Philippines	−0.82	1.42*	0.31	0.20	0.77*	0.87*
Africa	−0.21	2.95**	1.83*	−0.13	1.32*	1.16*
America	0.63	1.33*	2.98	1.23*	4.34*	2.75*
Asia	1.27***	2.15*	1.54*	1.23*	1.80*	1.74*
Europe	−1.69**	0.22	1.00	−1.49*	1.57*	0.24
Oceania	3.06**	−0.66	0.15	1.84**	0.18	0.34***
World	1.33*	1.55*	1.46*	1.32*	1.30*	1.35*

Source: Author's calculations based on FAO data

Note: Period 1980 implies (1980–9), 1990s (1990–9), 2000s (2000–9), Pre-(1980–94), Post-(1995–2009) and Total (1980–2009)

*Significant at 1%, **significant at 5% and ***significant at 10% level

and its use for processing. China, occupied first position in the aggregate consumption of cereals with 18 per cent share of world consumption, followed by the United States with 13 per cent share and India with 10 per cent share in aggregate world consumption. Among different regions, Asia constituted 47 per cent share, America 24 per cent, Europe 19.5 per cent and Africa 9 per cent of world consumption. It is evident from the data that out of total consumption of cereals, human consumption constituted less than half, as world consumption of cereals in 2007 was 1987 million tonnes, out of which human consumption was only 966 million tonnes. Between the two superior cereals, namely rice and wheat, China and India together accounted for half of the total as well as human demand for rice and around one-third of the total and human demand for wheat.

In the case of pulses, the total world human consumption increased from 28 million tonnes in 1980 to 43 million tonnes in 2007. The

Table 2.19 Share of different countries/regions in world consumption – rice

Countries/ regions	1980	1990	2000	2007	1980	1990	2000	2007
	Total demand				Human demand			
China	37.11	35.72	33.13	30.01	34.68	33.87	31.38	29.45
India	19.13	22.15	21.45	21.92	20.28	23.74	23.28	23.70
Indonesia	7.75	8.14	8.25	8.12	8.27	8.20	8.32	8.07
Bangladesh	4.99	5.59	6.14	6.73	5.41	5.98	6.61	7.23
Vietnam	3.18	3.56	4.28	4.36	3.21	3.48	4.07	4.09
Myanmar	2.75	2.52	2.95	3.51	2.72	2.18	2.24	2.21
Thailand	3.30	2.47	2.69	2.65	3.02	2.32	2.24	1.98
Japan	3.61	2.62	2.15	1.90	3.87	2.79	2.32	2.07
Brazil	2.26	2.10	2.08	1.90	2.17	2.14	2.05	1.81
Republic of Korea	2.14	1.35	1.15	1.00	2.34	1.46	1.24	1.04
Africa	3.09	3.52	4.18	5.15	3.09	3.56	4.37	5.38
America	4.71	4.78	5.20	5.11	4.45	4.61	5.03	4.94
Asia	90.55	90.45	89.61	88.68	90.69	90.55	89.49	88.57
Europe	1.58	1.18	0.93	0.97	1.69	1.20	1.01	1.01
Oceania	0.07	0.07	0.08	0.09	0.07	0.08	0.09	0.10
World	100.00	100.00	100.00	100.00	100.00	100.00	100.00	100.00
World *	388.89	501.09	576.39	615.32	329.64	428.91	487.53	522.59

Source: Author's calculations based on FAO data

Note: *Consumption is in million tonnes

aggregate consumption of pulses increased from 40 million tonnes in 1980 to 56 million tonnes in 1990. It came down to 55 million tonnes in 2000 but increased to 60 million tonnes in 2007. India occupied the dominant position in world consumption of pulses, both for aggregate as well as for human consumption. India's share in total human demand was 35 per cent, and in aggregate demand it was 30 per cent. Brazil was the second distant country with 7 per cent share of world human consumption. In aggregate demand, China occupied second position with 6 per cent share of world consumption. Given India's dominant position in consumption of pulses, Asia occupied more than 50 per cent share in human and aggregate demand of pulses in the world. Africa had

Table 2.20 Share of different countries/regions in world consumption – wheat

Countries/ regions	1980	1990	2000	2007	1980	1990	2000	2007
	Total demand				Human demand			
China	15.64	19.23	19.56	17.29	20.85	26.03	23.47	20.78
India	8.23	7.52	11.36	12.70	11.10	10.15	14.30	16.16
Russian Federation	24.91	21.36	6.59	5.86	12.62	11.67	4.62	4.38
United States	7.15	8.65	6.32	5.46	5.72	5.83	6.21	6.03
Pakistan	2.39	2.92	3.56	3.45	3.22	4.02	4.41	4.24
France	2.56	2.52	3.39	3.43	1.82	1.47	1.39	1.42
Turkey	3.59	3.30	3.17	3.11	3.26	3.40	3.20	3.21
Germany	2.72	2.29	2.78	2.94	1.92	1.52	1.49	1.56
Iran (Islamic Republic)	1.77	2.14	2.62	2.40	2.12	2.62	2.79	2.54
Brazil	1.53	1.31	1.54	1.83	2.14	1.84	1.87	2.34
Africa	5.69	6.02	7.22	8.27	7.61	8.00	8.79	10.02
America	11.26	12.56	12.89	12.28	13.09	12.55	13.06	13.19
Asia	36.75	40.10	49.56	49.80	47.49	52.81	58.59	58.12
Europe	45.54	40.59	29.47	28.55	31.27	26.21	19.13	18.23
Oceania	0.76	0.73	0.86	1.11	0.54	0.43	0.43	0.45
World	100.00	100.00	100.00	100.00	100.00	100.00	100.00	100.00
World *	427.68	537.17	565.17	599.15	282.33	353.61	408.67	433.88

Source: Author's calculations based on FAO data

Note: *Consumption is in million tonnes

more than 20 per cent share in human and total demand of pulses while America was third with less than 20 per cent share in both human and total demand of pulses. At the aggregate, human consumption constituted more than 70 per cent of the total consumption of pulses while seed, feed, wastage and processing constituted the rest of the 30 per cent demand for pulses.

World Human consumption of edible oils increased from 21 million tonnes in 1980 to 45.5 million tonnes in 2007. However, human consumption was only a minuscule proportion of total consumption of

Table 2.21 Share of different countries/regions in world consumption – cereals

Countries/regions	Total demand				Human demand			
	1980	1990	2000	2007	1980	1990	2000	2007
China	17.78	18.77	20.12	17.95	24.58	25.90	23.53	21.10
United States	11.89	12.85	13.61	13.38	3.17	3.51	3.71	3.57
India	8.03	8.83	9.68	10.11	15.94	16.68	17.43	18.40
Russian Federation	14.44	13.47	3.68	3.24	7.21	6.03	2.42	2.24
Brazil	2.44	2.30	2.90	3.23	2.16	2.05	1.93	2.25
Indonesia	1.82	2.11	2.53	2.52	0.00	0.00	2.42	2.24
Germany	2.83	1.96	1.97	1.96	1.24	0.95	0.93	0.97
France	1.89	1.53	1.80	1.78	0.87	0.79	0.77	0.76
Japan	2.52	2.28	1.96	1.71	2.47	2.01	1.72	1.52
Canada	1.66	1.51	1.66	1.68	0.34	0.31	0.41	0.41
Africa	6.00	7.09	8.34	9.36	10.08	11.02	12.56	14.29
America	20.31	20.96	23.24	23.72	10.53	10.64	11.21	11.35
Asia	39.86	43.10	48.25	47.21	61.90	64.23	65.34	64.16
Europe	33.40	28.32	19.51	19.04	17.21	13.86	10.64	9.94
Oceania	0.43	0.53	0.67	0.67	0.28	0.25	0.25	0.26
World	100.00	100.00	100.00	100.00	100.00	100.00	100.00	100.00
World *	1,408.16	1,663.80	1,822.51	1,987.37	630.13	787.71	894.33	965.57

Source: Author's calculations based on FAO data

Note: *Consumption is in million tonnes

Table 2.22 Share of different countries/regions in world consumption – pulses

Countries/ regions	1980	1990	2000	2007	1980	1990	2000	2007
	Total demand				Human demand			
India	22.86	24.44	25.32	29.78	27.00	35.44	32.34	35.09
China	16.63	7.66	8.08	5.82	17.86	8.01	4.99	3.99
Brazil	5.48	4.21	5.81	5.67	6.96	6.37	8.15	7.34
Nigeria	1.55	2.50	4.03	4.76	1.24	2.41	3.33	3.66
Mexico	4.41	2.44	2.71	2.56	5.68	3.63	3.67	3.24
United States	1.90	1.62	2.36	2.39	2.46	2.59	3.40	3.05
Russian Federation	13.15	15.85	2.23	2.15	2.82	1.79	0.45	0.52
Turkey	1.36	2.71	2.43	2.03	1.24	2.56	2.44	1.74
Italy	1.12	1.11	1.00	0.74	0.79	0.88	0.86	0.75
Ethiopia PDR	2.60	1.24	0.00	0.00	3.38	1.88	0.00	0.00
Africa	13.48	12.50	18.10	21.16	15.40	16.33	20.75	21.94
America	15.06	11.25	16.71	16.09	19.21	16.97	20.48	18.83
Asia	50.03	43.90	46.74	50.85	57.32	59.48	53.24	54.85
Europe	21.01	31.29	15.91	10.76	7.90	6.83	5.39	4.25
Oceania	0.42	1.06	2.54	1.14	0.17	0.40	0.14	0.14
World	100.00	100.00	100.00	100.00	100.00	100.00	100.00	100.00
World *	40.42	56.08	54.59	59.98	27.82	32.20	35.86	42.74

Source: Author's calculations based on FAO data

Note: *Consumption is in million tonnes

edible oils. Aggregate demand for edible oils was 202 million tonnes in 1980 that increased by more than twice to 470 million tonnes in 2007. Thus human demand for edible oils was less than 10 per cent of total demand. India and China were the highest consumers of edible oils for human consumption with 20 per cent share each in world consumption while Indonesia was third largest consumer with 13 per cent of world consumption share. In the total demand of edible oils, India was third biggest country after China and the United States. Among different regions, Asia occupied around 70 per cent share in human consumption

Table 2.23 Share of different countries/regions in world consumption – edible oil

Countries/ regions	1980	1990	2000	2007	1980	1990	2000	2007
	Total demand				Human demand			
China	11.01	13.63	17.44	18.39	25.86	22.18	23.50	18.65
United States	20.06	16.04	16.25	13.44	3.65	4.07	3.74	3.69
India	6.83	9.69	8.34	9.63	14.52	19.11	15.91	20.10
Brazil	7.59	7.15	7.14	8.07	2.79	2.81	5.84	7.32
Indonesia	4.62	5.51	5.03	4.80	10.84	12.41	15.36	12.96
Philippines	3.76	3.78	2.66	2.42	0.68	1.00	0.91	1.38
Russian Federation	6.10	5.09	1.15	1.71	2.30	1.77	0.33	0.69
Japan	3.07	2.81	2.17	1.48	4.82	4.09	3.03	2.73
Turkey	1.47	1.23	1.42	1.20	1.52	1.38	1.40	1.44
Republic of Korea	0.44	0.59	0.49	0.37	2.18	1.78	1.14	1.21
Africa	5.13	4.67	4.46	4.43	9.57	9.01	9.66	10.38
America	34.13	31.70	34.60	35.04	10.22	9.64	13.11	14.20
Asia	36.11	43.18	44.58	44.98	72.62	74.25	72.02	69.95
Europe	24.21	19.99	15.84	15.20	6.75	6.27	4.56	4.71
Oceania	0.43	0.46	0.52	0.35	0.84	0.83	0.65	0.75
World	100.00	100.00	100.00	100.00	100.00	100.00	100.00	100.00
World *	201.73	266.95	364.01	470.62	20.81	29.43	40.16	45.50

Source: Author's calculations based on FAO data

Note: *Consumption is in million tonnes

and 45 per cent share in aggregate consumption. America was in second position with only 14 per cent share in human consumption but a much higher 35 per cent share in total consumption. Europe was in third position in total demand of edible oils with 16 per cent share of world demand while Africa was third in human consumption with a share of 10 per cent in total world human consumption.

The above discussion shows that the proportion of human demand in total demand differs across different commodities and across space. It would be interesting to know the share of direct demand (human consumption) and indirect demand in total consumption of different commodities to see the percentage of components, namely seed, feed, waste and processing in the total indirect demand for different foodgrains across different countries over time. Tables 2.24 to 2.28 present percentage share of feed, seed, waste and processing and food demand in the total demand for foodgrains and edible oils. In the total world consumption of rice, human consumption constitutes 85 per cent share while around 6 per cent goes in for feed and wastage (during harvesting, threshing, transporting, etc.) each and less than 3 per cent is used for the seed purpose. Rice is largely consumed in Asia whereby India and China, the two largest consumers of rice use more than 85 per cent rice for human consumption alone.

Table 2.24 Percentage share of Seed, Feed and Wastage (SFW) and food in total demand in 2007 – rice

Countries/regions	Feed	Seed	Waste	Processing	Food	Total demand
Bangladesh	0.00	1.42	7.29	0.00	91.29	100.00
Brazil	0.00	1.86	11.28	5.94	80.91	100.00
China	8.23	3.58	4.75	0.11	83.33	100.00
India	2.14	2.45	3.22	0.37	91.82	100.00
Indonesia	5.25	1.10	9.24	0.00	84.42	100.00
Japan	1.30	0.40	1.89	3.98	92.42	100.00
Myanmar	27.34	4.63	14.55	0.00	53.48	100.00
Philippines	3.76	1.15	1.25	0.02	93.82	100.00
Korea	0.00	0.75	10.24	0.68	88.33	100.00
Thailand	15.77	4.13	14.77	1.78	63.56	100.00
United States	0.00	3.16	10.85	12.07	73.93	100.00
Vietnam	2.58	4.02	12.80	0.90	79.69	100.00
Africa	1.87	2.27	6.73	0.39	88.73	100.00
America	1.87	2.13	8.19	5.82	81.99	100.00
Asia	6.06	2.76	6.03	0.34	84.83	100.00
Europe	7.73	2.11	0.84	0.59	88.73	100.00
Oceania	0.00	0.67	0.79	0.84	97.70	100.00
World	5.64	2.69	6.12	0.62	84.93	100.00

Source: Author's calculations based on FAO data

Table 2.25 Percentage share of SFW and food in total demand in 2007 – wheat

Countries/Regions	Feed	Seed	Waste	Processing	Food	Total demand
Brazil	0.91	1.84	4.83	0.00	92.42	100.00
China	6.56	3.96	2.42	0.03	87.02	100.00
France	41.32	3.76	1.46	23.42	30.04	100.00
Germany	48.23	2.84	2.84	7.71	38.38	100.00
India	1.20	3.68	2.99	0.00	92.13	100.00
Iran (Islamic Republic)	13.94	4.10	5.28	0.00	76.68	100.00
Pakistan	2.26	6.20	2.56	0.01	88.98	100.00
Turkey	4.26	9.24	11.55	0.00	74.94	100.00
United States	12.48	7.29	0.00	0.19	80.04	100.00
Russian Federation	24.23	17.37	0.92	3.39	54.09	100.00
Africa	4.60	1.88	5.75	0.00	87.76	100.00
America	12.93	5.90	3.27	0.11	77.79	100.00
Asia	6.92	4.69	3.60	0.27	84.52	100.00
Europe	38.68	7.97	2.12	5.00	46.23	100.00
Oceania	55.84	10.37	2.45	2.13	29.21	100.00
World	17.07	5.61	3.30	1.60	72.42	100.00

Source: Author's calculations based on FAO data

Like rice, wheat was also largely used for human consumption. Out of total world consumption, 72 per cent of wheat was used for human consumption, 17 per cent for feed, 5 per cent for seed and around 3 per cent was wastage. Africa and Asia had the highest use of wheat for human consumption (around 85 per cent), while Europe and Oceania had its lowest share (20–5 per cent) for human consumption. The latter two regions had 39 and 56 per cent of their demand for wheat for feed purpose, respectively. Among the countries, India and Brazil had more than 90 per cent share of wheat as human consumption; France and Germany had less than 40 per cent of their share as human consumption. The latter two countries had 40 to 50 per cent of their wheat demand for feed purpose, while France also had 23 per cent share of demand for processing wheat products. The Russian Federation had 17 per cent of its wheat demand for seed purpose.

Table 2.26 Percentage share of SFW and food in total demand in 2007 – cereals

Countries/regions	Feed	Seed	Waste	Processing	Food	Total demand
Brazil	51.75	1.15	10.58	2.69	33.84	100.00
Canada	76.29	4.71	1.37	5.84	11.80	100.00
China	33.69	2.83	4.24	2.13	57.11	100.00
France	58.51	3.32	1.44	16.07	20.66	100.00
Germany	60.12	2.50	2.65	10.57	24.16	100.00
India	3.96	3.29	4.09	0.20	88.46	100.00
Indonesia	12.18	1.03	8.11	0.06	78.61	100.00
Japan	45.84	0.17	1.25	9.69	43.05	100.00
United States	60.95	1.29	0.15	24.65	12.96	100.00
Russian Federation	40.03	17.66	1.37	7.32	33.62	100.00
Africa	14.23	1.94	7.38	2.24	74.19	100.00
America	56.11	1.63	3.37	15.65	23.24	100.00
Asia	24.06	3.12	5.05	1.74	66.03	100.00
Europe	58.16	6.84	2.22	7.40	25.37	100.00
Oceania	67.99	7.26	2.27	3.71	18.78	100.00
World	37.53	3.39	4.31	6.18	48.59	100.00

Source: Author's calculations based on FAO data

Among total cereals, only 49 per cent of total world demand was for human consumption, while a whopping 38 per cent demand came for feed, 6 per cent for processing products, 3 per cent for seed and the remaining 4 per cent as wastes. The share of human consumption was highest in Africa (74 per cent) followed by Asia (66 per cent), Europe (25 per cent), America (23 per cent) and Oceania (19 per cent). Among countries, India had highest share of cereals for human consumption of 88 per cent, Indonesia 79 per cent and China 57 per cent. Canada and the United States had only 12 to 13 per cent share of cereal consumption for human use. Use of cereals for feed purpose out of total consumption lay in the range of 50 to 75 per cent in Brazil, France, Germany, the United States and Canada. In the whole regions of America, Europe and Oceania, feed demand for cereals lay between 50 to 68 per cent. The United States also had a 25 per cent demand of cereals for processing purposes. In the case of pulses, human demand constituted 71 per cent

Table 2.27 Percentage share of SFW and food in total demand in 2007 – pulses

Countries/regions	Feed	Seed	Waste	Processing	Food	Total demand
Brazil	0.00	4.77	2.98	0.00	92.25	100.00
China	39.75	7.82	3.64	0.00	48.79	100.00
Ethiopia PDR	0.00	0.00	0.00	0.00	0.00	0.00
India	8.20	4.54	3.31	0.00	83.95	100.00
Italy	19.68	4.42	3.45	0.00	72.45	100.00
Mexico	1.21	3.46	5.01	0.00	90.32	100.00
Nigeria	29.69	5.55	9.99	0.00	54.77	100.00
Turkey	25.58	9.45	3.88	0.00	61.10	100.00
United States	5.23	3.84	0.03	0.00	90.89	100.00
Russian Federation	60.38	17.37	5.11	0.00	17.14	100.00
Africa	11.65	6.88	7.61	0.00	73.86	100.00
America	5.86	7.21	3.56	0.00	83.37	100.00
Asia	14.17	5.40	3.59	0.00	76.84	100.00
Europe	59.03	8.82	3.34	0.64	28.16	100.00
Oceania	75.07	12.66	3.75	0.00	8.52	100.00
World	17.81	6.46	4.41	0.07	71.25	100.00

Source: Author's calculations based on FAO data

of total demand while feed demand had a share of 18 per cent, followed by 6 per cent demand for seed and 4 per cent of the produce going for wastage while demand for processing was negligible in pulses. Unlike cereals, America had the highest share of pulses demand for human consumption (83 per cent), followed by Asia (77 per cent) and Africa (74 per cent). The continents of Europe and Oceania had small share in total pulse consumption as was seen in the previous section, and out of their total consumption of pulses a major amount (around two-third) was accounted for by feed. India being the largest consumer of pulses had 84 per cent share of human demand, 8 per cent feed, 4 per cent seed and around 3 per cent wastage. Among edible oils, 80 per cent share of world demand was for processing purpose and human demand share was less than 10 per cent, with the remaining 10 per cent going for feed, seed and wastage. The above trends were more or less uniform across different regions and countries.

Table 2.28 Percentage share of SFW and food in total demand in 2007 – oilseeds

Countries/Regions	Feed	Seed	Waste	Processing	Food	Total demand
Brazil	1.04	2.38	0.77	87.04	8.77	100.00
China	7.10	2.54	2.34	78.21	9.81	100.00
India	7.29	2.63	3.65	66.27	20.17	100.00
Indonesia	0.00	0.27	9.45	64.19	26.09	100.00
Japan	3.50	0.11	1.34	77.18	17.87	100.00
Philippines	2.60	1.32	0.10	90.47	5.51	100.00
Republic of Korea	1.63	0.27	0.71	65.49	31.90	100.00
Turkey	0.02	0.91	2.62	84.90	11.55	100.00
United States	8.54	4.39	0.07	84.35	2.66	100.00
Russian Federation	8.34	5.61	4.16	77.97	3.91	100.00
Africa	0.96	3.47	4.57	68.35	22.66	100.00
America	5.48	3.10	1.16	86.34	3.92	100.00
Asia	5.76	1.97	3.14	74.10	15.04	100.00
Europe	7.47	1.26	1.26	87.01	3.00	100.00
Oceania	3.68	0.52	1.64	73.71	20.45	100.00
World	5.70	2.32	2.22	80.09	9.67	100.00

Source: Author's calculations based on FAO data

Tables 2.29 to 2.33 present per capita consumption of foodgrains and edible oils in different countries and regions. It is seen from the statistics that rice was mainly consumed in Asia with an average human consumption of 10 kilograms per capita per month during 2007 the latest year for which statistics is available. Wheat was consumed across all regions with an average world human consumption quantity of 5 kilograms per capita per month. Total cereal human consumption per capita per month was averaged around 12 kilograms per capita per month in 2007, which increased from 11.8 kilograms per capita per month in 1980. The human consumption varied from 12 kilograms per capita per month in Asia and Africa to 11 kilograms in Europe, 10 kilograms in America and only 6 kilograms in Oceania. Compared to human consumption total consumption of cereals variation was much higher, 43 kilograms per capita per month in America and Europe, 32 kilograms in Oceania, 19 kilograms in Asia and 16 kilograms in Africa. The highest amount

Table 2.29 Consumption per capita per month (kilogram) – rice

Countries/regions	1980	1990	2000	2007	1980	1990	2000	2007
	Total demand				Human demand			
China	11.95	12.73	12.26	11.38	9.47	10.33	9.82	9.49
India	8.85	10.58	9.78	9.57	7.96	9.71	8.97	8.79
Indonesia	16.64	18.44	18.58	17.92	15.06	15.89	15.85	15.13
Bangladesh	20.05	22.19	22.77	23.95	18.44	20.30	20.73	21.87
Vietnam	19.08	22.14	26.10	26.29	16.30	18.54	21.01	20.95
Myanmar	27.10	26.75	31.52	38.39	22.73	19.82	20.28	20.53
Thailand	22.54	18.05	20.47	20.02	17.50	14.50	14.38	12.72
Japan	10.08	8.95	8.20	7.71	9.17	8.14	7.50	7.12
Brazil	6.02	5.86	5.72	5.14	4.90	5.10	4.78	4.16
Republic of Korea	18.50	13.12	11.99	10.84	17.18	12.14	10.98	9.58
Africa	2.07	2.32	2.48	2.77	1.76	2.00	2.19	2.45
America	2.47	2.76	2.99	2.90	1.98	2.28	2.45	2.37
Asia	11.37	12.06	11.57	11.27	9.65	10.33	9.78	9.56
Europe	0.69	0.63	0.62	0.68	0.63	0.55	0.57	0.60
Oceania	1.00	1.09	1.24	1.30	0.90	1.01	1.16	1.27
World	7.29	7.88	7.84	7.70	6.18	6.75	6.64	6.54

Source: Author's calculations based on FAO data

of human consumption of cereals in 2007 was in Indonesia (14 kilograms) while the highest amount of total cereal consumption was found in Canada and the United States, 84 and 73 kilograms per capita per month, respectively. In India, human consumption of cereals per capita per month was 12.6 kilograms and total consumption was 14.3 kilograms in 2007. Although India constituted the highest share of pulses in total human consumption in the world, per capita consumption of pulses was higher in Brazil compared to India. Per capita human consumption of pulses in the world was measured at 0.53 kilograms per month. It was highest in Africa (0.82 kilograms) followed by America (0.74 kilograms), Asia (0.48 kilograms), Europe (0.21 kilograms) and Oceania (0.14 kilograms). India's human consumption of pulses per capita per month was recorded at 1.06 kilograms. In the case of edible

Table 2.30 Consumption per capita per month (kilogram) – wheat

Countries/ regions	1980	1990	2000	2007	1980	1990	2000	2007
	Total demand				Human demand			
China	5.54	7.35	7.10	6.39	4.88	6.55	6.16	5.56
India	4.19	3.85	5.08	5.40	3.73	3.42	4.62	4.98
Russian Federation	33.45	33.08	21.16	20.43	11.19	11.90	10.71	11.05
United States	11.09	15.28	10.54	9.02	5.86	6.78	7.49	7.22
Pakistan	10.60	11.67	11.62	10.47	9.43	10.60	10.40	9.31
France	16.95	19.88	27.07	27.71	7.96	7.66	8.04	8.32
Turkey	29.05	27.28	23.44	22.16	17.41	18.52	17.15	16.60
Germany	12.41	12.95	15.91	17.80	5.78	5.67	6.15	6.83
Iran (Islamic Republic of)	16.36	17.50	18.91	16.74	12.94	14.06	14.55	12.84
Brazil	4.48	3.92	4.16	4.83	4.13	3.63	3.65	4.46
Africa	4.20	4.24	4.19	4.33	3.71	3.71	3.69	3.80
America	6.51	7.76	7.27	6.77	4.99	5.11	5.33	5.26
Asia	5.07	5.73	6.28	6.16	4.33	4.97	5.37	5.21
Europe	21.96	23.39	19.09	19.43	9.96	9.94	8.96	8.98
Oceania	11.80	12.09	13.00	15.90	5.54	4.75	4.65	4.65
World	8.02	8.45	7.69	7.50	5.29	5.56	5.56	5.43

Source: Author's calculations based on FAO data

oils, per capita human consumption was highest in Oceania (0.82 kilograms) followed by Asia (0.66 kilograms), America (0.59 kilograms), Africa (0.41 kilograms) and Europe (0.24 kilograms). The aggregate consumption per capita of edible oils was much higher and it was highest at 15 kilograms in America and lowest at 1.8 kilograms in Africa. India's human consumption was 0.65 kilograms and aggregate consumption was 3.2 kilograms per capita per month.

Trends in consumption

This section presents human and total demand trends in the major countries and regions of the world for the period 1980s, 1990s,

Table 2.31 Consumption per capita per month (kilogram) – cereals

Countries/ regions	1980	1990	2000	2007	1980	1990	2000	2007
	Total demand				Human demand			
China	20.73	22.21	23.54	22.00	12.83	14.51	13.51	12.56
United States	60.71	70.34	73.18	73.28	7.24	9.09	9.80	9.50
India	13.47	14.01	13.95	14.26	11.96	12.53	12.32	12.61
Russian Federation	63.83	64.63	38.13	37.45	14.27	13.70	12.30	12.59
Brazil	23.49	21.30	25.29	28.15	9.33	8.98	8.23	9.53
Indonesia	14.15	15.84	17.98	17.95	12.73	13.68	14.58	14.11
Germany	42.40	34.36	36.39	39.34	8.32	7.89	8.42	9.50
France	41.18	37.43	46.30	47.79	8.52	9.15	9.67	9.87
Japan	25.53	25.87	23.62	22.44	11.18	10.79	10.22	9.66
Canada	79.32	75.39	82.10	84.38	7.24	7.44	9.89	9.95
Africa	14.59	15.47	15.61	16.25	10.96	11.39	11.54	12.05
America	38.63	40.13	42.28	43.38	8.96	9.65	10.01	10.08
Asia	18.12	19.07	19.70	19.38	12.59	13.46	13.09	12.80
Europe	53.03	50.54	40.77	42.98	12.23	11.71	10.91	10.90
Oceania	22.08	27.40	32.57	31.90	6.41	6.10	5.88	5.99
World	26.41	26.18	24.81	24.86	11.82	12.39	12.17	12.08

Source: Author's calculations based on FAO data

and 2000s and 1980–94 and 1995–2007. As in production trends our attention remains on the pre-liberalization (1980 to 1994) and post-liberalization periods (1995 to 2007). It is seen from the trend growth rate of cereals that world human consumption increased at a significant growth rate of around 2 per cent per annum during the pre-liberalization period and less than 1 per cent in the post-liberalization period. The overall demand for human consumption grew at the rate of 1.5 per cent per annum. The aggregate consumption of cereals increased at a significant rate of 1.4 per cent per annum in the pre-liberalization period and 1.1 per cent per annum in the post-liberalization period. For the whole period aggregate demand increased at the rate of 1.2 per cent per annum. In the supply section we noted that world production of cereals increased at a significant rate of 1.3 per cent

Table 2.32 Consumption per capita per month (kilogram) – pulses

Countries/ regions	1980	1990	2000	2007	1980	1990	2000	2007
	Total demand				Human demand			
India	1.10	1.31	1.09	1.27	0.89	1.09	0.92	1.06
China	0.56	0.31	0.28	0.22	0.41	0.18	0.11	0.11
Brazil	1.52	1.31	1.52	1.49	1.33	1.14	1.40	1.38
Nigeria	0.69	1.20	1.48	1.62	0.38	0.66	0.80	0.89
Mexico	2.16	1.35	1.23	1.17	1.91	1.16	1.10	1.06
United States	0.28	0.30	0.38	0.39	0.25	0.27	0.36	0.36
Russian Federation	1.67	2.56	0.69	0.75	0.25	0.17	0.09	0.13
Turkey	1.04	2.34	1.74	1.45	0.65	1.27	1.14	0.89
Italy	0.67	0.91	0.80	0.62	0.33	0.42	0.45	0.45
Ethiopia PDR	2.31	1.12	0.00	0.00	2.07	0.98	0.00	0.00
Africa	0.94	0.92	1.02	1.11	0.74	0.69	0.76	0.82
America	0.82	0.73	0.91	0.89	0.72	0.63	0.73	0.74
Asia	0.65	0.65	0.57	0.63	0.51	0.51	0.43	0.48
Europe	0.96	1.88	1.00	0.73	0.25	0.24	0.22	0.21
Oceania	0.62	1.84	3.71	1.64	0.17	0.40	0.14	0.14
World	0.76	0.88	0.74	0.75	0.52	0.51	0.49	0.53

Source: Author's calculations based on FAO data

per annum from 1980 to 2010. Thus, although production increased slightly more than increase in aggregate demand, demand for human consumption increased slightly more than that of production during the whole period. Except Europe, all other regions observed positive and significant growth in human as well as aggregate consumption of cereals. During the period 1980 to 2007, human demand increased at a rate of around 3 per cent per annum in Africa, 2 per cent per annum in America, 1.6 per cent per annum in Asia and 1.2 per cent per annum in Oceania. Only in Europe, human demand for cereals declined by −0.6 per cent per annum. For the corresponding period aggregate demand for cereals increased at 3.2 per cent per annum in Oceania, 2.9 per cent per annum in Africa, 1.9 per cent per annum in Asia and 1.8 per cent per annum in America. In Europe aggregate demand declined

Table 2.33 Consumption per capita per month (kilogram) – oil crop

Countries/ regions	1980	1990	2000	2007	1980	1990	2000	2007
	Total demand				Human demand			
China	1.84	2.59	4.07	5.33	0.45	0.46	0.61	0.52
United States	14.67	14.08	17.45	17.44	0.28	0.39	0.44	0.46
India	1.64	2.47	2.40	3.22	0.36	0.54	0.51	0.65
Brazil	10.48	10.62	12.42	16.68	0.40	0.46	1.12	1.46
Indonesia	5.15	6.65	7.14	8.10	1.25	1.65	2.41	2.11
Philippines	13.44	13.63	10.44	10.68	0.25	0.40	0.39	0.59
Russian Federation	3.86	3.91	2.38	4.69	0.15	0.15	0.08	0.18
Japan	4.45	5.12	5.24	4.58	0.72	0.82	0.81	0.82
Turkey	5.61	5.07	6.75	6.75	0.60	0.62	0.74	0.78
Republic of Korea	1.96	3.06	3.24	3.02	1.01	1.01	0.83	0.96
Africa	1.78	1.64	1.67	1.82	0.34	0.35	0.40	0.41
America	9.30	9.74	12.57	15.17	0.29	0.33	0.53	0.59
Asia	2.35	3.07	3.64	4.37	0.49	0.58	0.65	0.66
Europe	5.51	5.72	6.61	8.12	0.16	0.20	0.21	0.24
Oceania	3.12	3.78	5.04	4.01	0.63	0.75	0.70	0.82
World	3.78	4.20	4.95	5.89	0.39	0.46	0.55	0.57

Source: Author's calculations based on FAO data

at a rate of −1.1 per cent per annum, which was higher than that of human demand. Comparing the growth rates of consumption with that of production, growth in demand of human as well as total consumption was higher than that of production in Africa and America. Production growth was higher than human consumption but less than total consumption in Oceania and production growth was more than both human and total consumption in Asia. In Europe negative growth of human and total consumption was higher than the negative growth in production. Thus, overall production has barely been sufficient to meet the aggregate demand of cereals.

In the case of rice during the whole period, demand for human and aggregate consumption increased at a rate of 1.55 per cent per annum while production increased at a rate of 1.64 per cent per annum, slightly above the consumption rate. Similarly wheat demand for human consumption increased at a rate of 1.53 per cent per annum, total demand increased at a rate of 1.22 per cent per annum while wheat output increased at a rate of 1.05 per cent per annum that was less than both human and total consumption of wheat. For pulses, aggregate demand increased at 1.04 per cent per annum compared to 1.08 per cent per annum increase in world production during the whole period of the study. The human demand for the same time period increased at a little higher rate of 1.21 per cent per annum. It is interesting to note that aggregate demand for pulses increased at almost 2 per cent per annum in the pre-liberalization period that came down to less than 1 per cent in the post-liberalization period. In contrast, human demand growth was less than 1 per cent in the pre-liberalization period and increased to 1.5 per cent per annum in the post-liberalization period. The highest increase in human demand for pulses came from Africa, America and Asia, whereas aggregate demand increased at a rapid pace in Oceania during the whole period of the study.

In consonance with world production, world consumption of edible oils increased consistently throughout the period since the 1980s. The aggregate consumption of edible oils increased at 2.8 per cent per annum during the pre-liberalization, 3.5 per cent per annum during the post-liberalization period, which averaged around 3 per cent per annum during the whole period of the study. Human consumption demand pattern was almost opposite, around 3.5 per cent per annum in the pre-liberalization period, less than 2 per cent in the post-liberalization and slightly less than 3 per cent per annum during the whole period of the study. The growth in human as well as aggregate demand for edible oils was positive across all the continents and at the aggregate increased at around 3 per cent per annum during the whole period of the study in consonance with the growth rate of production of oilseeds.

Long run forecasts of world food situation

Despite the significant impact of the global financial crisis and economic slowdown in all sectors of the economy, agriculture is expected to be relatively better off as a result of the recent period of relatively high incomes and a relatively income-inelastic demand for food (USDA 2008). Continued weakness in the global economy will further dampen commodity prices over the next two to three years, which should then strengthen with economic recovery. The situation varies by commodity, but average prices in real terms (adjusted for inflation) for the next ten years are still projected at or above the levels of the decade prior to the 2007–8 peaks. Average crop prices are projected to be 10 to 20 per cent higher in real terms relative to 1997–2006, while for vegetable oils real prices are expected to be more than 30 per cent higher. Once economic recovery excels most of the growth in agricultural production and consumption will continue to come from developing countries. According to Food and Agricultural Policy Research Institute (FAPRI) projections, on average world total rice trade is projected to grow at 1.8 per cent annually, reaching 34.4 million tons by 2017–18. World consumption of rice is expected to grow at an average annual growth rate of 0.05 per cent from 2007–8 onwards and will reach 530.8 million tons in 2017–18. Rice production is expected to increase at the rate of 0.18 and expected to reach 461.3 million tons in the same year. Among the regions, the major share of demand as well supply shall remain with the countries of Asia alone, while share of all other regions will be only miniscule. Population growth will keep increasing world wheat demand for food use. During the decade from 2007–8 to 2017–18 world consumption would grow at a rate of 1.1 per cent per annum on an average, with the main source of the demand increase coming from Asian, African and Middle Eastern countries. By 2017–18, total world food consumption of wheat would reach 830 million tons from the base level of 727 million tons. Net trade would grow at 2.7 per cent annually on average, reaching 107.4 million tons in 2017–18. The world production of wheat would grow at little lower rate and is expected to grow at 0.98 per cent, annually. The aggregate production during 2017–18 is expected to touch 690 million tons. Region-wise, during the forecast years, demand for wheat will be high in Africa compared to other regions, while the major share will still be produced and consumed in Asia and Europe.

According to FAO-OECD forecasts, the total world production of rice in 2017 would touch 475 million tons. Although rice prices in the world market have been falling in recent periods, the decline has not always translated to lower domestic prices in importing countries, where they remain, in many cases, well above last year's level. World consumption of rice is expected to increase only by 14 per cent during the above-mentioned period. FAO's latest forecast for world wheat production in 2017 stands at 689.4 million tons up from 659 million tons in 2008 with 8.4 per cent total increase during a decade period, that is a rise of 0.67 per cent per annum. The wheat consumption is forecasted to reach up to 689.4 million tons, up almost by 8.5 per cent from the level of 2007–8. World production of coarse grains in 2017 is forecasted to increase more than enough to meet the expected utilization, paving way for a small recovery in inventories. World production and consumption of coarse grains are expected to increase from above 250 million tons in 2003 to more than 380 million tons in 2017. Demand for oils/fats is forecast to expand further, thanks to biofuel production, while growth in meal consumption could be constrained by ample availability of feed grains and subdued feed demand by the livestock sector. Under current forecasts, the global production will reach 1,217 million tons in the year 2017, a 30 per cent increment from the year 2003. While in the consumption, only 27 per cent increase has been seen form 953 million tons to 1,212 million tons in 2017.

Conclusions and policy implication

Growth in world food production, since 1950s, has kept ahead of population growth, despite the addition of some 3.5 billion extra mouths. The average per capita cereal production peaked at 371 kilograms in the early 1980s and again fell to around 350 kilograms in the mid-1990s. Since 1984, the world's population has been growing faster than cereal production. The fall in per capita production might have been the result of increasing volatility in the global harvest that has increased in the recent years because of adverse climate effect. Looking at the period 1980–2010, against the rising cereal production in the 1980s with some fluctuations in the 1990s, the area under cereals has moved in the opposite direction since the 1980s and with higher velocity in the 1990s.

The world production of cereals increased from 1.5 billion tonnes in 1980 to 2.4 billion tonnes in 2010. Area under cereals on the other hand, decreased from 717 million hectares in 1980 to 673 million hectares in 2000, and since then there has been slight increase in the area after 2006 up to 683 million hectares in 2010. During this three-decade period, world production of cereals increased at a significant rate of 1.3 per cent per annum while area decelerated at −0.2 per cent per annum. In the case of pulses, the total world production increased from 41 million tonnes in 1980 to 68 million tonnes in 2010 with wide fluctuations in the 1990s. Similarly, world area under pulses increased from 61 million hectares in 1980 to 76 million hectares in 2010 with similar fluctuations in area during the 1990s. Oilseeds (nine major oilseeds as per Indian standards) production saw the most spectacular increase during the past three decades. The world production (of nine major oilseeds) increased by threefold from 130 million tonnes in 1980 to 400 million tonnes in 2010. Area under oilseeds also increased during this period but by a lesser extent, only less than twofold from 109 million hectares to 196 million hectares.

The world human consumption of cereals increased from 630 million tonnes in 1980 to 966 million tonnes in 2007. The aggregate consumption increased from 1.4 billion tonnes in 1980 to more than 1.8 billion tonnes in 2000 and further to almost 2 billion tonnes in 2007. During this almost three-decade period, world aggregate consumption of cereals increased at a significant rate of 1.2 per cent per annum while human consumption increased at an even higher rate of 1.5 per cent per annum. It is interesting to note that whereas human demand constituted only 49 per cent of aggregate demand of total cereals, the proportion of human demand to total demand for rice and wheat was much higher, around 85 and 72 per cent, respectively. In other words, much higher proportion of coarse grains like millets, maize and barley are used either for feed for animals or for industrial processing including their use for manufacturing alcoholic beverages as well as their use in biofuel. The proportion of coarse grains used for human consumption directly (without processing) turns out to be only around 1 percent.

In the case of pulses, the total world human consumption increased from 28 million tonnes in 1980 to 43 million tonnes in 2007. The aggregate consumption of pulses increased from 40 million tonnes in 1980 to 56 million tonnes in 1990. It came down to 55 million tonnes in 2000 but increased to 60 million tonnes in 2007. World human consumption of edible oils increased from 21 million tonnes in 1980 to 45.5 million tonnes in 2007. However, human consumption was only a minuscule proportion of total consumption of edible oils. Aggregate demand for edible oils was 202 million tonnes in 1980 that increased more than twice to 470 million tonnes in 2007. Thus human demand for edible oils was less than 10 per cent of total demand.

For the whole period, aggregate demand for cereals increased at the rate of 1.2 per cent per annum. On the supply side, world production of cereals increased at significant rate of 1.3 per cent per annum from 1980 to 2010. Thus, although production increased slightly more than increase in aggregate demand, demand for human consumption increased slightly more than that of production during the whole period. Thus, overall production has barely been sufficient to meet the aggregate demand of cereals. For pulses, aggregate demand increased at 1.04 per cent per annum compared to the 1.08 per cent per annum increase in world production during the whole period of the study. The human demand for the same time period increased at a little higher rate of 1.21 per cent per annum. In consonance with world production, world consumption of edible oils increased consistently throughout the period since the 1980s. The growth in human as well as aggregate demand for edible oils was positive across all the continents and at the aggregate increased at around 3 per cent per annum during the whole period of the study in consonance with the growth rate of production of oilseeds.

To conclude, although increase in oilseeds production is quite impressive, the recent stagnation and possible fall in world grain production should be of serious concern because factors other than population growth will continue to push grain demand upwards. For example, the demand for grain as feed increases rapidly once incomes increase beyond a certain level. Whereas, projected growth in cereal consumption for food is very close to population growth, expected growth in feed grain demand is more than twice the expected population growth. The future of world food security looks grim; even as of now it is very difficult to say with certainty how much the adverse effect of the impending climate change will be, as its adverse impact is already visible in some way or the other.

Looking at the food security situation in India, we have seen that India's share in world area was much higher than her share in production in all the crops, namely cereal, pulses and oilseeds. This indicates that our yield per hectare is much lower compared to the world average. Not only was India's yield less than the world average, but it was less than that of most of the developed as well as developing countries as is seen from Tables 2.34 to 2.38. Thus, despite having more area under cultivation, India was producing much less than that of Brazil and China. Given the above comparisons, India needs concerted efforts in irrigation and use of other inputs to break the stalemate in productivity. Rising public investment in agriculture and increasing use of fertilizer and credit in the recent years is a positive move, but Indian agriculture needs a much bigger leap forward on a large scale to takeoff to achieve 4 per cent per annum growth rate in agriculture.

Table 2.34 Trend growth rate in rice consumption in major countries (per cent per annum)

Country/regions	1980s	1990s	2000s	Pre-	Post-	Total
Total demand						
China	2.00*	1.42*	−0.87**	0.95*	−0.22	0.69*
India	4.33*	1.37*	1.54*	3.44*	0.98*	2.00*
Indonesia	3.98*	2.14*	0.70*	2.42*	0.54*	1.60*
Bangladesh	2.95*	1.91*	1.73*	3.11*	2.89*	2.85*
Vietnam	3.24*	3.56*	1.32*	3.10*	1.98*	2.85*
Myanmar	1.95*	2.74*	3.72*	1.65*	3.56*	2.45*
Thailand	−0.08	1.13*	1.07**	−0.04	1.70*	0.88*
Japan	−0.68*	−0.62*	−0.82*	−0.62*	−0.99*	−0.69*
Brazil	2.38*	1.14	0.93	1.77*	1.35*	1.14*
Republic of Korea	−0.60***	−0.27	−1.01**	−1.27*	−1.09*	−1.06*
Africa	3.29*	2.92*	3.75*	3.69*	3.90*	3.64*
America	2.77*	2.19*	1.10***	2.62*	1.95*	2.21*
Asia	2.59*	1.66*	0.73*	1.87*	0.86*	1.45*
Europe	0.46***	−1.01	1.53*	−2.21*	2.36*	−0.59**
Oceania	1.98	3.75*	2.00**	2.83*	3.18*	3.47*
World	2.59*	1.71*	0.90*	1.91*	1.07*	1.55*
Human demand						
China	2.02*	1.26*	0.09	0.98*	0.38*	0.83*
India	4.52*	1.35*	1.56*	3.57*	1.00*	2.05*
Indonesia	3.89*	2.02*	0.72*	2.12*	0.66*	1.41*
Bangladesh	3.06*	1.92*	1.72*	3.05*	2.87*	2.80*
Vietnam	3.08*	3.23*	1.11*	2.89*	1.64*	2.55*
Myanmar	1.67*	1.95*	0.83*	0.80*	0.76*	0.97*
Thailand	−0.37	0.79*	−0.54**	0.12	−0.17	0.29*
Japan	−0.68*	−0.59*	−0.67*	−0.62*	−0.80*	−0.64*
Brazil	2.55*	1.01	0.48	1.87*	1.12***	1.06*
Republic of Korea	−0.57	−0.15	−1.26***	−1.29*	−1.86*	−1.30*
Africa	3.44*	3.16*	3.68*	3.83*	3.95*	3.79*
America	2.90*	2.22*	1.30**	2.68*	1.91*	2.19*

Country/regions	1980s	1990s	2000s	Pre-	Post-	Total
Total demand						
Asia	2.66*	1.54*	0.93*	1.90*	0.94*	1.45*
Europe	2.66*	1.54*	0.93*	1.90*	0.94*	1.45*
Oceania	2.28	3.80*	2.48*	3.10*	3.38*	3.66*
World	2.66*	1.62*	1.09*	1.94*	1.14*	1.55*

Source: Author's calculations based on FAO data

*Significant at 1%, **significant at 5% and ***significant at 10% level

Table 2.35 Trend growth rate in wheat consumption in major countries (per cent per annum)

Country/regions	1980s	1990s	2000s	Pre-	Post-	Total
Total demand						
China	4.17*	0.79*	−1.03*	3.37*	−0.88*	1.27*
India	4.70*	3.69*	2.15**	3.03*	2.20*	2.75*
Russian Federation	−0.25	−11.93*	−0.91	−4.74*	−0.49	−5.08*
United States	2.79*	−0.68	−0.90***	2.02*	−0.97*	0.40***
Pakistan	3.43*	3.05*	0.64	4.01*	0.76**	2.70*
France	0.64***	4.33*	0.59	1.40*	1.59*	2.49*
Turkey	1.01*	−0.12	0.30	0.72**	0.67*	0.47*
Germany	1.74*	2.52*	2.75***	0.28	2.55*	1.51*
Iran (Islamic Republic of)	5.08*	2.25*	−1.08*	4.43*	0.63	2.53*
Brazil	1.06***	2.82*	2.84*	0.94*	2.26*	1.90*
Africa	2.64*	2.46*	2.65*	2.61*	2.59*	2.58*
America	2.39*	1.01*	−0.11	2.31*	−0.26	1.12*
Asia	3.79*	2.06*	0.93*	3.38*	0.94*	2.18*
Europe	0.86*	−2.01**	0.41	−0.61	0.70*	−0.51*
Oceania	2.04*	2.31**	5.93*	1.27*	5.23*	2.72*
World	2.32*	0.80*	0.90*	1.75*	0.95*	1.22*

(*Continued*)

Table 2.35 (Continued)

Human demand						
China	4.39*	0.69*	−0.82*	3.41*	−0.95*	1.20*
India	4.72*	3.84*	2.31**	3.28*	2.34*	2.97*
Russian Federation	1.50*	−7.53**	−0.16	−3.56**	−0.27*	−3.57*
United States	2.42*	2.01*	0.45	2.64*	0.35***	1.86*
Pakistan	3.68*	3.09*	0.49	4.21*	0.60***	2.72*
France	0.35***	1.14*	1.43*	0.31**	1.29*	0.82*
Turkey	2.66*	0.50	0.46	2.41*	0.84*	1.34*
Germany	0.52**	0.91	1.01	0.29**	2.04*	1.01*
Iran (Islamic Republic of)	5.45*	1.79*	−0.84**	4.42*	0.93***	2.37*
Brazil	0.85	2.42*	3.40*	0.86*	2.48*	1.82*
Africa	2.54*	2.44*	2.67*	2.59*	2.62*	2.57*
America	1.77*	1.85*	0.93*	1.85*	1.00*	1.64*
Asia	4.09*	2.44*	0.72*	3.64*	0.63*	2.27*
Europe	0.74*	−1.64**	0.09	−0.56	0.19*	−0.61*
Oceania	−0.07	1.87*	0.97***	0.40***	0.29	0.82*
World	2.71*	1.46*	0.81*	2.25*	0.77*	1.53*

Source: Author's calculations based on FAO data

*Significant at 1%, **significant at 5% and ***significant at 10% level

Table 2.36 Trend growth rate in cereals consumption in major countries (per cent per annum)

Country/regions	1980s	1990s	2000s	Pre-	Post-	Total
Total demand						
China	1.72*	2.03*	−0.53*	1.99*	−0.28*	1.34*
United States	1.63**	1.37**	1.26**	2.00*	1.49*	1.58*
India	3.58*	1.80*	1.83*	2.67*	1.36*	1.91*
Russian Federation	0.77**	−13.87*	−0.90	−4.33*	−1.00*	−5.78*
Brazil	2.52*	2.93*	2.50*	2.69*	1.83*	2.39*

*Significant at 1%, **significant at 5% and ***significant at 10% level

Table 2.36 (Continued)

Country/regions	1980s	1990s	2000s	Pre-	Post-	Total
Total demand						
Indonesia	3.97*	2.87*	1.36*	2.94*	1.32*	2.37*
Germany	−0.79**	1.40**	1.55***	−1.91*	1.53*	0.07
France	−0.18	2.79*	0.59	−0.04	1.46*	1.24*
Japan	1.17*	−0.66*	−0.63*	0.65*	−0.73*	−0.22*
Canada	0.94	3.17*	0.57	0.93**	0.57	1.32*
Africa	3.64*	2.75*	3.05*	3.21*	2.66*	2.86*
America	1.69*	1.92*	1.60*	1.92*	1.70*	1.76*
Asia	2.54*	2.12*	0.91*	2.53*	0.83*	1.87*
Europe	0.19	−2.64*	0.57	−1.33*	0.40	−1.12*
Oceania	2.98*	3.60*	2.23***	2.48*	2.69*	3.16*
World	1.72*	1.01*	1.20*	1.39*	1.11*	1.17*
Human demand						
China	2.41*	0.84*	−0.42*	1.67*	−0.40*	0.75*
United States	3.23*	1.75*	0.53***	3.36*	0.43*	2.10*
India	3.70*	1.66*	1.86*	2.69*	1.46*	1.89*
Russian Federation	0.31*	−7.79**	−0.23	−4.21*	−0.26*	−3.91*
Brazil	1.82*	1.11*	3.27*	1.47*	2.55*	1.56*
Indonesia	3.88*	2.63*	1.07*	2.72*	0.59*	1.91*
Germany	0.92*	0.72	1.25***	−0.25	2.08*	0.64*
France	1.46*	1.08*	1.17*	0.86*	1.25*	0.97*
Japan	0.25***	−0.36*	−0.67*	0.12	−0.52*	−0.21*
Canada	2.16*	4.88***	1.27*	1.87*	2.13*	2.70*
Africa	3.31*	2.78*	2.95*	3.13*	2.56*	2.95*
America	2.41*	1.70*	1.31*	2.33*	1.44*	1.89*
Asia	2.83*	1.69*	0.84*	2.31*	0.71*	1.58*
Europe	0.28*	−1.40**	0.03	−0.72**	0.20*	−0.62*
Oceania	0.81*	1.66*	1.36**	1.09*	0.81*	1.23*
World	2.44*	1.45*	1.09*	1.97*	0.97*	1.48*

Source: Author's calculations based on FAO data

*Significant at 1%, **significant at 5% and ***significant at 10% level

Table 2.37 Trend growth rate in pulses consumption in major countries (per cent per annum)

Country/regions	1980s	1990s	2000s	Pre-	Post-	Total
Total demand						
India	3.37*	1.02	2.74**	1.85*	0.96***	1.26*
China	−3.79*	4.28	−3.27***	−6.53*	0.49	−1.40**
Brazil	0.48	1.80	0.71	1.65*	1.52**	1.54*
Nigeria	6.51*	5.29*	4.91*	8.48*	4.30*	6.64*
Mexico	−6.81*	1.49	0.49	−2.36**	−0.59	0.02
United States	1.79	3.00*	2.93**	3.13*	2.52*	2.99*
Russian Federation	5.82*	−23.24*	−0.10	−4.49***	1.64	−8.06*
Turkey	11.64*	−2.05**	−0.40	7.61*	−0.76	2.32*
Italy	4.14*	−2.80*	−0.96	3.45*	−0.71	0.68**
Ethiopia PDR	−6.74*	0.00	0.00	0.00	0.00	0.00
Africa	2.42*	3.28*	3.77*	2.88*	3.84*	3.37*
America	−0.73	2.88*	0.99*	1.54*	1.57*	2.02*
Asia	1.85*	1.35**	1.97*	0.60	1.26*	0.94*
Europe	8.90*	−6.41*	−3.06***	4.11*	−3.02*	−1.65*
Oceania	16.24*	15.97*	−9.23***	7.83*	−6.47*	6.27*
World	3.47*	0.34	1.28*	1.95*	0.93*	1.04*
Human demand						
India	3.68*	1.01	2.64**	2.02*	1.02***	1.35*
China	−5.18*	−1.30	−1.80	−8.27*	−1.38*	−4.34*
Brazil	0.39	2.23	0.76	1.79*	1.71**	1.79*
Nigeria	6.69*	5.13*	3.62*	8.46*	3.15*	6.19*
Mexico	−7.12*	1.86	0.83	−2.59**	−0.40	0.13
United States	2.34	3.20*	2.35***	3.61*	2.10*	3.09*
Russian Federation	−5.83*	−18.97*	7.41*	−5.16*	3.65***	−6.31*
Turkey	9.97*	−0.88	−1.03	7.49*	−0.37	2.97*
Italy	2.79*	0.66	0.52***	3.91*	0.52*	2.01*
Ethiopia PDR	−7.08*	0.00	0.00	0.00	0.00	0.00*
Africa	2.08*	3.32*	3.26*	2.47*	3.53*	3.10*
America	−0.84	2.26*	1.42*	1.16**	1.58*	1.74*

Country/regions	1980s	1990s	2000s	Pre-	Post-	Total
Total demand						
Asia	1.81*	0.58	2.04**	0.57	1.01*	0.64*
Europe	−0.21	−1.09***	−1.26*	0.30	−0.95*	−0.62*
Oceania	12.53*	−5.27	1.84	0.47	0.39	−1.33
World	1.27*	1.27*	2.02*	0.97*	1.52*	1.21*

Source: Author's calculations based on FAO data

*Significant at 1%, **significant at 5% and ***significant at 10% level

Table 2.38 Trend growth in oil crop consumption in major countries (per cent per annum)

Country/regions	1980s	1990s	2000s	Pre-	Post-	Total
Total demand						
China	3.64*	4.78*	4.73*	3.76*	5.93*	4.79*
United States	0.64	3.73*	1.60	1.70*	1.58*	2.29*
India	5.09*	2.17**	6.73*	6.19*	1.97***	3.70*
Brazil	1.78**	4.24*	4.95*	1.94*	4.74*	3.52*
Indonesia	5.10*	1.37*	2.66*	3.65*	2.67*	2.67*
Philippines	−0.02	−1.34	1.43	0.95	1.70	1.46*
Russian Federation	1.56*	−16.51*	11.04*	−8.03*	10.28*	−4.70*
Japan	2.12*	0.68*	−2.24*	1.25*	−0.81**	0.43*
Turkey	3.71***	5.26**	5.19***	2.04**	3.64*	3.41*
Republic of Korea	8.09*	1.92**	−1.68	5.31*	−0.20	2.49*
Africa	1.78*	3.61*	3.63*	2.12*	3.26*	2.99*
America	2.13*	4.65*	4.18*	2.64*	3.65*	3.52*
Asia	3.94*	3.01*	4.16*	4.03*	3.67*	3.69*
Europe	1.90*	0.90	2.89*	0.41	2.56*	1.25*
Oceania	3.59**	4.24*	1.08	2.75*	1.37	2.60*
World	2.78*	3.22*	3.93*	2.75*	3.46*	3.13*

(Continued)

Table 2.38 (Continued)

Human demand						
China	2.37*	5.06*	−1.38***	2.70*	−0.72	2.16*
United States	3.43	2.87***	0.88	1.67	2.15**	1.72*
India	5.21*	1.19	4.74*	7.02*	1.28	3.67*
Brazil	2.77*	11.19*	5.03**	4.45*	9.45*	8.06*
Indonesia	8.07*	4.19*	−0.44	3.90*	1.83*	2.81*
Philippines	2.89***	3.17*	7.14*	4.47*	4.38*	4.19*
Russian Federation	4.64*	−5.16	10.30*	−23.85*	17.23*	−5.43***
Japan	2.33*	0.18	0.42**	1.51*	0.33**	0.76*
Turkey	−0.61	2.40	7.49	2.49	5.79**	3.87*
Republic of Korea	1.56	0.32	1.53	0.34	3.71*	1.27*
Africa	1.93*	4.26*	2.93*	2.81*	3.36*	3.47*
America	2.18***	6.33*	2.79**	2.22*	5.30*	4.27*
Asia	4.26*	2.99*	1.42*	3.83*	1.13*	2.62*
Europe	4.38*	0.32	1.52**	0.80	2.50*	1.09*
Oceania	2.82*	0.41	3.37*	2.36*	2.23*	1.71*
World	3.83*	3.32*	1.78*	3.40*	1.94*	2.82*

Source: Author's calculations based on FAO data

*Significant at 1%, **significant at 5% and ***significant at 10% level

References

Bruntrup, Michael. 2008. 'Global Trends in Food Security', *Rural 21-Focus*, 3: 8–9.

FAO. 2001. 'Review of Basic Food Policies–2001'. By Espanol Francais, Food and Agricultural Organization, Rome.

FAO. 2002. 'Crops and Drops'. Food and Agricultural Organisation, United Nations Document.

FAO. 2003. 'Impact of Climate Change on Food Security and Implication for Sustained Food Production'. Committee on World Food Security, 29th Session, Food and Agriculture Organisation (FAO): http:www.fao.org/docrep/meeting/006/y9151e.htm.

FAO. 2008. 'The State of Food and Agriculture: Biofuels, Risks and Opportunities'. Food and Agriculture Organisation (FAO), Rome.

IMF. 2008. 'Primary Commodity Prices'. International Monetary Fund: http:www.imf.org/external/np/res/commod/index.asp.

OECD-FAO. 2007. 'Agricultural Outlook 2007–2016'. OECD, Rome and Paris.

USDA. 2008. 'USDA Agricultural projections to 2017: Long-term Projections Report'. OCE-2008–1,US Department of Agriculture, Washington, DC.

Von Braun, J. 2007. 'The World Food Situation: New Driving Forces and Required Actions'. International Food Policy Research Institute, Washington, DC.

Websites

Effects of the Financial Crisis on Vulnerable Households: Findings from Five Case Studies, http://www.reliefweb.int/rw/RWB.NSF/db900SID/MWAI-7SX5HG? OpenDocument.

USAID, http://www.usaid.gov/our_work/environment/water/food_security. html.

FAPRI, http://www.fapri.iastate.edu/outlook/2009.

FAO-OECD, http://www.fapri.iastate.edu/outlook/2009.

Chapter 3

Public and private investment in Indian agriculture

A study of inducement impact and some policy explorations

Surendra Meher

Despite rapid development of the Indian economy, especially in the past two decades, agriculture continues to play an important role in providing livelihood to the people in rural areas as more than half of the population still depends on agriculture for employment opportunities. Growth and development of the agricultural sector across regions and crops is, therefore, of crucial importance for the betterment of the majority of the population in terms of ensuring food security and providing gainful employment. It has also an important role to play in terms of supplying raw materials to industries and generating effective demand for the rest of the economy. But with the process of economic growth in India, the agricultural sector has been receiving inadequate attention. This is clear from the fact that its contribution to the gross domestic product (GDP) has been declining rapidly while the population depending on it has declined only marginally. Agriculture and allied sectors contribute only 14.6 per cent to the total GDP at 2004–5 prices (GoI 2010), while more than half of the total population depend on the agricultural sector for their livelihood. Moreover, the performance of agriculture in terms of growth rate has been poor especially in the post-globalization period. An estimate by Chand *et al.* (2007) reveals that the output of the total crop sector showed an annual growth of mere 0.79 per cent, while the agricultural sector excluding fisheries showed a growth rate of 1.65 per cent per annum from 1996–7 to 2004–5. As these growth trends are lower than the growth rates in rural populations and workforce employed in agriculture, this seems to be one of the factors for rising rural and agricultural distress in the country. The experiences of the first three years of the Eleventh Five Year Plan indicate that the agricultural sector including allied activities registered an annual growth of only 2.03 per cent per annum against a target of 4 per cent per annum (GoI 2010). Thus, the trade liberalization measures under the new macroeconomic policy initiated in India did not bring desired results for the agricultural sector. In other words, trade liberalization measures did not bring any significant growth in the agricultural sector especially after the mid-1990s.

The slowing down of agricultural growth has also been accompanied by huge interregional variations. In the post-liberalization period, agricultural growth decelerated sharply at the all India level as well as at the regional level. An estimate by Bhalla and Singh (2009) indicates that during the period 1990–3 to 2003–6, growth rate decelerated to only 0.48 per cent in the Southern regions and one per cent in the Eastern region from over three per cent during the period from 1980–3 to 1990–3 in both the regions. Thus, the worst affected was the Southern region, followed by the Eastern regions. The slowing down of agricultural growth accompanied by huge interregional variations has thus been a major concern for the policymakers and scholars. This would seriously affect the well-being of the farming community in particular and the rural sector in general. This is also true as the growth of agriculture and its allied activities has been considered essential for achieving inclusive growth as envisaged in the planning process. The Eleventh Plan identified public investment in agriculture as one of the important determinants of agricultural growth in India. It has been realized that public investment in agriculture has been grossly neglected since 1980, which is having a disastrous effect on agricultural growth.

Public investment in agriculture in the form of irrigation, research, education and extension, provision of formal credit, marketing and storages, creating rural infrastructure such as rural roads, transport, communications, etc., no doubt, plays an important role in accelerating agricultural growth on a sustainable basis. At the same time, public investment does induce private investment in agriculture and helps in maintaining the health of the rural economy. When it comes to the regional level, the weaker states especially the Eastern regions must be given adequate emphasis through higher doses of public investment in agriculture and creating adequate rural infrastructure, so that it would induce private investment to come up and maintain agricultural growth in this region.

This chapter examines the state level trends and magnitude of household components of investment in agriculture using the All India Debt and Investment Survey (AIDIS) data compiled by the Reserve Bank of India (RBI). It also examines the factors that influence private investment and output in agriculture at the state level. The chapter is organized in four sections. The first section presents a brief review of literature covering the discussion on the issue of the sources of data and the relationship between public and private investment in Indian agriculture. It also focuses on the recent trends of public investment based on the data revealed by the National Account Statistics, Central Statistical Organization (CSO). The second section analyses the trends in the household component of farm investment across the states, followed by a section examining the factors influencing private investment and output in agriculture at the state level. The last section presents the concluding remarks.

A brief review of past studies

Interest in studying investment in agriculture in India began during the 1960s when the country found shortage in foodgrain supply to feed the growing population. Tara Shukla's (1968) study, the first of its kind, showed that during the period 1920–60, the rate of increase in public investment was faster than the rate of increase in private investment, though the latter occupied a larger share during the same period. While traditional inputs such as bullocks constituted a major proportion of private capital formation, investment in irrigation projects constituted a major share of public sector capital formation. There were further evidences that private investment was pushed up as a result of public investment in various irrigation projects. Subsequently, the estimation of capital formation in various sectors of the economy has been undertaken by National Accounts Statistics of the CSO, Government of India. Using National Accounts Statistics, many scholars arrived at the conclusion that investment in Indian agriculture has shown a clear decline during the 1980s, compared to its previous two decades.[1] Postulating complementarities between public and private investment in Indian agriculture, Rath (1989), Rao (1994) and Alagh (1994) pointed out the inherent danger signal to agricultural growth and development due to decline in public investment which ultimately also leads to decline in private investment and thus ultimately to the growth process.

However, there has been a growing concern and dissatisfaction over the nature and coverage of data published in CSO on capital formation in Indian agriculture. The discussion focuses on the restrictive nature of the CSO series on public investment in agriculture, which is found to be largely consisting of investment in irrigation. It has been reported that 90 per cent of public investment in Indian agriculture in the CSO series comprises investment in irrigation (Rao 1997). Public investments on important infrastructure like marketing, storage, rural roads, rural electrification, etc., are not included in the CSO series. It was there-fore concluded that a decline in 'investment in agriculture' may not have necessarily led to a decline in 'investment for agriculture'. In other words, it may not necessarily imply a decline in investment for over-all infrastructure for agricultural development. Following this, Chand (2001) and Gulati and Bathla (2001) attempted to construct a broad series of investment in Indian agriculture by including investment on various items that are essential for agricultural growth and development. These studies reveal that public investment reported by the CSO covers only 48 per cent of the total public investment channelled into agricul-ture. Conversely, the CSO series excludes 52 per cent of public sector investment for capital formation in agriculture. It was also found that the broad series also showed declining trends, which started earlier than the decline in the CSO series. The alternative concepts of public capi-tal formation redefined and re-estimated indicated either stagnating or declining public sector investment since the mid-1980s.

The report of the Committee on Capital Formation in Agriculture, GoI (2003) brings out exclusive findings on some of the aspects of broadening the concept of capital formation in agriculture. It attempts to regroup the CSO estimates and obtain a composite figure of capital formation in agriculture. By regrouping, the report finds that the broad trends in gross fixed capital formation in agriculture, and for agriculture, are similar during the period 1980–1 to 2001–2. As a per cent of the total GDP, the 'GCF in agriculture' has declined from 3.4 in 1980–1 to 1.6 in 2001–2. And, the corresponding share of 'GCF for agriculture' declined from 4.3 per cent to 2.3 per cent during the same time period.

Most of the studies carried out during the 1980s and 1990s found a positive relationship between public and private investment in Indian agriculture. In other words, public investments have induced private investment in Indian agriculture. Chand and Kumar (2004) observed that the impact of agricultural subsidies on private investment was also positive but firmly concluded that long-term returns from public capital formation are more than double the returns from subsidies. It was also found that terms of trade for agriculture as well as institutional credit were a strong determinant of private sector capital formation. With broad series, Gulati and Bathla (2001) found that private investment is positively influenced by public investment in Indian agriculture.

Several other studies indicated that investment on rural infrastructure directly or indirectly meant for agricultural sector has an important role to play for enhancing agricultural investment and output. Binswanger and Khandker (1993) with the help of district level time series data found that education infrastructure and rural banks play an overwhelming role in determining investment, input and output decisions. The expansion of commercial banks into rural areas had a large effect on fertilizer consumption and on fixed private farm investment. Canal irrigation and rural electrifications have also significant impact on agricultural output. Fan *et al.* (1999), analysing the state-level data in India, showed that government spending on agricultural research and development, irrigation, and rural infrastructures including road and electricity have all contributed to the growth in agricultural productivity and reduction in rural poverty. In a similar study, Fan *et al.* (2002) worked out the effect of public expenditure on agricultural productivity and rural poverty reduction across Chinese provinces. Government spending on agricultural research and development substantially improved agricultural production followed by investment on rural education. Roy and Pal (2002) in a state-wise analysis of agricultural investment and productivity concluded that agricultural productivity is central to rural poverty alleviation and infrastructural and technological changes in turn play a key role in determining productivity. Kumar *et al.* (2006) also established a strong relationship between rural infrastructural development and the level of net agricultural state domestic product in the Indo-Gangatic Plain of India. It was concluded from the study that there is significant scope for increasing the value of output from agriculture in backward states by improving the rural infrastructure.

Trends of gross capital formation in Indian agriculture based on CSO

Investment in agriculture belongs to both the public sector and private sector or the corporate sector. The National Accounts Statistics of the CSO is the organized source of information on capital formation in the agricultural sector. However, it does not provide data on state-level estimates of public investment in agriculture. The private sector investment, on the other hand, comprises investment in the household sector as well as the corporate sector. The major share of investment is, however, accounted for by the household sector. Survey on the household component of private investment is usually done by the National Sample Survey (NSS) along with the RBI, once in ten years, popularly known as the AIDIS. The latest survey pertains to 1 July 2002 to 30 June 2003, in the NSS Fifty-Ninth Round.

Country-level estimates of gross capital formation (GCF) in Indian agriculture as revealed by the CSO are presented in Table 3.1. It may

Table 3.1 GCF and GDP (at constant prices)

Year	Public sector GCF as % of total GCF in agriculture	Private sector GCF as % of total GCF in agriculture	GCF in agriculture as % of total GCF	GCF in agriculture as % of total GDP	GDP in agriculture as % of total GDP	Total GCF as % of total GDP
1	2	3	4	6	7	8
1960–1	46.4	53.6	12.2	2.4	47.2	19.5
1970–1	37.2	62.7	13.5	2.7	40.9	20.3
1980–1	51.5	48.4	14.6	3.3	35.7	22.9
1990–1	29.6	70.3	8.9	2.1	29.5	23.9
2004–5	21.3	78.7	7.5	2.5	19.0	34.0
2009–10	17.7	82.3	7.7	2.9	14.6	38.5

Source: National Accounts Statistics, CSO, Various Issues

Note: Data up to 1990–1 is based on 1993–4 prices and 2004–5 onwards at 2004–5 prices

be noticed from the table that the GCF in agriculture as a percentage of total GCF increased steadily from 1960–1 to 1980–1, and thereafter it showed a continuous decline except a marginal recovery in the recent period, that is in 2009–10. The main reason for the decline in total investment in agriculture has been a declining trend of investment from public accounts during the 1980s. The proportion of public sector capital formation as a percentage of total capital formation in agriculture declined from 51.5 per cent in 1980–1 to 29.6 per cent in 1990–1 and further to 17.7 per cent in 2009–10. The percentage of GCF in agriculture to total GDP during 1960–1 stood out to be 2.4 per cent, which increased to 3.3 per cent in 1980–1, but declined further to 2.1 per cent in 1999–2000 and showed marginal improvement during 2009–10. The total capital formation as per cent of total GDP has also shown very encouraging trends after 1991 as is clearly evident from Table 3.1.

The growth rates of capital formation and GDP in agriculture is presented in Table 3.2. One can see from the table that GCF in agriculture (at 1993–4 prices) showed an increasing trend from 1960–1 to 1969–70, at the rate of 6.65 per cent and at the rate of 8.64 per cent per annum during 1970s. However, during 1980s, it registered a negative growth rate of (–0.69 per cent though it recovered marginally during

Table 3.2 Growth rate of GCF and GDP in agriculture (at constant prices)

Periods	GCF in agriculture	Public sector GCF in agriculture	Private sector GCF in agriculture	Total GDP	Total capital formation in the economy	GDP in agricultural sector
	1	2	3	4	5	6
1960–1 to 1969–70	6.65*	2.56***	9.90*	3.28*	3.99**	1.15
1970–1 to 1979–80	8.64*	9.64*	7.89**	3.51*	5.44*	1.85***
1980–1 to 1989–90	−0.69***	−4.28*	2.32**	5.43*	4.95*	3.03*
1990–1 to 1999–2000	1.85***	0.23	2.80***	6.16*	5.92**	3.27*
1999–2000 to 2009–10	8.61*	8.64*	8.14*	7.89*	12.46*	2.92*

Source: Computed from National Accounts Statistics, CSO

Note 1: *significant at 1%, **significant at 5%, ***significant at 10% level, respectively.
Note 2: Growth rate up to 1990–1 is based on 1993–4 prices and 2004–5 onwards at 2004–5 prices.

1990s, that is increased at a moderate rate of 1.85 per cent. The public sector capital formation, on the other hand, registered a sharp decline at a rate of −4.28 per cent during the 1980s. The growth rate of private sector capital formation, however, did not show as much fluctuation as it showed in the case of public investment. The aggregate capital formation in the economy grew at the rate of around five per cent during 1970s and 1980s and showed a healthy growth after the period of liberalization. The GDP in the economy registered a satisfactory growth after the initiation of economic reforms. The GDP accruing from the agricultural sector grew at the rate of 1.85 per cent during 1970s, and it recorded a growth of over three per cent per annum during 1980s and subsequently during 1990s. However, as it is evident from the table that growth rate in the agricultural sector has declined during the period from 1999–2000 to 2009–10. On the other hand, GCF in the agricultural sector showed a healthy growth of 8.61 per cent during the same period. Thus the slowdown in the agricultural sector during this period has been experienced in the midst of an increasing growth in public sector capital formation. One would however expect that the spurt in investment in agriculture during this period will bring about a beneficial impact for the entire farm sector in the coming years in view of long-term impact of public investment.

The attempt to increase public sector capital formation in the agricultural sector is nevertheless a part of the Eleventh Plan strategy of achieving inclusive growth in the country. The Eleventh Plan envisaged a substantial increase in public sector outlay on agriculture through massive expenditure on rural development. Some of these programmes are Rastriya Krishi Vikash Yojana (RKVY), Mahatma Gandhi National Rural Employment Guarantee Act (MGNREGA), Backward Region Grant Fund (BRGF) and rural infrastructure under Bharat Nirman and are expected to strengthen the growth impulse in the agricultural sector. The rural employment programme such as MGNREGA can help to boost agricultural growth through building rural infrastructure in the country. Construction of water bodies at a large scale in such programmes can help to improve irrigation facilities. Similarly, linking rural roads, one of the major components in the programme may help agriculture marketing and facilitate input delivery. Further, as Eleventh Plan mandate is growth to be inclusive, the agricultural strategy must focus on the overwhelming sections of small and marginal farmers who find it difficult to access inputs, credit and extension and to market their output.

The trends of plan outlay on agriculture, rural development, irrigation and flood control has been depicted in Table 3.3. The composition of expenditure under the head 'agriculture' covers several items, which includes crop husbandry, soil and water conservation, animal husbandry,

Table 3.3 Plan outlay agriculture and rural development (in percentage term from Sixth Plan – 1980–5 to Eleventh Plan – 2007–12)

Heads of expenditure	Sixth Plan 1980–5	Seventh Plan 1985–90	Eighth Plan 1992–7	Ninth Plan 1997–2002	Tenth Plan 2002–7	Eleventh Plan 2007–12
Agriculture	6.1	5.8	5.2	4.9	3.9	4.4
Rural development	6.4	7	7.9	8.7	8.0	7.8
Special area programme	1.4	1.6	1.6	0.4	1.4	1.2
Irrigation and flood control	10	7.6	7.5	6.5	6.8	6.2

Source: Economic Survey, Various Issues

dairy development, fisheries, plantations, agricultural research and education and agricultural financial institutions. Similarly, expenditure on irrigation and flood control, rural development programmes and special area programmes provide significant insights on the priority given to the primary sector.

When we look at the proportion of plan outlay on agriculture to total plan outlay over the successive plan periods, we find that till the end of Tenth Plan the outlay has been gradually declining, that is 6.1 per cent in the Sixth Plan to 3.9 per cent in Tenth Plan of the total plan outlay. The spurt has, however, taken place in the Eleventh Plan period. The hike in expenditure on rural development was substantial, but it started declining marginally after Ninth Plan. The proportion of expenditure on irrigation and flood control were declining till the end of Ninth Plan and showed a slight improvement during the Tenth Plan. There is therefore a need of continuous hike in public investment in agriculture to achieve the desired target of growth and to make growth truly inclusive.

Household component of private investment in agriculture: a state-wise analysis

Studies carried out on capital formation in Indian agriculture in the late 1950s and 1960s contend that the condition of agriculture in India remained predominantly subsistence and largely viewed this occupation as a way of life. There was no substantial investment on agricultural implements, irrigation and improved seeds during that period. Major proportion of the GCF of the cultivator households was related to bullocks alone and amounted to be nearly 80 per cent of the total investment (Shukla 1965). Even during 1971–2, one-fourth of the total capital expenditure was on the purchase of livestock, followed by 19.6 per cent on the purchase of agricultural implements, machinery and transport equipments (AIDIS 1971–2).

In the subsequent phases, the Government of India has taken necessary steps to provide required assistance to the farmers through planned outlay on agriculture and irrigation. Such intervention helped building up extensive irrigation potential by implementing major, medium and minor irrigation projects and required infrastructural facilities. This helped cultivators adopt new technological inputs, such as improved seeds, chemical fertilizers, etc., and create a new investment climate in their farm business. The pattern of farm investment among cultivating households, however, is largely determined by their entrepreneurial ability, soil and geographical conditions and more importantly the incentive provided to agriculture by the public sector. There are varying degrees of natural endowment required for cultivation in different parts of the country. Institutional strengths such as credit facilities, research and extension services and the land distribution pattern are also some of the factors that may influence farm investment and output. In this section, an analysis of private investment under the households component has been undertaken using the AIDIS data jointly carried out by NSSO along with RBI every ten years. It may be noted that the data on households' capital formation till 1971–2 is based on rural areas only; it is only from 1981–2 onwards that the same is available both for rural and urban areas. Therefore, for the sake of comparisons only the rural sector has been considered in the present study.

Table 3.4 presents the overall scenario of private fixed capital formation among the cultivator households, non-cultivator households and all rural households taken together. It may be noticed from the table that the proportion of households reporting capital formation under farm business has been gradually declining from 1961 to 2002. During 1961–2, 18.1 per cent of the total rural households have reported capital formation in farm business, while in the case of non-farm business and residential plots and house construction, the proportions stood out to be 2.3 per cent and 4.2 per cent, respectively. Relatively, slightly larger proportion of cultivator households (23.3 per cent) had reported capital formation in farm business during the same period. In subsequent decades, however, lesser proportions of rural households have been reporting capital formation in farm business. The proportion of rural households reporting capital formation declined to 14.9 per cent in 1971 and further to only 6.8 per cent in 2002. Similar trends were also observed in the case of cultivator households as it is evident in Table 3.4.

Capital formation for all categories of households in the rural sector is estimated to be Rs. 349.6 crores in nominal terms during 1961–2. Out of all the major rural economic activities, farm business accounts for 47.8 per cent, non-farm business 8.6 per cent, and residential plots and house construction account for 43.6 per cent. During 1971, the share of fixed capital formation in both farm business and non-farm business increased marginally, while the share of residential plots and house construction declined. But during subsequent decades, the share of investment in farm business was observed to have declined gradually. In the case of cultivator households as well, 52.5 per cent of total capital formation was accounted for by farm business in 1971–2, which declined to 29.1 per cent in 2002–3. In contrast, the respective shares of

Table 3.4 Overall scenario of private fixed capital formation – rural households 1961–2003

	Cultivator households				Non-cultivator households				All rural households			
	A	B	C	D	A	B	C	D	A	B	C	D
1961												
Farm business	23.3	32.7	165	51.1	3.6	1.1	2	8.1	18.1	24.3	167	47.8
Non-farm business	1.9	4.4	22	6.8	3.4	4.3	8	30.0	2.3	4.4	30	8.6
Residential plots and house construction	4.7	27	136	42.1	2.7	8.8	16	61.9	4.2	22.1	152	43.6
Total		64.1	323	100		14.2	26	100.0		50.8	349	100.0
1971												
Farm business	19.3	61.8	350	52.51	2.6	2.8	6	10.6	14.9	46.1	356	49.3
Non-farm business	1.9	10.9	62	9.26	3.0	6.2	13	23.2	2.2	9.7	74	10.3
Residential plots and house construction	4.4	44.9	255	38.22	2.8	17.7	36	66.2	4.0	37.7	291	40.3
Total		117.6	666	100		26.7	55	100.0		93.5	721	100.0
1981												
Farm business	16.0	176	1,266	37.6	3.58	14	32	10.1	13.1	138	1,298	35.2
Non-farm business	5.29	47	343	10.18	4.93	20	46	14.4	5.2	41	389	10.5
Residential plots and house construction	10.2	245	1,758	52.2	6.27	108	242	75.5	9.2	213	2,000	54.2
Total		468	3,366	100		142	321	100.0		392	3,687	100.0

	A	B	C	D	A	B	C	D	A	B	C	D
1991												
Farm business	11.9	545	4,199	38.27	1.8	52	205	8.4	8.5	378	4,400	32.8
Non-farm business	2.3	99	763	6.95	2.9	72	283	11.6	2.5	90	1,048	7.8
Residential plots and house construction	7.3	780	6,010	54.7	4.7	497	1,955	80.0	6.5	685	7,973	59.4
Total		1,424	10,972	100		621	2,443	100.0		1,153	13,415	100.0
2002												
Farm business	10.3	942	8,325	29.1	1.6	74	441	3.8	6.8	593	8,769	21.8
Non-farm business	1.7	372	3,288	11.5	2.6	403	2,400	20.7	2.1	384	5,681	14.1
Residential plots and house construction	5.9	1,923	16,995	59.4	4.9	1,474	8,779	75.6	5.5	1,742	25,773	64.1
Total	16.2	3,237	28,609	100.0	8.7	1,951	11,620	100.0	13.2	2,719	40,223	100.0

Source: AIDIS – various issues

A: Proportion of households reporting, B: Average value per cultivator (in Rs. at current prices), C: total value (in Rs. crore at current prices), D: Percentage of the total.

non-farm business and residential plots and house construction showed an increasing trend during this period. It may further be seen that about two-thirds of the resources were diverted to residential plots and house construction by the rural households during 2002–3. The capital formation of cultivator households followed the same trends as that of all rural households for the reason that the majority of households constituted cultivator in the rural sector. For instance, during 2002–3, 71 per cent of the total capital formation in rural sector was accounted for by the cultivator households for all purposes and about 95 per cent for farm business. Table 3.4 also brings out some of the important information regarding the average value of capital formation for cultivator households, non-cultivator households and all rural households. During 1991, the average value of capital formation for all rural households and for all purposes stood out to be Rs. 1,153 which increased to Rs. 2,719 during 2002 at current prices. For cultivator households alone, the average value was Rs. 1,424 during 1991 and increased to Rs. 3,237 in 2002 at current prices.

The growth rate of average value of fixed capital formation of the two occupational categories over the past five decades has been worked out and presented in Table 3.5. The growth rates are based on constant 1993–4 prices. It might be seen that the average value of capital formation in the rural sector has increased considerably during the decades 1971–2 to 1981–2. For all categories of households and all activities taken together, it increased at the rate of 14.7 per cent per annum during the above-mentioned period. The growth rate declined to 4.7 per cent during 1981–91 and further to 2.5 per cent during 1991–2002. For all rural households, the growth rate stood at 10.9 per cent in case of farm business. And, in case of non-farm business and residential plots and house construction, it grew at the rate of 14.8 per cent and 18.2 per cent, respectively during the period from 1971 to 1981. In subsequent decades the growth of the average value of capital formation in farm business declined considerably. In the post 1981–2 period, there was a declining preference of investment in farm business and increasing preference over non-farm business, indicating a broad diversification of rural households to the latter. This was also true in the case of cultivator households. The average value of capital formation in farm business registered a negative growth (–0.9 per cent) during the period 1991–2 to 2002–3 for all rural households; the decline was rather sharper for the non-cultivator households (–1.7 per cent). During this period, however, the growth of the average value of capital formation under non-farm business was satisfactory.

Table 3.5 Growth rate of average value of capital formation, 1961–2 to 2002–3 (at constant (1993–4) prices)

	1961–71	1971–81	1981–91	1991–2002
Cultivator households				
Farm business	5.9	10.4	5.2	–0.1
Non-farm business	8.8	15.0	1.2	6.6
Residential plots and house construction	4.6	17.8	5.5	2.9
Total	5.6	14.1	5.0	2.2
Non-cultivator households				
Farm business	9.1	16.8	7.1	–1.7
Non-farm business	3.1	11.7	6.8	10.2
Residential plots and house construction	6.6	19.1	9.5	4.5
Total	5.9	17.5	8.9	5.0
All rural households				
Farm business	6.0	10.9	3.9	–0.9
Non-farm business	7.6	14.8	1.6	7.7
Residential plots and house construction	4.8	18.2	5.6	3.2
Total	5.6	14.7	4.7	2.5

Source: Same as Table 3.4

Pattern of farm investment by cultivator households by different items

The AIDIS also provides rich information on the pattern of investment on different items in farm business. The survey report categorizes the components of farm investment into six broad heads, namely reclamation and land improvement, orchards and plantation, wells and other irrigation sources, agricultural implements and machinery, barn, golas and others. During 2002–3 surveys, 'livestock used as fixed asset' has been introduced. Therefore, for facilitating comparison with earlier decades, this component is added to agricultural implements and machinery heads as in most of the cases, livestock are used for agricultural purposes as an implement.

Table 3.6 brings out that since 1961–2, a major shift in resources has taken place to the investment on agricultural implements and machineries and wells and other irrigation resources. These two components combined together constituted around 83 per cent of the total investment during 2002–3. During the period 1961–2, reclamation and land improvements constituted about one-third of the total capital formation but showed a decline in subsequent decades. On the other hand, the investible resources diverted to irrigation and agricultural implements and machinery have registered an increase in subsequent periods. Thus, the composition of individual items of capital formation in farm business indicates increasing farm mechanization in Indian agriculture over the years. In other words, increase in productivity after the green revolution period has been mainly attributed to increasing adoption of modern farm practices.

The interregional variations of the household components of fixed capital formation in agriculture does bear significance in a sub-continent like India. Different states are endowed with different agroclimatic conditions, soil and land type, basic infrastructure and varying institutional arrangements. Table 3.7 brings out the magnitude of capital formation (average per cultivator household) across 17 major states at current prices. In the agriculturally developed states such as Gujarat, Haryana, Maharashtra, Punjab, Tamil Nadu and Rajasthan, the average value per

Table 3.6 Share of individual items of fixed capital formation in farm business – all India: cultivator household (figures in percentage)

NSS years	Reclamation and land improvements	Orchards and plantation	Well and other irrigation sources	Agricultural implements and machinery	Farm houses, barns and golas	Others	Total
1961	32.1	2.8	26.5	28.6	9.1	0.9	100.0
1971	16.5	1.8	27.1	43.2	10.3	1.1	100.0
1981	14.8	3.5	25.8	46.5	6.9	2.3	100.0
1991	14.3	1.9	31.8	45.6	4.2	2.1	100.0
2002	5.9	1.5	33.1	49.8	8.3	1.4	100.0

Source: Same as Table 3.4

Table 3.7 Statewise average value of fixed capital formation among cultivator households in farm business from 1961 to 2002 (in Rs. at current prices)

States	Average value of capital formation (in Rs. at current prices)				
	1961–2	*1971–2*	*1981–2*	*1991–2*	*2002–3*
Andhra Pradesh	44.3	29.9	187	399	944
Assam	22.6	26.1	51	51	139
Bihar	8.6	17.5	43	82	101
Gujarat	79.8	172.1	327	572	1,839
Haryana	*	*	652	876	3,870
Himachal Pradesh	*	*	103	426	1,325
Jammu and Kashmir	27.4	29.5	113	274	697
Karnataka	84.6	101.4	253	1,262	858
Kerala	22.3	22.8	136	378	961
Madhya Pradesh	18.6	54.8	151	1,028	461
Maharashtra	46.3	81	304	1,037	1,551
Orissa	24.6	16.9	38	90	431
Punjab	50.4	453.1	915	1,715	3,270
Rajasthan	27.2	70.8	234	956	1,791
Tamil Nadu	60.5	74.6	164	820	1,563
Uttar Pradesh	20	49.6	178	401	948
West Bengal	8.3	25.6	54	129	157
All India	32.7	61.8	176	545	942

Source: Same as Table 3.4

*: Not available

cultivator household was much higher than the national average during 2002–3. On the other hand, in the Eastern states, namely Orissa, West Bengal and Bihar, the average value of capital formation in farm business among the cultivator households is remarkably lower than the national average. There is, thus, a significant gap in the volume of investment in agriculture undertaken by the cultivator households in various regions of the country.

Factors influencing private investment and output in agriculture across states

The decision on investment in agriculture by the cultivator households is mainly influenced by their income potential and in most cases their eagerness to earn a reasonable living. Apart from this, conducive environment in a particular region also plays an important role in investment decision. The latter is also determined by a large chunk of public investment that can create such a conducive environment. For instance, private investment basically comes in the form of expenditure on irrigation tools, agricultural implements and machineries, livestock, etc. In order to make investment on these items, a cultivator would require credit impetus, price incentives, irrigation, power, transport and communication, etc. which are necessarily provided through public investment. Many scholars have tested the hypothesis of complementarity between public and private investment in Indian agriculture on the basis of both CSO data and broad estimates of public capital formation. In view of this, it has been interpreted that decline in public sector capital formation has simultaneously led to a decline in private sector capital formation. Chand and Kumar (2004) observed that trade and flow of institutional credit to agriculture was a strong determinant of private capital formation. Similarly, investment on rural infrastructure directly or indirectly meant for agriculture have an important role to play for enhancing agricultural investment and output and thereby poverty reduction.

In this section, an attempt has been made to analyse the factors influencing private investment in agriculture at the state level, considering several independent variables which are important for agricultural growth and development. Canal irrigation defined by the ratio of canal-irrigated area to gross cropped area has been taken as an important variable under public investment. Similarly, loan that is institutional credit per cultivator household is one of the important requirements for carrying farm investment in agriculture. Road density per square kilometre is an indicator of public investment on rural infrastructure. Private investment per cultivator household, in contrast, has been taken as a dependent variable in the regression model. The model at the state level is built taking a cross-section of data for the period 2002–3, for which the latest state level private investment data is available in the NSS. Results of the regression analysis are presented below.

$$PVTCF = -11813.7 + 0.46 \, (Canal.irrgn) + 0.81 \, (Rur.Lit)$$

$$(2.79)^* \qquad (4.97)\,^{***}$$

Adjusted $R^2 = 0.61$, F value = $(13.39)^{***}$, N = 17

PVTCF = 951.25 + 0.15 (Can. irrgn) + 0.59 (Loan)

(0.71)   (2.87)*

Adjusted $R^2 = 0.32$, F value = $(4.71)^*$, N = 17

PVTCF = 347.61 + 0.24 (Road density) + 0.40 (Land.pdv)

(1.03)   (1.70)

Adjusted $R^2 = (0.16)$, F value = 2.53, N = 17

Note: Figures in the parentheses indicates 't' values

***, ** and * indicate that the regression coefficients are significant at .01, .05 and .10 probability level, respectively.

The above results indicate that canal irrigation has a positive and significant impact on private investment in agriculture. It follows that states endowed with better canal irrigation facilities have an upper hand to keep the momentum of higher private farm investment. Positive and significant impact of canal irrigation on private investment suggests that it induces to acquire such agricultural assets as tractor, power tiller, improved plough, etc. because of assured irrigation and increasing production. Further, if the canal irrigation is protective in nature, it induces farmers to invest on private irrigation tools like well irrigations, tanks, etc. because of the improved water table as a consequence of canal irrigation. The regression equation also indicates that rural literacy has a positive and significant impact on private capital formation in agriculture. In other words, states with higher incidence of rural literacy have higher investment and output per cultivator household. In fact, the literate farmers are more alert in keeping updates on recent market trends, pest and input management and other information relating to farm production. They are also expected to accelerate adoption of new farm technology and to form farmers' interest groups to influence allocation of public resources in favour of agriculture (Roy and Pal 2002).

In the second equation, canal irrigations and loans have been taken as the independent variables. Both variables have the expected sign, though canal irrigation did not turn significant. In other words, both canal irrigation and institutional credit positively influence private investment in agriculture. Institutional credit availability to the farmers being a significant factor influencing private investment indicates that expansion of institutional credit across the rural areas in the country as well as developing an appropriate credit delivering mechanism is essential which is under the realm of public authority.

In the third equation, private investment has been considered as a function of road density and land productivity. The equation shows a poor R^2 value and low F value and none of the coefficients was significant. Nevertheless a positive sign indicates that both variables may induce private investment in agriculture. The development of roads helps farmers to carry agricultural crops to market yards and transporting various agricultural inputs namely, fertilizers and organic manures, seeds, etc. Further, the government must take adequate steps to enhance land productivity in terms of developing new varieties of seeds, by soil testing programmes and by expanding extension services and making their delivery mechanism more efficient.

The regression equations presented below suggest how government investment in agriculture through creating rural infrastructure is important for enhancing agricultural productivity in the country. In the first equation, per capita net state domestic product has been taken as the dependent variable as function of canal irrigation and rural literacy. The result indicates that both the variables have a positive and significant impact on agricultural output.

NSDP Agr (Per Capita) = −1947 + 0.58 (Canal.irrgn) + 0.46 (Rur.Lit)

(2.70)* (2.14)*

Adjusted R^2 = 0.40, F value= (4.66)*, N = 17

NSDP Agr (Per Capita) = 1233.59 + 0.38 (Canal irrgn) + 0.55 (Loan)

(2.01)*   (2.89)*

Adjusted R^2 = 0.43, F value = (7.04)**, N = 17

NSDP Agr (Per Capita) = 2249.26 + 0.13 (Road) + 0.76 (Elec.cons)

(0.76)   (4.43) **

Adjusted R^2 = 0.53, F value = (9.86) **, N = 17

Note: Figures in the parentheses indicates 't' values
***, ** and * indicate that the regression coefficients are significant at .01, .05 and .10 probability level, respectively.

In the second equation, loan per cultivator is added to canal irrigation, which raises the value of R^2. Both variables also turn out positive and significant. This suggests how important it is to extend credit facilities in order to enhance agricultural productivity. In the third equation, road density and consumption of electricity (KH per household) were taken as independent variables. Both variables bear positive signs, though only consumption of electricity turned out to be significant. It thus follows that investment on roads and creating power infrastructure are the essential components of increasing agricultural production and productivity.

Conclusion and policy explorations

The chapter concludes that there has been a clear decline of public investment in Indian agriculture based on the CSO series particularly during the 1980s. Even after broadening the concept of public investment by including several items that are essential for agricultural growth and development, the trend showed a clear decline as was seen in the review of literature. The government expenditure on agriculture and irrigation and on rural development programmes over the successive plan periods also suggests that the agricultural sector has been receiving little attention. The Eleventh Plan strategy of inclusive development envisaged a substantial increase in public sector outlay on agriculture through massive expenditure on rural development resulting in a hike in public investment in recent years.

One of the important components of this chapter was to analyse trends and determinants of private investment at the state level as per data revealed by RBI and NSSO. It has been seen that the proportion of cultivator households reporting capital formation in farm business declined from 19.3 per cent in 1971 to 10.3 per cent in 2002–3. Based on 1993–4 prices, from 1991–2 to 2002–3, the average value of fixed capital formation in farm business by cultivator household has shown a decline at the rate of –0.1 per cent. In case of non-farm business, on the other hand, there was an impressive growth rate of average value for both cultivator and non-cultivator households in rural sectors of the country. It is after the period 1981–2 that the trends indicate a broad diversification of rural households towards non-farm business. Thus, one of the important changes in the post-globalization era is that rural households including both cultivator and non-cultivators have diverted their resources from farm business to non-farm business.

There appears to be a large variation as far as the value of fixed capital formation per cultivator household is concerned across the states. In agriculturally developed states such as Gujarat, Haryana, Maharashtra,

Punjab, Tamil Nadu and Rajasthan, the average value per cultivator household was much higher than the national average in the latest round, that is in 2002–3. In contrast, in the Eastern states, namely Orissa, West Bengal and Bihar, the average value of capital formation in farm business among the cultivator households was remarkably lower than the national average. With the help of regression analysis it has been shown that cultivators in states having better agricultural infrastructure including canal irrigation, better roads, level of literacy and institutional credit tend to have higher investment in their farm business and higher output in their agriculture. On the other hand, cultivators in states lacking access to such infrastructure could not capitalize higher investment in their agriculture. Canal irrigation, as the study found, is the most important factor inducing private investment enhancing agricultural production in the country. Increased farm income under irrigated conditions would certainly induce farmers to invest on farm tools and implements which may further raise their income level and repaying capacity for the loan. It thus emerges that agricultural production and investment in agriculture would come up if a fruitful attempt is made to bridge interregional inequalities in the country in terms of improving access to rural agricultural infrastructure. The states especially in the Eastern region lag far behind as far as rural and agricultural infrastructure is concerned, and so public investment must be undertaken to improve and make their agriculture more productive and remunerative. Further, in the era of economic liberalization and globalization, the agricultural sector is required to be more competitive to sustain itself in the international market. For this reason, increased doses of public investment are required on agricultural research and development, and exploration of the possibilities of emerging areas of high-value products such as horticulture, dairy farming, bee-farming, fruit plantation, etc. Reduction of wasteful expenditure in the name of subsidy may be subsequently phased out, which could help to generate more resources for public investment.

In India, majority of the population still depends on agriculture. The poverty and malnutrition is widespread among those who directly or indirectly depend on agriculture for their livelihood. Public investment in agriculture by improving rural infrastructure is needed not merely to enhance private investment and agricultural production in the country, but to have the cumulative effect of increasing employment and betterment of large sections of the population who are depending on their livelihood from the unorganized non-farm sector. Increasing doses of public investment could therefore serve as a major social objective to reduce poverty, unemployment and malnutrition in the country.

Note

1 See, e.g. Krishnamurty (1985), Patnaik (1987), Rath (1989), Shetty (1990), Mallick (1993), Alagh (1994), Rao (1994), Gandhi (1996), Dhawan (1996), Mishra (1996).

References

Alagh, Yoginder K. 1994. 'Macro Policies for Indian Agriculture', in G. S. Bhalla (eds), *Economic Liberalisation and Indian Agriculture*, Institute for Studies in Industrial Development: New Delhi.

Alagh, Yoginder K. 1997. 'Agricultural Investment and Growth, Inaugural Address', *Indian Journal of Agricultural Economics*, 52(2): 279–87.

All India Debt and Investment Survey. 1998. 'Report on Capital Formation and Capital Expenditure', National Sample Survey 48th Round.

All India Debt and Investment Survey. 2003. 'All India Debt and Investment Survey, Report on Capital Formation and Capital Expenditure', National Sample Survey 59th Round.

Bhalla, G. S. and Singh, Gurmail. 2009. 'Economic Liberalisation and Indian Agriculture: A Statewise Analysis', *Economic and Political Weekly*, 44(52): 34–44.

Binswanger, P. Hans and Khandker, Shahidur R. 1993. 'How Infrastructure and Financial Institutions Affect Agricultural Output and Investment in India', *Journal of Development Economics*, 41(2): 337–66.

Chand, Ramesh. 2001. 'Emerging Trends and Issues in Public and Private Investment in Indian Agriculture: A State Wise Analysis', *Indian Journal of Agricultural Economics*, 56(2): 161–84.

Chand, Ramesh and Kumar, Parmod. 2004. 'Determinants of Capital Formation and Agriculture Growth, Some New Exploration', *Economic and Political Weekly*, 39(52): 5611–16.

Chand, Ramesh, Raju, S. S. and Pandey, L. M. 2007. 'Growth Crisis in Agriculture: Severity and Options at National and State Levels', *Economic and Political Weekly*, 42(26): 2528–33.

Dhawan, B. D. 1996. 'Relationship between Public and Private Investment, with Special Reference to Public Canal', *Indian Journal Agricultural Economics*, 51(1&2): 209–219.

Fan, Shenggen, Hazell, Peter and Thorat, Sukhadeo. 1999. 'Linkages between Government Spending, Growth and Poverty in Rural India', International Food Policy Research Institute, Washington, DC, Research Report No. 110.

Fan, Shenggen, Zhang, Linxiu and Zhang, Xiaobo. 2002. 'Growth, Inequality and Poverty in Rural China – The Role of Public Investment', International Food Policy Research Institute, Washington, DC, Research Report No. 125.

Gandhi, V. P. 1996. 'Investment Behaviour in Indian Agriculture', *Indian Journal of Agricultural Economics*, 51(4): 543–59.

Government of India. 2003. "Report of the Committee on Capital Formation in Indian Agriculture." Directorate of Economics and Statistics, Ministry of Agriculture, New Delhi.

Government of India. 2010. Economic Survey, Ministry of Finance, Government of India, New Delhi.

Government of India. (Various years). 'Agricultural Statistics at a Glance (Various Issues)', Department of Agriculture and Cooperation, Ministry of Agriculture, Government of India.

Gulati, Ashok and Bathla, Seema. 2001. 'Capital Formation in Indian Agriculture, Revisiting the Debate', *Economic and Political Weekly*, 36(20): 1697–708.

Krishnamurty, K. 1985. 'Inflation and Growth, a Model for India', in K. Krishnamurty and V. N. Pandit (eds), *Macro-Economic Modelling of the Indian Economy, Studies in Inflation and Growth*, Hindustan Publishing Corporation: Delhi.

Kumar, Ranjit, Singh, N. P., Singh, R. P. and Vasisht, A. K. 2006. 'Rural Infrastructure and Agricultural Growth: Interdependence and Variability in Indo-Gangetic Plains of India', *Indian Journal of Agricultural Economics*, 61(3): 469–480.

Mallick, S. K. 1993. 'Capital Formation in Indian Agriculture: Recent Trends', *Indian Journal of Agricultural Economics*, 48(4): 667–77.

Mishra, S. N. 1996. 'Capital Formation and Accumulation in Indian Agriculture since Independence', *Indian Journal of Agricultural Economics*, 51(1& 2): 193–219.

'National Accounts Statistics, CSO (Various Issues)', Ministry of Statistics and Programme Implementations, Government of India.

NSS (2003); Situation Assessment Survey of Farmers, Some Aspects of Farming, NSS 59th Round (January–December 2003) National Sample Survey Organisation, Ministry of Statistics and Programme Implementation, Government of India.

Patnaik, Prabhat. 1987. 'Recent Growth Experience of the Indian Economy: Some Comments', *Economic and Political Weekly*, 22(19/21): AN49 – An51 + AN54–AN56.

Rao, C. H. Hanumanta. 1994. *Agricultural Growth, Rural Poverty and Environmental Degradations in India*. Oxford University Press: Delhi.

Rao, C. H. Hanumantha. 1997. 'Agricultural Growth, Sustainability and Poverty Alleviation in India, Recent Trends and Major Issues of Reforms', Lecture Presented at International Food Policy Research Institute, Washington, DC, 10 December.

Rath, Nilakanth. 1989. 'Agricultural Growth and Investment in India', *Journal of Indian School of Political Economy*, 1(1): 1–16.

Report on the Committee on Capital Formation in Agriculture. (2003). Directorate of Economics and Statistics, Department of Agriculture and Cooperation, Ministry of Agriculture, Government of India.

Reserve Bank of India. (1972 and 1982). 'All India Debt and Investment Survey: Statistical Tables Relating to Capital Formation and Capital Expenditure and Capital Formation'.

Reserve Bank of India. 1977. 'All India Debt and Investment Survey, 1971–72 – Indebtedness of Rural Households and Availability of Institutional Finance', Bombay.

Roy, B. C. and Pal, Suresh. 2002. 'Investment, Agricultural Productivity and Rural Poverty in India', *Indian Journal of Agricultural Economics*, 57(4): 653–78.

Shetty, S.L. 1990. 'Investment in Agriculture: A Brief Review of Recent Trends', *Economic and Political Weekly*, 2(7&8): 389–98.

Shukla, Tara. 1965. 'Rates of Gross and Net Capital formation in Indian Agriculture and Factors influencing Them', *Indian Journal of Agricultural Economics*, 20(1).

Shukla, Tara. 1968. 'Investment in Agriculture', *Economic and Political Weekly*, 3(48): 1729, 1731–32.

Growth in fruit and vegetable crops

Emerging trends and patterns

Srinivasulu Rajendran

India is the largest producer of fruits and vegetables in the world; it accounted for 12.5 and 9.7 per cent, respectively, of the world's production in 2010 (FAO 2012). The share of fruits and vegetables to the real value (at 2004–5 prices) of agricultural output has increased from 19.2 to 26.3 per cent between 1981 and 2009. Growth rate of the value of fruits and vegetables annually has increased from 2.3 per cent to 4.3 per cent between 1981–90 and 1991–9 (CSO 2012). This is much higher than that of cereals and pulses. In 2009–10, fruits and vegetables formed the single-largest sub-sector in horticultural crops and accounted for 68.6 per cent of the area under horticulture (MoA 2011).

On the demand side, National Sample Survey data (MoSI&P 2012) show that the share of monthly per capita expenditure on fruits and vegetables has increased from 12.2 per cent in 1993–4 to 14.6 per cent in 2009–10 in rural areas, and from 14.9 per cent to 15.7 per cent in urban areas. With growing demand and a positive supply response, fruits and vegetables have assumed importance in Indian agriculture in terms of diversification towards horticultural crops (Birthal *et al.* 2008; Mittal 2007; Kumar 1998; Kumar and Mathur 1996; Singh *et al.* 2004). According to Chand *et al.* (2008), though the share of fruits and vegetables in Gross Cropped Area (GCA) increased from 2.8 per cent to 4.9 per cent and from 16.0 per cent to 25.8 per cent in output between 1980–1 and 2005–6, productivity growth decelerated after 2000–1. Conscious of the slowdown, the Government of India took a major initiative in 2004 under the National Horticulture Mission (NHM) to increase the share of horticulture in total food and non-food crops, improve yield and ensure better returns to farmers.

As per the Agricultural Census (2000–1), small farmers (<2 hectares) allocated 5.7 per cent of their total cropped area to horticultural crops, compared to 3.9 per cent by the large farmers (>4 hectares). Further, over the period, the share of horticultural crops in the total cropped area has increased proportionately more than that of the large farmers. This implies a rising tendency of diversification towards horticultural crops on large farms as well but at a slow pace. This situation may vary across horticultural crops. Fruits and vegetables, being the major constituents of horticultural crops, received considerable attention among other crops for being a frontrunner in providing highly attractive returns to producers as compared to other crops (Birthal *et al*. 2012; Birthal *et al*. 2008; Mittal 2007; Kumar 1998; Kumar and Mathur 1996; Singh *et al*. 2004). Especially, it contributed more to the well-being of the small-holders, as it is a labour intensive sector and generates more employment (Joshi *et al*. 2006).

Currently, the farm productivity in many Indian states is quite low as compared to their potential level. Particularly for fruits and vegetables, the yield has come down drastically and thereby there is large disparity in yield (Chand *et al*. 2008). Even though some disparity in yields are unavoidable due to differentials in climatic and other socio-economic factors, the current state of affairs indeed points towards the scope to raise crop production in the country by plugging the yield gaps in low-productive states through technological interventions (Chand *et al*. 2007). Under the given circumstances, increasing crop production, particularly of fruits and vegetables crops, through reducing the yield gaps by introducing technological interventions is an important concern for the policymakers, farmers and researchers. There are several studies in the literature that have analysed, (1) trends and pattern through growth analysis for major horticultural crops; (2) instability, acceleration and deceleration of growth of output (Chand *et al*. 2008; Sawant and Achuthan 1995) and (3) sources of growth through decomposition analysis (Birthal 2008; Chand *et al*. 2008; Chand, Raju and Pandey 2007; Kannan and Sundaram 2011; Kumar 2008; Pradeep 2009). However, based on literature this is the first study to examine and report the disaggregate level within fruits and vegetables at state level for the recent past.

In this background, (1) the study examines the patterns and trends emerging in fruits and vegetables growth across states in India, (2) verifies the existence of statistically significant acceleration in output growth and (3) examines the factors that contribute to growth and thereby adds value addition to the existing knowledge base studies for the policy implications. This chapter is organized in four sections. The first section discusses the sources of data and methodology. The second section focuses on performance of growth at the all-India level for horticulture crops, while the third section deals with performance of growth at the state level, the sub-sections of the third section describe the growth performance of fruits and vegetables separately during the pre- and post-2000 period. Finally the last section concludes with policy implications.

Data sources and methodology

The study evaluates the growth performance of fruit and vegetable crops for two decades, that is from 1991–2 up to 2009–10. The main focus of the study is on the comparison between two sub-periods, namely Period I – 1991–2 to 2000–1 and Period II – 2001–2 to 2009–10. The study uses the data published by the National Horticulture Board (NHB), Ministry of Agriculture, Government of India.

Compound Annual Growth Rates (CAGRs) have been estimated by fitting a simple trend function (1) to the time series of three years average of area, production and yield.

$$Log\ \Upsilon = a + bt \tag{1}$$

Where,

> Y's are the triennial averages of Y, the original observations of area, production and yield.
> t is the time variable, a is intercept and b is growth coefficient.

CAGRs are separately computed for two sub-periods for all the datasets related to the categories of fruits, vegetables, other horticulture crops and all horticulture crops. In addition to this, the same estimation is also done for the entire period for the above-mentioned horticulture crop categories. Besides, this study also attempted to verify the existence of statistically significant acceleration in output growth by estimating a quadratic function (2) in time variable:

$$Log\ \Upsilon = a + bt + ct^2 \tag{2}$$

This function is fitted to the time series of triennial averages of area, production and yield for fruits, vegetables, other horticulture crops and all horticulture crops. This exercise has also been undertaken for 18 states to ascertain emergence of acceleration or deceleration in their output growth. Finally the study estimates the effects of area and yield on the production of horticulture crops through decomposition analysis (Taffesse *et al.* 2008) at state and all India levels for the aforesaid periods.

The quantity of output of crop i (Q_{it}) is the product of yield (y_{it}) and acreage allocated to its production (A_{it}). Decomposition can thus take the following approximate form:

$$dQit \approx Aitdyit + yitdAit \tag{3}$$

The decomposition reveals the relative contribution of changes in acreage and yield to the overall change in the quantity of output. This is a policy-relevant issue to the extent that changes in acreage and yield reflect government interventions in the horticultural sector and the wider economy.

Horticultural sector – India

The results in Table 4.1 show that area under total horticultural crops has grown considerably from 12.9 million hectares (TE) in 1993–4 to 20.6 million hectares (TE) in 2009–10, registering a robust expansion of 59.6 per cent. The area has increased markedly at a 1 per cent level of significance at a CAGR of 3.3 per cent per annum during the reference period. During 2001–2 to 2009–10, the area under horticulture crops has grown by 29.6 per cent (from 15.9 million hectares (TE) to 20.6 million hectares (TE)) as compared to 19.4 per cent (from 12.9 million hectares (TE) to 15.4 million hectares (TE)) witnessed during 1993–4 and 2000–1. It shows that the expansion in area under horticulture crops has been relatively faster during 2001–2 to 2009–10 as compared to the previous decade. This is also reflected in the CAGR estimated for these two time periods, yet in both the periods area expansion has been highly significant at 1 per cent level of significance.

The CAGR for area under total horticultural crops has increased from 2.8 per cent to 3.3 per cent between 1993–4 to 2000–1 and 2001–2 to 2009–10, respectively. However, Table 4.2 which depicts the result of the quadratic trend function in time variable to ascertain the pace of growth deciphers that though there has been an expansion in area under these crops during 2001–2 to 2009–10, acceleration in the growth has moderated considerably at a 5 per cent level of significance. Nevertheless, it cannot be refuted that diversification is rapidly taking place in the Indian agricultural sector which has given further push to the cultivation of high value crops. Some studies (Birthal *et al.* 2012; Jha *et al.*

Table 4.1 CAGR for horticultural crops

Year	Indicator	Fruits	Vegetables	Other horticulture	Total horticulture
Growth rate					
(1993–4 to 2000–1)	Area	(3.2)*	(2.7)*	(2.7)*	(2.8)*
	Production	(4.1)*	(5.2)*	(3.3)*	(4.7)*
	Yield	0.9	(2.4)*	0.6	(1.8)*
(2001–2 to 2009–10)	Area	(6.5)*	(3.8)*	0.4	(3.3)*
	Production	(6.4)*	(5.5)*	(3.0)*	(5.5)*
	Yield	–0.1	(1.6)*	(2.6)*	(2.1)**
(1993–4 to 2009–10)	Area	(4.3)*	(2.9)*	(2.7)*	(3.3)*
	Production	(3.8)*	(4.5)*	(3.1)*	(4.1)*
	Yield	(–0.5)**	(1.5)*	0.4	(0.8)*
Coefficient of variation					
(1993–4 to 2000–)	Area	7.6	6.9	6.6	6.9
	Production	9.9	12.8	8.2	11.2
	Yield	3.7	6.3	2.8	4.7
(2001–2 to 2009–10)	Area	17.2	10.7	9.9	9.1
	Production	17.7	15.3	9.5	15.2
	Yield	3.9	4.7	8.4	8
(1993–4 to 2009–10)	Area	23	15.3	16.3	16.4
	Production	20.8	22.8	16	21.3
	Yield	5.1	7.7	6.2	6.9

Source: NHB and Author's Calculation

Note: (*) and (**) Significant at 1 per cent and 5 per cent levels, respectively

2009; Joshi *et al.* 2007; Mittal 2007) emphasized that this change has primarily been demand driven due to change in the lifestyle, change in consumption pattern, improving health consciousness, importance of balanced diet and marked improvement in affordability. Besides, change in the focus of government policies away from basic food sufficiency to ensure availability of nutritional and wholesome balanced food has led to immense thrust on the production of horticulture crops particularly fruits and vegetables.

The results further show that though the area under total horticulture crops has increased significantly at 1 per cent level of significance, it is fruits and vegetables which have witnessed the highest area expansion at a 1 per cent level of significance. In fact, between 1993–4 and 2009–10, area under fruits and vegetables expanded at an accelerated significant pace at 1 per cent level. Area under fruits has nearly doubled from 3,088 thousand hectares (TE) in 1993–4 to 6,096 thousand hectares (TE) in 2009–10 growing at a CAGR of 4.3 per cent per annum while acreage under vegetables has grown at a relatively slower rate of 2.9 per cent during 1993–4 and 2009–10. The area under vegetables has grown from 5,171 thousand hectares (TE) to 7,940 thousand hectares (TE) during the reference period. Post-2000–1, fruits followed by vegetables with a CAGR of 6.5 per cent and 3.8 per cent, respectively have played a critical role in enhancing the total area under horticulture crops while other horticulture crops have not witnessed any significant expansion in area.

With the expansion of area, production of horticulture crops has also increased tremendously. The total production had risen by 39.8 per cent from 106.2 million tonnes in TE 1993–4 to 148.5 million tonnes in TE 2000–1. In the subsequent decade, the horticulture production further increased to new heights from 148.4 million tonnes in TE 2001–2 to 216.4 million tonnes in TE 2009–10, registering a growth of 45.8 per cent (6.0 per cent higher over the first decade). It is also found that in the second decade, moderation in area growth under these crops did not have any virtual impact on their production growth. Robust CAGR of 5.5 per cent during 2001–2 to 2009–10 and 4.7 per cent during 1993–4 to 2000–1 has averaged out the CAGR to around 4.1 per cent during 1993–4 to 2009–10. Consequently, production nearly doubled from 106.2 million tonnes (TE) to 216.4 million tonnes (TE). Though, both area and production increased considerably throughout the period, there is huge variation as manifested in high coefficient of variation (CV). In fact, there has been massive increase in CV during the period from 1993–4 to 2000–1 and 2001–2 to 2009–10. CV in area has moved up from 6.9 per cent to 9.1 per cent and that in production from 11.2 per cent to 15.2 per cent which shows increase in instability in the way both area and production have taken shape in the past two decades.

The reason could be attributable to too much dependency on factors such as weather condition, lack of area-specific latest technology, instability in the prices of output and input commodities, reduced capital formation particularly by public sector, injudicious usage of inputs and animal behaviour linked to short-term price gains. Due to these factors, rise in area has been unequally translated into rise in yield, thereby escalating the overall variation in horticulture production. The CV in overall horticulture yield also nearly doubled from 4.7 per cent in the first decade to 8.0 per cent in the second decade.

Further Table 4.1 indicates that during 1993–4 and 2000–1 all three crops categories namely, fruits, vegetables and other horticulture crops performed exceptionally well in terms of production at 1 per cent level of significance. The study also measured the acceleration and deceleration in area, production and yield based on quadratic functions. The results show (Table 4.2) that in the case of vegetables, between 1993–4 and 2000–1, both area and yield improved, but yield had accelerated while area showed signs of deceleration. Faster rise in the former over the latter, resulted in a faster rise in production at 1 per cent level of significance. During this period, productivity grew by nearly 24.0 per cent from 12.1 metric tonnes (TE) in 1993–4 to 15.0 metric tonnes (TE) in 2000–1. However, 2001 onwards, the scenario underwent a change. Growth in vegetable yield gained momentum and remained significant at 1.0 per cent. Like vegetables, fruits also experienced area expansion, albeit at a decelerated rate. This together with other factors such as high dependency on monsoon, poor soil fertility and weak extension services had impacted the yield and, therefore, production increased at a declining pace. The CAGR of fruits yield continued to remain insignificant and in fact, it turned negative from 0.9 per cent during 1993–4 to 2000–1 to –0.1 per cent during 2001–2 to 2009–10 as rise in production could not keep pace with expansion in area due to sizeable lack of advanced techniques and weak extension services as inferred from in exorbitantly high CV. Though the decline in yield remained statistically significant during 2001–2 and 2009–10, if it continues for a while, it may lead to significant plunge in yield in years to come.

Other horticulture crops (category) have shown a remarkable progress in the CAGR of yield between two time periods, from positively insignificant growth of 0.6 per cent during 1993–4 to 2000–1 to a highly significant CAGR of 2.6 per cent during 2001–2 to 2009–10.

Table 4.2 Estimates of quadratic in time variable fitted to triennial average of area, production and yield: all India

Dependent/ independent variable	Fruits			Vegetables		
	Area	Production	Yield	Area	Production	Yield
Growth rate (1993–4 to 2000–1)						
Constant	7.9091	10.1148	2.2057	8.5456	11.0084	2.4627
t	(0.0439)*	(0.1180)*	(0.0741)**	−0.0152	0.0053	0.0205
t_sqr	−0.001	(−0.0060)*	(−0.0050)**	0.0032	(0.0035)*	0.0003
R_sqr	0.99	0.99	0.76	0.95	0.99	0.86
Growth rate (2001–2 to 2009–10)						
Constant	7.3356	11.0056	3.67	8.713	11.7473	3.0343
t	0.0917	−0.0844	(−0.1761)*	−0.0233	−0.0827	−0.0594
t_sqr	−0.001	(0.0049)*	(0.0058)*	0.002	0.0045	(0.0025)**
R_sqr	0.98	0.99	0.82	0.96	0.96	0.93
Growth Rate (1993–4 to 2009–10)						
Constant	8.034	10.4789	2.4449	8.4844	10.964	2.4796
t	0.0032	0.0037	0.0006	0.0109	(0.0318)*	(0.0208)**
t_sqr	(0.0018)*	(0.0015)**	−0.0003	(0.0008)*	0.0005	−0.0003
R_sqr	0.98	0.93	0.29	0.98	0.97	0.89

(Continued)

Table 4.2 (Continued)

Dependent/ independent variable	Other horticultural crops			Horticultural crops		
	Area	Production	Yield	Area	Production	Yield
Growth Rate (1993–4 to 2000–1)						
Constant	8.3099	9.0298	0.7199	9.3839	11.4379	2.054
t	(0.0481)*	(0.0989)*	0.0508	0.0222	(0.0497)*	0.0275
t_sqr	–0.0017	(–0.0051)*	–0.0034	0.0004	–0.0003	–0.0007
R_sqr	0.99	0.97	0.63	0.98	0.99	0.85
Growth Rate (2001–2 to 2009–10)						
Constant	6.1498	7.4939	1.3441	8.5048	12.0144	3.5096
t	(0.3616)**	(0.2703)*	–0.0913	(0.1471)*	–0.0504	(–0.1975)**
t_sqr	(–0.0119)**	(–0.008)*	0.0039	(–0.0038)**	0.0035	(0.0073)**
R_sqr	0.59	0.91	0.82	0.96	0.98	0.85
Growth Rate (1993–4 to 2009–10)						
Constant	8.1974	9.174	0.9766	9.3504	11.5401	2.1897
t	(0.0705)*	(0.0436)*	–0.0269	(0.0302)*	(0.0241)**	–0.0061
t_sqr	(–0.002)**	–0.0006	(0.0014)**	0.0001	0.0007	0.0007
R_sqr	0.8	0.93	0.35	0.98	0.97	0.43

Source: NHB and Author's Calculation

Note: (*) and (**) Significant at 1 per cent and 5 per cent level, respectively

This clearly points towards strong technological advancements made during 2000s and perhaps good availability of extension services, for such crops could demonstrate relatively better stability in their production as compared to fruits and vegetables. However, robust productivity growth during 2001–2 and 2009–10 could not offset the sluggish growth of the 1990s. Hence, for the entire two decades, the growth in yield remained insignificant at 0.4 per cent. There is a need to nurture these crops with further advanced agricultural inputs and improving the knowledge of farmers through extension services. The other major factor contributing to the above trend could be the relatively less perishability of other horticultural crops vis-à-vis fruits and vegetables.

To validate the aforesaid argument, the present study also measured area and yield effects through decomposition analysis (Table 4.3). The results reveal that both area and yield effects are almost similar for total horticulture crops during 1991–2 to 2009–10, whereby pre- and post-2000s also show similar effect. However, the scenario changed for fruits. The relative contribution of change in yield effect is higher than the

Table 4.3 Decomposition analysis for horticulture crops at all India level – 1991–2 to 2009–10

Categories	Variable	Area effect	Yield effect
Total horticulture	Overall	1.002***	1.0108587***
	Pre 2000	0.980***	0.991***
	Post 2000	1.008***	1.010***
Fruits	Overall	0.904***	1.025***
	Pre-2000	0.971***	0.975***
	Post-2000	0.832***	0.942***
Vegetables	Overall	0.998***	0.928***
	Pre-2000	0.985***	0.880***
	Post-2000	0.974***	0.995***
Other horticulture	Overall	1.054***	0.898***
	Pre-2000	0.993***	0.970***
	Post-2000	1.136***	0.927***

Source: NHB and Author's Calculation

Note: Overall (1991–2009), pre-2000 (1991–2000), post-2000 (2001–9)
Legend: *$p<0.05$; **$p<0.01$; ***$p<0.001$

area effect in improving the production of fruits during both decades pre- and post-2000s. However, the magnitude of effect has come down during 2001–2 and 2009–10. As far as vegetables are concerned, area effect remained dominant during the overall period. But during 1990s, production was improved by area expansion, whereas in the post-2000s it was yield that played a vital role in improving the production of vegetables. The reason for the same could be the ongoing several programmes that could have impacted area expansion but were lacking in their focus on technology. Therefore, in case of both fruits and vegetables, the government policies had an impact on area expansion, but it appears that they failed in promoting technology innovation necessary for the improvement in yield and production. So, it is necessary to focus more on technology innovations to improve production of fruits and vegetables. Nonetheless, in the category of 'other horticulture crops'[1] post-2000, the growth rate of yield has gone up, which is a clear indication of technology upgradation that played a vital role for improving their production. To validate this decomposition analysis shows that in the post-2000s, although both effects were significantly positive at 1 per cent level, the coefficients of yield effect remained lower than that of the area effect.

State-level analysis: fruit and vegetable crops

Fruits category

(1) During the 1990s

Statewise CAGR and CV of Area, Production and Yield for fruits are presented in Tables 4.4 and 4.5, respectively. Table 4.4 shows that during 1993–4 and 2000–1, area expansion under fruits in the majority of the states led to 3.2 per cent growth in total area at the all India level. Fastest rise was seen in Haryana (9.4 per cent) followed by Gujarat (8.5 per cent), Maharashtra (7.3 per cent), Orissa (6.6 per cent), Tamil Nadu (6.0 per cent), Karnataka (5.3 per cent) and Himachal Pradesh (5.2 per cent). In all these states not only was growth high, it was statistically significant as well. The pace of area expansion in these states was well above that of the national average. On the other hand, states like Jammu and Kashmir, Kerala, Madhya Pradesh, Rajasthan and Tripura experienced shrinkage in area under fruits as the growth rate had been negative. The shrinkage in area in these states could be due to diversion of some land into other horticultural crops.

Table 4.4 Statewise CAGRs of area, production and yield for fruits (per cent)

States	CAGRs for 1993–4 to 2000–1			CAGRs for 2001–2 to 2009–10			CAGRs for 1993–4 to 2009–10		
	Area	Production	Yield	Area	Production	Yield	Area	Production	Yield
Andhra Pradesh	(3.2)*	1.0	(−2.1)*	(8.1)*	(10.5)*	(2.2)*	(6.9)*	(5.9)*	(−0.9)*
Assam	(1.7)*	(2.0)*	0.2	(1.8)**	(2.5)*	0.8	(0.9)*	(1.3)*	(0.5)*
Bihar	(1.4)*	0.8	−0.6	0.1	1.1	1.0	0.05	(−1.1)*	(−1.2)*
Gujarat	(8.5)*	0.5	(−7.5)*	(9.6)*	(14.3)*	(4.2)*	(7.6)*	(7.6)*	−0.1
Haryana	(9.4)*	(8.8)*	−0.6	1.6	(1.4)*	−0.2	(4.7)*	(5.2)*	0.5
Himachal Pradesh	(5.2)*	−0.5	(−6.0)*	−0.4	(8.3)*	(8.6)*	0.6	(5.0)*	(4.4)*
Jammu and Kashmir	−0.2	(3.3)*	(2.9)*	(5.4)*	(6.4)*	0.8	(2.1)*	(4.1)*	(1.8)*
Karnataka	(5.3)*	(5.7)*	0.5	1.2	(2.3)**	(1.0)*	0.6	0.4	−0.2
Kerala	−2.1	−1.6	−0.2	(7.2)*	(9.9)*	(2.9)*	(2.6)*	(2.3)*	−0.6
Madhya Pradesh	−0.6	2.3	(2.9)*	3.2	4.2	1.1	−1.0	1.2	(2.2)*
Maharashtra	(7.3)*	(7.5)*	−0.04	(14.4)*	(3.2)*	(−10.2)*	(12.5)*	(7.0)*	(−4.8)*
Orissa	(6.6)*	(4.8)*	(−1.8)*	(3.2)*	(1.3)*	(−1.8)*	(3.2)*	(1.3)*	(−1.8)*
Punjab	−3.4	−1.2	(3.8)*	(8.5)*	(11.6)*	(2.8)*	(−3.4)*	1.4	(4.9)*
Rajasthan	−0.3	(17.5)*	(17.8)*	(7.1)*	(10.6)*	3.6	(3.1)*	(6.8)*	(3.8)*

(Continued)

Table 4.4 (Continued)

States	CAGRs for 1993–4 to 2000–1			CAGRs for 2001–2 to 2009–10			CAGRs for 1993–4 to 2009–10		
	Area	Production	Yield	Area	Production	Yield	Area	Production	Yield
Tamil Nadu	(6.0)*	(7.2)*	1.4	(4.3)*	(8.3)*	(3.8)*	(3.4)*	(3.9)*	0.5
Tripura	(–7.0)*	(3.2)*	(10.7)*	(2.9)*	(2.5)*	–0.4	(–1.6)**	(3.3)*	(4.8)*
Uttar Pradesh	0.3	2.9	2.5	(2.0)*	(5.2)*	(3.2)*	–0.1	1.1	(1.2)*
West Bengal	0.2	(3.8)*	(3.5)*	(4.8)*	(6.3)*	(1.4)*	(3.6)*	(5.9)*	(2.2)*
All India	(3.15)*	(4.07)*	0.9	(6.48)*	(6.36)*	–0.1	(4.34)*	(3.78)*	(–0.53)**

Source: NHB and Author's Calculation

Table 4.5 Statewise CV of growth rates for fruits (per cent)

States	CV for (1993–4 to 2000–1)			CV for (2001–2 to 2009–10)			CV for (1993–4 to 2009–10)		
	Area	Production	Yield	Area	Production	Yield	Area	Production	Yield
Andhra Pradesh	7.9	6.5	6.5	21.1	27.2	6.3	35.3	34.6	8.5
Assam	4.8	5.5	1.1	8.0	9.2	3.7	7.1	8.8	3.4
Bihar	3.7	10.5	10.6	1.9	5.2	5.2	2.9	11.6	11.2
Gujarat	19.5	6.8	21.3	24.6	35.6	11.5	37.5	45.7	16.3
Haryana	21.8	21.3	2.8	10.3	4.9	7.8	23.6	24.6	7.0
Himachal Pradesh	13.9	8.0	18.0	4.8	24.1	26.6	9.8	31.0	33.0
Jammu and Kashmir	4.3	9.1	7.7	15.0	16.8	3.7	14.3	21.8	9.6
Karnataka	12.5	13.9	3.0	9.1	10.7	3.2	10.5	12.3	3.7
Kerala	11.0	7.8	13.7	21.3	28.8	10.2	21.1	23.8	13.2
Madhya Pradesh	3.7	10.7	9.4	22.3	27.0	6.9	16.7	21.0	12.7
Maharashtra	18.7	26.3	10.9	33.8	8.9	34.6	60.6	33.2	28.1
Orissa	15.8	12.4	4.6	9.2	5.0	5.9	16.1	9.3	9.3
Punjab	15.7	10.1	13.4	22.1	31.9	9.8	30.3	23.9	25.0
Rajasthan	2.2	35.2	35.5	20.2	32.3	17.6	20.4	37.6	26.3

(Continued)

Table 4.5 (Continued)

States	CV for (1993–4 to 2000–1)			CV for (2001–2 to 2009–10)			CV for (1993–4 to 2009–10)		
	Area	Production	Yield	Area	Production	Yield	Area	Production	Yield
Tamil Nadu	14.3	18.1	9.7	12.8	25.9	13.1	17.8	25.8	11.2
Tripura	18.9	8.5	24.6	8.1	7.2	3.7	16.6	16.3	23.7
Uttar Pradesh	2.1	12.4	10.3	7.3	18.1	11.5	5.6	15.3	11.0
West Bengal	4.5	13.0	10.0	12.8	17.0	5.2	19.7	30.0	11.7
All India	7.6	9.1	4.3	17.2	17.7	4.0	23.0	21.4	4.1

Source: NHB and author's calculation

There are however some exceptions. During 1990s, Rajasthan despite experiencing deceleration in area attained the highest production growth of 17.5 per cent among all the other states. It is followed by Haryana (8.8 per cent), Maharashtra (7.5 per cent), Tamil Nadu (7.2 per cent) and Karnataka (5.7 per cent). In all these states, production growth has been statistically significant leading to more than 4.0 per cent growth in fruit production at the all India level. Jammu and Kashmir and Tripura like Rajasthan also recorded a high growth in production of 3.2 per cent even with declining area growth, which was an outcome of improvement in the yield in these states. In fact, Rajasthan and Tripura had the highest yield growth among all states during 1993–4 and 2000–1.

In general, yield performance had largely been unsatisfactory during 1993–4 and 2000–1 for the majority of the states under study due to technology gap, high dependence on monsoon, poor soil fertility due to excessive usage of fertilizers, pesticides, poor quality of seeds and other factors. However, Rajasthan and Tripura were able to maintain a robust growth in the yield of 17.8 per cent and 10.7 per cent, respectively, while fruit yield in other states grew at a slower pace and for some it was negligible, as production grew at a slower pace in comparison to the expansion in area. Punjab is an exceptional case where even positively significant growth in yield could not augment production due to large contraction in area under fruits.

(2) During the 2000s

During 2001–2 and 2009–10, at the all India level, the yield came down to –0.1 per cent from 0.9 per cent in the previous decade owing to decline in the large number of states such as Jammu and Kashmir, Madhya Pradesh, Maharashtra, Rajasthan, Tripura, West Bengal and Punjab. The fall however had been hard hitting in Maharashtra, Rajasthan, Tripura, West Bengal and Jammu and Kashmir. The major reasons behind the gloomy performance were the lack of advanced and appropriate technology and increased marginalization of land holdings which erodes the benefits of large-scale production. Negative yield in Haryana, Maharashtra, Orissa and Tripura had contributed to overall stagnancy in all India yield growth. The fall in the yield was particularly disturbing in Maharashtra and Orissa with –10.2 per cent and –1.8 per cent, respectively. In Maharashtra, area growth doubled in the 2000s from 7 per cent in the 1990s to 14 per cent in the 2000s but production declined by half from 7.5 per cent to 3.2 per cent during the same time period. Whereas, in Orissa, production plunged more due to contraction in area under fruits as yield continues to fall at the same rate experienced in the previous decade.

On the other hand, Himachal Pradesh with 8.6 per cent and Gujarat with 4.2 per cent were the best performing states and to an extent Uttar Pradesh and Tamil Nadu. Himachal Pradesh has shown marked improvement in production on the back of robust increase in yield despite fall in area. This shows that technological intervention by the government had been successful in its objective. In 2005, the government of India has introduced the Technology Mission for Integrated Development of Horticulture in Himachal Pradesh along with Jammu and Kashmir, Uttaranchal and eight other North-Eastern states.

Overall poor yield growth in the 1990s and 2000s was manifested in a significant deceleration in yield at 5.0 per cent level of significance during the entire period. Yet production managed to grow at a statistically significant rate of 3.8 per cent which points towards a magnificent role played by area expansion. Nearly half of the states exhibited a negatively significant yield during the 2001–2 and 2009–10 ranging between –0.1 and –4.8 per cent. Maximum plunge was, however, noticed in Maharashtra and followed by Orissa and Bihar. In Himachal Pradesh, yield growth improved remarkably on account of the technology factor as compared to area in the 2000s which had pulled the yield growth for the entire period (1993–4 and 2009–10). Bihar happened to be the only state which lagged behind its counterparts both in terms of slow growth in area expansion under fruits and production of fruits. There was insignificant increase in area while production declined significantly at 1.0 per cent growth rate in the past two decades.

The statewise CV (Table 4.5) shows that in general the fluctuation in area and production had been higher in the 2000s and in upward direction, which means that both the area and production increased notably in the states, but the pattern had been unsteady. States like Bihar, Haryana, Himachal Pradesh, Karnataka, Orissa and Tripura have shown moderation in area growth during 2001–2 and 2009–10 as compared to 1993–4 and 2000–1, which is also associated with the downward stability in production and yield.

(3) Overall Period (1993–4 to 2009–10)

During 1993–4 and 2009–10, variation in both area and production scaled up at an all India level triggered by instability in area expansion and production while yield remained nearly stable. Invariably high volatility in area is found in Maharashtra (60.6 per cent) followed by Gujarat,

Andhra Pradesh and Punjab between 30 and 38.0 per cent. In production, variability is mainly led by variability in area under fruit cultivation in Gujarat, Andhra Pradesh and Maharashtra. Himachal Pradesh, West Bengal and Rajasthan are special cases where wide fluctuations in production are associated with both area and technology.

As far as fruits are concerned, the decomposition analysis (Table 4.6) shows that there are many states where technical intervention is much more important than area expansion in order to improve fruit production. On the other hand, there are some states namely Haryana, Himachal Pradesh, Kerala and Rajasthan, where the results reveal that the relative contribution of changes in area needs to be expanded to increase the production of fruits. In Haryana and Himachal Pradesh the area growth rate came down between pre- and post-2000 (Table 4.5); therefore, there is room to increase area expansion. However, in states like Kerala and Rajasthan the growth rate of area increased drastically and significantly between pre- and post-2000; hence, there appears to be less room for more area expansion under fruits. Nevertheless, the results of decomposition analysis show that in order to increase the production of fruits in these states (i.e. Kerala and Rajasthan), it is necessary to increase area effect by further increasing the area under fruits.

Vegetables category

(1) During the 1990s

Statewise CAGRs and CV of area, production and yield for vegetables are presented in Tables 4.7 and 4.8, respectively. Vegetables also experienced rise in both area and production at a statistically significant rate of 2.7 per cent and 5.2 per cent, respectively. Though the rate of growth of area expansion was slower as compared to 3.2 per cent growth in area under fruits, vegetables had a better yield growth of 2.3 per cent, more than double of the 0.9 per cent witnessed in fruits which led to higher production growth as compared to the 4.1 per cent growth in fruit production. Most of the states, barring Bihar, Rajasthan, Maharashtra and Punjab, showed positive growth in yield. However, highest yield was attained in Jammu and Kashmir at a growth of 12.0 per cent, trailed by West Bengal (7.2 per cent), Tamil Nadu (5.2 per cent), Andhra Pradesh (3.8 per cent) and Tripura (3.0 per cent) where yield growth rate had been well above the national average of 2.3 per cent. Except few states, vegetable yield growth was far better than that of fruits in most of the states. Further, in most of these states production had increased on account of significant rise in area and to an extent by technology improvements. Whereas in

Table 4.6 Decomposition analysis for total fruits crop at state level – 1991–2 to 2009–10

State	Overall		Pre-2000		Post-2000	
	Area effect	Yield effect	Area effect	Yield effect	Area effect	Yield effect
Andhra Pradesh	0.975***	1.041***	0.992***	1.084***	0.958***	1.001***
Assam	1.122***	1.048***	0.991***	1.093***	1.117***	1.017***
Bihar	0.976***	1.056***	0.976***	1.037***	0.989***	1.084***
Gujarat	0.827***	0.995***	0.776***	1.053***	0.917***	0.946***
Haryana	0.899***	0.853***	0.913***	1.003***	0.899***	0.855***
Himachal Pradesh	0.983***	0.746***	0.988***	0.964***	0.971***	0.644**
Jammu and Kashmir	0.936***	0.849***	0.937**	0.805**	0.970***	0.987***
Karnataka	0.958***	0.958***	0.954***	0.996***	0.931***	0.952***
Kerala	1.113***	0.732***	1.025***	0.705***	1.452***	0.570**
Madhya Pradesh	1.057***	1.041***	1.047***	0.986***	1.046***	1.044***
Maharashtra	0.716***	1.353***	0.865***	0.967***	0.741**	1.471***
Orissa	0.940***	1.133***	0.916***	1.161***	0.946***	1.038***
Punjab	1.004***	0.671***	1.173**	0.692***	0.943***	0.970***
Rajasthan	0.897***	0.846***	1.050***	0.938***	0.872***	0.807**
Tamil Nadu	0.993***	0.985***	0.983***	0.933***	1.002***	1.019***
Tripura	0.954***	0.583***	0.998***	0.565***	0.965***	1.026***
Uttar Pradesh	1.026***	1.021***	1.003***	1.098***	1.027***	1.003***
West Bengal	0.965***	0.992***	0.973***	1.040***	0.963***	0.955***
All India	0.904***	1.026***	0.971***	0.975***	0.832***	0.942***

Source: NHB and author's calculation

Note: Overall (1991–2009); Pre2000 (1991–2000); post-2000 (2001–9)
Legend: *p<0.05; **p<0.01; ***p<0.001

Table 4.7 Statewise CAGRs of area, production and yield for vegetables (per cent)

States	CAGRs for (1993–4 to 2000–1)			CAGRs for (2001–2 to 2009–10)			CAGRs for (1993–4 to 2009–10)		
	Area	Production	Yield	Area	Production	Yield	Area	Production	Yield
Andhra Pradesh	(7.1)*	(11.2)*	(3.8)*	(4.2)*	(9.8)*	(5.4)*	(4.4)*	(7.1)*	(2.6)*
Assam	(3.1)*	(6.0)*	(2.7)*	(3.8)**	(7.0)*	(3.0)*	(2.1)*	(4.5)*	(2.3)*
Bihar	(–5.8)*	(–6.0)*	–0.3	(4.0)*	(6.4)*	(2.4)*	0.2	1.1	(0.9)*
Gujarat	(7.7)*	(9.0)*	0.9	(9.4)*	(13.0)*	(3.3)*	(8.3)*	(10.1)*	(1.5)*
Haryana	(8.9)*	(9.2)*	0.3	(10.2)*	(7.9)*	(–2.1)*	(9.8)*	(8.4)*	(–1.2)*
Himachal Pradesh	(2.2)*	(3.8)*	1.6	(8.1)*	(8.7)*	0.5	(3.8)*	(6.0)*	(2.2)*
Jammu and Kashmir	–13.3	1.9	(12.0)*	(6.2)*	(11.5)*	(5.2)*	0.1	(7.1)*	(5.7)*
Karnataka	0.2	(2.4)*	1.4	(3.1)*	(6.2)*	3.0	(2.3)*	1.4	–1.1
Kerala	(–4.9)**	(–0.6)**	4.9	(5.3)*	(4.6)*	–0.7	(–3.8)*	(0.9)**	(4.8)*
Madhya Pradesh	(3.9)*	(6.7)*	(2.5)*	4.2	(4.0)**	–0.1	0.3	1.3	(1.0)*
Maharashtra	(8.8)*	(6.1)*	(–2.6)*	(1.7)*	(3.7)*	2.0	(4.7)*	(4.4)*	–0.4
Orissa	1.3	(3.3)*	(1.9)*	–0.1	(1.1)*	1.2	(–1.8)*	–0.2	(1.6)*
Punjab	(5.0)*	(3.9)*	–1.1	(3.8)*	(3.8)*	–0.01	(4.1)*	(4.4)*	0.3

(Continued)

Table 4.7 (Continued)

States	CAGRs for (1993–4 to 2000–1)			CAGRs for (2001–2 to 2009–10)			CAGRs for (1993–4 to 2009–10)		
	Area	Production	Yield	Area	Production	Yield	Area	Production	Yield
Rajasthan	(6.8)*	(3.9)*	(−2.7)*	(4.7)*	(11.5)*	(6.5)*	(4.9)*	(6.8)*	(1.8)*
Tamil Nadu	−2.1	(8.5)*	(5.2)*	(4.4)*	(6.5)*	(2.0)*	1.7	(5.2)*	(2.2)*
Tripura	−5.0	−2.5	(3.0)*	(0.7)*	(2.6)*	(1.7)*	0.2	(1.4)*	(1.1)*
Uttar Pradesh	(0.7)*	(3.3)*	(2.6)*	(3.7)*	(4.7)*	0.9	(2.7)*	(4.3)*	(1.5)*
West Bengal	(15.1)*	(23.3)*	(7.2)*	(2.3)*	(2.6)*	0.4	(6.7)*	(9.2)*	(2.5)*
All India	(2.7)*	(5.2)*	(2.3)*	(3.8)*	(5.4)*	(1.5)*	(2.9)*	(4.5)*	(1.5)*

Source: NHB and author's calculation

Legend: *p<0.05; **p<0.01; ***p<0.001

Jammu and Kashmir and Tamil Nadu, yield enhanced purely due to the introduction of advanced technology as growth in area showed a declining trend. Tripura and Kerala, however, were special cases where significant contraction in area outstripped the positive yield effect growth, thereby resulting in a significant decline in production of vegetables. In Bihar, production declined considerably on account of decline in both area and yield, but the contribution of area in the decline was higher than that of yield rate. In Maharashtra and Rajasthan, significant increase in production was purely led by statistically significant increase in acreage; yield declined significantly, which reflect either the limitation of soil fertility to respond to technological changes or the absence of appropriate technological interventions during the 1990s in these states.

(2) During the 2000s

During 2001–2 and 2009–10, though area increased under vegetables to 3.8 per cent from 2.7 per cent during the 1990s, the increase was marginal. Further it was comparatively lower than that of fruits (6.5 per cent) during this period which clearly highlights the growing popularity of fruits among farmers and the thrust laid by central and state governments. But there had been substantial difference in terms of yield growth rate of fruits and vegetables. The yield growth of fruits showed stagnancy with a negative growth of 0.1 per cent while that of vegetables had been positively significant (1.5 per cent), which lead to growth in production accordingly. It can be said that vegetable production growth was attributable to both increase in area and technology as compared to mainly area expansion in case of fruits. Higher productivity for vegetables as compared to fruits shows the existence of far better technological innovations for improving the productivity of vegetables as compared to fruits. This could be due to several reasons such as better adaptability of vegetables in adverse climatic conditions in comparison to fruits, better adaptability to soil condition and other such factors.

In Rajasthan vegetable production grew by almost three times. This is remarkable in a dry state as increase in production came from rise in yield as area moderated. In fact, it had reported the highest yield growth of 6.5 per cent from –2.7 per cent growth registered during 1993–4 and 2000–1. Area growth in Rajasthan was moderated to 2.1 per cent from 6.8 per cent in the 1990s to 4.7 per cent in the next decade. The next highest yield growth was recorded by Andhra Pradesh (5.4 per cent) and Jammu and Kashmir (5.2 per cent). In Jammu and Kashmir, the cumulative effect of both area and yield which increased at a statistically significant rate of 6.2 per cent and 5.2 per cent, respectively, led to a robust surge in production. Production expanded by 11.5 per cent. But in comparison to the 1990s, yield growth remained half during 2000s, which points towards growing ineffectiveness of the available technology and makes the case for technological upgradation subjected to regional needs. Bihar and Tripura made a comeback in 2001–2 and 2009–10 by registering positively and significant growth in area, yield and production. In Tripura, though yield remained positively significant, it has grown at a lower rate vis-à-vis in the 1990s. It is also important to highlight that during 2001–2 and 2009–10, Andhra Pradesh, Tamil Nadu and Gujarat excelled fairly well in both fruits and vegetables unlike others and attained statistically significant growth in area, yield and production.

In the majority of the states including bigger states such as Haryana, Madhya Pradesh, Punjab and Kerala, faster rise in area over yield led to rise in production. This clearly brings to the fore the need to lay greater focus on promoting better technological innovation, scientific soil treatment to improve soil productivity and expanding the availability of assured irrigation.

(3) Overall period (1993–4 to 2009–10)

Nearly stable performance during the 1990s and 2000s led to stable growth in area and yield during the entire period 1993–4 to 2009–10 amounting to 2.9 per cent and 1.5 per cent, respectively. Jammu and Kashmir and Kerala emerged as the top performing states in terms of yield growth with a growth of 5.7 per cent and 4.8 per cent, respectively, with virtually no significant expansion in area under vegetable cultivation. Other states mostly experienced yield growth in the range of 0–2.6 per cent. Though Haryana, Karnataka and Maharashtra exhibited subdued yield performance, production surged owing to decent growth in area.

The CV (Table 4.8) shows that area remained highly unstable in both decades. However, increased fluctuations in 2001–2 and 2009–10 accentuated the instability for the entire period. However, like fruits, yield showed relatively less volatility as in most of the states even with increase in the area, yield failed to deliver on the expected lines. For a good number of the states, dramatic surge in area during 2000s scaled up the CV. On the other hand, in production, a similar scenario prevailed and is in upward direction except in Tripura, Orissa and West Bengal, which showed considerable downward moderation in volatility. During 1993–2010, Haryana, Jammu and Kashmir, Kerala and

Table 4.8 Statewise CV of CAGR for vegetables (per cent)

States	CV for (1993–4 to 2000–1)			CV for (2001–2 to 2009–10)			CV for (1993–4 to 2009–10)		
	Area	Production	Yield	Area	Production	Yield	Area	Production	Yield
Andhra Pradesh	17.6	25.5		10.9	12.2	26.6	15.4	21.7	36.1	15.9
Assam	7.8	15.1		7.7	15.0	24.5	11.2	14.4	27.5	13.2
Bihar	15.7	17.9		4.2	11.3	17.5	7.0	13.1	17.8	6.8
Gujarat	18.2	21.8		5.4	24.0	32.7	9.4	40.5	50.5	9.5
Haryana	21.4	22.9		2.5	25.9	20.7	6.7	46.7	39.6	7.3
Himachal Pradesh	5.7	9.4		5.3	21.2	22.9	2.3	22.7	32.2	11.6
Jammu and Kashmir	69.5	25.2		25.9	19.8	33.8	16.1	49.6	43.9	27.3
Karnataka	6.8	8.1		9.9	8.7	21.9	14.7	13.2	16.9	15.3
Kerala	16.1	2.4		20.0	17.6	13.5	6.2	29.1	10.0	26.3
Madhya Pradesh	10.8	16.7		6.3	18.8	16.7	4.8	15.3	16.1	6.7
Maharashtra	21.6	17.8		8.6	6.4	15.0	8.5	23.0	23.6	8.7
Orissa	5.8	8.5		5.7	3.2	4.3	3.3	12.2	7.7	8.3
Punjab	11.8	11.2		5.8	10.1	11.7	4.1	20.1	22.4	5.3
Rajasthan	16.2	10.0		7.1	12.8	29.7	18.1	23.6	38.4	16.1
Tamil Nadu	35.8	20.8		14.4	14.1	19.9	6.0	25.3	27.2	12.3
Tripura	14.1	10.3		7.5	5.2	7.8	5.2	10.4	11.3	6.9
Uttar Pradesh	6.2	9.8		7.3	10.2	13.0	3.7	14.9	21.9	8.3
West Bengal	35.5	49.7		17.4	6.2	8.5	4.4	30.1	38.0	14.3
All India	7.0	12.8		6.1	10.7	15.3	4.7	15.3	22.8	7.7

Source: NHB and author's calculation

Orissa showed less moderation in production as compared to area but still on the higher side. States like Jammu and Kashmir, Kerala, Rajasthan, Andhra Pradesh and Karnataka showed high variation in yield. The decomposition analysis for vegetables (Table 4.9) reveals that almost all

Table 4.9 Decomposition analysis for total vegetables crop at state level

State	Overall		Pre-2000		Post-2000	
	Area effect	Yield effect	Area effect	Yield effect	Area effect	Yield effect
Andhra Pradesh	0.946***	0.967***	0.935***	0.933***	0.9720***	1.022***
Assam	0.948***	0.937***	0.961***	1.029***	0.980***	0.905***
Bihar	0.948***	0.984***	0.952***	1.042***	0.847***	0.969***
Gujarat	0.946***	0.943***	0.936***	0.884***	0.9150***	0.989***
Haryana	0.899***	0.995***	0.890***	0.963***	0.908***	1.000***
Himachal Pradesh	0.901***	0.934***	1.013***	0.935***	0.805**	0.884***
Jammu and Kashmir	1.190***	0.470***	1.340**	0.443***	0.917***	1.007***
Karnataka	1.017***	0.659***	1.094***	0.697***	0.957***	.963***
Kerala	1.035***	0.886***	0.765*	0.574*	1.101***	1.168***
Madhya Pradesh	1.021***	1.048***	0.976***	0.894***	0.960***	1.069***
Maharashtra	0.893***	1.042***	0.878***	1.034***	0.934***	1.018***
Orissa	0.977***	0.994***	0.983***	0.996***	0.947***	0.997***
Punjab	0.967***	0.993***	0.969***	0.973***	0.961***	1.035***
Rajasthan	0.964***	0.994***	1.001***	0.992***	0.954***	0.993***
Tamil Nadu	1.629***	0.288***	1.691***	0.282***	0.929***	1.010***
Tripura	0.825***	0.989***	0.538*	0.880***	0.920***	1.005***
Uttar Pradesh	1.01***	0.969***	1.022***	0.958***	0.967***	1.015***
West Bengal	0.885***	0.810***	0.718***	0.893***	0.988***	1.011***
All India	0.998***	0.928***	0.983***	0.879***	0.974***	0.995***

Source: NHB and author's calculation

Note: Overall (1991–2009); Pre-2000 (1991–2000); Post-2000 (2001–9)
Legend: *p<0.05; **p<0.01; ***p<0.001

the states must necessarily focus on technology intervention to improve production of vegetables rather than on area expansion.

Conclusion

As highlighted by several studies (Chand 2008; Joshi *et al.* 2007; Mittal 2008) the horticulture sector in India got a real boost only post-1990s backed by both strong demand and supply-side factors. Demand-side determinants such as change in lifestyle, change in food habits, increasing health consciousness, importance of balanced diet and growing affordability have driven demand for such high value crops in general and that for fruits and vegetables in particular (Kumar 1998; Mittal 2008). While on the supply side, a catalytic role is being played by government policies, higher profitability and improvement in infrastructure, which expanded the focus from attaining basic food sufficiency to ensure availability of nutritional and wholesome balanced food and has turned out to be a booster for the horticulture sector particularly fruits and vegetables (Birthal *et al.* 2008; Joshi *et al.* 2004). Though considerable diversion of cropped area has taken place from basic crops towards horticulture crops by farmers due to better returns, yet supply has lagged to keep pace with the demand (Birthal *et al.* 2012; Chand and Shinoj 2012; Joshi *et al.* 2007).

The study shows that extensive area had been brought under fruit and vegetable cultivation in almost all the states; however, the proportion of land under fruits and vegetables in total horticulture crops varies across states. In states like Himachal Pradesh, Maharashtra, Jammu and Kashmir, Andhra Pradesh and Tripura nearly half of the horticulture land was devoted to fruit cultivation by 2009–10. On the other hand, in Haryana, West Bengal, Bihar, Punjab, Uttar Pradesh, Assam and Orissa, where vegetables form a major part of people's diets, more than half of their horticulture land was already under vegetable crops by 2000–1, which further increased by 2009–10. The reasons behind massive area expansion under vegetables include quick returns, more labour and shorter gestation period (Birthal *et al.* 2008; Birthal *et al.* 2012).

The results show that in the past two decades there had been significant increase in the area under horticulture crops, particularly fruits and vegetables, spearheaded by faster expansion during the 2000s as compared to 1990s. It is further observed that surge in the production of these crops collectively and individually was more an outcome of improvement in yield than that of area expansion during 1993–4 and 2000–1. Increased use of modern seeds, chemical fertilizers and electricity together contributed to increase in productivity (Birthal *et al.* 2008; Kannan and Sundaram 2011). This scenario somewhat changed during 2000s; all horticulture crops experienced expansion in production due to both area and yield, yet more through area expansion. While, relatively weak growth in the yield of fruits indicates technological gaps and weak extension services during this period (Chand *et al.* 2008). In addition, high CV during 2001–2 and 2009–10 in area, production and yield as compared to the 1990s clearly emphasized that there was relatively high instability in area, production and yield. This instability in yield could be due to many factors such as sluggish growth in inputs, deterioration of soil fertility due to inefficient use of chemicals, slow seed replacement cost, choice of right seeds, absence of strong extension services, lack of training of farmers, growing marginalization of farm holding, inefficiency in transfer of technology in fields, depleting water table and price volatility (Birthal *et al.* 2008). It also points to the fact that the NHM, which was introduced in 2005 for developing the horticulture sector, largely remained lopsided in its outcome. It has so far remained highly successful in expanding the area but failed to scale up the productivity levels that it was expected to promote. This result was also supported by the decomposition analysis; coefficients of yield effect were found to be higher than the area effect on changes in production and thereby leading to the inference that technology should have played a vital role in improving the level of production in the post-2000 period.

Further to this, one of the quickest expansions in area under both fruits and vegetables witnessed between 2001–2 and 2009–10 in states like Maharashtra, Andhra Pradesh, Punjab, Uttar Pradesh, Tamil Nadu, Karnataka and Madhya Pradesh (Chand *et al.* 2008) was an outcome of the state-specific government policies as well. The pro-horticulture initiatives and rise in prices have led to the rapid diversification towards horticulture crops, mainly fruits and vegetables. To increase the production of high value crops unused land is also being brought under cultivation to the extent possible. For example, Tamil Nadu exhibits a peculiar trend, unlike other states there has been an almost equal expansion in the area under fruits and vegetables in this state in the past ten years. This state has in fact been one of the important drivers in augmenting the overall horticulture production in India. This also underscores the role of the state government in developing Tamil Nadu as the major hub of horticulture crops and is also a reflection of efficient management of resources and climatic conditions for the maximization of output. Maharashtra is at the bottom with negative productivity in spite of the highest increase in acreage under fruits and vegetables collectively. Among all states, Rajasthan can be a good case study. The state government's policies have lent a tremendous support to the flourishing horticulture sector in the desert, which includes amendment of the Agricultural Produce Market Committee (APMC) Act for fostering direct purchase and contract farming of horticulture production, massive upscaling of micro-irrigation, establishment of 19 specific commodity markets and promotion of crop-specific cluster in the regions.

In a nutshell it can be said that this sector has a huge potential and can assume an important role in uplifting the socio-economic conditions of people living in rural areas in developing countries like India. But in order to realize its full potential, it is imperative to address the issues of decline or stagnancy in the fruit and vegetable yield given that land will become a scarce resource in years to come. Until now, government policies remained overtly supportive to area expansion over technology improvement and its real time use at the farm level. At present the challenge is not only to augment productivity through region-specific technological advancement, improving soil fertility, establishment of a strong extension services network, assured irrigation and growing marginalization of land, among others, but challenges are also posed from fast-shrinking agricultural land due to its diversion to non-farm activities and the fast-evolving occupational structure in the country where mass exodus is taking place from rural areas to urban areas in search of better jobs.

Note

1 Excludes fruits and vegetables in horticulture crops.

References

Birthal, Pratap Singh. 2008. 'Linking Small Holder Livestock Producer to Market: Issues and Challenges', *Indian Journal of Agriculutral Economics*, 63(1): 19–37.

Birthal, Pratap Singh, Joshi, Pramod Kumar, Chauhan, Sonia and Singh, Harvinder. 2008. 'Can Horticulture Revitalise Agricultural Growth?', *Indian Journal of Agricultural Economics,* 63(3): July–September.

Birthal, Pratap Singh, Joshi, Pramod Kumar, Roy, Devesh and Thorat, Amit. 2012. 'Diversification in Indian Agriculture toward High-Value Crops: The Role of Small Farmers', *Canadian Journal of Agricultural Economics* 61(1): 195–229.

Brajesh, Jha, Tripathi, Amarnath and Mohanty, Biswajit. 2009. 'Drivers of Agricultural Diversification in India, Haryana and the Greenbelt Farms of India', Working Paper Series No. E/303, Institute of Economic Growth: Delhi.

Chand, Ramesh. 2008. 'Progress and Potential of Horticulture in India', *Indian Journal of Agricultural Economics*, 63(3): 299–309.

Chand, Ramesh and Parappurathu, S. 2012. 'Temporal and Spatial Variations in Agricultural Growth and Its Determinants', *Economic and Political Weekly*, June 30, XLVII(26–27): 56–64.

Chand, Ramesh, Raju, S.S. and Pandey, L.M. 2007. 'Growth Crisis in Agriculture: Severity and Options at National and State Levels', *Economic and Political Weekly*, 42(26): 2528–33.

Chand, Ramesh, Raju, S.S. and Pandey, L.M. 2008. 'Progress and Potential of Horticulture in India', *Indian Journal of Agricultural Economics*, 63(3), July–September.

CSO. 2012. 'Statewise and Cropwise Estimates of Value of Output from Agriculture (1980–2009)', Central Statistical Organization, Ministry of Statistics and Programme Implementation, Government of India (GoI).

FAO. 2012. 'Food and Agriculture Organization Statistics', Food and Agriculture Organization of the United Nations, Rome, Italy.

Joshi, P. K., Gulati, A., Birthal, P. S. and Tewari, L. 2004. 'Agriculture Diversification in South Asia: Patterns, Determinants and Policy Implications', *Economic and Political Weekly*, June 12–18, 39(24): 2457–2467.

Joshi, P. K., Gulati, A. and Cummings, Ralph, Jr. 2006. 'Agricultural Diversification and Smallholders in South Asia', Academic Foundation: New Delhi.

Joshi, P. K., Gulati, A. and Cummings, Ralph, Jr. 2007. 'Agricultural Diversification and Smallholders in South Asia', Academic Foundation: New Delhi.

Kannan, Elumalai and Sujata, Sundaram. 2011. 'Analysis of Trends in India's Agricultural Growth', Working Paper – 276, Bangalore: The Institute for Social and Economic Change.

Kumar, Praduman. 1998. 'Food Demand and Supply Projections for India', Agricultural Economics Policy Paper 98–01, IARI Monograph, New Delhi, India: Indian Agricultural Research Institute.

Kumar, Praduman and V.C. Mathur. 1996. 'Structural Changes in Demand for Food in India', *Indian Journal of Agricultural Economics*, 51(4): 664–73.

Kumar, Praduman, Mittal, Surabhi and Hossain, Mahabub. 2008. 'Agricultural Growth Accounting and Total Factor Productivity in South Asia: A Review and Policy Implications', *Agricultural Economics Research Review*, 21(2): 145–72.

Kumar Praduman, Mruthyunjaya and Pratap S. Birthal. 2007. 'Changing Consumption Pattern in South Asia' in P. K. Joshi, A. Gulati and Ralph

Cummings Jr. (eds), *Agricultural Diversification and Smallholders in South Asia*. Academic Foundation, New Delhi.

Mittal, Surabhi. 2007. 'Can Horticulture Be a Success Story for India?', Working Paper No. 197, New Delhi: Indian Council for Research on International Economic Relations.

Mittal, Surabhi. 2008. 'Need for Export Oriented Horticultural Growth', *Business Standard*, January 1.

MoA. 2011. 'Land Use Statistics at a Glance 2010', Directorate of Economics and Statistics, Ministry of Agriculture (MoA), Government of India (GoI).

MoSI&P. 2012. 'Household Consumption of Various Goods and Services in India, 2009–10', NSS 66th Round, Report No 541, Ministry of Statistics and Implementations and Programmes (MoSI&P).

Pradeep, Kumar Mehta. 2009. 'Diversification and Horticultural Crops: A Case of Himachal Pradesh', Unpublished PhD dissertation, University of Mysore.

Sawant, S. D. and Achuthan, C. V. 1995. 'Agricultural Growth across Crops and Regions: Emerging Trends and Patterns', *Economic and Political Weekly*, 30(12): A2–13.

Singh, H. P., Nath, Prem, Dutta, O. P., and Sudha, M. 2004. 'Volume 11: Horticulture Development', in *State of the Indian Farmer: A Millennium Study*, pp. 254–68, New Delhi: Academic Foundation.

Taffesse, Alemayehu Seyoum, Dercon, Stefan, Hill, Ruth Vargas and Zeitlin, Andrew. 2008. 'Decomposition of Growth in Cereal Production in Ethiopia', Paper prepared for the DFID funded study on 'Understanding the constraints to continued rapid growth in Ethiopia: the role of agriculture', Ethiopian Economics Association, December.

Chapter 5

Total factor productivity growth and its determinants in agriculture

A case of Karnataka

Elumalai Kannan

Karnataka is one of the developed Indian states placed above the median level of social and economic development (Bhalla and Singh 2001; Deshpande 2004). The growth and structure of Karnataka's economy have undergone dramatic changes since the introduction of the new economic policy in the 1990s. The state economy has registered an impressive average annual growth rate of over 7.0 per cent during 1999–2000 to 2007–8 with a major share of this high growth coming largely from the booming services (tertiary) sector. With structural change, the share of agriculture and allied sectors in the Gross State Income (at 1999–2000 prices) declined from 28.0 per cent in 1999–2000 to 15.0 per cent in 2011–12, while the share of industry increased only marginally from 27.2 per cent to 28.3 per cent. However, the contribution of the services sector increased significantly from 44.9 per cent to 56.7 per cent between 1999–2000 and 2011–12. The structural changes observed in the state economy are largely in line with the changes evident at the national level.

Considering the fact that the overall economy has been greatly influenced by the tertiary sector with an anticipated decline in the contribution of the agriculture and allied sectors to state income, the structural transformation should have substantially transferred people dependent on agriculture to the non-agricultural sector. However, this has not happened at both the state and national levels. According to the 2011 Population Census, agriculture supported 13.74 million workers, who constituted about 49.28 per cent of the total workforce in the State of Karnataka. A decline in income share combined with a large dependent workforce on agriculture has hindered productivity gains in this sector over time. Further, despite considerable efforts made by the state government to augment the irrigation potential, area irrigated to gross cropped area (GCA) has remained low at 32 per cent.

The green revolution technology introduced in the late 1960s in the form of high yielding varieties (HYV) seeds and chemical fertilizers greatly helped to increase crop production in the state. This was made possible with higher public investment in agricultural research, education and training, irrigation and other infrastructures. However, the technological gains could not spread evenly across regions and crops in the state due to diverse agroclimatic conditions and varying natural resource endowments. The growth performance of the agricultural sector has also been varied with wide fluctuations. Meanwhile, there were concerns on stagnation in production and productivity of crops during 1980–1 to 1989–90. An expert committee constituted by the state government in 1993 concluded that investments made in agriculture during 1980s were not optimally utilized to sustain the growth momentum witnessed during the 1970s. While analysing the impediments to agricultural growth, Deshpande (2004) contended that both public and private investments have not adequately been made in the backward regions particularly in the unirrigated plateau zone of Northern Karnataka and that of Southern Karnataka to spur the growth process. There is also empirical evidence to suggest that productivity growth measured by total factor productivity (TFP) declined during the 1980s (Ananth et al. 2008). But, there is lack of research evidence to show whether declining productivity growth in the crop sector has reversed during the recent years. This is particularly important from the point of view of renewed efforts made by the state government through various developmental programmes for accelerating growth in the agricultural sector. This, in fact, forms the motivation for the present study to estimate and analyse trends in the TFP of important crops in the State of Karnataka. From the policy perspective also, it is important to assess and understand the determinants of TFP so as to take appropriate initiatives for accelerating agricultural output growth. More specifically, the present study estimates the TFP growth of major crops in Karnataka and analyses the factors affecting TFP at the state level.

The rest of the chapter is organized as follows. The first and second sections discuss data and analytical methods. Changes in cropping pattern and growth in area, production and yield of crops are presented in the third and fourth sections, respectively. The fifth section analyses trends in public investment in Karnataka's agricultural sector. The cost structure of major crops is discussed in the sixth section. The seventh and eighth sections discuss growth in input, output and TFP index, and determinants of TFP, respectively, followed by concluding remarks in the final section.

Database and methodology

In the present study, TFP is estimated taking into account two output and nine input series. Output index includes main product and by-product. The input index comprises seed, fertilizer, manure, human labour, animal labour, machine labour, pesticide, irrigation and land. Data on quantity and value of output and inputs for ten major crops, namely paddy, jowar, maize, ragi, arhar, groundnut, sunflower, safflower, cotton and sugarcane have been compiled from the Cost of Cultivation of Principal Crops published by the Ministry of Agriculture, Government of India and the Department of Agriculture, Government of Karnataka. However, for some of the inputs only value is available, the quantity of such inputs is measured through indirect methods. For instance, the quantity of by-product has been generated by using grain-straw ratios as given by Nirman *et al.* (1982) and Kolay (2007), while machine labour is measured as number of four-wheeled tractors. Land has been measured as the total area under respective crops. The wholesale price index of pesticides and electricity consumption in agriculture has been used to derive the quantity of pesticides and irrigation, respectively. Further, for constructing aggregate (weighted) output, input and TFP indices for all crops in Karnataka as a whole, the share of area of respective crops in the GCA have been used as weights.

To analyse the determinants of TFP, the data on government expenditure on research, education, extension, farmers training, rural literacy, canal irrigation, rainfall and fertilizer consumption have been compiled from published sources. The Combined Finance Accounts published by the Comptroller and Auditor General of India provides data on expenditure on research, education and extension. Information on canal irrigation, fertilizer consumption, rainfall and rural literacy has been compiled from the Statistical Abstract of Karnataka published by the Directorate of Economics and Statistics, Government of Karnataka.

Analytical method

In simple terms, productivity is defined as the ratio of output to input. The partial productivity measures like labour productivity and land productivity are of limited use in the presence of multiple outputs and multiple inputs as they do not indicate the overall productivity when considered in isolation. When the productivity concept is extended beyond single output and single input, an alternative approach for aggregating outputs and inputs is used. The TFP relates the aggregate output index to aggregate input index. Growth accounting (index number method) is commonly used for measuring TFP in the agricultural sector, as it is easier to implement without econometric estimation (Desai and Namboodiri 1997; Elumalai and Pandey 2004; Evenson *et al.* 1999; Kumar and Mruthynjaya 1992; Kumar and Rosegrant 1994; Kumar *et al.* 2004; Mukherjee and Kuroda 2003; Murgai 2005). Under the growth accounting method, TFP measures growth in output which is not accounted for growth in inputs. In other words, the residual productivity is considered as a measure of technical change, which indicates a shift in the production function.

Among index number methods the Tornqvist–Theil index, which is an approximation to the Divisia index, is widely used for constructing the aggregate output index and aggregate input index. The properties and difficulties in using the Divisia index in its original integral form are expounded in Hulten (1973). The popularity of the Tornqvist–Theil index can be attributed to the fact that it is exact for linear homogenous translog production function and such an index is called 'superlative' by Diewert (1976). Further explanation on theoretical properties and issues in measurement can be found in Diewert (1978, 1980), Christensen (1975), Capalbo and Antle (1988) and Coelli *et al.* (2005).

The Tornqvist–Theil output, input and TFP index in logarithmic form can be expressed as follows:

Output Index

$$\ln\left(Q_t / Q_{t-1}\right) = 1 / 2 \sum_j \left(S_{jt} + S_{jt-1}\right) \ln\left(Q_{jt} / Q_{jt-1}\right)$$

Input Index

$$\ln\left(X_t / X_{t-1}\right) = 1 / 2 \sum_i \left(S_{it} + S_{it-1}\right) \ln\left(X_{it} / X_{it-1}\right)$$

TFP Index

$$\ln\left(TFP_t / TFP_{t-1}\right) = \ln\left(Q_t / Q_{t-1}\right) - \ln\left(X_t / X_{t-1}\right)$$

Where S_{jt} is the share of output j in total revenue, Q_{jt} is output j, S_{it} is the share of input i in total input cost, X_{it} is input i and all specified in time t.

For constructing the TFP index, chain index is preferred to fixed base index (Coelli *et al.* 2005). Chain index combines annual changes in productivity to measure changes in productivity over a period of time. Formally, let $I(t + 1, t)$ be an index for the period $t + 1$ with the base period t. This index is applied to time series $t = 0$ to T. A comparison between period t and fixed base 0 is made by following the chain indexing of successive periods.

$$I(0, t) = I(0, 1) \times I(1, 2) \times I(2, 3) \times\ldots\ldots\ldots \times I(t{-}1, t)$$

Changes in cropping pattern

Foodgrain crops dominate the cropping pattern accounting for about two-thirds of the total GCA in Karnataka (Table 5.1). Among foodgrains, coarse cereals occupy a prominent place in the cropping pattern. Nevertheless, per cent area under foodgrains has declined from 71.9 per cent in the triennium ending 1962–3 to 60.0 per cent in the triennium ending 2007–8. However, the decline in area under foodgrains was offset by an increase in area under oilseeds and other cash crops (which includes coconut, arecanut, chillies and coffee). Data on horticultural crops are compiled by the Directorate of Economics and Statistics, Government of India and the National Horticultural Board (NHB). However, data compiled by these two government agencies do not match due to differences in the method of data collection. The coverage of crops by them also differs. As per NHB data, the share of area under fruits and nuts in the GCA has marginally declined during recent years. However, the share of area under vegetables has increased to 3.1 per cent in 2007–8 from 1.0 per cent in 1992–3.

During 2007–8, jowar and rice occupied a predominant position in the cropping pattern followed by sunflower and maize. Despite accounting for a relatively high share, the area under jowar declined drastically since the early 1960s. A similar pattern could be noticed with respect to other coarse cereals like bajra, ragi and small millets. In fact, jowar and small millets seem to have lost their area by over 50 and 80 per cent, respectively between 1962–3 and 2007–8. However, crops like maize, arhar (pigeon pea) and gram have gained in their relative area during the study period. Maize constituted only 0.1 per cent of GCA in 1962–3, which has steadily increased to reach 1.4 per cent in 1982–3 and then

Table 5.1 Changes in cropping pattern in Karnataka (percentage share of GCA)

Crop	TE 1962–3	TE 1972–3	TE 1982–3	TE 1992–3	TE 2000–1	TE 2007–8
Rice	9.9	10.7	10.3	10.3	11.9	11.2
Jowar	28.0	21.8	19.2	18.0	15.4	11.3
Bajra	4.8	4.6	5.4	3.3	2.6	3.3
Maize	0.1	0.7	1.4	2.3	4.9	7.8
Ragi	9.6	9.8	9.8	8.8	8.1	6.2
Wheat	2.9	2.9	3.0	1.7	2.2	2.1
Small millets	4.2	4.1	3.2	1.1	0.6	0.3
Cereals	59.7	55.4	52.4	45.5	46.6	42.2
Arhar	2.7	2.5	3.3	3.9	4.3	4.9
Gram	2.5	1.4	1.3	1.7	2.8	4.4
Pulses	11.9	11.0	13.2	13.8	15.8	17.6
Foodgrains	71.9	68.3	66.6	59.4	62.4	59.7
Groundnut	8.4	9.2	7.6	10.5	9.3	7.1
Sunflower	–	–	1.0	8.6	4.9	9.6
Total oilseeds	9.7	11.0	12.2	22.7	17.3	19.5
Cotton	9.3	10.2	9.0	5.0	4.7	3.1
Sugarcane	0.7	1.0	1.6	2.2	3.1	2.2
Tobacco	0.4	0.3	0.5	0.4	0.6	0.8
Fruits and nuts	–	–	–	1.2	2.6	2.1
Vegetables	–	–	–	1.0	2.8	3.1
Others*	0.7	1.3	4.6	4.8	6.7	7.2
GCA	100.0	100.0	100.0	100.0	100.0	100.0

Source: Government of Karnataka (various issues)

Note: *includes coconut, areca nut, chillies and coffee

to 7.8 per cent in 2007–8. Similarly, per cent area under arhar in total cropped area has increased from 2.5 per cent in 1972–3 to 4.9 per cent in 2007–8. Although the share of area under gram decelerated during the 1970s and early 1980s, it started picking up since the 1990s.

Groundnut is one of the traditional crops grown in Karnataka both under irrigated and rain-fed conditions. The per cent area under this crop declined sharply since 2000 due to persistent drought-like conditions prevailing in the state. However, share of area under sunflower registered sharp increase from 1.0 per cent in 1982–3 to 9.6 per cent in 2007–8. Among cash crops, the area under cotton declined drastically over time. However, sugarcane area increased considerably from the 1960s to the 2000s, but showed a declining trend since 2001–2. It emerges from the analysis that there has been a marked shift in area from cereals to pulses, oilseeds and high-value crops like vegetables and plantation crops.

Growth in area, production and yield

The compound annual growth in area, production and yield of major crops grown in Karnataka is given in Table 5.2. Growth rates have been computed for four different periods, namely pre-green revolution (1960–1 to 1966–7), green revolution (1967–8 to 1979–80), post-green revolution (1980–1 to 1989–90) and economic reforms (1990–1 to 2007–8). The compound annual growth in area under foodgrains was 0.3 per cent during the pre-green revolution period, but it declined to −0.1 per cent during the green revolution period. However, growth in foodgrains production was high at 3.5 per cent during the green revolution period. This high growth rate has largely come from growth in yield (3.8 per cent) when compared to pre-green revolution period during which growth in production was contributed by growth in area. However, during the post-green revolution period growth in area under foodgrains was positive at 0.4 per cent, but growth in its production has declined due to fall in growth in yield. During the period of economic reforms, foodgrains production grew at a respectable rate of 2 per cent per annum, which was mainly contributed by growth in yield. These results broadly indicate that the growth in yield of foodgrains has fallen during the 1980s and consequently impacted production. Interestingly, decline in growth in production and yield has got reversed during the recent period.

However, the cropwise analysis of growth rates is more revealing. During the pre-green revolution period, growth in area for most of the food crops was negative except rice (2.5 per cent), maize (12.0 per cent), ragi (3.5 per cent) and arhar (0.7 per cent), while growth in yield was negative for rice, maize, ragi, small millets and wheat. However, the situation has changed from the mid-1960s to the 1970s during which

Table 5.2 Compound annual growth rates of area, production and yield of major crops

Crop	1960–1 to 1966–7			1967–8 to 1979–80			1980–1 to 1989–90			1990–1 to 2007–8		
	Area	Production	Yield	Area	Production	Yield	Area	Production	Yield	Area	Production	Yield
Rice	2.5	1.7	–1.0	–0.4	1.9	2.2	0.2	0.0	–0.2	0.4	1.7	1.3
Bajra	–0.3	1.7	1.9	3.0	5.6	2.6	–2.9	0.4	3.2	0.2	1.7	1.5
Jowar	–1.0	3.0	3.8	–2.5	0.8	3.5	1.4	–0.1	–1.5	–2.5	–1.4	1.1
Maize	12.0	2.2	–8.1	12.0	15.0	3.0	6.1	7.0	0.8	8.6	7.9	–0.7
Ragi	3.5	–7.2	–10.3	0.9	8.4	6.7	0.9	0.6	–1.7	–1.7	–0.6	1.1
Small millets	–2.9	–5.3	–2.5	2.3	8.0	5.6	–6.9	–5.8	1.2	–7.0	–6.2	0.9
Wheat	–3.4	–8.5	–6.3	2.3	7.1	4.7	–3.8	–6.4	–5.5	1.3	1.9	0.6
Cereals	0.3	0.3	0.0	–0.3	3.5	4.2	0.2	0.4	0.2	–0.7	1.9	2.1
Arhar	0.7	2.9	2.0	1.3	5.3	3.9	4.2	2.0	–2.1	5.7	6.3	3.5
Gram	–12.9	–4.2	8.8	–1.7	–2.1	–0.3	6.1	3.0	–3.9	2.7	8.1	2.3
Pulses	–2.1	1.5	0.0	2.2	3.4	2.5	1.7	0.1	–1.0	1.2	3.9	2.7
Foodgrains	0.3	0.4	0.1	–0.1	3.5	3.8	0.4	0.4	0.1	0.4	2.0	1.6
Groundnut	0.3	3.2	0.1	–1.0	–1.6	–0.6	5.0	7.1	2.0	–2.7	–4.6	–1.9
Sunflower	–	–	–	–9.0	–11.2	–2.4	32.1	26.8	–4.0	0.3	1.6	1.4
Total oilseeds	–1.4	1.2	1.5	3.4	3.3	–0.1	7.7	9.2	0.8	–1.2	–1.8	–0.5

(Continued)

Table 5.2 (Continued)

Crop	1960–1 to 1966–7			1967–8 to 1979–80			1980–1 to 1989–90			1990–1 to 2007–8		
	Area	Production	Yield	Area	Production	Yield	Area	Production	Yield	Area	Production	Yield
Cotton	0.1	–7.3	–6.2	0.3	4.9	3.9	–7.3	1.7	9.7	–3.1	–2.8	0.3
Sugarcane	4.1	6.6	2.1	4.2	2.0	–2.1	4.7	5.4	0.6	–0.3	–0.5	–0.2
Tobacco	–1.9	–9.5	–8.6	1.4	5.4	4.7	–0.6	1.4	1.9	4.3	1.0	–3.2
Fruits and nuts	–	–	–	–	–	–	–	–	–	0.6	0.2	–0.4
Vegetables	–	–	–	–	–	–	–	–	–	1.8	–0.2	–2.0

Source: Government of Karnataka (various issues)

Karnataka agriculture has started benefiting from the new seed and fertilizer technology. In fact, this period can be called the golden period of Karnataka agriculture with relatively high growth in the production of most crops. Although area growth under certain crops declined, remarkable achievements were made on the front of production and yield growth. Except gram, the yield of all other foodgrain crops recorded positive growth during this period.

However, the momentum in yield growth in foodgrains did not appear to continue during the 1980s with most of the crops registering negative growth rates. Only bajra, maize and small millets witnessed positive growth in yield. Except gram, growth in production of food crops declined. However, during 1990–1 to 2007–8, there was a reversal in growth in yield of foodgrain crops. Only maize registered negative growth in yield, but its production growth was impressive at 7.9 per cent, which was contributed by high growth in area. Despite positive growth in yield, production of jowar, ragi and small millets was negative due to drastic decline in their area.

The performance of oilseeds appeared better during the 1980s with the introduction of the Technology Mission of Oilseeds. The growth in area under total oilseeds was negative at 1.4 per cent during the pre-green revolution period but increased positively to 3.4 per cent in the green-revolution period which further increased to 7.7 per cent during the post-green revolution period. Although growth in yield of oilseeds has not changed in the same manner as the expansion in area, it has registered a positive growth of 0.8 per cent during 1980s. However, growth momentum did not continue during the 1990–1 to 2007–8 period. The growth in area, production and yield of all oilseeds was negative. Among individual oilseed crops, growth in area, production and yield of sunflower was positive, while that of groundnut was negative.

In the case of cotton, growth in area has declined continuously since the 1980s. However, it is encouraging to note that growth in yield of cotton has increased from –6.2 per cent in the pre-green revolution period to 3.9 per cent in the green-revolution period and 9.7 per cent in the post-green revolution periods. Unfortunately, it has again declined during the recent period. Meanwhile, the growth in production of sugarcane was found to be largely driven by increase in area during the pre-green revolution, green revolution and post-green revolution periods. But, negative growth in its area as well as yield has resulted in decline in production during the reforms period. Area under tobacco has showed high growth rate during the recent period, which has helped to register positive growth in its production. Overall, the growth analysis indicates that the yield of most crops particularly foodgrains have declined during 1980–1 to 1989–90 leading to stagnation in production. Interestingly, during 1990–1 to 2007–8, there is reversal in growth rate in production and yield for some food and non-food crops. Among various growth-promoting factors, the public investment in agriculture seemed to have played an important role in accelerating growth, and this merits some discussion here.

Public investment in agriculture

Public investment in agriculture takes place in the form of provision of basic infrastructure like irrigation, market, roads, storage facilities and research and technology. Table 5.3 presents public investment in agriculture and allied sectors in Karnataka. In absolute terms, average public investment in agriculture amounted to Rs. 673.7 million during the triennium ending 1976–7 at 1999–2000 prices, which declined steadily to Rs. 240.5 millions in the triennium ending 1992–3. Although there was a reversal in trends during the recent years, it had never reached the level registered during 1976–7. Similar trends are observed in per hectare investment as well. In fact, capital expenditure per thousand hectares of net sown area was Rs. 67,490 in 1976–7, and thereafter it declined continuously till the late 1990s.

The decline in public investment seems to have adversely affected growth in the agricultural sector during the 1980s and early 1990s.

Table 5.3 Public investment in agriculture and allied sectors

Year	Capital expenditure (Rs. millions)		Capital expenditure/1000 ha of net sown area (Rs.)	
	Current prices	Constant prices (1999–2000)	Current prices	Constant prices (1999–2000)
TE 1976–7	107.7	673.7	10,806	67,490
TE 1982–3	135.5	568.9	13,320	55,985
TE 1992–3	136.8	240.5	12,946	22,780
TE 2002–3	275.3	257.1	27,208	25,400
TE 2008–9	848.4	612.2	81,755	59,007

Source: Comptroller and Auditor General of India (various issues)

According to the Report of the Expert Committee (1993) constituted by the Government of Karnataka, decline in investment along with its non-optimal utilization has resulted in stagnation in agricultural productivity. Public investment in agricultural infrastructure has the potential to attract private investment, which might help to make improvements in farming activities. Understandably, increase in public investment in the agricultural sector during the early 2000s has provided some hope for the revival of growth in the sector. It is also quite encouraging to note the seriousness of the state government to invigorate agricultural research and education for developing and disseminating better technology to farmers. This is evident from a high growth in public investment in agricultural research and education by 10.1 per cent during 2000–1 to 2007–8, which otherwise has been declining continuously from 15.8 per cent in the 1970s to 6.8 per cent in the 1980s and 4.7 per cent in the 1990s (Kannan and Shah 2010).

Changing cost structure of principal crops

The cost structure of crops has changed with the advent of new technology, machinery and management practices. The availability of modern inputs at affordable rates and their increased use determine crop productivity. In this section, an attempt has been made to analyse the trends in cost structure of major crops like paddy, jowar, arhar, groundnut and cotton. Traditional inputs like land and human labour have accounted for over 50 per cent of the total cost of paddy cultivation in Karnataka (Table 5.4a). The cost share of seed was 4.5 per cent during triennium ending 1982–3, which declined to about 3.2 per cent in 1992–3 and further down to 2.8 per cent in 2007–8. The decline in cost of seed might be due to supply of seeds at a subsidized rate by the state government through developmental programmes and schemes.

While the per cent cost share of animal labour has declined, the share of machine labour has increased over time. The share of pesticides by and large, has increased between 1982–3 and 2000–1. However, the share of fertilizers in the total cost of cultivation has showed a declining trend. The cost share of 'others' that includes land revenue, cess and taxes, interest on working and fixed capital, depreciation on farm implements and buildings by and large, showed a declining trend over time.

Jowar is one of the major coarse cereals cultivated in Karnataka. Out of total cost of cultivation of jowar, land and human labour together accounted for about 50 per cent (Table 5.4b) share. Given the fact that jowar is cultivated largely under dry land conditions, the use of modern

Table 5.4a Trends in cost structure of paddy (per cent)

Items	TE 1982–3	TE 1992–3	TE 2000–1	TE 2007–8
Traditional inputs				
Land	28.4	31.1	27.5	27.5
Seed	4.5	3.2	3.1	2.8
Manure	6.8	3.9	4.7	2.0
Human labour	25.8	30.1	31.7	29.0
Animal labour	9.8	7.7	4.8	5.4
Modern inputs				
Pesticides	0.3	2.0	2.8	2.2
Irrigation	2.2	2.2	2.2	3.0
Fertilizers	10.8	9.3	11.8	13.3
Machine labour	0.6	2.2	6.2	9.2
Others	10.9	8.4	5.3	5.7
Total cost	100.0	100.0	100.0	100.0

Source: Government of India (various issues)

Table 5.4b Trends in cost structure of jowar (per cent)

Items	TE 1982–3	TE 1992–3	TE 2000–1	TE 2007–8
Traditional inputs				
Land	25.4	30.0	21.9	22.1
Seed	3.3	2.0	2.2	1.9
Manure	4.7	2.7	3.4	1.1
Human labour	25.9	24.8	28.9	32.0
Animal labour	16.8	9.9	15.9	19.2
Modern inputs				
Pesticides	0.3	0.8	0.4	0.0
Irrigation	0.9	1.1	0.7	0.3
Fertilizers	6.4	9.4	9.7	8.2
Machine labour	1.0	2.2	5.6	5.7
Others	15.5	17.3	11.3	9.5
Total cost	100.0	100.0	100.0	100.0

Source: Government of India (various issues)

inputs like fertilizers, pesticides and irrigation were limited. The share of pesticides and irrigation together was less than one per cent of the total cost. Animal labour accounted for relatively higher cost share when compared to that of machine labour. Further, the cost share of seed came down marginally over time due to the operation of state government subsidy schemes for distribution of seeds to small and marginal farmers. Overall, traditional inputs accounted for about three-fourths of the total cost.

Arhar is also largely cultivated under dry land conditions. The availability of improved varieties and favourable prices has induced farmers to expand the area under arhar in recent times. Traditional inputs accounted for about two-third of the total cost. Land and human labour together accounted for a relatively high cost share (Table 5.4c). The cost share of pesticides was little over 11 per cent until 1992–3, which has come down during the recent years. Further, the share of fertilizers has showed an increasing trend over time. Although use of machine labour has increased, animal labour continues to dominate operations in the cultivation of arhar.

Table 5.4c Trends in cost structure of arhar (per cent)

Items	TE 1982–3	TE 1992–3	TE 2000–1	TE 2007–8
Traditional inputs				
Land	29.1	26.3	22.2	26.0
Seed	4.9	3.8	3.4	3.1
Manure	3.5	3.7	3.8	3.8
Human labour	25.8	28.2	27.9	25.0
Animal labour	12.6	10.8	11.3	13.5
Modern inputs				
Pesticides	11.7	11.5	7.0	9.0
Irrigation	0.0	0.0	0.6	0.0
Fertilizers	3.1	4.6	7.3	5.9
Machine labour	0.0	0.7	4.6	4.6
Others	9.2	10.3	11.9	9.2
Total cost	100.0	100.0	100.0	100.0

Source: Government of India (various issues)

Groundnut is an important oilseed crop cultivated in Karnataka. Among the cost components, seed cost accounted for about one-fifth of the total cost of cultivation (Table 5.4d). The share of seed cost increased during 1992–3, but thereafter showed a more or less declining trend. Human labour and animal labour accounted for about 23.9 per cent and 10.4 per cent, respectively, of the total cost in 2007–8. Since, this crop is cultivated largely under dry land conditions, the share of improved inputs like pesticides, irrigation and machine labour is found to be low. However, the cost share of fertilizers has, by and large, increased over time. Further, use of machinery in the cultivation of groundnut has increased considerably from 0.2 per cent in 1982–3 to 4.9 per cent in 2007–8. The cost share of 'others' showed a declining trend over time. The share of 'others' was 11.4 per cent in 1982–3, which declined to 9.5 per cent in 1992–3, 8.9 per cent in 2000–1 and then to 8.1 per cent in 2007–8.

The cost structure of cotton is presented in Table 5.4e. Traditional inputs constituted about 70 per cent of the total cost. Among

Table 5.4d Trends in cost structure of groundnut (per cent)

Items	TE 1982–3	TE 1992–3	TE 2000–1	TE 2007–8
Traditional inputs				
Land	23.0	27.8	19.4	22.7
Seed	21.5	22.9	19.4	20.2
Manure	5.7	4.8	4.0	1.7
Human labour	21.7	20.8	29.2	23.9
Animal labour	9.7	7.2	9.0	10.4
Modern inputs				
Pesticides	0.2	1.0	0.4	0.4
Irrigation	0.3	0.9	1.1	1.7
Fertilizers	6.4	4.9	6.3	6.0
Machine labour	0.2	0.3	2.3	4.9
Others	11.4	9.5	8.9	8.1
Total cost	100.0	100.0	100.0	100.0

Source: Government of India (various issues)

Table 5.4e Trends in cost structure of cotton (per cent)

Items	TE 1982–3	TE 1992–3	TE 2000–1	TE 2007–8
Traditional inputs				
Land	25.6	30.6	20.6	27.4
Seed	3.6	5.8	6.3	10.0
Manure	2.2	4.1	4.1	2.9
Human labour	27.1	20.5	30.4	26.9
Animal labour	4.7	9.7	11.4	8.3
Modern inputs				
Pesticides	14.0	6.9	6.4	3.3
Irrigation	0.1	0.3	0.9	0.8
Fertilizers	16.6	9.5	8.7	8.7
Machine labour	2.3	2.0	1.7	5.2
Others	3.6	10.5	9.6	6.6
Total cost	100.0	100.0	100.0	100.0

Source: Government of India (various issues)

traditional inputs, land and human labour accounted for 50 per cent. Interestingly, the cost share of animal labour has declined, while that of machine labour has increased. The share of pesticides has declined considerably during recent years at 3.3 per cent in 2007–8 compared to 6.4 per cent in 2000–1. The cost share of pesticides was 14 per cent in 1982–3 and 6.9 per cent in 1992–3. This might be due to the rapid spread of genetically modified cotton technology in the state. Fertilizers and others constitute about 8.7 per cent and 6.6 per cent, respectively. In Karnataka, cotton is mostly cultivated on the black soils of rain-fed areas with little supplementary irrigation. The share of irrigation cost accounted for less than one per cent of the total cost.

It is clear from the analysis of cost structure that traditional inputs have accounted for higher cost shares than modern inputs. However, the share of modern inputs like machine labour and fertilizers have by and large, increased over time. As expected, the cost share of irrigation is found to be low for major crops grown in Karnataka.

Growth in output, input and TFP index

Average annual growth in output, input and TFP index for ten major crops across different periods is presented in Table 5.5. The period of analysis for different crops is guided by the availability of data on inputs and output from the cost of cultivation study. It can be observed from the table that the TFP of paddy has registered positive growth during 1980–1 to 1989–90 (1980s), 1990–1 to 1999–2000 (1990s) and 2000–1 to 2007–8 (2000s). Higher output growth triggered by technological change has resulted in positive TFP growth. Annual growth in TFP was impressive at 1.48 per cent in the 1990s and 2.68 per cent in the 2000s when compared to 0.42 per cent during the 1980s. For the entire period of analysis, that is 1980–1 to 2007–8 TFP has risen at 1.49 per cent. Overall, the contribution of TFP to output growth was found to be 60.02 per cent. The contribution of technological change to paddy output growth was positive and respectable across sub-periods. This indicates that productivity growth rather than input growth is the main driver of paddy production in Karnataka.

Jowar registered output growth of 2.7 per cent in the 1980s. But, a higher growth of inputs over output during the 1990s resulted in negative TFP growth. However, TFP rose positively during 2000–1 to 2007–8. During 1980–1 to 2007–8 annual growth in TFP was 2.03 per cent, which contributed over 80 per cent of jowar output growth. A similar growth pattern could also be observed in the case of maize. Growth in the maize output index was impressive at 2.52 per cent in the 1980s, but it declined to 0.56 per cent in the 1990s. However, turnaround in higher output growth in the recent period has been commendable. Overall, TFP of maize has grown at 1.12 per cent contributing 62.22 per cent of output growth.

In the case of ragi, except in the 1980s both output and TFP registered positive growth rates across all other periods of analysis. During the 1990s and 2000s, it showed an impressive output growth of 2.66 and 6.56 per cent, respectively. Annual growth in TFP during the corresponding periods was 0.82 per cent and 7.75 per cent. For the entire period of analysis, TFP has recorded an annual growth rate of 1.39 per cent contributing 68.25 per cent of total output growth.

As for arhar, except during the 1990s output growth was mainly driven by technology. In fact, output growth of arhar was impressive at 7.10 per cent and 7.29 per cent during the 1980s and 2000s, respectively. Growth in TFP during the corresponding periods was 5.47 per cent and 7.14 per cent, respectively. Overall, growth in TFP of arhar

Table 5.5 Annual growth in input, output and TFP index of various crops in Karnataka (per cent)

Crop	Input	Output	TFP	Share of TFP in output growth
Paddy				
1980–1 to 1989–90	0.42	0.84	0.42	50.20
1990–1 to 1999–2000	2.99	4.47	1.48	33.19
2000–1 to 2007–8	−0.87	1.82	2.69	147.53
1980–1 to 2007–8	0.99	2.48	1.49	60.02
Jowar				
1980–1 to 1989–90	1.71	2.70	0.99	36.56
1990–1 to 1999–2000	0.45	−0.90	−1.35	150.55
2000–1 to 2007–8	−0.97	6.45	7.42	115.00
1980–1 to 2007–8	0.45	2.48	2.03	81.74
Maize				
1980–1 to 1989–90	0.54	2.52	1.98	78.60
1990–1 to 1999–2000	0.79	−0.56	−1.35	241.98
2000–1 to 2007–8	0.69	3.91	3.23	82.46
1980–1 to 2007–8	0.68	1.79	1.12	62.22
Ragi				
1980–1 to 1989–90	0.95	−2.70	−3.65	135.22
1990–1 to 1999–2000	1.84	2.66	0.82	30.83
2000–1 to 2007–8	−1.19	6.56	7.75	118.17
1980–1 to 2007–8	0.64	2.03	1.39	68.25
Arhar				
1980–1 to 1989–90	1.63	7.10	5.47	77.06
1990–1 to 1999–2000	2.12	−0.75	−2.87	382.89
2000–1 to 2007–8	0.15	7.29	7.14	97.89
1980–1 to 2007–8	1.37	4.25	2.88	67.65

(Continued)

Table 5.5 (Continued)

Groundnut				
1980–1 to 1989–90	3.27	3.83	0.56	14.70
1990–1 to 1999–2000	−1.59	−3.27	−1.68	51.29
2000–1 to 2007–8	−1.01	10.97	11.98	109.18
1980–1 to 2007–8	0.20	3.32	3.12	93.93
Sunflower				
1980–1 to 1989–90	11.49	12.04	0.55	4.57
1990–1 to 1999–2000	−1.16	−1.28	−0.12	9.48
2000–1 to 2007–8	3.02	6.38	3.35	52.59
1980–1 to 2007–8	4.30	5.43	1.13	20.85
Safflower				
1980–1 to 1989–90	5.77	15.20	9.43	62.02
1990–1 to 1999–2000	−1.52	1.45	2.97	205.06
2000–1 to 2007–8	0.41	1.74	1.32	76.19
1980–1 to 2007–8	1.48	6.12	4.64	75.77
Cotton				
1980–1 to 1989–90	0.34	4.00	3.67	91.59
1990–1 to 1999–2000	−0.56	−4.98	−4.42	88.77
2000–1 to 2007–8	−1.77	15.62	17.39	111.34
1980–1 to 2007–8	−0.62	4.12	4.74	115.04
Sugarcane				
1980–1 to 1989–90	−7.03	−0.34	6.69	Negative
1990–1 to 1999–2000	6.04	0.78	−5.27	Negative
2000–1 to 2007–8	−0.55	0.97	1.51	156.45
1980–1 to 2007–8	−0.27	0.46	0.73	157.93
All crops				
1980–1 to 1989–90	1.72	1.81	0.09	4.95
1990–1 to 1999–2000	0.42	−0.56	−0.98	174.27
2000–1 to 2007–8	0.13	5.01	4.88	97.47
1980–1 to 2007–8	0.77	1.88	1.11	59.26

Source: Author's calculations

was 2.88 per cent with a contribution of 67.65 per cent to output growth.

Barring 1990–1 to 1999–2000, the growth in output and TFP of groundnut was positive in all other periods under study. TFP has registered a positive growth rate of 0.56 per cent in the 1980s. But, it has decelerated to –1.68 per cent in the 1990s. During the entire period of analysis, the respective growth in output and TFP was 3.32 per cent and 3.12 per cent. TFP has contributed about 93.93 per cent to output growth indicating that technology has played a greater role in augmenting the production of groundnut in Karnataka.

With respect to sunflower production, use of inputs seems to be relatively high. The growth in inputs was the main driver of output growth during the 1980s and 1990s. Interestingly, during the 2000s growth in output as well as TFP of sunflower was positive at 6.38 per cent and 3.35 per cent, respectively. Obstinately, the growth pattern of TFP appears to be different for safflower with both output and TFP rising positively across all periods. However, growth in TFP has decelerated from 9.43 per cent in the 1980s to 2.97 per cent in the 1990s and then to 1.32 per cent in the 2000s.

For cotton, input, output and TFP have shown positive growth rates during 1980s. TFP has registered a healthy growth rate of 3.67 per cent with its contribution of 91.59 per cent to output growth. However, during the 1990s all the three indices have registered negative growth. But output and TFP grew impressively in the 2000s, which could be attributed to the spread of Bt cotton technology. For the entire period of analysis, growth in output and TFP was 4.12 and 4.74 per cent, respectively. Technological change seems to have played an important role in increasing cotton output growth in Karnataka.

In the case of sugarcane, the input and output indices showed negative growth during the 1980s. However, high input growth as compared to output growth has resulted in a negative TFP growth of 5.27 per cent in 1990–1 to 1999–2000. During the 2000s growth in output and TFP was 0.97 and 1.51 per cent, respectively. Overall, TFP of sugarcane has registered positive growth of only 0.73 per cent, indicating that sugarcane production is input based with technology playing little role in it.

With regard to Karnataka state as a whole, during the entire period of analysis, input and output indices have registered a growth rate of 0.77 and 1.85 per cent, respectively. TFP has risen at 1.09 per cent per annum, and it has contributed 58.67 per cent to total output growth. Low TFP growth implies that there is huge scope for increasing agricultural production through new technological breakthrough. Among sub-periods, growth in TFP was found negligible during the 1980s supporting the contention that the crop sector in Karnataka had witnessed stagnation in growth during that period. Even though output and TFP have showed negative growth rates in the 1990s, they have improved remarkably during the 2000s. In fact, the deceleration in TFP growth in Indian agriculture during 1990s has been well documented in Kumar *et al.* (2004, 2008).

Determinants of TFP

In this section, an attempt has been made to analyse the determinants of the TFP of the crop sector in Karnataka. The analysis has been carried out at the state level by aggregating the cropwise TFP index using area share as weights. To examine the determinants of TFP, a multiple regression technique in double log functional form was carried out.

The TFP index was regressed on the following variables.

TFP = f (RES_EXP, EXT, RURALLIT, CANALIRR, KHRAIN, PNR)

Where

RES_EXP is Government expenditure on research and education (Rs. per hectare of GCA)
EXT is Government expenditure on extension and farmers training (Rs. per hectare of GCA)
RURALLIT is Rural literacy in per cent
CANALIRR is Per cent canal irrigated area
KHRAIN is Kharif rainfall
PNR is Ratio of P_2O_5 to N nutrients

The estimated regression results are presented in Table 5.6. Except rural literacy, the coefficient of other variables appeared with expected signs. Results indicate that government expenditure on agricultural research and education has positive and significant impact on TFP. The coefficient associated with extension was positive and significant. It implies that public expenditure on agricultural research, education and extension assumes a greater role in accelerating productivity in agriculture. Canal irrigation, relatively an assured source of irrigation has positive and significant effect on TFP. In Karnataka, a substantial cropped area falls under rain-fed agriculture. The coefficient of Kharif rainfall (April–September) was positive and significantly impacting productivity.

Table 5.6 Determinants of TFP in Karnataka agriculture: 1980–1 to 2007–8 (Dependent variable: TFP Index at state level)

Variable	Regression coefficient	Standard error	't' ratio	Level of significance
Research expenditure	0.2304	0.0765	3.0100	0.0070
Extension	0.1280	0.0592	2.1600	0.0420
Rural literacy	−0.0103	0.0031	−3.2900	0.0030
Canal irrigation	0.0159	0.0058	2.7400	0.0120
Kharif rainfall	0.2420	0.0442	5.4800	0.0000
P_2O_5 to N ratio	0.2519	0.0518	4.8700	0.0000
Constant	1.9060	0.5112	3.7300	0.0010
Adjusted R-squared	0.9911			
D-W statistics	1.7819			

Source: Author's calculations

The ratio of phosphoric to nitrogen nutrients was taken as proxy for the balanced use of fertilizer. The coefficient of this variable appeared positive and significant implying that the balanced use of plant nutrients enhance soil health and thus increase crop productivity. However, the effect of rural literacy was found to be negative and significant. The possible explanation for such a result is the migration of rural literates to urban areas due to availability of increased non-farm employment opportunities and distress like conditions in the agricultural sector. Thus, they may not contribute directly to increasing agricultural productivity.

On the whole, the analysis of TFP shows that most crops have registered a decline in productivity growth during the 1990s. Interestingly, during 2000–1 to 2007–8, all crops have showed positive growth in TFP. Further, the analysis of determinants of TFP indicates that the government expenditure on research, education and extension, canal irrigation, rainfall and balanced use of fertilizers are the important drivers of crop productivity in Karnataka.

Summary and conclusion

The present study has estimated the TFP growth of ten major crops in Karnataka and analysed the factors affecting it at the state level.

The widely used Tornqvist–Theil Index was utilized for constructing aggregate output and aggregate input indices of individual crops. Two outputs and nine inputs have been used to construct output and input indices. The cropping pattern has undergone visible changes since the 1960s with a shift in area from cereals to pulses, oilseeds and high-value crops like vegetables and plantation crops. The growth analysis has revealed that the yield of most crops in particular foodgrains has declined during 1980–1 to 1989–90 leading to stagnation in production. However, during 1990–1 to 2007–8 there is a reversal of growth in production and yield for some food and non-food crops. Among various growth-promoting factors, public investment in agriculture seemed to have played an important role in accelerating growth.

Although TFP of most crops has registered decline in productivity growth during the 1990s, there has been a revival in terms of positive TFP growth in the recent period. For Karnataka state as a whole, input and output indices have registered a growth rate of 0.77 and 1.85 per cent, respectively during 1980–1 to 2007–8. TFP has risen at 1.09 per cent per annum contributing about 58.67 per cent to the total output growth. Further, the analysis of determinants of TFP indicate that government expenditure on research, education and extension, canal irrigation, rainfall and the balanced use of fertilizers is the important driver of crop productivity in Karnataka. A low TFP growth implies that there is huge scope for increasing agricultural production through new technological breakthrough by enhancing investment in research and technology, and rural infrastructure. More public and private investment should be encouraged in under-developed regions of the state through providing incentives and a favourable policy environment.

References

Ananth, G. S., Chengappa, P. G. and Janaiah, Aldas. 2008. 'Research Investment on Technology Development in Peninsular India', in Keijiro Otsuka and Kaliappa Kalirajan (eds), *Agriculture in Developing Countries Technology Issues,* pp. 46–60, Sage Publications: New Delhi.

Bhalla, G. S. and Singh, Gurmail. 2001. *Indian Agriculture Four Decades of Development,* Sage Publications, New Delhi.

Capalbo, S. M. and Antle, John M. (eds). 1988. *Agricultural Productivity Measurement and Explanation,* Resources for the Future, Washington DC.

Christensen, L. R. 1975. 'Concepts and Measurement of Agricultural Productivity', *American Journal of Agricultural Economics,* 57(5): 910–15.

Coelli, Timothy J., Prasada Rao, D. S., O'Donnell, Christopher J. and Battese, George E. 2005. *An Introduction to Productivity and Efficiency Analysis*, Springer: USA.

Comptroller and Auditor General of India [Various Issues]. 'Finance Accounts', Government of India Press, New Delhi.

Desai, Bhupat M. and Namboodri, N. V. 1997. 'Determinants of Total Factor Productivity in Indian Agriculture', *Economic and Political Weekly*, 32(52): A165–171.

Deshpande, R. S. 2004. 'Agricultural Development of Karnataka: Promises to Keep.' Research Report. Agricultural Development and Rural Transformation Centre (ADRTC). Bangalore: Institute for Social and Economic Change.

Diewert, W. E. 1976. 'Exact and Superlative Index Numbers', *Journal of Econometrics*, 4: 115–45.

Diewert, W. E. 1978. 'Superlative Index Numbers and Consistency in Aggregation', *Econometrica*, 46(4): 883–900.

Diewert, W. E. 1980. 'Capital and Theory of Productivity Measurement', *The American Economic Review*, 70(2): 260–7.

Elumalai, K. and Pandey, U. K. 2004. 'Technological Change in Livestock Sector of Haryana', *Indian Journal of Agricultural Economics*, 59(2): 249–58.

Evenson, Robert E., Pray, Carl E. and Rosegrant, Mark W. 1999. 'Agricultural Research and Productivity Growth in India', Research Report 109, International Food Policy Research Institute, Washington, DC.

Government of India [Various Issues]. 'Cost of Cultivation of Principal Crops in India', Ministry of Agriculture, Government of India Press, New Delhi.

Government of Karnataka [Various Issues]. 'Statistical Abstract of Karnataka', Government of Karnataka Press, Bangalore.

Hulten, Charles R. 1973. 'Divisia Index Numbers', *Econometrica*, 41(6): 1017–105.

Kannan, E. and Shah, Khalil. 2010. 'Determinants of Stagnation in Productivity of Important Crops in Karnataka', Research Report: XI/ADRTC/127, Agricultural Development and Rural Transformation Centre, Institute for Social and Economic Change, Bangalore.

Kolay, A. K. 2007. *Manures and Fertilisers*, Atlantic Publishers and Distributors: New Delhi.

Kumar, Praduman and Mruthynjaya. 1992. 'Measurement and Analysis of Total Factor Productivity Growth in Wheat', *Indian Journal of Agricultural Economics*, 47(3): 451–8.

Kumar, Praduman and Rosegrant, Mark W. 1994. 'Productivity and Sources of Growth in Rice in India', *Economic and Political Weekly*, 29(53): A183–88.

Kumar, Praduman, Kumar, Anjani and Mittal, Surabhi. 2004. 'Total Factor Productivity of Crop Sector in the Indo-Gangetic Plain of India: Sustainability Issues Revisited', *Indian Economic Review*, 34(1): 169–201.

Kumar, Praduman, Mittal, Surabhi and Hossain, Mahabub. 2008. 'Agricultural Growth Accounting and Total Factor Productivity in South Asia: A Review and Policy Implications', *Agricultural Economics Research Review*, 21: 145–72.

Mukherjee, A.N. and Kuroda, Y. 2003. 'Productivity Growth in Indian Agriculture: Is There Evidence of Convergence Across States?' *Agricultural Economics*, 29(1): 43–53.

Murgai, Rinku. 2005. 'The Green Revolution and Productivity Paradox: Evidence from Indian Punjab', *Agricultural Economics*, 25(2–3): 199–209.

Nirman, K. P. S., Singh, Shivtar and Raut, K. C. 1982. 'Estimation of Crop Residues Using Grain to Straw Ratios', *Agricultural Situation in India*, 37(3): 32–43.

Report of the Expert Committee. 1993. *Stagnation of Agricultural Productivity in Karnataka during 1980's*, Government of Karnataka Press: Bangalore.

Chapter 6

Agricultural input subsidy in Haryana

Some critical aspects

Sachin Kumar Sharma

India introduced seed-water-fertilizer technology during the 1960s with an objective to achieve self-sufficiency in food grain production. The Indian government provided these inputs at a subsidized rate in order to make them available, accessible and affordable to the farmers. Both input subsidies and support price for the output were used as complementary instruments of the twin policy of promoting productivity and stabilizing the agricultural prices. Over time these subsidies have been questioned on the basis of unsustainable burden on the finances of the central and state governments, distortions in cropping pattern in favour of water intensive crops, adverse environmental effects and interregional/inter-personal disparities in development (Gulati and Sharma 1995; Rao and Gulati 1994; Singh and Joshi 1989). Subsidy on irrigation through electricity and canal water has caused distortion in cropping patterns in favour of water-intensive crops like paddy in Punjab, Haryana, and sugarcane in Maharashtra. In a case study of Gujarat, Shaheen and Shiyani in 2005 conclude that flat tariff rate is the major factor of groundwater overexploitation in the region as subsidization of electricity for pumping ground water reduces the marginal cost of extraction to near zero and thereby encourages the farmers to use this resource inefficiently. On the equity issue, it is well-established now that most of the benefits of these subsidies are appropriated by well-developed irrigated regions and large farmers.[1] The issue of input subsidies also came into the limelight due to subsidy commitments under the Agreement on Agriculture (AoA). Recent notifications to WTO (World Trade Organization) on domestic support to the agricultural sector show that India has no obligation to reduce agriculture subsidy. However, due to problems associated with input subsidies at the domestic front, there is a demand for the rationalization of agricultural subsidies (Gulati and Narayan 2003; Rao 2001).

Given the context, this chapter analyses some of the issues and problems related to input subsidies to the agricultural sector with a case study of Haryana. The study focuses on estimation of three inputs namely electricity, canal irrigation and fertilizer. Haryana is chosen because it is an agriculturally developed state, having considerable surplus of foodgrain. Adoption of green revolution technology during the mid-1960s marked a significant breakthrough in domestic supply of basic food at a time when India was facing food shortage and hunger. Haryana was a forerunner to adopt green revolution technology and it recorded significant growth in foodgrain production. However, intensive use of subsidized inputs has led to many problems like water logging, salinity, overexploitation of ground water and fiscal burden on exchequer of electricity boards and irrigation departments.

This study is broadly divided into six sections. Section two, three and four are related to estimation of fertilizer, electricity and canal subsidy, respectively, during the past two and half decades. Section five presents composition, magnitude and trend of total input subsidy, whereas the last section provides the main findings.

Fertilizer subsidy

Fertilizer subsidy extended to the agricultural sector consists of support provided on imported and indigenously produced fertilizers. The oil crisis of 1973–4 motivated the government to develop the Retention Price Scheme (RPS), fixing a fair price for fertilizer based on prescribed efficiency norms and a controlled price affordable to farmers, while at the same time giving a reasonable level of return to the industry. After implementing the RPS for nitrogen producers in 1977, RPS was implemented for phosphate fertilizers during the next few years. This scheme not only attracted considerable investment in fertilizer production but also led to manifold increase in fertilizer subsidy due to high fertilizer demand and stagnant retail prices of fertilizer. A joint (parliamentary) committee on fertilizer pricing was formed in 1991 to review the method of computation of retention prices for different manufactures of fertilizers and to suggest whether there was any scope for reducing fertilizers within the existing scheme or whether a new methodology for fertilizer pricing could be evolved without causing undue strain to the exchequer and at the same time assuring fair prices to the farmers and a fair return to the manufacturers. The main conclusion and recommendations of the committee were that the rise in subsidy had been mainly due to rise in the process of inputs which were not reflected in the farm gate prices, increase in the cost of imported fertilizers, devaluation of the rupee in July 1991 and the stagnant farm gate prices from 1980 to 91. The committee did not favour total decontrol of all fertilizers but recommended to decontrol price and distribution of the phosphate and potassium fertilizers along with a marginal 10 per cent reduction in consumer price of urea. Based on the recommendation, the prices, movement and distribution of all phosphate and potash fertilizers were decontrolled in 1992. As a result of the decontrol, the retail prices of these fertilizers increased significantly. With a view to partially compensate the increased cost of decontrolled fertilizer, an ad hoc concession (later termed as concession) was announced in 1992. The rates of concession were revised from time to time in the later years. At present the Indian government gives fertilizer subsidy on Nitrogen (N), Phosphorous (P) and Potash (K).

Examining the issue of fertilizer subsidy in relation to efficiency considerations, many studies have decomposed fertilizer subsidy between the agriculture and the industry sectors. These studies indicate that estimates of subsidies do not actually reflect the subsidies to the farmers. Fertilizer subsidies reflect, in part the high cost of fertilizer produced by some inefficient producers. It reports that, the economic subsidy on fertilizer to cultivators (measured as the difference between the import parity price and what farmers actually pay) is about half of what is delineated in the budget documents. The other half goes to fertilizer industry in terms of price for its existence beyond what the norms of efficiency would permit (Acharya 2000; Gulati and Kalra 1992).

About the agricultural sector in Haryana, it is one of the highest users of fertilizer and ranks third in terms of per hectare fertilizer consumption among major states (Figure 6.1). Wheat, rice and sugarcane are the main crops in Haryana that require intensive use of fertilizer and water. Fertilizer subsidy to agriculture in Haryana is estimated by multiplying the per ton subsidy on N, P and K with their respective consumption figures.

Due to intensive use of inputs, fertilizer subsidy has increased substantially over the period. For example, in 2009–10, fertilizer subsidy was recorded at Rs. 52,980 crore and Rs. 2,375 crore in India and Haryana, respectively. The share of gross cropped area (GCA) of Haryana in total GCA all India increased from 3.14 per cent in 1981–2 to 3.37 per cent in 2008–9. In a similar fashion, the share of fertilizer subsidy in Haryana to the total fertilizer subsidy at the all India level also increased from 4.16 per cent in 1981–2 to 5.78 per cent in 2008–9. Thus, the agricultural sector in Haryana enjoys more than a proportionate share of total fertilizer subsidy at the all India level when compared to its proportionate share in the GCA of India.

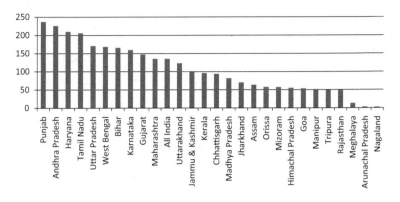

Figure 6.1 Fertilizer consumption per hectare

Source: Fertilizer statistics in India (various issues), Fertilizer Association of India, New Delhi.

Table 6.1 Fertilizer subsidy

Year	India			Haryana				
	N	P & K	Total	N	P & K	Total	Share in total subsidy	Share in total area
	Rs. Million						%	%
1981–2			3,750			156	4.16	3.30
1985–6			19,237			842	4.38	3.14
1990–1			43,890			2,050	4.67	3.19
1995–6	62,350	5,000	67,350	3,726	169	3,895	5.78	3.19
2000–1	94,810	43,190	138,000	6,202	1,613	7,815	5.66	3.29
2005–6	118,640	65,960	184,600	7,902	2,435	10,337	5.60	3.37
2006–7	159,240	102,980	262,220	9,787	3,663	13,450	5.13	3.32
2007–8	230,560	169,340	399,900	14,333	6,472	20,805	5.20	3.31
2008–9	310,480	655,550	966,030	19,469	22,893	42,362	4.39	3.32
2009–10	180,280	349,520	529,800	11,130	12,621	23,751	4.48	

Source: Fertilizer Statistics in India (various issues), Fertilizer Association of India, New Delhi.

Table 6.2 Comparison of fertilizer subsidy: India and Haryana

Year	India	Haryana	India	Haryana
	Rs./hectare		As a percentage of GDP	
1981–2	21	27	0.77	0.80
1985–6	108	150	2.66	2.88
1990–1	236	346	3.18	3.46
1995–6	359	652	2.89	3.61
2000–1	743	1,278	3.37	4.56
2005–6	957	1,589	3.44	5.00
2006–7	1,362	2,104	4.34	5.07
2007–8	2,049	3,222	5.58	6.46
2008–9	4,951	6,533	12.08	11.44
2009–10			5.64	5.93

Source: Fertilizer Statistics in India (various issues), Fertilizer Association of India, New Delhi.

Per hectare fertilizer subsidy in Haryana is almost 1.5 times of what the agricultural sector at the all India level receives (Tables 6.1 and 6.2). As a percentage of agricultural gross domestic product (GDP), fertilizer subsidy at the all India level as well as in Haryana has shown upward trends over the past three decades. The major share of fertilizer subsidy was in the form of N followed by P and K.

Fertilizer policies in India have grossly distorted the relative prices of the three major plant nutrients. These policies have kept the maximum sale price of N low relative to P and K, particularly since the deregulation of the P and K markets in August 1992. As a result, the nitrogen usage has increased sharply compared to P and K. The cost of such distortion adds considerably to the subsidy bill. It is also harmful to the health of the soil with respect to the long-term implications of the unbalanced use of fertilizers. Here, it is worth mentioning that the recommended consumption ratio of N: P: K is 4: 2: 1. This ratio is much distorted in Haryana in comparison to the ratio prevailing at the all India level (Table 6.3). This distorted consumption ratio has resulted in many problems such as stagnation in productivity, soil sickness, widespread deficiency of secondary and micronutrients, spread in salinity and alkalinity of the soil. It is noteworthy that the Government of India constituted a 'Task Force

Table: 6.3 NPK consumption ratio

Year	N	P	K	N	P	K
	India			Haryana		
1981–2	6.04	1.96	1.00	19.00	2.91	1.00
1985–6	7.01	2.48	1.00	49.33	11.50	1.00
1990–1	6.02	2.43	1.00	88.60	27.60	1.00
2000–1	6.97	2.69	1.00	73.88	21.34	1.00
2005–6	5.27	2.16	1.00	29.55	8.81	1.00
2009–10	4.29	2.00	1.00	15.86	5.49	1.00

Source: Fertilizer Statistics in India (various issues), Fertilizer Association of India, New Delhi.

on Balanced Use of Fertilizers', under the Chairmanship of A. K. Singh to review the policies on use of fertilizers. The committee recommended the restoration of NPK use ratio at the macrolevel by increasing the use of P and K, instead of reducing the intake of nitrogen. However, at the microlevel, the application of nutrients has to be soil, crop and climate specific.

Electricity subsidy

The power sector is in the concurrent list of the Indian constitution. The central and state governments are jointly responsible for the overall development of the power sector. The state governments have consti-tuted the State Electricity Boards (SEBs), which are autonomous bodies and responsible for power generation and distribution. The perfor-mance of the power sector mainly depends on the functioning of the SEBs. The power sector in India has been witnessing major changes. The growth of the power sector in India since independence has been noteworthy. However, demand for power has been outstripping the availability. The high level of technical and commercial losses and lack of commercial approach in the management of utilities have led to unsus-tainable financial operations. Cross-subsidies have risen to unsustain-able levels. Such conditions led to the enactment of the Electricity Act (2003), which provides an enabling framework for accelerated and more efficient development of the power sector. However, the financial and commercial viability of the electricity sector, to a great extent, depends on the trend and magnitude of electricity subsidy given to the agricultural sector. The Haryana Electricity Regulatory Commission (HERC) was established on 17 August 1998 as an independent statutory body corporate as per the provisions of the Haryana Electricity Reforms Act, 1997. Haryana was the second state in India to initiate the process of reforms and the restructuring of the power sector in India.

The quantum of total electricity subsidy to the agricultural sector is calculated by multiplying the total unit of electricity consumed in agriculture by per unit subsidy provided. Per unit subsidy to the agricultural sector is estimated as the difference between per unit average cost of electricity sold and its per unit recovery from the agricultural sector. Data for this purpose has been taken from the Annual Report on the Working of SEBs and Electricity Departments, Planning Commission (various issues). However, these reports provide data only up till 2001–2, and this period onwards subsidy data for India has been taken from Agriculture Statistics at a Glance. For Haryana State, electricity subsidy data for the recent years has been taken from various orders of the HERC.

Due to intensive use of the electric tube well and low electricity tariff for agriculture purposes, electricity subsidy has substantially increased. During 2008–9, electricity subsidy was recorded at Rs. 27,489 crore and Rs. 2,370 crore in India and Haryana, respectively. The share of electricity subsidy for agriculture in Haryana as a proportion of total electricity subsidy to agriculture in India increased from 4.73 per cent in 1981–2 to 9.07 per cent during 2008–9. Per acre electricity subsidy to agriculture in Haryana is more than that for all of India. As a percentage of agricultural GDP, electricity subsidy at the all India level as well as in Haryana has shown upward trends over the past three decades (Tables 6.4, 6.5 and 6.6).

It is important to note that electricity subsidy data suffers from a lot of problems. Various orders of the Haryana Electricity Regulation Commission mentioned the incorrectness of consumption data for agriculture purpose. The quality of electricity service is not good. Power supply is so unreliable, inadequate and of such poor quality that the farmers are highly dissatisfied. Another important point related to power subsidy is the practice of the flat rate system in the agricultural sector. This system implies that the marginal cost of additional unit of electricity used is negligible. In Haryana, tariff per unit for agriculture purpose is 25 paise per unit and Rs. 35 per bhp per month at a flat rate. Flat rate system provides an incentive to the farmer to go for water intensive crops.

Flat tariff rate is the major factor of groundwater overexploitation in the region as subsidization of electricity for pumping ground water

Table 6.4 Electricity subsidy in India

Year	Electricity consumption for agricultural purpose Million KWH	Cost of power supply Paisa per unit	Average tariff Paisa per unit	Subsidy per unit	Total subsidy Rs. million
1981–2	16,465.00	47.59	20.26	27.33	4,500
1985–6	23,422.00	74.59	18.04	56.55	13,245
1990–1	50,321.00	108.59	15.10	93.49	47,045
1995–6	85,732.00	179.60	19.00	160.60	137,686
2000–1	84,729.00	327.10	35.38	291.72	247,171
2001–2	81,673.00	349.90	41.54	308.36	251,847
2005–6	–	–	–	–	194,310
2006–7	–	–	–	–	197,290
2007–8	–	–	–	–	206,610
2008–9	–	–	–	–	274,890

Source: (1) Annual Report on the Working of State Electricity Board and Electricity Departments, Planning Commission (Various issues).
(2) Agriculture Statistics at Glance (Various issues)

Table 6.5 Electricity subsidy in Haryana

Year	Cost	Tariff	Subsidy	Electricity consumption	Total subsidy
Unit	Paisa/unit	Paisa/unit	Paisa/unit	Million KHW	Rs. Millions
1981–2	47.27	20	27.27	1,159	316
1985–6	71.57	20	51.57	1,366	704
1990–1	103.66	22.98	80.68	2,796	2,256
1995–6	208.7	51.9	156.8	4,150	6,507
2000–1	403.7	37.02	366.68	4,756	17,439
2001–2	411.9	47.71	364.19	4,622	16,833
2005–6					12,315
2006–7					14,649
2007–8					18,738
2008–9					23,700
2009–10					27,386

Source: (1) Annual Report on the Working of State Electricity Board and Electricity Departments, Planning Commission (Various issues).
(2) Statistical Abstract of Haryana (Various Issues)
(3) HERC (http://herc.gov.in/, accessed on 20 June 2012)

Table 6.6 Comparison of electricity subsidy: India and Haryana

	India	Haryana	India	Haryana	Share
	Per hectare Rs.		As a percentage of GDP		
1981–2	25	54	0.92	1.63	7.02
1985–6	74	126	1.83	2.41	5.32
1990–1	253	381	3.41	3.81	4.80
1995–6	734	1,089	5.90	6.02	4.73
2000–1	1,331	2,852	6.04	10.18	7.06
2005–6	1,008	1,894	3.62	5.96	6.34
2006–7	1,025	2,291	3.26	5.52	7.43
2007–8	1,059	2,902	2.88	5.82	9.07
2008–9	1,409	3,655	3.44	6.40	8.62

Source: (1) Annual Report on the Working of State Electricity Board and Electricity Departments, Planning Commission (Various issues).
(2) Statistical Abstract of Haryana (Various Issues)
(3) Agriculture Statistics at Glance (Various issues)
(4) HERC (http://herc.gov.in/, accessed on 20 June 2012)

reduces the marginal cost of extraction to near zero and thereby encourages the farmers to use the resource inefficiently. As a result, in the low rainfall area or where groundwater reserves are inadequate, especially in dry districts of Haryana, the availability of water gets depleted beyond the recharge level.

Canal irrigation subsidy

Water has been an essential input for agricultural development. There is a widespread concern about the growing magnitude of recurring losses on irrigation projects due to subsidized water rate (Tables 6.7 and 6.8). As the irrigation water rate is levied by the state governments, it varies from state to state as well as for crops and seasons. The rates have not been revised in many states since a long time. The revenue from public irrigation works does not cover even the cost of operation and maintenance. There has been a general complaint that the standards of maintenance are poor and the situation is further worsening resulting in deterioration in the quality of service. In this context, it is interesting to estimate the trends and magnitude of subsidy on canal irrigation as it

Table 6.7 Irrigation subsidy in India

Year	Major and medium				Minor				Total subsidy
	GR	W.E	W.E-GR	Recovery	GR	W.E	W.E-GR	Recovery	
				%				%	
1981–2	120	681	561	17.65	28	267	239	10.58	800
1985–6	224	1,169	945	19.15	21	472	451	4.44	1,396
1990–1	224	2,452	2,228	9.14	42	975	933	4.30	3,161
1995–6	495	4,819	4,324	10.28	112	1,756	1,644	6.35	5,968
2000–1	754	8,762	8,009	8.60	80	2,004	1,924	4.00	9,933
2004–5	854	12,230	11,376	6.98	117	2,864	2,747	4.09	14,123
2005–6									14,280
2006–7									16,978
2007–8									19,457
2008–9									23,665

Source: (1) Water and Related Statistics, Central Water Commission (Various issues).
(2) Financial Aspects of Irrigation Projects in India, Central Water Commission (Various issues).
(3) Agriculture Statistics at Glance (Various issues)
(4) Statistical Abstract of Haryana (Various issues)

has implications for the overall fiscal situation of the central and the state governments' efficiency in domestic resources.

Subsidy on canal irrigation is computed as the difference between the gross revenue and the working expenses Operational and Maintenance (O&M expenses, depreciation and total interest on capital employed) on major, medium and minor irrigation projects. Irrigation subsidy data for India from 2005 to 6 onwards, has been taken from *Agriculture Statistics at a Glance*. Due to high working expenses, on the one hand, and low revenue on the other, irrigation subsidy has increased in India as well as in Haryana. The share of irrigation subsidy given by Haryana in the total irrigation subsidy given at the all India level has been around 12 per cent according to the latest data. Per acre electricity subsidy to the agricultural sector in Haryana is more than that of the all India level. As a percentage of agricultural GDP, canal subsidy at the all India level as well as in Haryana has shown an upward trend over the past three decades (Table 6.9).

Table 6.8 Irrigation subsidy in Haryana (Rs. millions)

Year	Working expenses	Gross receipts	Difference	Interest on cumulative capital	Total subsidy
1981–2	207.20	108.10	99.10	42.85	141.95
1985–6	294.00	120.90	173.10	72.93	246.03
1990–1	444.10	173.10	271.00	118.06	389.06
1995–6	849.10	210.00	639.10	170.03	809.13
2000–1	809.60	543.00	266.60	308.29	574.89
2004–5	2,171.60	700.00	1,471.60	397.27	1,868.87
2005–6	2,354.01	774.90	1,579.11	436.60	2,015.71
2006–7	2,551.75	857.81	1,693.94	479.82	2,173.76
2007–8	2,766.10	949.60	1,816.50	527.33	2,343.82

Source: (1) Water and Related Statistics, Central Water Commission (Various issues).
(2) Financial Aspects of Irrigation Projects in India, Central Water Commission (Various issues).
(3) Agriculture Statistics at Glance (Various issues)
(4) Statistical Abstract of Haryana (Various issues)

Table 6.9 Comparison of canal subsidy: India and Haryana

Year	India	Haryana	India	Haryana	Share
	Per hectare Rs.		As a percentage of GDP		
1981–2	5	24	0.16	0.73	17.75
1985–6	8	44	0.19	0.84	17.63
1990–1	17	66	0.23	0.66	12.31
1995–6	32	135	0.26	0.75	13.56
2000–1	53	94	0.24	0.34	5.79
2004–5	74	291	0.30	0.93	13.23
2005–6	74	310	0.27	0.98	14.12
2006–7	88	340	0.28	0.82	12.80
2007–8	100	363	0.27	0.73	12.05
2008–9	121		0.30		

Source: (1) Water and Related Statistics, Central Water Commission (Various issues).
(2) Financial Aspects of Irrigation Projects in India, Central Water Commission (Various issues).
(3) Agriculture Statistics at Glance (Various issues)
(4) Statistical Abstract of Haryana (Various issues)

Canal irrigation is also suffering from poor quality and unreliable service. Subsidy on canal irrigation also increased due to low recovery of working expenses. The quality of service provided by irrigation agencies is not satisfactory. Farmers have the capacity to pay for higher irrigation charges, and many are also willing to pay, but they need to be assured of better irrigation services and plugging of leakage in irrigation funds. Acharya (2000) pointed out that raising the irrigation charges should not be considered as panacea to solve all these problems. In fact, improvement in the efficiency of the management system should receive prime attention. Once the system is improved and farmers are assured of the timely supply of water, there may not be any resistance to the increase in water rates.

Aggregate subsidy

Tables 6.10 and 6.11 give information about the estimated total input subsidy to the agricultural sector in India and Haryana. Total subsidy in India as well as in Haryana has increased over the past three decades. Share of agricultural subsidy in Haryana as a proportion of all India at present is around 6 per cent (Table 6.12). Per acre electricity subsidy to the agricultural sector in Haryana is more than 1.5 times that of the all India level. As a percentage of agricultural GDP, electricity subsidy at

Table 6.10 Total input subsidy in India (Rs. millions)

Year	Fertilizer	Electricity	Irrigation	Total
1981–2	3,750	4,500	800	9,049
1985–6	19,237	13,245	1,396	33,878
1990–1	43,890	47,045	3,161	94,096
1995–6	67,350	137,686	5,968	211,003
2000–1	138,000	247,171	9,933	395,105
2005–6	184,600	194,310	14,280	393,190
2006–7	262,220	197,290	16,978	476,488
2007–8	399,900	206,610	19,457	625,967
2008–9	966,030	274,890	23,665	1,264,585
2009–10	529,800			

Source: Tables 6.1–6.8

Table 6.11 Total input subsidy in Haryana (Rs. millions)

Year	Fertilizer	Electricity	Irrigation	Total
1981–2	156	316	142	614
1985–6	842	704	246	1,793
1990–1	2,050	2,256	389	4,695
1995–6	3,895	6,507	809	11,211
2000–1	7,815	17,439	575	25,829
2005–6	10,337	12,315	2,016	24,668
2006–7	13,450	14,649	2,174	30,272
2007–8	20,805	18,738	2,344	41,887
2008–9	42,362	23,700		66,062
2009–10	23,751			23,751

Source: Tables 6.1–6.8

Table 6.12 Comparison of total subsidy: India and Haryana

	India	Haryana	India	Haryana	Share
	Per hectare Rs.		As a percentage of GDP		
1981–2	51	105	1.85	3.17	6.78
1985–6	190	320	4.68	6.13	5.29
1990–1	507	793	6.82	7.93	4.99
1995–6	1,126	1,877	9.04	10.38	5.31
2000–1	2,128	4,224	9.66	15.07	6.54
2005–6	2,039	3,793	7.32	11.94	6.27
2006–7	2,475	4,735	7.88	11.42	6.35
2007–8	3,208	6,486	8.74	13.00	6.69
2008–9	6,482	10,188	15.82	17.84	5.22

Source: Tables 6.1–6.8

the all India level as well as in Haryana has shown an upward trend over the past three decades.

Here it is worth mentioning about some of the primary survey results conducted in three districts of Haryana with a sample size of 324 farmers during 2005–6. Many farmers had mentioned that the price of inputs increased at a higher rate than the growth rate of output prices during the past few years. This directly affects their capacity to buy inputs like fertilizer. In the case of electricity subsidy, all the sample households reported the problem of fluctuations in voltage and irregular supply of electricity in accessing subsidy. The average number of hours of power supply for agriculture per day was recorded as 4.10 hour only (average of hours reported by all sample households). Due to this, many farmers owned both diesel and electrical pump sets, which increased the cost of cultivation of different crops. All sample households were totally dissatisfied with the poor quality of power, which led to the high degree of motor burnouts. Many sample households also mentioned cumbersome administrative procedure for a new electricity connection and high initial cost to install an electric tube well. In the case of canal subsidy, 95.9 per cent of sample households complained about the poor quality of service. Due to this many sample households had resorted to costlier alternatives like diesel pump sets or buying water from other farmers. All the farmers had agreed to pay high irrigation charges if the quality of service improved given the fact that canal irrigation is much cheaper than other alternative sources of irrigation such as diesel pump sets or buying water from other farmers. It is noteworthy that farmers from Panipat and Bhiwani districts of Haryana reported the problem of soil salinity. Subsidy on irrigation through electricity and canal water causes distortion in cropping pattern in favour of water-intensive crops like paddy and sugarcane. Input subsidies, by encouraging the intensive use of inputs in limited pockets, have led to lowering the productivity of inputs, reducing employment elasticity of output through the substitution of capital for labour and environmental degradation such as water logging and salinity on the one hand, and the lowering of the water table on the other.

The above results reveal that input subsidy on fertilizer, power and irrigation have placed an unsustainable burden on the finances of the central and state governments. It has negative impact on the capital formation in the agricultural sector. The period after 1991, saw a fall in public sector capital formation. There had been a widespread decline across the board in all the states in public sector capital expenditure for agriculture during the whole period of the 1990s and early 2000s. (Chand 2006; Rao and Gulati 2005). However, there is a related question about the efficiency of public investment and subsidy. On the question of efficient instrument to attain high agricultural growth, Roy and Pal (2006) used the two-stage least square model to conclude that investment is a better instrument than subsidization. This does not necessarily mean that agricultural subsidies are wasteful expenditure. However, the marginal benefit from one rupee investment in agriculture is higher than that on subsidy. Since public investment in agriculture has a larger productivity enhancement effect than subsidy, the state governments should restrain themselves from diverting resources to subsidize at the cost of more productive investment. However, just reducing the subsidy will not serve the purpose. The reduction in subsidy should be planned in a judicious manner in view of the various sensitivities involved. The report on Central Government Subsidies presented by the Ministry of Finance in 2004 recommends public investment as an effective instrument to promote the use of fertilizers. The report is of the opinion that the application of fertilizer is more dependent on technological and non-price factors than on price or agro-economic variables. The report finds that increase in urea prices may not translate into lower production. It recommends rationalization of urea price would have a salutary impact on the balanced application of N, P and K. Many studies like Guleria and Singh (2001), Gulati and Sharma (1995), Kalirajan and Shand (2006), Chand (2006), and others recommended that there is need for large-scale price and institutional reforms to relieve the pressure of subsidies on the exchequer and also to release resources for higher investments in the agricultural sector. There is an urgent need to target the subsidies more effectively to benefit small and marginal farmers for whom these were originally intended and also to improve the efficacy of public investments in agriculture so that they serve the desired purpose.

Concluding remarks

The results of this study show an upward trend of input subsidy in Haryana over the past three decades. The subsidies have placed an unsustainable burden on the finances of the central and state governments, which have severely limited the public sector capacity for financing investment in agriculture and irrigation. The pricing policy of various inputs leads to cultivation of water-intensive crops in Haryana, which further leads to the problem of water logging and salinity in certain areas. Subsidies on irrigation through canal water and electricity have led to the distortion of the cropping pattern in favour of water-intensive crops. Similarly, underpricing of electricity has led to the depletion of ground water in some areas. The need of the hour is institutional reforms and substitution of subsidy to public investment that should be targeted to small and marginal farmers. However, before increasing user charges or rationalization of input subsidies, there is a need to improve the quality of services as farmers are willing to pay if they are assured of reliable services. The present situation if not improved may lead to unsustainable agriculture with lots of problems like soil erosion, salinity, low productivity, etc.

Note

1 See, for example, Roy and Bumb (2000), Subbarao (1985), Singh (2004), Jain (2006), Tuteja (2004), Sinha and Prasad (1980) and Gupta (2002).

References

Acharya, S.S. 2000. 'Subsidies in Indian Agriculture and their Beneficiaries', *Agriculture Situation in India*, August.

Chopra, Kanchan. 2006. 'Withdrawal of Subsidies from Irrigation and Fertiliser: Impact on Small and Marginal Farmers', in R. Radhakrishna, S.K. Rao, S. Mahendra Dev and K. Subbarao (eds), *India in a Globalising World*, Academic Foundation: New Delhi.

Gulati, Ashok and Kalra, G.D. 1992. 'Fertiliser Subsidy: Issues Related to Equity and Efficiency', *Economic and Political Weekly*, March 28.

Gulati, Ashok and Narayanan, Sudha. 2003. *The Subsidy Syndrome in Indian Agriculture*. Oxford India Private Limited: New Delhi.

Gulati, Ashok and Sharma, Anil. 1995. 'Subsidy Syndrome in Indian Agriculture', *Economic and Political Weekly*, September 30.

Guleria, Amar S. and Singh, Nagesh. 2001. 'WTO and the Prospects of Indian Agriculture', in G.K. Chadha (ed), *WTO and the Indian Economy*, Deep & Deep Publication: New Delhi.

Gupta, Rajesh Kumar. 2002. *Agricultural Subsidies and their Economic Implications*. Deep and Deep Publication: New Delhi.

Jain, Varinder. 2006. 'Political Economy of Electricity the Subsidy: Evidence from Punjab', *Economic and Political Weekly*, September 23.

Kalirajan, K.P. and Shand, R.T. 2006. 'Sources of Output Growth in Indian Agriculture', in N.A. Majumdar and Uma Kapila (eds), *Indian Agriculture in the New Millennium*, Academic Foundation: New Delhi.

Rao, C.H. Hanumantha. 2001. 'WTO and Viability of Indian Agriculture', *Economic and Political Weekly*, September 8.

Rao, C.H. Hanumantha and Gulati, Ashok. 1994. 'Indian Agriculture: Emerging Perspective and Policy Issues', *Economic and Political Weekly*, December 31.

Rao, C.H. Hanumantha and Gulati, Ashok. 2005. 'Indian Agriculture: Emerging Perspective and Major Policy Issues', in C.H.Hanumantha Rao, B.B.Bhattacharya and N.S.Siddharthan (eds.), *Indian Economy and*

Society in the Era of Globalisation and Liberalisation, Academic Foundation: New Delhi.

Roy, B.C. and Pal, Suresh. 2006. 'Investment, Agricultural Productivity and Rural Poverty in India: A State-Level Analysis', in N.A. Majumdar and Vma Kapila (eds), *Indian Agriculture in the New Millennium*, Academic Foundation: New Delhi.

Shaheen, F.A. and Shiyani, R.L. 2005. 'Water Use Efficiency and Externality in the Groundwater Exploited and Energy Subsidised Regime', *Indian Journal of Agriculture Economics*, July–September.

Singh, A.J. and Joshi, A.S. 1989. 'Economics of Irrigation in India with Special Reference to Punjab', *Indian Journal of Agricultural Economics*, July–September.

Singh, Richa. 2004. 'Equity in Fertiliser Subsidy Distribution', *Economic and Political Weekly*, January 17.

Sinha, S.P. and Prasad, Jagdish. 1980. 'Special Programmes for Weaker Sections-Evaluation: A Case Study of Programmes in Musahari Block, District Muzaffarpur, Bihar', *Indian Journal of Agriculture Economics*, 35(4).

Subbarao, K. 1985. 'Incentive Policies and India's Agricultural Development: Some Aspects of Regional and Social Equity', *Indian Journal of Agricultural Economics*, October–December.

Tuteja, Usha, 2004. 'Utilisation of Agricultural Input Subsidies by Scheduled Caste vis-à-vis Non-Scheduled Caste Farmers in Haryana', *Indian Journal of Agriculture Economics*, October–December.

Part II

Farm labour, livelihood diversification and non-farm employment

Chapter 7

Determinants of agricultural wages

A panel data analysis

Promodita Sathish[1]

In labour-surplus developing economies it is generally noticed that a positive or non-zero wage exists with large-scale unemployment or underemployment particularly in the agricultural sector. There may also be a situation where a perfectly elastic supply of labour with rigid wage, corresponding to a subsistence-level wage, exists. This may be due to various structural and institutional factors. It is also possible that stable or even rising wages exist with large-scale unemployment. The basic question is why unemployment among workers does not put pressure on wages to push them down to a market-clearing level. In this context, it is interesting to find out the factors that determine wages in a labour-surplus economy like India. The majority of the workforce in India resides in rural areas and works in the agricultural sector. A disproportionately large number of workers dependent on this sector are a reflection of uneven development of other sectors, which are unable to absorb labour. The pressure to absorb labour falls on the agricultural sector. This is compounded with increasing population, resulting in large-scale unemployment and underemployment prevailing with low subsistence-level wages.

Various factors have affected real wages and their growth rate in the agricultural sector in India. These inter alia, include positive changes brought about by the green revolution, tightening of the labour supply on account of the diversification of workers into the non-agricultural sector, exogenous factors like reduction in investment in agricultural sector particularly in irrigation during the 1990s and state-specific factors. Hence it is interesting to explore the reasons or factors which affect the real wages and growth in real wages in Indian agriculture.

This chapter attempts to find out the reasons within the basic framework of demand and supply of labour. It will be meaningful if an analysis is undertaken at the state level incorporating all major states of India.

To this effect, panel data regression analysis has been adopted to identify the determinants of wages for the period 1960–1 to 2005–6. The
significance of panel data analysis is that it helps in controlling for all
state-specific factors. Further to see whether the determinants have
changed over time, the entire period has been divided into sub-periods,
such as initial period – 1960–1 to 1974–5, pre-reform period – 1975–6
to 1990–1 and post-reform period – 1991–2 to 2005–6. At the outset it
may be mentioned that there are number of factors other than the market forces, such as institutional and non-institutional factors influencing
the determination of wages. Such factors, inter alia, include migration of
labour, prevalence of bonded labour, existence of labour union and state
intervention. However, exploring such factors falls outside the scope of
this chapter, which is primarily confined to exploring factors of determination of real wages within the neoclassical demand and supply framework thus ignoring various institutional and non-institutional factors.

The chapter is arranged in five sections. The first section estimates the
growth rate of real wages in 14 major states of the Indian economy for
the period 1960–1 to 2009–10. The next section briefly reviews some
of the relevant studies that detail the factors explaining variation in real
wages within the demand and supply framework. The third section presents an analysis of the variables of determinants of real wages. Section
four deals with the model and its interpretation, while the last section
presents brief conclusions of the study.

Growth in real wages

The growth of real wages of agricultural workers has been worked out
by taking a trend growth in real wages.

$$\ln y = a + bt$$

where

    $\ln y$ = logarithm of real wage at constant (1999–2000) prices
    t = time
    b = coefficient.

Statewise growth of annual average daily real earnings of agricultural
workers in various agricultural occupations is presented in Table 7.1.
It is evident from the table that considerable differences persisted in
the growth of real wages across the states during 1960–1 to 2009–10.

Table 7.1 Growth rates of real wages (per cent)

	1960–1 to 1974–5	1975–6 to 1990–1	1991–2 to 2009–10	1960–1 to 2009–10
Andhra Pradesh	–0.36	4.76*	2.67*	2.53*
Bihar	–0.11	2.83*	2.68*	2.22*
Gujarat	–1.26**	2.36*	3.17*	2.15*
Haryana	1.80**	2.04*	0.84**	0.17*
Karnataka	–1.30***	–0.54	5.40*	2.04*
Kerala	1.50**	4.17*	5.99*	3.74*
Madhya Pradesh	–1.67*	4.05*	1.80*	2.43*
Maharashtra	–0.87	5.41*	–0.49	1.79*
Orissa	–1.73*	3.33*	2.61*	2.15*
Punjab	2.07*	2.40*	–0.63	1.05*
Rajasthan	–0.85	3.09*	1.89*	2.11*
Tamil Nadu	1.09**	2.15*	3.69*	2.55*
Uttar Pradesh	1.68	2.22*	3.08*	2.39*
West Bengal	–0.85	5.41*	1.74*	2.68*
All India	0.21	3.72*	2.74*	2.41*

Source: Author's calculations

*Significant at 1 per cent level; **Significant at 5 per cent level; ***Significance at 10 per cent level

During 1974–5 to 1990–1, the real wages of agricultural workers increased by 3.72 per cent per annum at the all India level. In subsequent years, however, the growth was only 2.74 per cent per annum. For the entire period 1960–1 to 2009–10, the growth rate was 2.41 per cent per annum.

It is clearly visible from the table that during the first period of 1960–1 to 1974–5, the initial beneficiary states of the technological breakthrough in Indian agriculture, that is Punjab, Haryana and Uttar Pradesh were the ones which recorded low to moderate growth in real wages relative to other states. Increased agricultural operations, resultant of technological breakthrough, might have enhanced the demand for agricultural workers thereby impacting real wages favourably. The new technology involved mainly a new biochemical input combination,

High Yielding Variety (HYV) seeds, water and chemical fertilizer, and increases in yield were associated with increase in labour absorption (Bhalla 1991).

During 1975–6 to 1990–1 all states, except Karnataka, recorded positive and significant growth in real wages. The highest growth of 5.41 per cent was recorded by both Maharashtra and West Bengal. Besides these two states a few other states including Andhra Pradesh and Kerala recorded impressive growth in real wages. However, during this period, Punjab and Haryana did not witness any significant increase in real wages relative to other states. Besides, the base year effect in real wages (for both Haryana and Punjab) it can be pointed out that in these states Green Revolution embarked during the mid-sixties leading to a substantial increase in real wages. Any further enhancement in real wages in the subsequent years, translating into growth in real wages, was subject to the base year effect (i.e., mid-1960s). An initial response was increased labour use per hectare, peaking in the mid-1970s. This, however, declined in subsequent years. Rising real wage rates of agricultural workers in Haryana and Punjab may have tilted the scales in favour of labour-saving technology during the early to mid-1970s. During the second phase of the green revolution, mechanization was increasingly adopted partly but not entirely in response to rising real product wage rates due to timeliness which required obtaining maximum yield in the case of the crops like rice, cotton and sugarcane (Bhalla 1997). Maharashtra witnessed a remarkable growth of 5.41 per cent in real wage rates during 1975–6 to 1990–1 over the previous period of negative growth (–0.87 per cent). The persistence of government programmes such as the Rural Employment Guarantee Schemes introduced in the state since the mid-1970s has been a prominent factor exerting an upward influence on rural wages in Maharashtra (Acharya and Panwalkar 1988).

During the period 1991–2 to 2009–10 a deceleration in the growth of real wage rates was observed across states with the exception of a few states. At the all India level, growth in real wages decelerated to 2.74 per cent during 1991–2 to 2009–10 from 3.72 per cent witnessed during 1975–6 to 1990–1. Out of 14 states, nine states observed deceleration in growth rate. Another feature witnessed during this period was that a few states like Andhra Pradesh, Maharashtra, Madhya Pradesh and West Bengal which observed striking growth during 1975–6 to 1990–1 recorded a strong deceleration during 1990–1 to 2009–10. The reasons for deceleration may be attributed to various factors. These may inter alia include structural retrogression of the total workforce in the 1990s, the deceleration in agricultural output and steep rise in food prices in the early years of the 1990s (Parthasarthy 1996; RadhaKrishna and Sharma 1998). It may be observed from the table that states such as Gujarat, Karnataka, Kerala, Tamil Nadu and Uttar Pradesh recorded significant growth in real wages during 1991–2 to 2009–10. One of the reasons among others may be the implementation of the Mahatma Gandhi National Rural Employment Guarantee Act (MGNREGA) 2005, which was subsequently extended to cover all the districts with rural area with effect from 2008. MGNREGA not only provided a social security net by creating a source of employment, but it also moderated seasonal migration of casual workers to other parts of the state and to the country, thereby contributing a sense of well-being (Sinha 2012). The MGNREGA has contributed to the agricultural sector in at least two ways. First in many parts of the country, MGNREGA wages have started setting the floor wages for casual workers in rural and semi-urban areas (Sinha 2012). This in turn, may have also benefited agricultural workers by setting a benchmark wage in the agricultural sector in many states. Second, the availability of work opportunities outside the agricultural sector or diversification of workers into sectors other than agriculture has tightened the labour market. This has led to a decline in the supply of agricultural labour relative to the demand and has also tightened the agriculture labour market. Consequently, there has been upward movement of wages of agricultural workers in states.

Factors explaining variation in real wages: the background

Several studies have been undertaken to analyse different factors affecting the wage rate in Indian agriculture. Variation in the real wages has been attributed to several factors: first, wage rate is linked to agricultural production (Acharya 1989; Herdt and Baker 1972; Jha 2007; Jose 1988; Lal 1976; Narayanamoorthy and Deshpande 2003; Srivastava and Singh 2005, 2006); second, wage rate has been related to cereal prices and the cost of living index (Baby 1997; Bhalla 1993b; third, the movement of wage rates has been linked to trade unions (Bardhan 1970); fourth, studies deal with the supply-side factors affecting availability of labour. These include growth of population, occupational diversification, landlessness and labour-land ratio (Bhalla 1993a, 1997; Jha 2007; Parthasarathy 1996; Sarmah 2002; Sharma 2001, 2005; Vaidyanathan 1994a); fifth, institutional forces like in-migration and hired labour (Acharya 1989; Jose 1988; Sharma 2005) and possible alternative sources of income are other factors to which variations in wage rate have been attributed. Some studies suggest that intervention by the state in the form of fiscal expansion and capital formation also have significant impact on wage determination (Bhalla 1997). Last, poverty-alleviation programmes, relief works, etc. also affect wages (Unni 1997).

Most of the earlier studies have focused on the demand and supply framework while explaining variations in real wages over time. The demand-side variables considered by the earlier studies are related to productivity, be it land productivity or labour productivity, while the supply-side variables are the relative size of agricultural workers available for the agricultural operations to total workers. The studies of Bardhan (1973a), Jose (1988), Lal (1976), Narayanamoorthy and Deshpande (2003), Papola and Misra (1980), Sarmah (2002) emphasized demand-side important variables. These include irrigation, increase in cereal output, cropping pattern, variations in the level of output across states, gross cropped area (GCA) per worker, cropping intensity and production of foodgrain per agricultural labour.

A more accepted version of the view emphasizing demand-side variables has been put forward by Lal (1976). In order to capture the impact of the green revolution in agriculture, he took percentage increase in cereal output as representing demand variables, while percentage increase in male agricultural labour between 1961 and 1971 was taken as the supply variable. Similarly, Sheila Bhalla (1979) while analysing the interdistrict variations in Punjab found that the productivity of male agricultural labourers accounted for significant variation in real wages during the early 1970s. Further, it has also been emphasized that in the labour market, the forces of demand and supply acquired increasingly greater importance in the determination of the real wage rate during the green revolution decade. Similarly, Jose (1988) while analysing the strength of the link between money wages and output per worker for 1970–1, 1977–8 and 1984–5 found a significant relationship between the two. Large parts of the variation in wages were explained by variation in levels of output across states. Growth of agricultural output leading to growth in real wage rates seems to have held true in as many as 9 out of 16 states.

Increase in productivity affecting real wages as a consequence of the demand effect has been analysed by Acharya (1989). While studying the male and female wage differentials separately at a disaggregated level for 58 agroclimatically homogenous regions covering the period from 1970–1 to 1984–5, he found that real wages are sensitive to general upswings and downswings in the economy such as agricultural production and inflation. However, over time, especially during the 1990s, diversification in production has emerged as an important factor over time affecting real wages, especially during the 1990s. Bhalla (1993a) shows that for most states for the period 1971–2 to 1983–4 (time-series analysis) availability of non-farm work turns out to be a dominant factor affecting real wages and second is the change in the cost of living. While for cross-section data for the year 1982–3 (13 states), variation in labour productivity constitutes the most significant factor in explaining variation in real wage rates. The incidence of poverty among self-employed agricultural households was found to have significant impact, while employment structure (diversification) had no significant role in explaining interstate variations during the same time period. She concludes that over time, rising labour productivity did not make a decisive contribution to the observed rise in real wage rates, instead its role was that of an enabling factor. The prime mover in all the states seems to have been workforce diversification rather than labour productivity.

Similarly, Parthasarathy (1996) and Sharma (2001) have also found that labour productivity and diversification explain large part of variation in wages. Sarmah (2002) took urbanization, male literacy and child mortality as variables apart from irrigation and non-agricultural labour, in order to explain variations. He found that variables such as irrigation and diversification were found to be significant and positively correlated with the wage rate. However, urbanization, literacy and child mortality were found negatively correlated with the wage rate.

Srivastava and Singh (2005, 2006) co-opted capital investment along with other variables such as agricultural productivity, agricultural diversification, non-farm diversification, capital investment and percentage of agricultural labourers to total rural workers. The findings of their studies reflect that all the variables are significant and have the expected signs. The major impact on agricultural wages appears to have come from the diversification of workforce away from agriculture, and the responsiveness of wages to diversification has increased in the post-reform period. However, diversification has not been able to offset the diminished impact of agricultural growth on wages leading to significant deceleration in real agricultural wages.

The effect of diversification on wages along with labour productivity has also been analysed by Sharma (2005) and Jha (2007) as demand-side variables in their models. The proportion of agricultural labour households to rural households and labour-land ratio were used as supply-side variables to explain the variation in real wages. These studies find that important demand-side variables are irrigation, cropping pattern, GCA, capital investment, agricultural output, labour productivity and yield, while land-labour ratio, diversification, percentage of agricultural labourers to total rural workers and proportion of landless have emerged as important variables affecting supply of agricultural workers.

Another study by Ahmed (1981) observed that production uncertainty and proportion of agricultural wage labour to total rural workers negatively affected the supply of workers.

Determinants of real wages: an analysis of the variables

Many studies have attempted to find the determinants of agricultural wages within the conventional supply and demand framework. A consensus reached by most of the earlier studies is that productivity is an important demand-side variable while agricultural workers (availability of worker) is the important supply-side variable. The size of worker is in turn determined by diversification of workers into other occupations. This chapter considers some selected variables used in the earlier studies. It however, believes that it is the aggregative or cumulative effect of technological breakthrough on these variables which increases the demand for labour leading to increase in the productivity of labour and hence wages. The chapter analyses the impact of the most important demand- and supply-side variables operating in the Indian economy. Among supply-side variables, those affecting the availability of labour or relative size of labour, diversification and net sown area per thousand workers are being analysed. On the demand side, output per worker and irrigation have been considered to be the important ones.

Model and results

Specification of model

A panel data analysis has been taken up to prove the working of real wages within the demand and supply-side framework. The main hypothesis is that the changes in real wages are affected by demand and supply variables, that is there exists a functional relationship between real wage per worker and its determinants. The regression model has been constructed by pooling all the cross-section data related to different variables over time. The advantage of panel data is that it can be used for controlling the individual heterogeneity of the real wages. It is more informative, more reliable and more efficient and has greater degrees of freedom. The cross-sectional information relates to statewise data of different variables used. This cross-sectional information reflects the differences between subjects, whereas time-series data show the statewise different variables. The data period covered for the present study is 1960–1 to 2005–6. This would reflect the changes within the subject as well as over time.

With repeated observation of enough cross-sections, panel analysis permits the researcher to study the dynamics of change with short time series. The combination of time series with cross-sections enhances the quality and quantity of data in ways that would be impossible using only one of these two dimensions (Gujarati 1995). Panel analysis can provide a rich and powerful study of a set of people if one is willing to consider both the space and time dimensions of the data.

The general equation for explaining the behavioural pattern of real wages may take the following form:

$$Y_{it} = \alpha + \beta X_{it} + \varepsilon_{it} \tag{1}$$

$$rw_{it} = \alpha + \beta X_{it} + \varepsilon_{it} \tag{2}$$

where

rw = real wage in rupees at 1999–2000 prices
X = array of independent variables
Y is dependent variable. In present chapter, real wage is dependent variable.
β = array of coefficients of the variables
i = 1, 2, 3, ... 14 for the 14 major states.
t = time period of the study, 1960–1 to 2005–6
ε_{it} = white noise

Equation (1) is the constant coefficient model where we have assumed constant coefficient referring to both intercepts and slopes, that is neither significant statewise nor temporally. In the above pooled equations, we have not controlled for heterogeneity of the 14 major states. To control the heterogeneity of states, panel data model which signifies the error term u_{it} as a composite residual is taken up as:

$$u_{it} = \mu_i + \lambda_t + \varepsilon_{it} \tag{3}$$

Equation (3) consists of first time-invariant state-specific components u_i which capture various characteristics of the states, which are not observable but have a significant impact on their wage determination. Second, states' invariant unobservable time – specific effects λ_t which are not included in the regression and third, the remainder stochastic disturbance term ε_{it}, which is assumed to be serially uncorrelated with mean zero and is possibly homoscedastic. The equation for the panel data model can be specified as:

$$rw_{it} = \alpha + \beta X_{it} + \mu_i + \lambda_t + \varepsilon_{it} \tag{4}$$

Estimation of determinants of agricultural real wages

By incorporating time and time interaction dummies with the variables, equation (1) which is a pooled equation is developed into the following;

$$\ln rw_{it} = \alpha + \beta X_{it} + \lambda t + \varepsilon_{it} \tag{5}$$

$$\ln rw_{it} = \alpha + \beta X_{it} + \delta_1 D_2 + \delta_2 D_3 + \lambda t + \varepsilon_{it} \tag{6}$$

$$\ln rw_{it} = \alpha + \beta_1 X_{it} + \gamma D_2 \, X_{it} + \omega D_3 X_{it} + \delta_1 D_2 + \delta_2 D_3 + \lambda t + \varepsilon_{it} \tag{7}$$

where

rw = real daily wages in rupees at 1999–2000 prices
X = array of independent variables
β_1 = array of coefficients of the variables
i = 1, 2, 3, ... 14 for the 14 major states.
t = time period of the study, 1960–1 to 2005–6
ε_{it} = white noise
λ = the coefficient of time variable
ω = coefficient of time interaction slope dummy for 1991–2 to 2005–6
γ = coefficient of time interaction slope dummy for 1975–6 to 1990–1
D_2 = 1 for 1975–6 to 1990–1; otherwise 0
D_3 = 1 for 1991–2 to 2005–6 ; otherwise 0
$D_2 \beta X_{it}$ = time interaction slope dummy for period 1975–6 to 1990–1;
$D_3 \beta X_{it}$ = time interaction slope dummy for period 1991–2 to 2005–6;
δ_1 = array of coefficient of time dummy
δ_2 = array of coefficient of time dummy

The time interaction model signifies the temporal effect on the set of variables characterizing cross-sectional unit over a particular time span. D_2 and D_3 depict the pre-and post-economic reform periods, respectively. In the model, we have taken 14 major states for 46 years and errors (e) term may or may not be independent and homoscedastic, that is $E(\mu_i) = 0$ for all observation and $E(rw_{it}) = (\mu_i + \beta X_{it}) + E(e_i)$, when $e_i = 0$

$E(rw_{it}) = \mu_i + \beta X_{it}$

Similarly, var $(e) = E\{(e_i. E(e_i)\}^2 = \sigma^2$ = constant.

var $(e) = \sigma e_i^2$ = not constant.

$\sigma_1^2 = \sigma_2^2 = \ldots\ldots\ldots = \sigma_{16}^2.$

To take into account the above, three types of models namely pooled, fixed effect and random effect models have been examined for the determinants of agricultural real wages within the demand and supply framework.

Model I

Model 1, which is pooled regression, labour productivity, diversification and net area irrigated to GCA have been used as the explanatory variables with time and slope dummies.

$$\ln rw_{it} = \alpha + \beta\, X_{it} + \gamma D_2 \beta X_{it} + \omega D_3 \beta X_{it} \\ + \alpha_1 D_2 + \alpha_2 D_3 + \lambda t + \varepsilon_{it} \tag{8}$$

rw = real wage daily wages in rupees at 1999–2000 prices
X_{it} = array of independent variables such as lnlp, div, nigc
lnlp = refers to logarithm of labour productivity
div = refers to ratio of non-agricultural workers to the total workers
nigc = refers to ratio of net area irrigated to GCA
β_1 = array of coefficients of the variables
i = 1, 2, 3, ... 14 for the 14 major states.
t = time period of the study, 1960–1 to 2005–6
λ = coefficient of time variable
γ = coefficient of time interaction slope dummy for 1975–6 to 1990–1
ω = coefficient of time interaction slope dummy for 1991–2 to 2005–6
D_2 = 1 for 1975–6 to 1990–1; otherwise 0
D_3 = 1 for 1991–2 to 2005–6 ; otherwise 0
$D_2 \beta X_{it}$ = time interaction slope dummy for period 1975–6 to 1990–1;
$D_3 \beta X_{it}$ = time interaction slope dummy for period 1991–2 to 2005–6;
δ_1 = array of coefficient of time dummy
δ_2 = array of coefficient of time dummy
ε_{it} = white noise

The results have been estimated by STATA 8.1 econometric package and are given in Tables 7.2 to 7.4. The pooled regression analysis shows that all the three variables like labour productivity, diversification and net irrigated area to GCA are statistically significant for the entire

Table 7.2 Pooled regression results (dependent variable: Lnrw)

Source	SS	df	MS		Number of Obs =	644
Model	107.60	12.00	8.97		$F(12, 631) =$	186.44
Residual	30.35	631.00	0.05		Prob>F=	0.000
Total	137.94	643.00	0.21		R-Squared =	0.780
					Adj R-Squared =	0.776
					Root MSE =	0.219

Variable	Coef.	Std. Err.	t	P>|t|	[95% Conf.Interval]	
Lnlp	0.462	0.038	12.170	0.000	0.388	0.537
Div	0.003	0.002	1.740	0.082	0.000	0.007
Nigc	0.007	0.001	5.150	0.000	0.004	0.010
d2lnlp	−0.066	0.050	−1.330	0.185	−0.164	0.032
d3lnlp	−0.132	0.054	−2.460	0.014	−0.237	−0.027
d2div	0.002	0.003	0.830	0.404	−0.003	0.008
d3div	0.003	0.003	1.250	0.211	−0.002	0.009
d2nigc	−0.002	0.002	−1.250	0.210	−0.006	0.001
d3nigc	−0.009	0.002	−4.680	0.000	−0.013	−0.005
d2	0.566	0.410	1.380	0.168	−0.239	1.370
d3	1.368	0.447	3.060	0.002	0.490	2.246
T	0.009	0.002	4.520	0.000	0.005	0.013
Constant	−1.159	0.314	−3.690	0.000	−1.776	−0.542

Source: Author's calculations
ln *rw* = logarithm of real wages in rupees at constant (1999–2000) prices
lnlp = logarithm of labour productivity in rupees at constant (1999–2000) prices
div = ratio of non-agricultural workers to the total workers in per cent
nigc = ratio of net area irrigated to GCA.
d_2 = 1 for 1975–6 to 1990–1; otherwise 0
d_3 = 1 for 1991–2 to 2005–6; otherwise 0

period, that is 1960–1 to 2005–6. However, diversification of workers into non-agricultural sector is significant at 10 per cent level. The time trend is statistically significant for the entire period and post-reform period. The pooled regression analysis also includes time interaction dummies. It is evident from the table that time interaction effect is positive and significant only with labour productivity with coefficient

Table 7.3 Panel data regression analysis (fixed effect model)

Fixed-effects (within) regression					Number of obs =	644
Group variable (i): statecode					Number of groups =	14
R-sq within = 0.8265					Obs per group: min =	46
between = 0.6163					avg =	46
overall = 0.7250					max =	46
					F(12,618) =	245.33
corr(u_i, Xb) = .1068					Prob > F =	0.000

	Coef.	Std. Err.	T	P>|t|	[95% Conf.Interval]	
Lnlp	0.266	0.046	5.740	0.000	0.175	0.357
Div	0.006	0.003	1.760	0.078	−0.001	0.012
Nigc	0.011	0.002	4.310	0.000	0.006	0.016
d2lnlp	−0.080	0.036	−2.250	0.025	−0.151	−0.010
d3lnlp	−0.198	0.039	−5.120	0.000	−0.273	−0.122
d2div	0.004	0.002	2.090	0.037	0.000	0.008
d3div	0.010	0.002	4.840	0.000	0.006	0.014
d2nigc	−0.001	0.001	−0.490	0.625	−0.003	0.002
d3nigc	−0.006	0.001	−4.940	0.000	−0.009	−0.004
d2	0.621	0.296	2.100	0.036	0.040	1.201
d3	1.716	0.337	5.090	0.000	1.054	2.379
T	0.009	0.002	5.050	0.000	0.006	0.013
Constant	0.480	0.439	1.090	0.274	−0.381	1.342
sigma_u	0.205742					
sigma_e	0.144498					
rho	0.669675					

F test that all u_i=0: F(13, 618) = 64.26 Prob > F = 0.0000

Source: Author's calculations

Table 7.4 Panel data regression analysis (random effect model)

Random effects GLS regression				Number of obs =		644
Group variable (i): statecode				Number of groups =		14
R-sq within = 0.8265				Obs per group: min =		46
between = 0.6399				avg =		46
overall = 0.7372				max =		46
Random effects u_i ~ Gaussian				Wald chi2(12)=		2964.04
corr(u_i, X) = 0 (assumed)				Prob >chi2 =		0.000

	Coef.	Std. Err.	T	P>|t|	[95% Conf.Interval]	
Lnlp	0.289	0.044	6.630	0.000	0.203	0.374
Div	0.006	0.003	2.280	0.023	0.001	0.012
Nigc	0.010	0.002	4.400	0.000	0.006	0.014
d2lnlp	−0.086	0.035	−2.470	0.014	−0.155	−0.018
d3lnlp	−0.204	0.038	−5.390	0.000	−0.278	−0.130
d2div	0.004	0.002	2.090	0.037	0.000	0.008
d3div	0.009	0.002	4.680	0.000	0.005	0.013
d2nigc	−0.001	0.001	−0.470	0.639	−0.003	0.002
d3nigc	−0.007	0.001	−5.030	0.000	−0.009	−0.004
d2	0.677	0.289	2.340	0.019	0.110	1.243
d3	1.795	0.327	5.480	0.000	1.154	2.437
T	0.009	0.002	5.220	0.000	0.006	0.013
Constant	0.265	0.404	0.660	0.512	−0.527	1.057
sigma_u	0.1984947					
sigma_e	0.1444979					
rho	0.6536213					

Source: Author's calculations

0.33. It is however negative but significant in case of net area irrigation −0.20. All other variables with time interaction effect are insignificant.

The above pooled regression analysis is a constant coefficient model where constant coefficient is assumed with respect to both intercept and slope, that is there are neither statewise nor temporal differences for 14 major states over 46 years. Further, in the pooled model, we have not controlled for heterogeneity of the 14 states. This may lead to biased and inefficient results. There are variables which are state specific but unobservable over time. Likewise time-specific statewise unobservable variables also affect the wage determination across the states. To take into account the heterogeneity of states, the panel data analysis with fixed and random models has been considered in this chapter. The intercept is allowed to vary which takes into account the state-specific factors. Further, by taking time dummies and time interaction dummies an attempt is made to capture factors determining wages during the pre- and post-reform periods and change occurred, if any, over time. With the fixed effect model or random effect model, the adjusted R square improves. To decide between the fixed effect model and random effect model, the Hausman test was applied.

In Tables 7.3 and 7.4 it may be seen that all the variables are statistically significant and corroborate our a priori expectations. The Hausman test has been applied in order to decide whether the random effect model is to be accepted against the fixed effect model or not. The result of the Hausman test statistic of 23.98 rejects the null hypothesis of the difference in coefficients not being systematic and favours the fixed effect model which takes into account the heterogeneity of individual states. The adjusted R^2 improves with the fixed effect model to 0.82 from 0.77 of pooled regression analysis.

Variables like labour productivity, diversification and net area irrigated are found to be statistically significant with expected positive association with real wages. The temporal effect in the model is positive and statistically significant for the overall period of 46 years. It is found to be significant during the pre- (at 2 per cent level) and post-reform periods.

The time interaction of the effect of the variables on wages is significant in the case of all variables taken up in the model both in the pre- and post-reform periods. The regression coefficients of the model show the following:

(1) One per cent increase in the labour productivity results in 0.27 per cent increase in the real wages. The time interaction effect of labour productivity is significant but negative during both pre- (at

2 per cent level of significance) and post-reform periods. This indicates that in both the periods pre- and post-reform, that is the period 1975–6 to 1990–1 and 1991–2 to 2005–6, respectively, the responsiveness of real wages to labour productivity declined. In the pre-reform period, 1 per cent increase in the labour productivity results in only 0.19 per cent increase in real wages in agriculture. The responsiveness of real wages to labour productivity, however, declines to 0.07 per cent in the post-reform period. The result is in conformity with the statewise analysis where labour productivity turns out to be a significant variable with correct sign in explaining variations in real wages (Acharya 1989; Jha 2007; Parthasarthy 1996; Sharma 2001). It is also in line with other studies that have reported a decline in the effect of labour productivity over time (Jha 2007; Sharma 2005; Shrivastava and Singh 2005, 2006).

(2) The proportion of non-agricultural main workers to total main workers away from the agricultural sector signifies diversification. Diversification for the entire period, that is 46 years has the correct sign and is statistically significant at 10 per cent. Further, the time interaction effect of diversification on wages has improved significantly during both pre-, that is 1975–6 to 1991–6, and post-reform, that is 1991–2 to 2005–6, periods. It may be noted that the time interaction effect is of higher magnitude in the post-reform period.

A one percentage point increase in diversification leads to a 0.60 per cent increase in real wages for the entire time period, that is over 46 years from 1960–1 to 2005–6. In the pre-reform period, a one percentage point increase in diversification explains 1.00 per cent variation in real wages (significant at 0.3 per cent). The result is in conformity with the findings of studies in which diversification emerged as the prime mover of real wages since the mid-1970s (Bhalla 1993b, 1997; Parthasarthy 1996; Unni 1997). The responsiveness of real wages to diversification increases to 1.6 per cent in the post-reform period. The results are in conformity with the findings of other studies which have reported a positive effect of diversification of workers on real wages of agricultural workers and the increase in the responsiveness of real wages to diversification in the post- reform period (Sharma 2005; Srivastava and Singh 2005, 2006). The results show that responsiveness of real wages increase over time and had greater impact during the post-reform period.

(3) A one percentage point increase in net area irrigated to GCA increases the real wages by 1.1 per cent for the overall period. Though, the time interaction effect is negative in both the periods, that is pre- and post-reform, it is significant only in the post-reform period. Further, the responsiveness of real wages to net area irrigated to GCA declines over time which indicates an increase in GCA under irrigation and explains less variation in real wages during the post-reform period. A one percentage point increase in net area irrigated to GCA explains only 0.5 per cent variation in real wages during the post-reform period. The above result is consistent with the findings of studies reporting decline in the responsiveness of the real wages to irrigation (Srivastava and Singh 2005, 2006).

Summary and conclusion

The results of the panel data analysis show that occupational diversification is the most important determinant of real wages in the agricultural sector during 1960–1 to 2005–6. The results also delineate the changing nature of the relationship between the variables and real wages over time, especially during the pre- and post-reform periods. The responsiveness of real wages to demand-side variables has declined during the pre-reform period and with much higher magnitude during the post-reform period. Consequently, major agricultural variables like labour productivity and irrigation have less impact on agricultural wages during the pre-reform period and even smaller impact during the post-reform period. Further, the effect of labour productivity in determining the real wages has decreased over time. The responsiveness of wages to irrigation, which is in the form of public investment, has declined over time. The main reason for this is decline in public investment in the agricultural sector during the 1990s, which not only affected agricultural growth but also dried up one of the main sources of growth of agricultural wages.

Diversification emerges as the most important determinant of real wages in the agricultural sector, and its responsiveness increases over time especially, during the pre- and post-reform periods. The result suggests that occupational diversification and irrigation, that is public investment which boosts agricultural infrastructure, are effective ways of enhancing agricultural wages. The policy implication is that only small parts of gains in labour productivity get translated into wage increase. Any land or output-based strategy directed towards the betterment of agricultural workers has significantly limited or smaller impact on real wages. Efforts should be focused on the promotion of non-farm opportunities which would siphon off excess workers from the agricultural sector, thus contracting the supply to the agricultural sector and thereby enhancing the wages of agricultural workers. The study also delineates the importance of public investment in irrigation to boost agricultural growth and also enhance wages in the agricultural sector.

Note

1 The author is grateful to R. K. Sharma, Jawaharlal Nehru University, Promod Kumar, Institute for Social and Economic Change and R. Sathish, Ministry of Finance, GoI, for their invaluable help. The views expressed here are the author's own and not of the organization to which she belongs.

References

Acharya, Sarthi. 1989. 'Agricultural Wages in India: A Disaggregated Analysis', *Indian Journal of Agricultural Economics,* 44(2), April–June, 122–39.

Acharya, Sarthi and Panwalkar, V. G. 1988. 'The Maharashtra Employment Guarantee Scheme: Impacts on Male and Female Labour', The Population Council Regional Research Papers, South and East Asia, Bangkok.

Ahmed, Iqbal. 1981. 'Wage Determination in Bangladesh Agriculture', *Oxford Economic Papers, New Series,* 33(2), July: 298–322.

Baby, A. A. 1997. 'Trends in Agricultural Wages in Kerala: 1960–1990', *The Indian Journal of Labour Economics,* 40(2): 263–77.

Bardhan, Kalpana. 1977. 'Rural Employment, Wages and Labour Market in India – A Survey of Research III', *Economic and Political Weekly,* XII(28), July 9: 1108.

Bardhan, Parnab. 1970. 'Green Revolution and Agricultural Labourers', *Economic and Political Weekly,* V(Special No.), July: 1239–46.

Bardhan, Parnab. 1973a. 'Factors Affecting Wage Rate for Agricultural Labourer', *Economic and Political Weekly,* II(26), Review of Agriculture, June: 56–64.

Bardhan, Parnab. 1973b. 'Variations in Agricultural Wages – A Note', *Economic and Political Weekly,* VIII (Special Article No. 21), May 26: 947–8.

Bhalla, Sheila. 1979. 'Real Wage Rates of Agricultural Labourers in Punjab, 1961–77 – A Preliminary Analysis', *Economic and Political Weekly,* Review of Agriculture, June: A57–68.

Bhalla, Sheila. 1981. 'Work Force Structure 1981: The Turning of the Tide?', in G. P. Mishra (ed.), *Regional Structure of Development and Growth in India,* Vol. 1, pp. 363–91, Ashish Publishing House: New Delhi.

Bhalla, Sheila. 1993a. 'The Dynamics of Wage Determination and Employment Generation in Indian Agriculture', *Indian Journal of Agricultural Economics*, 48(3), July–September: 448–70.

Bhalla, Sheila. 1993b. 'Test of Some Propositions about the Dynamics of Changes in the Rural Workforce Structure', *Indian Journal of Agricultural Economics*, XXXVI(3): 428–439.

Bhalla, Sheila. 1997. 'Trends in Poverty, Wages and Employment in Rural India', *The Indian Journal of Labour Economics*, 40(2), April–June: 213–23.

Gujarati, Damodar N. 1995. *Basic Econometrics: 3rd edition*. McGraw Hill International Edition: New York.

Herdt, Robert W. and Baker, Edward A. 1972. 'Agricultural Wages, Production and the High-Yielding Varieties', *Economic and Political Weekly*: A-23–30.

Jha, Brajesh. 2007. 'Agricultural Wages in India: A State Level Analysis', *The India Journal of Labour Economics*, 50(2): 293–302.

Jose, A. V. 1973. 'Wage Rates of Agricultural Labourers in Kerala', *Economic and Political Weekly*, Annual No. February: 281–8.

Jose, A.V. 1974. 'Trends in Real Wages Rates of Agricultural Labourers', *Economic and Political Weekly*, ix(13), Review of Agriculture, March: A25–30.

Jose, A.V. 1978. 'Real Wages, Employment, and Income of Agricultural Labourers', *Economic and Political Weekly*, Review of Agricultural, March 30: A16–20.

Jose, A.V. 1988. 'Agricultural Wages in India', *Economic and Political Weekly*, June 25: A46–58.

Lal, Deepak. 1976. 'Agricultural Growth, Real Wages, and the Rural Poor in India', *Economic and Political Weekly*, Review of Agriculture, June: A47–60.

Naryanamoorthy, A. 2001. 'Irrigation and Rural Poverty Nexus; A State wise Analysis,' *Indian Journal of Agricultural Economics*, 56(2), January–March: 40–56.

Narayanamoorthy, A. and Despande, R. S. 2003. 'Irrigation Development and Agricultural Wages an Analysis across States', *Economic and Political Weekly*, August 30: 3716–22.

Nayyar, Rohini. 1977. 'Wages, Employment and Standard of Living of Agricultural Labourers in Uttar Pradesh', International Labour Organisation, Poverty and Landlessness in Rural Asia, Geneva.

Papola, T.S. and Misra, V.N. 1980. 'Labour Supply and Wage Determination in Rural Uttar Pradesh', *Indian Journal of Agricultural Economics*, 35(1), January–March: 106–20.

Parthasarathy, G. 1996. 'Recent Trends in Wages and Employment of Agricultural Labour', *Indian Journal of Agricultural Economics*, 51(1 and 2), January–June: 145–67.

Radhakrishna, R. and Sharma, Alakh N. 1998. 'Empowering Rural Labour in India: Market, State and Mobilisation', Institute of Human Development, New Delhi, pp. 203–19.

Reddy, P. Prudhvikar. 1998. 'Trends in Agricultural Wages – An Inter-Regional Analysis in Andhra Pradesh', *Economic and Political Weekly*, March 28: A15–19.

Sarmah, Sasank. 2002. 'Agricultural Wages in India: A Study of States and Regions', *The Indian Journal of Labour Economics*, 45(1): 89–116.

Sharma, H. R. 2001. 'Employment and Wages Earnings of Agricultural Labours: A State-wise Analysis', *The Indian Journal of Labour Economic*, 44(1): 27–38.

Sharma, H. R. 2005. 'Economic Conditions of Agricultural Labour household in 1990s: A State Level Analysis of Wage Earning and Indebtedness', *The Indian Journal of Labour Economics*, 48(2): 425–36.

Sinha, N. K. 2012. 'Mahatma Gandhi National Rural Employment Guarantee Act, Intentions, Practice, and Correctives for the Future', in Rajeev Malhotra (ed.), *Policies for India's Development, A Critical Decade*, pp. 353–57, Oxford University Press.

Srivastava, Ravi and Singh, Richa. 2005. 'Economic Reform and Agricultural Wages in India', *The Indian Journal of Labour Economics*, 48(2), April–June: 407–23.

Srivastava, Ravi and Singh, Richa. 2006. 'Rural Wages during the 1990s: A Re-estimation', *Economic and Political Weekly*, September 23: 4053–62.

Unni, Jeemol. 1988. 'Agricultural Labourers in Rural Labour Households, 1956–57 to 1977–78 – Changes in Employment, Wages and Incomes', *Economic and Political Weekly*, June 25: A59–68.

Unni, Jeemol. 1997. 'Employment and Wages among Rural Labourers: Some Recent Trends', *Indian Journal of Agricultural Economics*, 52(1), January–March: 59–72.

Vaidyanathan, A. 1986. 'Labour Use in Rural India: A Study of Spatial and Temporal Variations', *Economic and Political Weekly*, Review of Agriculture, 21(52), December 27.

Vaidyanathan, A. 1987. 'Irrigation and Agricultural growth' (Presidential Address), *Indian Journal of Agricultural Economics*, 42(4), October–December: 503–27.

Vaidyanathan, A. 1994a. 'Employment Structure: Some Emerging Perspective', *Economic and Political Weekly*, 29(50), December 10: 3147–56.

Vaidyanathan, A. 1994b. 'Second India Studies Revisited: Food, Agriculture and Water', Madras Institute of Development Studies, Madras, January.

Williamson, J. G. 1965. 'Regional Inequality and Process of National Development: A Description of the Patterns', *Economic Development and Cultural Change*, 13: 3–45.

Wooldridge, Jeffrey M. 2006. *Introductory Econometric and a Modern Approach*. 3rd ed. South-Western Cengage Learning. Akash Press. Cengage Learning, India PLtd. Alps Building 1st Floor, Janpath, New Delhi-1.

Census and reports

Area and Production of Principal Crops in India, (Various issues), Director-
ate of Economic and Statistic, Ministry of Agricultural, Government of
India, New Delhi.
Indian Agricultural Statistics, (Various issues), Directorate of Economic and
Statistics, Ministry of Agricultural, Government of India, New Delhi.
Agricultural Wages in India, (various issues, 1960–1 to 2010–11), Director-
ate of Economics and Statistics, Ministry of Agriculture, Government of
India, New Delhi.
Census of India, 'General Economic Tables', 1961, 1971, 1981, 1991,
2001, Part II B(i). Registrar General of India, Ministry of Home Affairs,
Government of India.
Census of India (1971), Series I Indian Miscellaneous Studies, Paper I of
1974, Report of Resurvey on Economic Questions – Some Results, Reg-
istrar General of India, Ministry of Home Affairs, Government of India.
The Statistical Abstract of India: (various issues), Central Statistical Organi-
sation, Government of India, New Delhi.

Papers presented in seminars

Bhalla, Sheila. 1991. 'Speeding up Agricultural Growth Implications for
Labour Absorption', Paper Prepared for the National Seminar on Rural
Development (26–7 April 1991), Lucknow.
Singh, Ajit Kumar. 1989. 'Changes in the Structure of Rural Workforce in
Uttar Pradesh: A Temporal and Regional Studies', Paper presented to the
seminar on Non-Agricultural Employment in India: Trend and Prospects,
Ahmedabad, March 1989.

Appendix – I

Table 7.1A Sources of variables and methodology of estimation

Sl No.	Variables name	About variable	Methodology of estimation	Sources
1	RW	Real wage in rupees at 1999–2000 prices	(1) Real wage is calculated from money wage which is deflated by the CPI-AL at constant (1999–2000) base. (2) Monthly average of daily money wage is taken statewise. (3) These monthly wages are aggregated to arrive at a simple annual average of daily money wages.	Money wages have been taken from the various publications of Agricultural Wages in India, published by the Directorate of Economics and Statistics, Ministry of Agriculture.
2	LP	Labour productivity has been defined as output per worker in rupees across the states at constant (1999–2000) prices	(1) Statewise and cropwise value of agricultural output at different constant prices were estimated at 1999–2000 prices using the splicing method. (2) Labour productivity is calculated by statewise value of output of 36 crops at 1999–2000 prices, which is divided by the statewise total main agricultural worker for the period 1960–1 to 2005.	(1) Statewise value of agricultural output from the Central Statistical Organization (2) Data on Agricultural workers obtained from the Census of India, 1961, 1971, 1981, 1991 and 2001

3	DIV	Proportion of non-agricultural workers to the total workers	Diversification has been defined as the proportion of non-agricultural main workers in total main workers (in per cent).	(1) Census of India, 1961, 1971, 1981, 1991 and 2001 (2) To arrive at time series we have interpolated the data set 1961–71, 1971–81, 1981–91, 1991–2001 and 2001–6
4	NIGC	Net area irrigated to GCA	Ratio of net area irrigated to GCA (in per cent).	Various issues of Agricultural Statistics – At a glance, Directorate of Economics and Statistics, Ministry of Agriculture
5	NSTW	Net sown area per thousand workers	To arrive at net sown area per thousand workers, net sown area (in hectares) was divided by the agricultural main workers across the states over the years.	Various issues of Agricultural Statistics – At a glance, Directorate of Economics and Statistics, Ministry of Agriculture

Appendix II

Table 7.2A List of agricultural outputs – Crops

1	Rice
2	Wheat
3	Jowar
4	Bajra
5	Barley
6	Maize
7	Ragi
8	Small millets
9	Gram
10	Tur (arhar)
11	Urd
12	Moong
13	Masoor
14	Linseed
15	Sesamum
16	Ground nut
17	Rapeseed (mustard)
18	Castor
19	Coconut
20	Sugarcane
21	Other sugar
22	Kapas
23	Jute
24	Mesta
25	Tea
26	Coffee
27	Tobacco
28	Dry chillies
29	Black pepper
30	Areca nut
31	Banana

Chapter 8

The state, labour and reproduction of low-wage space

Experience from Kerala

S. Mohanakumar

Wage level and its movements are central to the theory of distribution. Wage studies, therefore, entail exploration in every branch of the economy. The market wage or spot wage for labour in the unorganized sector is reported to be considerably different for different districts within a geographical entity and further intra-state wage differential for the same type of labour and work is found persisting for a long period (Jose 1978). This chapter addresses the question of why the daily wage rates for rural labour, particularly for those in the unorganized segment of the farm sector, differ significantly across districts in a relatively small geographical entity like Kerala. The question of spatial wage differentials assume significance in the context of Kerala for two reasons, namely (1) unorganized segment of the rural labour market is well organized under radical political movements in the local state; (2) daily wage labourers (labouring poor) in the state are rather known for their work-related mobility within and outside the state, implying that the labour would move to high-wage zones from low-wage zones. It is argued in the chapter that the state, in general, creates and maintains peripheries by keeping wage low in certain localities within the geographical boundaries of the state. The conventional wage determination model fails to capture the intervention of the state on behalf of capital in the rural labour market. The discussion is organized as follows. The first section reviews how different schools of thought addressed the wage question and the spatial wage differentials, followed by a brief description of the area and sample selection procedure adopted for the study in the second section. In section three, discriminatory policies and programmes of the state (local state in this context) to reproduce and perpetuate low-wage zones and labouring poor within the jurisdiction of a sub-state is analysed. The difference in the living standard of workers in low- and high-wage districts are analysed in the fourth section, followed by the last section presenting the conclusions of the study.

The wage question in a historical perspective

The studies on wage level and its movements encompass a protracted history of development. The wage question arises under specific historical context. Any discussion on wage and wage theory has to be discussed in the backdrop of the historical evolution of different stages through which production relations passed through, before they attained the present state of development of the society concerned. In the past, prior to when a systematic and scientific knowledge on wage labour and labour market existed, political economists had made serious attempts to explain wage movements and their determinants, particularly of workers in the unorganized sector in the context of developed countries (Brown 1987). Often changes in money wages were explained by primarily relating them to labour supply induced changes (Dobb 1943). For instance, upswing in real wages of building workers in Southern England in the fifteenth century was attributed to the periodic occurrence of famines caused by bad harvest. The wage question assumed economic and political importance when the Mercantilist School of thought had emerged as the plenipotentiary of the commercial capital at its fledgling phase in the sixteenth and seventeenth centuries in Britain (Rubin 1979). Mercantilists were the first group of thinkers to give a systematic treatment to the newly emerged capitalist system of production while justifying the economic policy of the state. Protagonists of the school nurtured an economic ideology, the origin of which could be traced back to the development and growth of commercial capital in the continental countries. The emergence of commercial bourgeoisie and its gradual transformation into a potential industrial capitalist class necessitated the supply of a cheap and abundant labour force for the youthful capitalism to be efficient and competitive in the world market, particularly with respect to the cloth industry. Material conditions required for the supply of cheap labour force came into being with the penetration of capitalistic production relations in agriculture, necessitated by the growth of trade, particularly of wool to the cloth industry in Italy and Flanders (Rubin 1979: 19–39). Small peasants and farmers lost the agricultural lands and grazing fields for their cattle and were left with little option but to swell the numerous ranks of beggars and vagabonds. Decaying feudal production relations in the countryside and speedy spread of merchant capital laid out the material condition much needed for the transformation of commercial capital into industrial capital. The group of people who were engaged in the service of middlemen or brokers turned into the manufacturing side. Independent craftsmen were deprived of their means of livelihood and they were left with little option but to join the ranks of wage labourers. It was under such circumstances that the Mercantilist School emerged to champion the cause of the fledgling commercial capital by arguing for active state patronage for the nascent bourgeoisie to grow by declassing the peasants and independent craftsmen in England during the sixteenth and the seventeenth centuries. Mercantilists upheld the position that a rise in the price for food articles would erode the purchasing power of labourers which would force them to work harder. Their declared policy on wage and wage labour was 'cheap bread makes workers lazy'. Mercantilists argued that if bread is cheap, workers would work only for two days and spend the rest of the days in a week '*carousing*'. Conversely, if labourers were made to taste the biting lash of famine (by the compulsion of high price of corn), landlords and industrial capital would be able to avail uninterrupted supply of labourers. Barring a few differences, the commercial bourgeoisie and landlords in England were fully in agreement particularly with respect to the wage policies of the mercantilists, and they succeeded in convincing different social classes that *dear corn would make labour cheap and vice versa*. Mercantilists wanted the state to fix minimum wages to workers in areas which they thought would discipline the labour force, who had been thrown out from their wonted living style with the capitalist development in agriculture and industry. However, the wage policy of mercantilists may be perceived against the backdrop of the specific questions thrown up by the youthful capitalism in England and the practical solutions to them offered by mercantilists.

Physiocrats theorized wage as advance for subsistence, and they developed the concept of a uniform wage.[1] The issue of regional differences in the daily wage level of workers surfaced in the discussion on wages for the first time, and debate evolved out of the material conditions prevailing in France and its competitors in the international market. By the second half of the eighteenth century, the Industrial Revolution took root on a large scale in Europe particularly in England and most parts of Western Europe, while France, remained predominantly an agrarian economy. Against the backdrop of a sagging agrarian economy in France, the Physiocrats conceptualized *natural wage*, which comprised the sum of the bare subsistence of the labouring households. The market for farm products produced in France originated mostly from its neighbouring countries, and the relatively lower wage rate prevailing in the neighbouring

countries did exert a cost escalation effect on the major exportables produced in France as compared to its import destinations. Precisely for this
reason, the Physiocrats argued for a uniform wage rate. Adam Smith dis-
tinguished between natural and market wage (Smith 1976). The natural
rate of wage is the subsistence wage, which is indispensable for a labourer
to meet his bare subsistence. A wage rate higher than the natural rate
would lead to a rise in population and a consequent decline in wage rate
to levels below the natural rate, resulting thereby in a decline in population and labour force. The market rate of wage is the rate fixed by the
market, and it is influenced by the supply of and demand for labourers.
The natural rate of wage is the prime cost of reproduction of labour and
the concept originated from the labour theory of value. The value of
labour is thus measured by the value of necessities which had gone into
subsistence for the maintenance of the labour force. Depending on the
conditions in the market, the price of labour may vary to a level above or
below his subsistence requirements, which is the market price of labour. ·
However, the assumption of a long-term tendency of the wage rate to
align with the natural wage or subsistence wage is based on the premise
that a change in wage above the natural wage causes an increase in population followed by a swell in labour supply, which in turn takes the wage
level back to its original level of subsistence. The classical economists in
general had subscribed to an earlier version of the theory of population
change and wages fund doctrine, which was later developed by Malthus
as the theory of population change and John Stuart Mills as the Wage
Fund Doctrine. However, Smith visualized a class society in which the
buyer and the seller of labour power existed, and the wage rate above
the subsistence level was fixed by bargaining or contract. Adam Smith
sought to explain spatial wage differentials for the same type of labour
and work across nations in terms of the pace at which capital accumulation takes place. Though Britain was more prosperous and opulent than
North America, the wage rate in North America was higher because
the state of advancement of North America was much faster than that
of Britain. In a thriving economy like America, the demand for labour
would be higher than its supply, and it was the demand for labour, which
keeps the market wage rate rising. Smith said:

> But though North America is not yet so rich as England, it is much
> more thriving, and advancing with much greater rapidity to the fur-
> ther acquisition of riches. The most decisive mark of the prosperity
> of any country is the increase of the number of its inhabitants.
>
> (Smith 1976: 79)

The concept of wage, and its different dimensions developed by Ricardo owed much to the tradition of Adam Smith. Sharing the tradition of Smith, Ricardo too conceptualized the recompense to labour in terms of natural wage and market wage. Deviation from subsistence wage was explained by the supply of and demand for labour, which determined the market wage (Ricardo 1957). Natural wage represented the wage base or necessary minimum subsistence wage and the market wage was the actual wage or the spot wage received by a labourer. The Ricardian wage concept incorporated the element of customs and habits in the nitty-gritty of the natural price of labour. It means labourers might cut down their diet, at times when the wage rate fell below the cost of necessities, but not the expenditure patterned by customs and habits (Dobb 1943). It underlines the fact that labourers will be reproduced at a constant cost, and that the constant cost is the equilibrium in which any economy should function – an assertion which implies that like any other commodity, labour is also produced at its long run cost and the supply of labour will be perfectly elastic at its long run supply price or subsistence wage (based on assumptions of Malthusian theory of population and Wage Fund Doctrine).

Can the natural price of labour be consistently above the market rate for a fairly long period? Primarily, the demand for and supply of labour and the price of necessaries upon which the wage income is expended influence the natural wage rate. Ricardo defines market wage rate as the rate determined by the supply of and demand for labour. Market wage rate can be kept consistently above the natural wage rate for an indefinite period only in an 'improving' society characterized by rapid growth in the pace of accumulation, giving increasing stimulus to the demand for labour, which in turn outweighs the rate of growth of population. However, if the pace of accumulation is gradual and constant, the rate of population growth will exceed the demand for labour driving the market wage down to its natural wage rate. Ricardo related wages to that part of the capital stock which is destined for the payment to labourers for their maintenance and that part being always a constant proportion of total capital stock. Ricardo believed that wage base or natural wage is neither fixed nor constant, but subject to variation in relation to the material base of the subsistence wage. The very content of subsistence wage does undergo considerable change over time as the productive forces and the wealth created in the society attain higher stages of development. Ultimately, reasons for the upward shift in the content of subsistence wage gets boiled down to the demand factor for labourers. Ricardo attributed the material difference in natural wage to the habits and customs of people, and he sought to explain the differences in natural wage by comparing the customs and habits of people in England and elsewhere. He says:

> An English labourer would consider his wage under their natural rate, and too scanty to support a family, if they enabled him to purchase no other food than potatoes, and to live in no better habitation than a mud cabin; yet these moderate demands of nature are often deemed sufficient in countries where man's life is cheap and his wants easily satisfied.
>
> (Ricardo, 1957: 55)

Although the above statement has reference with respect to national differences in wages, the conceptualization throws light on factors which might influence wage levels in different locations within a geographical entity. The observation is in conformity with the general laws governing the social and economic development of a socio-economic formation in a particular historical epoch and the nature of living and the very mode of satisfying them do vary across nations. The limitation of the above observation is the assumption that the state on behalf of the ruling class has little to do with the upkeep and maintaining of the different modes of living of different social and economic groupings within a socio-economic formation at a specific historical juncture. Ricardo lacks on account of the following: (1) Following Smith, Ricardo's major concern too was industrial labour; (2) the wage question was located and addressed at the national level and therefore the intra-state differences were not a matter of concern; (3) classical economists, in general, were the protagonists of capital rather than labour and therefore the issues and concerns related to labour have either been of secondary importance to them or to a great extent ignored.

Major criticism against the tradition of classical political economists, including Marx, William Petty, François Quesnay, Adam Smith, David Ricardo, Pierie Boisgwilletert (France), Simonde de Sismondi, was that they were unable to understand the dual nature of labour. Marx analysed the value of labour power by distinguishing it from other commodities.[2] Unlike Smith and Ricardo, Marx dealt with in greater detail national differences in wages to focus attention on the different facets of the wage system and stated rather categorically that the quantum of the means of subsistence in which the value of labour power is embedded may fluctuate independently of the variations in price, which is obviously a corrected position upon Smith. Analysis of national wage calls for taking into account all such factors that influence the magnitude of the value of labour power:

> In the comparison of wages in different nations, we must therefore take into account all the factors that determine changes in the amount of value of labour-power; the price and the extent of prime necessaries of life as naturally and historically developed, the cost of training the labourers, the part played by the labour of women and children, the productiveness of labour, its extensive and intensive magnitude.
>
> (Marx 1954: 559)

Marx's contribution to the wage theory is the categorical division brought into it. Neither his predecessors nor could the neoclassical economists envision it. In a socio-economic formation characterized by different and mutually opposing groups, it is not worth seeking a single way of life or material standard of living. It implies that the mode of satisfying basic needs may be different for a different sub-set of the population within a geographical entity. However, the observation does not explain the significant difference in wage levels across districts in a small geographical entity, and it is possible with the active intervention of the state to constantly reproduce geographical locations of cheap labour force. Various forms of intervention by the state in reproduction and perpetuation of geographical space have not figured in any meaningful way in the Marxian framework too. This is primarily on account of the fact that Marx analysed the wage question in a capitalist society in which the state performs its functions solely on behalf of capital. It means a separate analysis of the antagonistic relationship between capital and labour was not essential at the fledgling phase of capitalism. However, the Marxian method of analysis can be employed to explain regional wage differences for any social and economic grouping in a geographical entity.

In the debate on wage question, the Marginal Productivity Theory (MPT) of the late 1880s made a breakthrough and supplied an effective weapon to the employers to argue that the wage was low because it was linked to productivity. A low-wage rate for a particular set of labourers could be empirically and convincingly linked to the marginal productivity of labour. Its political implication was that collectivization of labour, and their collective bargaining has little influence on wage levels. Further, the MPT exonerated the state and capital from any form of anti-labour laws, regulations and wage reduction because the MPT did empirically prove that labourers received wage in proportion to their marginal productivity, and the only way of increasing wage level is to push up the productivity. Productiveness of labour is socially evolved overtime as an outcome of the judicious mix of several historical, social and economic factors. In the modern world, the policies and programmes of the government is crucial while the MPT is silent on the question of why the daily wage rate is significantly different across districts in a local state or, in other words, how the marginal product of labour is different for the same category of workers in adjacent districts. Often inter- and intra-state difference in the daily wage of workers in the unorganized sector are explained with reference to supply of labour measured in terms of number of agricultural labour per unit of land, proportion of Scheduled Caste (SC) and Scheduled Tribe workers in the total, level of class consciousness and collective bargaining, development of the labour market and influence radical political movements. The theoretical postulates underlined in the reasons for the spatial wage differentials, irrespective of the paradigm, equally assign a neutral role to the state in the reproduction and perpetuation of low-wage spaces and thereby the prevalence of low-wage zones in relatively small geographical entities. It is important, therefore, to analyse different ways that the central and local states intervene to create and upkeep low-wage peripheries within the geographical boundaries of local states.

The background, locale and sample of the study

Kerala, the southernmost state in India, was formed in 1956. The erstwhile princely states of Travancore in the south and Cochin State in the centre of Kerala were amalgamated in 1949. Later, the Malabar region in the north, which was part of the Madras Presidency was annexed to the Travancore–Cochin State and formed the State of Kerala. Although the influence of radical political movements on farm workers and peasants is more or less comparable across districts in the state, the daily wage rates for workers in the unorganized sector do vary significantly across districts in the state. The southern part or erstwhile Travancore and Central Kerala or the princely states of Cochin had inherited relatively better developed land and labour markets as compared to the Northern part (Malabar) of the state. The farm workers were better organized under left-wing radical political movements and unleashed historic struggles against the state and landlords in South Kerala. On the contrary, in the Northern part, farmers and workers had put up a joint fight against the oppressive policies of the imperial government, and, therefore, labour unions were in for better working conditions and wages, for farm workers did have a relatively late origin in North Kerala as compared to the

South. The intra-state differences in the daily wage of farm workers, semi-skilled and unskilled workers in the non-farm segment of the rural labour market not only differ, but their magnitude of difference is such that the daily nominal wage for farm workers in the low-wage districts constitutes less than half the wage rate in high-wage districts. Further, the difference in wage level is found to have persisted historically.

Table 8.1 shows the nominal wage rate for different categories of farm and non-farm workers prevailing in different districts in the state. Based

Table 8.1 Daily wage of labour in the unorganized rural sector in Kerala by districts January – 2011 (Rs.)

District	Agricultural labour (general)	Carpenter	Mason
Idukki	200	450	450
Wayanad	190*	375*	375*
Alappuzha**	263	430	405
Kottayam	275	375	375
Kasargod**	275	460	460
Kozhikode	283	387.5	387.5
Ernakulam	283	450	475
Thrissur	300	422	422
Palakkad**	320	300	300
Kannur	335	375	375
Kollam	350	450	450
Thiruvananthapuram	350	425	425
Malappuram	395	500	450
Pathanamthitta	400	500	500
Kerala	350	422	417

Source: Department of Economics and Statistics, Government of Kerala

Note: *For the collection of wage statistics, centres from Wayanad District is not included. Wage data for Wayanad from the sample Gram Panchayat (Mananthavady) was collected directly for the study.
**Average working hours for agricultural labour in Kerala is eight hours a day. However, there are exceptions to the general rule. Kasargod-Hosdurg centre (five hours), Palakkad Alappuzha-Chittur and Palakkadu centres (seven hours), Kollam-Karthikappally centre (six hours). The publication, *Agricultural Wages in India*, publishes the same data collected by the Department of Economics and Statistics, Government of Kerala.

on the daily wage rate in the farm and non-farm sector in rural areas, districts can broadly be classified under high-wage and low-wage zones. Districts with a daily wage of less than 75 per cent of the wage of state average in the reference year are classed under low-wage zone, and districts above 125 per cent of the state's average wage are included under the high-wage zone. High-wage and low-wage zones exist in South and North Kerala. In order to incorporate the historical and political elements in the evolution, development and formation of the rural labour market and the wage system, the state is geographically stratified into South and North Kerala. South Kerala comprises the erstwhile Travancore–Cochin part constituting present South and Central Kerala and North Kerala included in the erstwhile Malabar region. From each geographical stratum, two *Gram Panchayats* were randomly picked up to represent low- and high-wage districts. Accordingly, Idukki and Wayanad districts represented low-wage zones in South and North Kerala, respectively, while Thiruvananthapuram and Malappuram districts were high-wage districts, respectively, from South and North Kerala. *Venganoor* (Thiruvananthapuram), *Santhanpara* (Idukki), *Thavanoor* (Malappuram) and *Mananthavadi* (Wayanad) were sample *Grama Panchayats* selected for the study from the respective districts. The study is based on a primary survey of 300 rural households selected from low and high-wage zones in South and North Kerala. A multistage stratified random sampling with household as the ultimate unit was used for the study. The sample size was distributed proportionate to the relative share of cultivators and agricultural labourers of sample districts. The primary survey was conducted in 2006, and the data consists for the reference period the financial year/Calendar year 2005/2006.

The state and reproduction of labour

In its crude form the state is defined as a machine for the oppression of one class by another (Lenin 1980). Although, there exist different approaches to politically locate and interpret the content, character and acts of the state, it has been widely accepted that the state protects and promotes the interest of the dominant class and its elementary function includes creation and upkeep of the environment for extension of capitalist relations of production and capital accumulation. A primary condition for the expansion of capitalist production relations includes creation and upkeep of a vast reserve army of labour for the capital. As the pace of accumulation increases, the capital employs more labour while displacing a part of the existing labour force because of the technological change in production. The reserve labour force is therefore not a homogeneous and composite mass of unemployed youth as usually is envisaged but comprises different categories of labour force, namely floating, latent and stagnant. Displaced workers constitute the floating reserve army of labour, and the pool is drawn down when the accumulation process is in its recovery phase or the production process creates more jobs than it destroys. Under the capitalist production process, the floating component in the reserve army of labour is a transitory phenomenon, and its pool is drawn down and replenished in tune with the cyclical movement of the economy. The *latent* component of the reserve labour force, who reproduce outside capitalist relations of production (traditional agriculture governed by the purpose of producing for the family and subsistence rather than for the market) are pushed into selling their labour power as their traditional source of livelihood (agriculture and handicrafts) has been destroyed with the expansion of capitalist production. The *latent* labour forces along with new entries from female folk into the rural labour market are a potential source of cheap labour power. Another component in the relative surplus population is the *stagnant* reserve labour. They have never been in the capitalist production arena as their skills and manpower do not suit the technique of production and, therefore, their labour power deteriorates and skills remain undeveloped. The *stagnant* reserve labour force reproduce on the extreme margins of social production and organized social life. In a socio-economic formation, the cost of socially determined subsistence standard of living of labour is determined by the physical and socially determined cultural reproduction cost of the floating and latent reserve army of labour. Although there is an average value of labour power in a particular epoch for a socio-economic formation, it does vary across districts within the geographical boundaries of a local state. If the wage differential persists for a long period across districts, there could be factor(s) other than supply and demand for labourers. The value of labour power is kept low by denying a socially determined average standard of living to labourers in certain regions/areas where the labourers live or constituents of the ruling class are less.

It is important to examine how the state by its strategies, policies and programmes replenishes a relative surplus population and keeps the standard of living of labour low in certain regions in relation to the socially determined average standard of living of the sub-state. To recapitulate, the subsistence wage of classical economists, the equilibrium wage of the Marginalist School and the socially determined standard of living of Marx do mean the cost of reproduction of value of labour power measured in terms of cost of living in a particular epoch in a nation or in a region within the nation. As labour is a social product, the consumption basket or the standard of living of labour comprises a physical and a cultural component. How does the state intervene in the determination of subsistence standard of living? The value of labour power is formed by two components: (1) physical component and (2) historically evolved and socially determined cultural component. The physical component is the ultimate limit, comprising the necessaries of life, which are absolutely indispensable for labourers to subsist and perpetuate. Perhaps, it could be expressed in calories required to subsist and work along with other necessaries of life and under comparable climatic conditions. The basket of necessaries which are deemed to be indispensable for the subsistence of the labourer and his family varies significantly from region to region and also from one historical epoch to another. The second element in the cost of reproduction of labour is the traditional standard of living of a social formation, which is nothing but the value of commodities consumed by labour to satisfy desires springing from the social conditions in which people are reared up in whichever way they live. In shaping the social needs of a particular social formation, historical tradition and social habitude play an important role. Historical tradition refers to the stage of development of the productive force and the past struggle of labourers to transform the system from serfdom to its current status. In agrarian economies, the evolutionary stage of development from caste-based organization of production to wage labour-based capitalistic production, relations could vary from region to region. Marx cites the example of interdistrict differences in average wages across agricultural districts in England.

The other element in the reproduction cost of labour is the necessary wants and the mode of satisfying them. The mode of satisfying needs depends on habits and the degree of comforts, which the society in general enjoys. The difference in the degree of civilization is the product of development of the productive force, which in itself is a manifestation of the stage of development of the socio-economic formation. To put it differently, under uniform production relations, can the value of labour power differ significantly across districts within a relatively small geographical entity? The state policies and programmes are crucial in deciding the social and cultural cost of reproduction of labour or the value of labour power. Although the cultural cost of reproduction is more abstract in nature rather than concrete, the abstract term can be examined to an extent, empirically, by analysing factors influencing the social cost of reproduction.

The state's strategy is to keep the physical and cultural components in the social cost of reproduction of the value of labour power at its possible minimum. There is a biological limit to reduce the cost of reproduction of labour, and if the price of labour falls below the minimum required for renewing the vital energy, the labour force can be maintained and developed only in a crippled state. As social production advances, the cultural component in the subsistence living standard too increases. The scale and magnitude of the value of labour power is determined by the mode of satisfying the physical and cultural needs of labour. The cultural component in the reproduction cost includes amenities in life, education, health, communication, transport and other comforts in life which the society has developed and has been enjoying. It in turn means that the physical and cultural cost of reproduction of labour is determined by the supply of infrastructure and facilities available for different classes of people in a society. In the jurisdiction of a local state, there exists economically and socially backward areas/districts, and the availability and accessibility of infrastructure is discriminated spatially and socially. Often, backward districts in less developed nations have the following characteristic features: (1) daily wage of workers in the unorganized segment of the rural labour market are less than the state's average; (2) size of surplus population (particularly *latent* and *stagnant* reserve army of labour) is relatively large in backward districts; (3) proportion of socially backward communities in the population, farm workers and cultivators in the total workforce are significantly higher than the average for the state; (4) the share of plantation crops (export-oriented cash crops) and value added from the primary sector in the total of the district income is relatively higher in backward regions. In terms of social and cultural cost of reproduction of labour, backward districts attract less private investment because of low purchasing power of the majority of the population in those districts. Backwardness can be measured in terms of infrastructure for health, roads and educational institutions.

In the following text, the above-mentioned characteristics of backwardness are empirically verified for the state of Kerala. The state has a population of 33.39 million (2011) distributed across 14 districts. In terms of population, Malappuram District tops the rank, while Idukki and Wayanad rank thirteenth and fourteenth, respectively. Although, Idukki and Wayanad Districts have a relatively low population size, the latter was the second lowest in per capita income at constant prices, while Idukki District ranked seventh in 2010–11. Table 8.2 compares the relative share in the population and farm dependent workforce by districts in Kerala. Three districts, namely, Wayanad, Idukki and Palakkad together accounted for 14.22 per cent of the total population in the state while

Table 8.2 District-wise proportion of agriculture-dependent population in Kerala – 2011 (per cent)

Travancore			Malabar		
District	Total population –2011	Agriculture-dependent population (2001)	District	Total population –2011	Agriculture-dependent population (2001)
Thiruvanantha-puram	10.16	9.01	Thrissur	9.34	6.74
Kollam	8.12	7.43	Palakkad	8.22	16.91
Pathanamthitta	3.88	5.11	Malappuram	11.39	8.89
Alappuzha	6.62	5.34	Kozhikode	9.04	3.89
Kottayam	6.14	5.64	Wayanad	2.45	6.12
Idukki	3.55	9.84	Kannur	7.57	6.34
Ernakulam	9.75	6.16	·		

Source: (1) Economic Review, Government of Kerala, 2012
(2) Government of India. (2001). 'Census of India 2001, Series-33. Kerala, Provisional population totals, Paper-3 of 2001', Distribution of workers and non-workers, Directorate of Census operations, Kerala.

the combined share of these three districts in the total farm dependent population of Kerala was 32.87 per cent. Another specific feature of these districts was the dominance of *Dalits* and *Adivasis* in the population. These three districts with a population share of 14.27 per cent together house about 34.91 per cent of *Dalits* and 23.24 per cent of *Adivasis* in the state population. The observed higher population proportion of *Dalits* and *Adivasis* in these districts may be viewed against their higher representation in unskilled and low-paid rural agricultural labour force (latent and stagnant labour force) in Kerala. Table 8.3 supplements relative share in population with area under plantation crops in respective districts. Labour-intensive and export-oriented plantation crops, namely, tea, coffee, cardamom and pepper cultivation can be considered a characteristic feature of backward agrarian economies. The export-oriented plantation crops are grown in low-wage zones, Wayanad and Idukki Districts.

Comparative infrastructure in low-wage and high-wage zones

As mentioned elsewhere, subsistence standard of living consists of physically and socially determined and historically evolved cultural

Table 8.3 Proportion of Dalits and Adivasis and area under plantation crops by districts – 2001

District	% of Dalits	% of Adivasis	% of area under plantation crops – 2008
Thiruvananthapuram	11.47	0.65	2.29
Kollam	12.49	0.20	3.63
Pathanamthitta	13.13	0.53	1.72
Alappuzha	9.45	0.15	0.62
Kottayam	7.69	0.94	3.71
Idukki	14.11	4.51	31.87
Ernakulam	8.48	0.32	2.33
Thrissur	11.91	0.16	1.60
Palakkad	16.53	1.52	3.34
Malappuram	7.87	0.34	3.12
Kozhikode	6.98	0.21	3.91
Wayanadu	4.27	17.43	22.45
Kannur	4.11	0.83	6.38
Kasargod	7.49	2.52	7.87
Kerala	9.81	1.14	100.00

Source: Census (2001) and Statistics for Planning (2009)

components. The magnitude of the value that goes into the reproduction of labour is greatly determined by accessibility to the average comforts that exist at a particular point of time. For the comparison of access to various infrastructure for human development and comforts in life, the following indicators are considered. Health, education, state investment in industrial sector measured in terms of industrial establishments by Kerala Small Industrial Development Corporation Ltd (SIDCO) and road length per square kilometre by districts. These indicators are compared for an assessment of geographical discrimination by the local state to keep the living standard of labours different. The number of hospital beds available per 1,000 population across districts is presented in Figure 8.1. It is found that the number of hospital beds per 1,000 population was lowest in Kasargod District, followed, respectively, by Palakkad, Idukki and Wayanad Districts – four relatively backward and low-wage

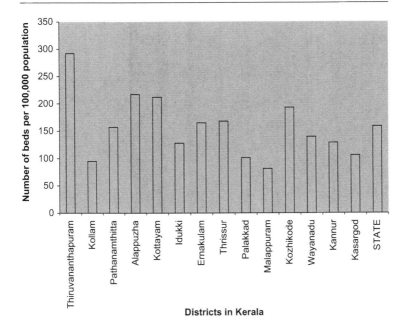

Figure 8.1 Hospital bed per lakh population

Source: Statistics for Planning, Government of Kerala

zones in South and North Kerala. Figure 8.2 compares infrastructure availability measured in terms of road length per square kilometre area in all the districts. It is found that the socially and economically backward districts have relatively less road length per square kilometre area, and empirical observation further confirms that there is spatial discrimination by the state between developed and backward districts in Kerala. Another indicator influencing wage level is the size of surplus population measured in terms of different types of reserve labour. A higher density of industrial establishments reduces the pressure in the rural labour market. Table 8.4 gives the number of major industrial estates by districts established by SIDCO. It is worth mentioning that out of 775 major industrial establishments in Kerala, Wayanad and Idukki, the two low-wage districts in Kerala, have no industrial establishment (SIDCO). Although there are several factors influencing the decision to establish industrial units in a district by the government agency (SIDCO), conspicuous absence of major industrial units in three districts, of which

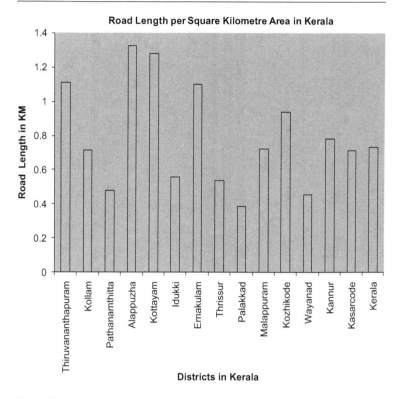

Figure 8.2 Road per square kilometre area

Source: Statistics for Planning, Government of Kerala

two districts, namely Idukki and Wayanad turned out to be the low-wage zone districts from the South and North Kerala point towards geographical discrimination.

The implication is that the relative surplus population competes in the labour market for fewer jobs in the farm sector. In the value of labour power, education is crucial and the content of labour changes with the expenditure on education. Table 8.5 provides a district-wise comparison of number of arts and science colleges (government and private) by districts in Kerala for 2011. The low-wage zones, namely Wayanad, Idukki and Kasargod Districts are ranked twelfth, thirteenth and fourteenth, respectively, in the availability of colleges in Kerala, and the observation again confirms the hypothesis that the state discriminates in proving (or denying) infrastructure to improve the quality of labour. The economic

Table 8.4 Number of major industrial estates under SIDCO – 2011

District	Working units	% share
Kottayam	141	18.19
Thrissur	134	17.29
Kollam	94	12.13
Thiruvanthapuram	78	10.06
Palakkad	73	9.42
Alappuzha	68	8.77
Kasaragod	58	7.48
Kozhikode	49	6.32
Kannur	35	4.52
Malappuram	25	3.23
Idukki	0	0
Wayanad	0	0
Ernakulam	20	2.58
Total	775	100.00

Source: Economic Review, 2011, Volume Two, Appendix Tables

and social status of people is an important element influencing the quality of education in a region, and the proportion of dropouts at the primary and high school level is an indirect indicator of the educational backwardness of a region. Table 8.6 gives the percentage of drop outs at the primary and secondary level of schools by districts in Kerala in 2011. It is observed that the backward districts of Wayanad and Idukki rank first and second in students' dropping out at the primary school level, and the same trend is followed at the high school level as well. The foregoing analysis clearly showed a positive association between backwardness in terms of infrastructure for human development and daily wage rates for workers in the unorganized sector. It is argued therefore that the stretch of backwardness is known and is a cultivated characteristic feature of low-wage geographical spaces.

Living standard in low- and high-wage zones

In this section, information elicited from rural households on their standard of living, way of life in high-wage and low-wage zones are

Table 8.5 Number of arts and science colleges (government and private) in Kerala – 2011

District	Number of colleges	Rank
Ernakulam	25	1
Kottayam	22	2
Thiruvananthapuram	20	3
Thrissur	20	4
Kozhikode	14	5
Malappuram	13	6
Kollam	13	7
Alappuzha	12	8
Palakkad	11	9
Kannur	11	10
Pathanamthitta	9	11
Idukki	8	12
Wayanad	6	13
Kasargod	5	14
State	189	

Source: Statistics for Planning, Government of Kerala

compared. Indicators used for comparison are (1) consumption pattern, (2) housing, (3) basic amenities of life and (4) possession of consumer durables. It is hypothesized that the above four living standard indicators for farmer and labour households in high-wage zones is higher than in low-wage zones. The findings of the primary survey support the argument that the local state enforces geographical discrimination, creates peripheries and maintains low-wage zones.

Caste composition of low-wage and high-wage zones

Caste is a crucial institutional variable in the wage determination process because the mass base of the state comprises a combination of class and caste. In the high-wage zone in South Kerala (Venganoor Gram Panchyat (GP) in Thiruvananthapuram district), 30 per cent of labour households belonged to the *Paraya* and *Pulay* community, two castes

Table 8.6 Number of schools per 1,00,000 population by district in Kerala – 2011

District	Students density	% of Dropouts In primary class	% of dropouts in high school
Pathanamthitta	61.56	0.44 (6)	0.38
Kannur	51.20	0.33 (9)	0.54
Kottayam	46.02	0.33 (8)	0.73
Idukki	43.16	0.86 (2)	1.56
Kasargod	42.53	0.68 (3)	1.93
Kozhikode	40.04	0.24 (13)	0.45
Alappuzha	35.96	0.27 (11)	0.69
Malappuram	35.81	0.3 (10)	0.90
Wayanad	35.76	0.88 (1)	1.64
Kollam	35.25	0.24 (12)	0.70
Palakkad	34.58	0.46 (5)	0.80
Thrissur	32.44	0.23 (14)	1.28
Ernakulam	30.83	0.35 (7)	0.78
Thiruvananthapuram	29.90	0.51 (4)	0.38
Kerala	37.89	0.38	0.85

Source: Economic Review, 2011, Volume Two, Appendix Tables

in the lowest rung of the caste hierarchy (SC). The second largest community supplying labour force to the farming sector in the GP is *Nadars* (Other Backward Caste – OBC). On the contrary, among farmer households, 47 per cent were *Nairs (upper caste)* closely followed by *Nadars* (42 per cent). It is rather strange to note that households from the SC (*Paraya* and *Pulay)* category constituted only 5 per cent of the farming community in the high-wage zone in South Kerala. The low-wage zone in south Kerala – Santhanppara GP in Idukki District presents a different scenario. The original inhabitants of Santhanppara village (low-wage zone in South Kerala) were *Thevar, Chettiyar* (Tamil origin), *Devankar* and other lower castes of Tamil origin. Farmers in the village migrated to the place by 1970s from the border area of Tamil Nadu and other parts of the Idukki District. The farming community comprises *Nairs,* Christians and Muslims, who were attracted to the place by cheap labour and land. The *Pulaya* community alone accounted for 47 per cent of the total labour households; another caste under the SC category, *Kanakar*, formed the second largest source of supply of labourers. Among farmer households, *Nairs* was the single largest category and *Ezhava* was the second largest group followed by the *Namboodiris*. The high-wage zone in North Kerala is Tavanoor GP in Malappuram District. Labour from the SC community supply a major share of labour to the agricultural sector in Tavanoor. Among farmer households, Christian and Muslim communities constituted 50 per cent of the farmer households in the village. The low-wage zone in North Kerala (Manathavady GP in Wayanad District) gets the supply of farm labour chiefly from the Adivasi community. *Adivasis* and *dalits* are aboriginals in the village, and Christian, *Nairs* and Muslims are migrants from the mainland, who were attracted to the place by the availability of cheap labour and land.

Consumption pattern: high-wage zone

Daily household expenditure on food and non-food items is a direct indicator of the consumption levels of households. The mode of satisfying social needs is an indicator of the state of development of the productive force of a socio-economic formation. In the sample survey, we collected information on food and non-food expenditure of both labour and farmer households in sample villages (Table 8.7). The high-wage zones included Venganoor GP in Thiruvananthapuram (South) and Tavanoor GP in Malappuram (North) districts. The daily household food expenditure in high-wage zones ranged from Rs. 20 to Rs. 200. It does not include electricity charges, house rent (commuted rent), expenditure on education, clothing, gifts and contributions, marriage expenses and expenditure incurred on other special occasions. Important observations on consumption pattern as observed from Table 8.7 are: farmer and labour households in these high-wage zones begin the day with bed coffee or red tea, followed by a reasonably good breakfast with items such as *Idli, Dosa* or some other breakfast items made usually of rice or wheat. Between 1 p.m. and 2 p.m., invariably, both farmer and labour households take lunch with not less than two side dishes. By evening, around 5 p.m. all members take milk tea, occasionally with snacks. Male members may sometimes go out to the village centre for their evening tea and snacks or a glass of country liquor. In the night, labour and farmer households alike take square meals consisting of fish curry with one or two other side dishes. After working hours or having completed the work, adult male members pay regular evening visits to the village centre wearing pressed or at least neatly washed clothes and spend three

Table 8.7 Percentage distribution of labour and farmer households (HH) by daily expenditure on food and non-food items

| Expenditure class | Travancore | | | | Malabar | | | |
| | High-wage zone Thiruvananthapuram (Venganoor GP) | | Low-wage zone Idukki (Santhanpara GP) | | High-wage zone Malappuram (Tavanoor GP) | | Low-wage zone Wayanad (Mananthavadi GP) | |
	Labour HH	Farmer HH	Labour HH	Farmer HH	Labour HH	Farmer HH	Labour HH	Farmer HH
≤ 50	26.09	5.88	45.28	26.47	23.08	12.90	75	25.00
51–75	45.65	41.18	30.19	35.29	23.08	9.68	13	12.50
76–100	13.04	41.18	24.53	20.59	32.05	45.16	12	25.00
101–25	8.70	0	0	0	1.28	0	0	12.50
126–50	6.52	5.88	0	11.79	17.95	19.35	0	12.50
> 151	0	5.88	0	5.88	2.56	12.90	0	12.50
Total	100	100	100	100	100	100	100	100

Source: Sample Survey

to four hours on socialization at village centres. For a six-member family, a labour household spends between Rs. 3,000 and Rs. 5,000 on clothes annually, and the amount increases with the income levels and with number of young children at home.

Consumption pattern: low-wage zone

Living standards and consumption patterns in low-wage zones, namely Santhanppara GP in Idukki District and Mananthavady GP in Wayanad Districts have many commonalities. In Santhanppara, labour and farmer households are mostly of Tamil origin. Tamilians are the aboriginals of the village. Farmers from nearby places migrated to the village during 1970s and the early 1980s primarily enticed by cheap and abundant land. Labourers live in hut-type houses, and the average estimated cost of a hut is below Rs. 5,000. On average, a farmer's house is not distinctly different from that of a labourer. Labourers work in estates, which are not covered under labour laws or minimum wage legislation, of areas ranging between 25 acres and 50 acres. Crops mostly grown in the GP are pepper, cardamom and coffee. Labour households do not cook breakfast and lunch separately like in the high-wage zones. They take black tea or coffee (low priced and locally available) in the morning and cook rice for the day. Along with rice, *chutney,* made of locally available leaves is prepared. During working days, they cook rice in the morning and carry tiffin containing cooked rice and *chutney* for brunch around 11 a.m. On their return, supper is cooked. Supper too contains rice and one side dish. If they do not have work, rice will be cooked around 11 a.m. and the cooked rice is eaten between 1 p.m. and 2 p.m. However, they are not habituated to have lunch or breakfast at specific hours; adults particularly women, limit their food intake to one meal a day. Only on special occasions do they buy non-vegetarian items. On working days, on their way back home in the evening, labour households purchase vegetables costing about Rs. 5 for a family. While shopping, labourers may take black tea and snacks from a nearby tea shop in the village centre, which functions only in the mornings and the evenings. Labourers, to a certain extent, use neem-stick for brushing teeth. Labour households of Tamil origin send their children to Bodimettu in Tamil Nadu for education as there are not many good schools in the area. Girl children of the Tamil labour households are sent to work in cloth mills in Coimbatore for a daily wage rate of Rs. 15 to Rs. 20 per day.

In the low-wage zone in the Malabar region, Mananthavady Panchayat, labourers are drawn mainly from *Adivasi* communities. The *Advasi* community usually live together, and their habitation is called *Ooru*. Like Santhanppara, employment in Mananthavady Grama Panchayat is seasonal as crops grown in the village are annuals: pepper and coffee. However, Mananthavady town is a relatively large urban centre with all facilities. The sample village is an extension of the urban centre. Unlike Santhanppara, public transport system is developed and buses ply to the sample village rather frequently. Unlike Santhanppara, considerable difference could be observed in Mananthavady in the standard of living. Labourers cook rice in the morning and skip breakfast. The cooked rice is eaten around 11 a.m., and supper is served with one side dish. They do not take or cook breakfast; instead they drink black tea in the morning. Farmer households belong to communities such as *Nair* and *Ezhavas*, Christian and Muslim. Living standards of farmers in Mananthavady village is much lower than the standard of living of farmers of the same size class in the high-wage zone. Nonetheless, farmer households cook breakfast, lunch with sufficient side dishes and take evening tea and supper in the low-wage zone.

Possession of consumer durables

Possession of consumer durables is yet another indicator of the state of development of a society or mode of living. Table 8.8 gives five major items used to ease the task in daily life. It is found that 34 per cent of labour households and 64 per cent of farmer households in the high-wage zone in South Kerala have television sets at home, whereas neither farmer nor labour households have television sets in the low-wage zone in South Kerala. It is because electricity has not reached the village which was taken as sample in the GP. Though the difference between the low- and high-wage zone in North Kerala is not as startling as in South Kerala, there is difference between low-wage and high-wage zones in North Kerala too. The basic needs of life such as drinking water, electricity and sanitation facilities are also compared in Table 8.9. In the high-wage zone, both farmer and labour households have near total facilities including sanitation, while less than 9 per cent of labour households have electricity in their houses in the low-wage zone. The difference in basic amenities in life between the low-wage and high-wage zones holds key for the geographical production of low-wage zones. Table 8.10 compares the type of houses where labourers live in low-wage and high-wage zones. In low-wage zones labourers have mostly tiled or thatched houses as compared to their counterparts in high-wage zones.

Table 8.8 Percentage distribution of labour and farmer households by the possession of consumer durables

Expenditure class	Travancore				Malabar			
	High-wage zone Thiruvananthapuram (Venganoor)		Low-wage zone Idukki (Santhanpara)		High-wage zone Malappuram (Tavanoor)		Low-wage zone Wayanad (Mananthavadi)	
	Labour HH	Farmer HH	Labour HH	Farmer HH	Labour HH	Farmer HH	Labour HH	Farmer HH
Car or jeep	0	0	0	0	0	16	0	6
Two wheeler	0	6	0	0	2.5	26	0	12
Other vehicles	0	0	0	0	1	3	0	0
Television	34	64	0	0	16	83	13	69
Fridge	2	6	0	0	1	60	0	25
Washing machine	0	0	0	0	1	13	0	25

Source: Sample Survey

Table 8.9 Percentage distribution of farmers and labourers having basic amenities

| Item | Travancore | | | | | Malabar | | | |
| | High-wage zone Thiruvananthapuram (Venganoor GP) | | Low-wage zone Idukki (Santhanpara GP) | | | High-wage zone Malappuram (Tavanoor GP) | | Low-wage zone Wayanad (Mananthavadi GP) | |
	Labour HH	Farmer HH	Labour HH	Farmer HH		Labour HH	Farmer HH	Labour HH	Farmer HH
Drinking water	100	100	22	67		42	100	51	100
Electricity	91	100	9	29		67	100	75	100
Toilet	93	100	32	58		91	100	60	100

Source: Sample Survey

Table 8.10 Percentage distribution of farmers and labourers by type of houses

Expenditure class	Travancore				Malabar			
	High-wage zone Thiruvananthapuram (Venganoor GP)		Low-wage zone Idukki (Santhanpara GP)		High-wage zone Malappuram (Tavanoor GP)		Low-wage zone Wayanad (Mananthavadi GP)	
	Labour HH	Farmer HH	Labour HH	Farmer HH	Labour HH	Farmer HH	Labour HH	Farmer HH
Terrace	19	59	4	23	20	76	9	56
Tiles	22	23	96	73	59	24	24	32
Thatched	20	18	Nil	4	21	Nil	Nil	Nil
Hut	9	Nil	Nil	Nil	Nil	Nil	21	6
Sheet	21	Nil	Nil	Nil	nil	Nil	15	6
Panchayat house	9	Nil	Nil	Nil	Nil	Nil	31	Nil
Total	100	100	100	100	100	100	100	100

Source: Sample Survey

Conclusion

Wage theories, in general, envisage that the value of labour power tends to the socially determined standard of living or the natural wage rate in the long run. Deviation from the natural wage or long run cost of reproduction of labour (value of labour power) is short-lived and is corrected by the supply-demand conditions in the market. Spatial or regional differences in the value of labour power or wage level within a geographical entity therefore, have not been of much significance to both classical and neoclassical frameworks of analysis. The conceptualization of Marx on the value of labour power gives the scope for an analysis of spatial differences in wages by bringing in the state as an active player in the process of wage determination. The value of labour power is composed of physical and cultural components. A lower level of consumption, in its quantity and quality, for satiating the physical and cultural needs of labour would keep the cost of reproduction of labour (value of labour power) in certain areas relatively less as compared to the socially determined subsistence standard of living of the society at that historical epoch. To a great extent, the state, by its programmes and policies, geographically discriminates areas by denying basic infrastructure facilities for human development in order to keep the value of labour power to its minimum possible. Less investment in auxiliary means of production and the modern industrial sector in such backward areas would add onto the size of relative surplus population, which in turn prevents the wage level from rising. The question why the state geographically discriminates is answered from its class bias that often socially and economically vulnerable sections live in backward areas within the jurisdiction of a local state. The intra-regional differences in wage in Kerala confirmed the hypothesis that the spatial difference in wage is an outcome of the state's bias against the class which is outside the mass base of the ruling class. Although, unionization, collective bargaining and past struggles of the working class are important to keep the wage level high, along with other demand-side variables in the wage determination process, the role of the state is one of the most influential actors in the determination of the value of labour power. The conventional wage analysis ignores that dimension of the issue. A close perusal of infrastructure facilities for human development by districts in Kerala revealed that industrial establishments by government agencies are fewer in low-wage districts (backward areas) as compared to high-wage districts. A comparison made between high- and low-wage zones on consumption expenditure and its pattern, house type and other basic amenities of life showed that those indicators were significantly different for both farmer and labour households in high-wage and low-wage zones. The empirical observation that low-wage zones are created and nursed by the state on behalf of the capital for the supply of cheap labour confirms the hypothesis that regional wage differentials are an outcome of a state act as other factors influencing the wage levels.

Notes

1 The history of the development of agriculture in every part of the world was characterized by the simultaneous existence of pre-capitalist relations of production along with fully developed capitalistic production relations. The *peonage* system prevailed in Mexico in the seventeenth and eighteenth centuries was a variant of such pre-capitalistic relations of production.

2 Karl Marx categorized thinkers in the political economy tradition into three, namely bourgeoisie political economist, which comprised William Betty, Franco Quesney, Adam Smith and David Ricardo. The tradition opened up by Malthus, J.B. Say and Bastiat were labelled as vulgar bourgeoisie political economists; Sisimondi and Proudhan represented the petty bourgeoisie political economist. They, while criticizing the capitalist production system, argued for a return to the old and archaic economic formation. However, they were protecting the interest of petty- bourgeoisie in urban and rural areas.

References

Brown, P.H. 1987. 'Origin and Development of Money and Real Wages', in John Eatwell, Murray Milgate and Peter Newman (eds), *The New Palgrave Dictionary of Economics,* Vol. 1, pp. XX–XX. Macmillan Press Ltd: London.

Dobb, M. 1943. *Wages.* NISBET & Co. Ltd, Cambridge University Press: Cambridge.

Hobsbawm, E. 2006. 'From Feudalism to Capitalism', in P. Sweezy, *et al.* (eds), *The Transition from Feudalism to Capitalism,* pp. XX–XX. Aaakar Books: Delhi.

Jose, A. V. 1978. Agricultural Labour in Kerala: A Historical Cum Statistical Analysis. Unpublished Ph.D thesis. Centre for Development Studies, Thiruvananthapuram.

Lenin, V. I. 1980. *The State and Revolution.* Collected Works, Vol. 25, Progress Publishers: Moscow.

Marx, K. 1954. *Capital,* Vol. 1. Foreign Language Publishing House: Moscow.

Ricardo, D. 1957. *The Principles of Political Economy and Taxation.* J. M. Dent & Sons Ltd: London.

Rubin, I. I. 1979. *A History of Economic Thought*. Ink Links Ltd: London.
Smith, A. 1976. *An Enquiry into the Nature and Causes of Wealth of Nations*. Vol. 1. The University of Cambridge: Chicago.
Travancore. 1935. 'Report of the Agriculture Debt Redemption Committee', Thiruvananthapuram.

Chapter 9

Law, income and child labour in South Asia

Shakti Kumar

The International Conference on Child Labour in Agriculture (28–30 July 2012, Washington. D.C.) reconfirmed the 'slowing down of the global pace of reduction of child labour'. The reason behind it was the breaking down of the socio-economic conditions of the world, in general, and that of South Asia, in particular. Therefore, the goal of the UNO to 'Secure Right of Child' and 'Decent Work for All' has been retargeted to achieve in 2016 rather than in 2015.

South Asia shares more than 50 per cent of the world's child labour with the highest intensity in agriculture, which is the source of food and employment. India, Pakistan, Bangladesh, Sri Lanka and Nepal are characterized by the highest concentration of labour force in this sector with declining share of agriculture in gross domestic product (GDP) (Myron 1993). All these facts suggest the failure of Lewis theory of transformation in South Asia, whereby with development labour transfers from primary sector to secondary and tertiarry sectors. What steps have been taken yet, in this direction, needs a thorough analysis?

Literature review

The pace of quantum change of child labour depends on national policies and actions in the area of eradication of child labour (Mirium 2003). National actions should be directed towards raising of awareness regarding the negative effects of child labour (Oliveira 2003). There should be penal provision of a country's law for banning child labour (Mehrotra and Biggeri 2002). Hiring a live-in person to undertake domestic household chores is an integral part of South Asian tradition (Sharma 2001). If law and actions do not work for combating child labour through raising income, government fails. The Indian government has failed to free those in bonded child labour who are bound to work in exchange for loans to their families (Coursen and Zama 2003).

Therefore, poverty and income stability are key determinants of children's work (Dalep 2010). Poverty is the major cause of child labour (Maitra and Ray 2010). Child labour falls with rise in GDP per capita (Joelle 2010). Poverty alone is not the only factor, but there are some other factors that compel children to work (Heather 2011).

The above literature reviews suggest that child labour exists mostly in poor countries and among the people who are poorer. Therefore, one should go through the socio-economic conditions of South Asian countries. Table 9.1 shows these conditions showing population, number of children, literacy rate, enrolment ratio, per capita GDP and poverty ratio. It clearly infers that poverty exists in South Asia, which is characterized by concentration of labour force along with declining share of agriculture in GDP despite having agriculturally dominated area.

No literature is available showing law, income and child labour in an area which is characterized with concentration of labour force in agriculture along with declining share in GDP without labour transfer from agriculture to industry. Therefore, the present study has been carried out to find out the solution to combat child labour in South Asia, meeting above characteristics.

The present study has been divided into four sections. The first section deals with quantum of child labour in South Asia. The second section deals with countries' laws followed in South Asia. The third section shows a model of how a country's law combats child labour. The final section presents conclusions and policy implications.

Table 9.1 Socio-economic characteristics of South Asian countries in 2008

Socio-economic conditions	Sri Lanka	Pakistan	India	Nepal	Bangladesh
Population (mn)	19.1	168	1,134	27	153
Children (5–14 years) million	3.180	40	210	6.23	35.06
Literacy rate of youth (15–24 years age) in %	95.6	65.1	76.4	70.1	63.6
Net primary enrolment ratio (%) male:female	98:97	74:57	90:87	91:87	87:91
Per capita GDP (US$)	4,595	2,370	3,452	1,550	2,050
Below poverty line population (%)	25.0	32.6	28.6	42.0	49.8

Source: (1) UNDP *Human Development Report 2008*
(2) ILO. International Programme on the Elimination of Child Labour

Quantum of child labour in South Asia

South Asia comprises 21.69 million child labourers, which is 7.36 per cent of total children and 1.56 per cent of its total population (1,387 million) as shown in Table 9.2. Sri Lanka comprises the lowest proportion of children (age ranges between 5 and 14 years) as well as child labour available in South Asia while this proportion is highest for India. The ILO (International Labour Organization) study of intra-country child labour shows that India shares only 6.0 per cent as child labour in total number of children. This figure is almost one-third of India for Sri Lanka. It infers that child labour gets affected not only by population but also by other factors.

The major factors responsible for child labour in different countries are explained in the following paragraphs.

(1) Major factors responsible for child labour in Pakistan

   (a) High population growth rate with average family size of eight
   (b) Popularity of subsistence agricultural activities which provide livelihood to three-fourths of the total population.
   (c) High poverty and low productivity per labour

Table 9.2 Magnitude of child labour in South Asia (Mn) as a proportion of total children (5–14 years age group)

Country	Total no. of children (TC)	Child labour (CL)	CL as % of TC
Sri Lanka	3.180 (1.10)	0.475 (2.05)	14.94
Pakistan	40.00 (13.58)	3.30 (14.29)	8.25
India	210.00 (71.31)	12.60 (54.58)	6.00
Nepal	6.225 (2.11)	1.660 (7.19)	26.66
Bangladesh	35.060 (11.90)	5.050 (21.89)	14.40
Total	294.465 (100*)	11.275 (100*)	7.36

Source: (1) Bangladesh Bureau of Statistics; Report on National Child Labour Survey *2002/2003*, ILO, Baseline Survey on Child Labour in Bangladesh, 2006
(2) Registrar General, Government of India: Census of India, 2001
(3) Report from Migration and Employment, Nepal, 1997
(4) Federal Bureau of Statistics, Pakistan, 1996
(5) Department of Census and Statistics, Sri Lanka, 1999
(6) ILO, International Programme on the Elimination of Child Labour

Note: *Parentheses show percentage share of respective country in South Asia

(d) Comparatively smaller number of educational institutions than required

(e) Discriminatory social attitude between girls and boys to have education

(2) Major factors responsible for child labour in Bangladesh

(a) Vicious cycle of parental poverty
(b) Rapid growth rate of population
(c) Lack of enforcement of minimum wages
(d) Low quality of education
(e) Lack of enforcement of legal provisions
(f) Gender discrimination

(3) Major factors responsible for child labour in Sri Lanka

(a) One-fifth of total population below poverty line
(b) Lack of sufficient number of schools to meet the demand
(c) Girls are forced to stay home
(d) Lack of support and guidance from parents

(4) Major factors responsible for child labour in Nepal

(a) Lack of enforcement of legal provision
(b) Parental poverty and subsistence livelihood
(c) Illiteracy of parents
(d) Low perceived value of education
(e) Civil war, with parents sending their children to work in urban areas for fear of them being caught in crossfire or being the victim of Maoists

(5) Major factors responsible for child labour in India

(a) Parental poverty and illiteracy
(b) Lack of enforcement of legal activities
(c) Discrimination between the male and female child
(d) Dependency of parents on agriculture for livelihood
(e) High growth of population
(f) Fewer number of schools and infrastructure

From above one can easily entail that there are a number of factors responsible for generating child labour in the South Asia. First, there is parental poverty almost in all the countries of South Asia. Second, illiteracy is common to all South Asian countries. Third, existing social and economic circumstances encourage having more number of children.

Fourth, lack of access to basic and meaningful qualitative educational facilities deprive children of even primary education.

Constitutional protection

In the era of globalization and economic liberalization, the state has reduced its responsibility from many areas, and consequently some of these areas of responsibility have moved away to the corporate sector. One such area is school education, and as a result child labour has become a source of profit at the cost of socio-economic welfare. In this case, constitutional protection of child labour is required to save the social as well as economic welfare of the global economy. There are three types, namely ILO, SAARC and Government (constitutional), of protection from child labour in South Asia.

ILO constitutional protection

The UN's millennium goal is 'securing rights for children' and providing 'Decent Work for All' by 2015. In this connection, ILO takes child labour not as an isolated issue but as an integral part of national efforts for economic and social development. The following major steps are taken by the ILO to achieve this goal.

(1) ILO convention number 05 (1919): In the first International Labour Conference, the minimum age of a child to work in industry was decided.
(2) ILO convention number 29 (1930): Adopted first Forced Labour Convention.
(3) ILO Abolition of Forced Labour Convention number 105 (1957)
(4) ILO convention number 138 (1973): Minimum age of child labour was decided.
(5) UN Convention on the Rights of the Child (UNCRC) – 1989.
(6) International Programme on the Elimination of Child Labour (IPEC, 1992): awareness programmes were organized in all South Asian countries regarding prevention of child labour and resettlement of rehabilitated children.
(7) Stockholm declaration (1996): Child labour was declared as a crime.
(8) ILO declaration on Fundamental Principles and Right at Work (1998): Four major steps were taken in this declaration – freedom of association, abolition of forced labour, end of discrimination in the workplace and elimination of child labour.

(9) ILO Worst Forms of Child Labour Convention number 182 (1999): focused on eradication of child labour working in hazardous industries which are damaging them physically, mentally or morally.
(10) Prevention of trafficking of Child Labour – 2000.
(11) World Day against Child Labour (2002): 12 June has been declared as world Day against Child Labour.
(12) Global Economic Study on the costs and benefits of eliminating Child Labour (2004): Through combating child labour, the benefit can be raised seven times more than cost and hence global benefit will be US$5.1 trillion.

Despite these efforts made by ILO, all South Asian countries have not taken it seriously to combat child labour as shown in Table 9.3. Sri Lanka has ratified all five conventions, while India has only three conventions to combat child labour.

SAARC constitutional protection

Among South Asia countries, Sri Lanka is the only one which has ratified all ILO Conventions related to combating child labour. The Colombo Resolution (1992, SAARC), Rawalpindi Resolution (1996, SAARC) and Male Resolution (1997, SAARC) made pathways to reach the milestone of the Kathmandu Resolution (2002, SAARC). During the eleventh SAARC summit (January, 2002) in Kathmandu, all SAARC

Table 9.3 ILO conventions on child labour and their ratification status in South Asia

Country	ILO convention no. 138	ILO convention no. 182	ILO convention no. 29	ILO convention no. 105	UNCRC
Sri Lanka	√	√	√	√	√
Pakistan	√	√	√	√	√
India			√	√	√
Nepal	√	√	√		√
Bangladesh		√	√	√	√

Source: ILO, International Programme on Elimination of Child Labour

Note: UNCRC-United Nations Convention on the Rights of the Child

members (Bangladesh, India, Nepal, Pakistan, Sri Lanka, Bhutan and Maldives) undertook the following steps to eradicate child labour.

(1) The SAARC convention on preventing and combating trafficking in women and children for prostitution.
(2) The SAARC convention on regional arrangements for the promotion of child welfare in South Asian countries.

On the basis of these two conventions, the SAARC members developed Regional Plans of action to eradicate child labour.

Government constitutional protection

The respective governments with combined efforts of ILO, UNICEF and NGOs took various steps to combat child labour.

Pakistan:

(1) Article 11(1) of the constitution of Pakistan forbids slavery and states that no law permits or facilitates its introduction into Pakistan in any form. Article 11(2) prohibits all forms of forced labour and traffic in human beings. Article 11(3) prohibits employment of children below 14 years of age.
(2) The Employment of Children Act (1991) prohibits employment of children in any organized sector, particularly in hazardous industry.
(3) The Bonded Labour System Abolition Act (1992) abolishes bonded labour with immediate effect.
(4) The Prevention and Control of Human Trafficking Ordinance (2002) defines human trafficking as buying or selling a person for exploitative entertainment. In this case parents and any person involved in trafficking are liable to get punishment of seven years.
(5) The National Policy and Plan of Action (2002) prevents child labour by offering alternate education and ensuring primary education and skills training to the target children.
(6) The Government of Pakistan has established a fund for the education of working children and rehabilitation of freed bonded labour.
(7) The Government Reduction Strategy Paper (2003) of Pakistan gives due consideration to the issue of child labour through poverty eradication.

(8) The Ministry of Education launched the National Plan of Action for education for all (2003) for achieving universal primary education by 2015.
(9) The National Commission for Child Welfare and Development has initiated a national pilot project for rehabilitation of children involved in labour.

Bangladesh:

(1) Both the Employment of Children Act (1938) and Factories Act (1965) prohibit employment of children under 12 and 18 years of age, respectively.
(2) In 1990, Bangladesh passed the Primary Education Act.
(3) In 1993, it made compulsory primary education for children aged 6 or above.
(4) The preparatory phase of the Time-Bound Programme was launched in March 2004.

Sri Lanka:

(1) Under the Constitution of Sri Lanka, 1978, Article 27 (13) the Government promotes special care in the interest of children to ensure employment.
(2) The Draft Constitution (2000), Article 22 protects children from abuse to have free education.
(3) Section 360 of the Penal Code stops (a) prostitution and sexual abuses of children, (b) forced labour, (c) removal of organs of children and (d) child trafficking
(4) School attendance became compulsory, w.e.f., 1997 Regulation of Education.
(5) President Task Force (1996) controls child labour.
(6) National Child Protection Authority (1999) rehabilitates protected children.

Nepal:

(1) The Constitution of Nepal confers the fundamental right to education on children.
(2) The Children's Act (1992) protects the rights and interests of Nepalese children and ensures their physical, mental and intellectual development.

(3) The Labour Act (1992) and Labour Rules (1993) prohibit employment of children in any hazardous industries.
(4) The Child Labour Prohibition and Regulation Act (1999) makes provision for punishment to employers of children.
(5) Citizen's Right Act (1955) stops child trafficking.

India:

A number of constitutional protections have been given to child labour in India. These are enumerated below:

(1) *Indian Factory Act (IFA, 1881):* It fixed the minimum age of employment at seven and maximum number of working hours at nine per day with four months holidays in a year. IFA-1891 and 1954 disallowed the employment of children during night time.
(2) *Whitely Commission (1929):* Rege Committee (1944) and Gurupadswamy Committee (1979) recommended regulating child labour. Based on these committees, the Child Labour Prohibition and Regulation Act was passed by the Government of India in 1986.
(3) *Indian Constitution (1950):* Article-14, 15, 15(3), 19(1), 21, 21(A), 23, 24, 45, 36-e, 39-f and Directive Principles are certain constitutional protections which are adopted in India to prevent child labour. Through implementation of these constitutional provisions, India reiterates its commitment to the protection, safety and well-being of children. Both article-24 and the Directive Principles prohibit child labour in factories, mines and other hazardous occupations. Article-24 clearly states 'no child below the age of fourteen years shall be employed to work in any factory or mines or in any hazardous employment'. Article-45 makes provision of free and compulsory education for children up to the age group of 14. Article-39-e lays down that no child be forced by economic necessity to enter unsuited occupations. Article-39-f makes a provision to provide healthy opportunities to children to maintain their dignities.
(4) *Bonded Labour Abolition Act (1976):* It purports to abolish all debt agreements and obligations arising out of India's longstanding bonded labour. It orders the economic rehabilitation of freed bonded labourers by the state.
(5) *Child Labour Prohibition and Regulation Act (1986):* It bans employment of children working in hazardous occupations. It defines child as a person who has not completed 14 years of age. It lays down

penalties for the violation of this provision. This Act accepts that child labour cannot be abolished as long as poverty exists.

(6) *The National Child Labour Policy (1987):* All the children released from employment in hazardous industries are provided educational services, non-formal, under the centrally sponsored National Child Labour Project (NCLP). It is operational in 100 districts in 13 states, in the areas of high concentration of child labour throughout the country.

(7) *Ratification of UNCRC – 1989 (1992):* India ratified the United Nations Convention on the Right of the Child (UNCRC) in 1992 according to which India is bound to have international standards for children's rights. It provides the following principles for examining the implementation of the convention: (a) the principle of non-discrimination (Article-2), (b) best interests of the child (Article-3), (c) the right to life, survival and development (Article-6) and (d) respect for the views of the child (Article-12).

(8) *Unnikrishnan vs State of Andhra Pradesh (1993):* The Supreme Court of India lays down a provision according to which the right to education for children is to be considered a fundamental right. It brought state initiatives to educate child labour.

(9) *M.C. Mehta vs State of Tamilnadu (1996):* When gross violation of Article-24 takes place due to employment of child labour, Article-32 is imposed to stop child labour. The Supreme Court of India gave direction for immediate identification of children in hazardous occupations and their subsequent rehabilitation, including providing appropriate education to the released children.

(10) *Ratification of UN convention:* India has ratified only three conventions, namely the ILO Convention No.29, 105 and UNCRC.

Model showing effect of constitutional protection on quantum of child labour

The effective implementation of the Constitutional Protection (CP) and declining magnitude of child labour (M) will raise the welfare (W) of the households of South Asia (SA). In this case, one can rightly observe that:

$$W\ (SA) = U\ (CP) - U\ (M)$$

According to the Marshallian theory, at equilibrium, $W' = 0$ and hence $U'\ (CP) = U'\ (M)$. It shows a critical state of the income distribution, where total welfare will be maximum. However, $U''\ (CP) > 0$ and U''

(M) < 0 infers that the second condition of welfare maximization does not exist. It entails that once a critical state of income (Y_C) is achieved, the welfare of the South Asian households is bound to increase with declining magnitude and rising constitutional protection.

Figure 9.1 entails following two facts:

(1) When constitutional protection is effectively implemented, the welfare of the household rises because welfare is positively associated with it. It raises human capital through encouraging children to attend school. In this case, U' (CP) moves rightward to U' (2CP) in a range where income effect outweighs substitution effect, and hence critical income rises to Y_{2C}. It shows that welfare can be raised through raising the income of the family.

Model: Policy implication

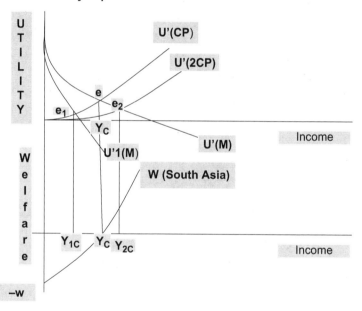

21

Figure 9.1 Model to increase welfare through combating child labour

Source: Mehrotra S. and Biggeri M. (2002), *The Subterranean Child Labour Force: Subcontracted home based manufacturing in Asia*, UNICEF.

(2) A rise in the magnitude of the child labour decreases the welfare of the household. In this case, U' (M) shifts downward to U' (1M) at e_1 in a range where substitution effect outweighs income effect, and hence it encourages parents to send their children to work because critical income declines. It further raises child labour.

Criticism of constitutional protections

Despite efforts made through constitutional enforcement, there exists child labour exploitation in South Asia due to the following flaws:

(1) Almost all laws, in practice, are enforced only in the organized sector where only 8 per cent of total child labourers are employed. It ignores the unorganized sector where 92 per cent of total child labourers are employed.

(2) So long as the child is not forced to work in an exploitative environment, the state does not take legal action.

(3) The Act provides a list of hazardous occupations. It does not define what constitutes hazardous work (except the 1936 Indian Factory Act.).

(4) It does not clarify what should happen to child labour once the employer is prosecuted. However, after the initiative of the Supreme Court of India a provision for the rehabilitation of child labour has been made but separate budgetary provision has not been made yet.

(5) Under the law, the employer is supposed to notify the Labour Department of any children working in the establishment. This is akin to asking the murderer to report the crime.

(6) The implementation of the Act depends on the state's ill-equipped bureaucratic machinery.

(7) The education of the child is important more for society rather than parents. Therefore, law empowers the state to take punitive action against parents who do not send their children to school. In practice, the law should empower parents to do so.

(8) Illiteracy is common in South Asian countries. It is a hurdle in getting the benefits of constitutional protections.

(9) Fees and fines charged to employers for violating law is a small part of profit generated by employing child labour. It encourages employers to employ child labour.

(10) Constitutional protections are unable to encourage political wills to combat child labour.

Conclusion and policy implication

The child labour law of South Asia passes on the responsibility of combating child labour from society or nation to parents. However, due to poverty, parental income in South Asia is not sufficient to meet children's needs. Therefore, rather than pass on the responsibility from the nation to parents, it should be collectively carried out by all three because children are the assets of the parents, society and nation as a whole.

References

Coursen, N. and Zama, N. 2003. 'Small Change: Bonded Child Labour in India's Silk Industry', *Human Right Watch Publications*, 15(2).

Dalep, E. 2010. 'Economic and Cultural Forces in the Child Labour Debate: Evidence from Urban Bangladesh', *Journal of Development Studies*, 37(4): 1–22.

Heather, C.F. 2011. 'Child Labour: A Review of Recent Theory and Evidence with Policy Implications', *Journal of Economic Survey*, 25(2): 234.

Joelle, S.L. 2010. 'A Cross National Study of Child Labour and Its Determinants', *The Journal of Developing Areas*, 44(1): 325–44.

Maitra, P. and Ray, R. 2010. 'The Joint Estimation of Child Participation in Schooling and Employment', *OXFORD*, 30: 41–62.

Mehrotra, S. and Biggeri, M. 2002. 'The Subterranean Child Labour Force: Subcontracted Home Based Manufacturing in Asia', *UNICEF*, P-73.

Mirium, B. 2003. 'Quantitative Study on Child Labour in Guatemala: Final Report', *ILO*, P-96.

Oliveira, A.M. 2003. 'National Survey on Child and Adolescent Labour in Nicaragua', *ILO*, P-148.

Sharma, S. 2001. 'Nepal Situation of Domestic Child Labour in Kathmandu: A Rapid Assessment', *ILO*, P-153.

Weiner, Myron. 1991. *The Child and the State in India: Child Labor and Education Policy in Comparative Perspective*. Princeton: Princeton University Press, 1991.

Chapter 10

Diversification in rural livelihood in Uttarakhand

Rajendra P. Mamgain

There is a rich body of literature which shows how rural households undertake multiple activities to support their livelihoods. The motives behind such diversification may vary sharply; at one extreme, households diversify their activities for maximizing income, whereas at the other extreme, they do so just to maintain their subsistence living as a coping mechanism (Agarwal 1991; Ellis 1998; Walker and Ryan 1990). Diversification in livelihood essentially has two main aspects: one is the number of different income-earning activities, which a household (or an individual) undertakes (Jodha *et al.* 1977); the other is the relative proportion of income gained from each activity (Ellis 2000). Most of the studies on rural diversification deal with the changes in the structure of employment and income, and the causes for the shift in employment towards non-farm occupations are analysed around growth-induced versus distress-led theoretical strands of diversification (see, Bhalla 1990; Chadha 1994; Harris 1991; Viadyanathan 1986). At the household level the process of diversification, however, is complex. A household may be involved in a number of occupations, yet in terms of their contribution to household income, just one or two may be the major contributors. Thus, to what extent will it be appropriate to term such households a case of diversified livelihoods? In order to fill this gap in the literature, this chapter examines the livelihood diversification among rural households in Uttarakhand, both in the context of number of occupations and their relative contribution to household income. It measures the intensity of diversification in livelihoods, analyses the underlying factors for determining such diversification and examines the impact of diversification in livelihoods on income levels of households in the rural areas of Uttarakhand. It also examines whether diversification in livelihoods is a risk mitigating strategy arising out of vulnerability in the nature of assets which a household poses or a profit maximization process wherein a household switches to more secure and high-income earning livelihoods.

Brief overview of Uttarakhand economy

Before examining the above issues, it will be appropriate to briefly highlight the major features of the economy of Uttarakhand. The state was created on 19 November 1999 after a long struggle by the people of Uttarakhand on the plank of economic backwardness. The state comprises 13 districts out of which 10 districts have hilly and mountainous topography. According to the 2011 Population Census, the total population of Uttarakhand is 10.11 million. Nearly 47.9 per cent of the population of the state is residing in the hilly districts. These districts are predominantly rural as over 82.9 per cent of population therein resides in rural areas. With a literacy rate of over 79.6 per cent, the state is much ahead of many other Indian states (Table 10.1).

The higher participation of the population in economic activities, generally referred to as work participation rate (WPR) is yet another

Table 10.1 Selected features of Uttarakhand economy

SI No.	Variable	Value
1	Total population (in million) 2011	10.11
2	Decadal population growth (2001–11)	19.17
3	% share of hill districts in population (2011)	47.9
4	% share of rural population in hill districts (2011)	82.9
5	Literacy rate (2011)	79.63
6	Rural WPR (2009–10)	43.0
7	Male	46.1
8	Female	39.9
9	% of workers employed in agriculture	66.05
10	% share of agriculture in GSDP	24.96
11	% of rural population under poverty (2004–5)	32.7
12	% of out-migrants	14.9

Source: For population and literacy, Population Census, 2011; for workers, NSSO, 2011; for poverty and migration, Mamgain (2004)

feature of the state. Nearly 43 per cent of population constitutes the workforce in the rural areas of Uttarakhand. This high participation in the workforce is largely attributed to comparatively higher participation of females in the workforce in the state as compared to other states (Table 10.1). The WPR for males in rural areas is comparatively low in Uttarakhand than the national average. The low WPR in the case of males is largely associated with the lack of employment opportunities in the rural areas of the state, and to some extent, their higher participation in education. The high WPR for females is largely due to their heavy engagements in agriculture and animal husbandry related work. In fact, women are the backbone of hill agriculture.

Uttarakhand is diverse in its topography. About 93 per cent of the geographical area of the state is hilly and mountainous. Over 64 per cent of the geographical area of the state is under forests, and about 14 per cent of the area is under cultivation. Thus, the availability of per person agricultural land is quite low in the state, 0.09 hectare as compared to 0.17 hectare in India during the year 2000. This has decreased over the years with the growing population from 0.15 hectare and 0.21 hectare in 1981 for Uttaranchal and India, respectively (Mamgain 2004). The land is fragmented and scattered in hill districts of the state, which requires comparatively higher amounts of labour and animal power as compared to plain areas. Only 35 per cent of the cultivated land is irrigated in the hill districts, which leaves a large proportion of farming households dependent on the vagaries of the monsoon. This results in abysmally low levels of farm productivity (Mamgain 2004). It has been estimated that agriculture provides only five to six months of food security to the farming households, thus causing widespread poverty, underemployment and resultant out-migration.

Resorting to multiple employments is a common feature in the hill districts of Uttarakhand. Nearly half of the principal status workers are engaged in more than one economic activity intermittently. The extent of resorting to such multiple employments is highest for cultivators, casual wage labour and petty traders. This shows the scarcity of stable employment opportunities in the region.

Owing to lack of remunerative employment opportunities and poor resource base such as land, there is a widespread poverty in the rural areas of Uttarakhand. Nearly one-third of the rural population was living in poverty in the state. Mamgain (2004) estimates that about 40 per cent of the rural population in the hill regions of Uttarakhand live in poverty.

Due to widespread poverty, vulnerable livelihoods and lack of basic amenities, the pace of out-migration has accelerated over the years from the hill districts of Uttarakhand. This has been largely in search of remunerative employment opportunities and education, to some extent (Bora 1996; Mamgain 2004). The comparatively lower decadal growth of population in the rural areas of hill districts during the period 2001–11 strongly indicates the increased pace of such out-migration even after the formation of the new state of Uttarakhand. In fact, two hilly districts, namely Almora and Pauri Garhwal have recorded a sizeable absolute decline in their population over the decade 2001–11, suggesting huge out-migration of households in search of better livelihoods. The emergence of the new state and its widely appreciated higher economic growth could not ameliorate the livelihood issues of those residing in the rural areas of hill districts.

With this brief overview, the next section of this chapter analyses the diversity in livelihood options and their relative contribution to household income. The determinants of livelihood diversification are discussed in the last section. The analysis is based on a field study of 399 rural households in the hill districts of Uttarakhand undertaken during 2001–2 (see more details for methodology, Mamgain 2004).

Diversity in livelihood options

In International Crops Research Institute for the Semi-Arid Tropics (ICRISAT) villages, Jodha et al. (1977) argued that small farm households were more likely to have more than one source of income than larger ones, as they were more vulnerable to the exigencies of drought and unreliable yields. However, over the years diversification has become a common strategy among rural households irrespective of the size of their operational land holdings to reduce their vulnerability to risks within the agricultural sector. This has been observed by Dev et al. (2002) for the same set of villages during 1990s and later years.

Given the scarcity of income earning assets as a source for secured livelihood, resorting to multiple occupations (livelihood sources) is a common feature of the rural households in the mountain region of Uttarakhand. As is seen in Table 10.2, almost all the sample households have at least two or more livelihood sources. The large majority of households (nearly about 70 per cent) are engaged in three to four occupations. About 13 per cent of the households are even engaged in more than four occupations (sources of livelihoods). A distinguishing feature that clearly emerges in Table 10.1 relates to the increasing percentage of households taking up four or more occupations with the increase in land size. The number of livelihood sources is comparatively

Table 10.2 Range of livelihood options for different household groups (per cent)

Household group	Number of occupations (livelihood sources)						Number of house-holds
	1	2	3	4	More than 4	Total	
Land class (in acres)							
Landless	18.42	26.32	28.95	18.42	7.89	100.00	38
Up to 0.5	0.68	17.69	44.22	27.89	9.52	100.00	147
0.5 to 1.5	0.00	18.75	41.41	26.56	13.28	100.00	128
1.5 to 2.5	3.92	11.76	33.33	33.33	17.65	100.00	51
2.5 to 5.0	3.13	0.00	37.50	34.38	25.00	100.00	32
>5.0	0.00	33.33	0.00	66.67	0.00	100.00	3
Per capita income class (Rs.)							
Less than 2,500	7.69	35.90	41.03	12.82	2.56	100.00	39
2,500–5,000	3.79	18.94	39.39	31.06	6.82	100.00	132
5,000–7,500	0.00	8.54	40.24	32.93	18.29	100.00	82
7,500–12,500	2.60	7.79	38.96	31.17	19.48	100.00	77
12,500–22,500	2.27	11.36	38.64	25.00	22.73	100.00	44
22,500 and above	0.00	40.00	40.00	16.00	4.00	100.00	25
Total	2.76	16.79	39.60	28.07	12.78	100.00	399

Source: Mamgain (2004)

lower among the landless, poor and very rich households; nearly 45 per cent among them have up to two livelihood sources. Nearly one-fifth of the landless households have a single source of livelihood. On the other hand, the number of livelihood sources is highest among households belonging to the middle-income group with nearly half among them having four and more occupations.

It would be interesting to analyse the livelihood sources in terms of their contribution to household income. We treat major occupation (income source) as that which contributes more than half of the total household income. Viewed in this context, it is most likely that in a subsistence hill economy a fairly large number of households have to fetch their income from multiple sources without any source being a prominent one. It is seen that for a highest 40 per cent sample households there is not a single main source of income, while casual wage labour (non-agriculture) is the main source of income for about 13 per cent sample households. Non-agricultural self-employment and animal husbandry are the major sources of income for another 11 per cent and about 7 per cent households, respectively. Cultivation, on the other hand, is the main source of income for less than one-tenth sample households, even though it is being pursued by an overwhelming majority of the rural households (Table 10.3). This also accounts for the underlying pressure to diversify livelihoods among most of the sample households. However, due to scarce employment opportunities outside agriculture, a large majority of workers are engaged in agriculture in the sample households.

Table 10.3 Percentage distribution of households by their main source* of income and average number of sources of income

Main source of household income	Households (%)	Average number of livelihood sources per household
Cultivation	7.27	2.28
Animal husbandry	7.02	3.18
Agricultural labour	3.51	3.36
Non-agricultural labour	12.53	2.86
Non-agricultural self-employment	10.78	2.81
Caste-based occupations	1.50	3.33
Regular salaried jobs	9.27	3.22
Remittances	6.27	3.00
Pension	2.01	3.55
No major source	39.85	3.75
All households	100	3.33
Number of households	399	–

Source: Mamgain (2004)

Note: Any source of income contributing more than half the household income is treated as the main source of income

A look at the average number of occupations (livelihood sources) per household (Table 10.3) across main sources of household income provides some interesting insights. The average number of livelihood sources is highest at 3.8 among the households, who have no main source of income. The next average number of occupations is highest among households for whom pension is the main source of income. As against this, the average number of livelihood sources is lowest among households whose main source of income is cultivation. This also means that there is a significant number of households who have diversified their livelihood sources from agriculture to non-agricultural occupations.

Before analysing the diversification in sources of livelihoods, it will be appropriate to analyse the income from different livelihood sources.

Income from livelihood options

According to Singh and Asokan (1981), income is defined as net returns to family-owned resources, encompassing land, livestock, labour and capital. It also includes income through wages, salaries and transfer income through rent, remittances and pensions. Both monetary and imputed values of all traded and non-traded goods such as crop by-products figure in the computation of household income.

Before analysing the data, a few remarks are made about the household income of selected households. It was observed that income was invariably under-reported by some of the households, particularly those who were better off and those who were very poor. Second, the poor reporting was due to memory lapses or because of rough guesswork by the households as households hardly keep any written records. Despite these limitations, some interesting features emerge from the income data, which are analysed in the following section.

Composition of household income

In our sample, the farm sector contributes about one-third of the total household income, which comprises 14.6 per cent through cultivation, 14.4 per cent through livestock and 3.8 per cent through agricultural wage labour. The non-farm sector is thus the major contributor to the household income, its share being as much as 58 per cent. The share of self-employed in trade and business in the household income is highest at about 33 per cent, followed by salary income (16.6 per cent). About 8.4 per cent of household income is contributed through non-agricultural wage labour (Table 10.4). The low share of agriculture in total

Table 10.4 Composition of household income by households' per capita income class

Sector	Per capita annual income class (Rs.) (At 1999–2000 Prices)						
	Less than 2,500	2,500– 5,000	5,000– 7,500	7,500– 12,500	12,500– 22,500	22,500 and above	Total
Agricultural and allied activities							
Cultivation	23.58	18.48	20.70	17.92	16.66	3.98	14.63
Animal husbandry	26.13	23.47	24.27	16.87	11.16	2.31	14.45
Agricultural labour	4.71	8.70	9.12	2.77	1.26	0.00	3.83
Sub-total	54.42	50.64	54.10	37.56	29.08	6.29	32.91
Non-agricultural sector							
Self-employed	8.10	8.88	11.64	16.58	34.08	74.01	33.16
Salaried jobs	2.78	4.42	7.81	25.33	26.43	18.04	16.55
Non-agricultural labour	18.54	26.72	11.84	5.07	3.92	0.08	8.42
Sub-total	29.43	40.03	31.28	46.97	64.43	92.14	58.13
Transfer income							
Remittance	16.15	7.24	10.02	9.23	4.55	1.38	6.27
Pension	0.00	2.09	4.60	6.25	1.94	0.20	2.69
Sub-total	16.15	9.34	14.62	15.47	6.49	1.58	8.96
Total	100.00	100.00	100.00	100.00	100.00	100.00	100.00
%sample households	13.03	32.33	25.06	15.54	8.52	5.51	100.00

Source: Mamgain (2004)

household income despite being the major employing sector is also reconfirmed by the data pertaining to district domestic product for the hill districts of Uttarakhand.

This broad structure of household income, however, does not hold true when we analyse the composition of household income across households grouped by their income class. For households belonging to the lowest three-income strata, the contribution of agriculture and allied activities is more than half. Animal husbandry is an important source of livelihood for such households as it alone contributes about one-fourth of the household income. Casual wage labour (both agricultural and non-agricultural) is another important source of income as it contributes between 21 and 35 per cent of the income in the lowest three income strata households. Thus, agriculture, animal husbandry and casual wage labour together contribute more than 70 per cent of household income in those households belonging to the lowest three income strata (Table 10.4). This itself explains their low levels of income.

The share of non-farm income in total household income tends to increase with the rise in the income strata of households. This emerges clearly in Table 10.4. In the middle-income group (Rs. 7,500–12,500) households, about one-fourth of the household income is contributed by salaried employees and another 14 per cent by the non-agricultural self-employed in petty trade. In the higher income group households, the self-employed in petty trade and business are dominant contributors to household income. As expected, the contribution of remittances to household income is substantive (more than one-tenth) in low-income group households.

It merits mention here that in some households diversification in livelihood sources comes though improvement in education and/or asset-holding capabilities of their members, that is a risk averting and capital accumulation strategy. Essentially, the end objective of diversification in livelihood sources is to attain a comparative increase in their income level. For households who resort to such diversification, non-farm income becomes a major contributor to the household income.

Extent of livelihood diversification

As mentioned in the beginning of this chapter, another way to measure diversification in the sources of livelihood is to look into the relative contribution of each livelihood option to household income. For this, we have used the Herfindahl Index and Entropy Index. The Herfindahl Index (H) is defined as the sum of squares of all 'n' proportions. It is the measure of concentration. For increasing diversification, 'H' decreases. It is bounded by '0' (indicating complete diversification) and '1' (indicating complete specialization). To put it algebraically:

$$H = \sum p_i^2, \ p_i = A_i / \sum A_i$$

Where p_i = proportion of ith source of income, A = income from i^{th} source.

Entropy Index, popularized by Theil (1967) is a measure of diversification. Algebraically

$$E = \Sigma pi \log (1/pi).$$

It is decomposable and has all the desirable properties of good measure (Kackbark and Anderson 1975). There is a positive relationship between the Entropy Index (E) and the extent of diversification. It takes the value zero when there is complete specialization and log N (maximum possible) when there is perfect diversification. Thus, it is bounded by zero and log N.

Table 10.5 shows the extent of diversification of livelihood sources and per capita income across various groups of sample households. The diversification is presented under three different scenarios based on the location of sample households/villages, that is peri-urban (scenario I), semi-interior (scenario II) and interior (scenario III) (Appendix Table 10.1A). Peri-urban villages are those which are located nearer to rural markets, have better infrastructure facilities like road, electricity and a relatively higher percentage of area under commercial production. Semi-interior and interior villages are characterized by a predominance of traditional cereal-based agriculture, limited access to infrastructure and a high incidence of out-migration.

Overall, livelihood sources among the rural households in Uttarakhand are highly diversified, the Entropy Index value being 0.39,

Table 10.5 Diversification in livelihoods

Location of household	Entropy Index	Herfindahl Index	Per household mean value of productive assets other than land (Rs. '000) (At 1999–2000 prices)	Mean occupations (No.)	Per capita mean income (Rs.) (At 1999–2000 prices)
Peri-urban	0.29	0.61	37.84	2.81	12,853
Semi-interior	0.44	0.44	14.17	3.68	8,504
Interior	0.42	0.45	13.98	3.41	5,909
All	0.39	0.49	21.16	3.33	8,890

Source: Mamgain (2004)

whereas the average number of sources of livelihoods per household stands at more than three. The highest possible value of the Entropy Index is 0.52, that is log of N number of occupations (Table 10.5).

The extent of livelihood diversification is observed to be comparatively low in peri-urban villages as compared to those in interior villages (Table 10.5). The average number of occupations is less than three in peri-urban villages, whereas it is more than three in interior villages. On the other hand, per capita income is more than double in peri-urban villages. It can be inferred that commercial farming and non-farm self-employment in peri-urban villages have significantly improved the per capita income levels across all land holdings so that the need to resort to multiple occupations is reduced. Thus, most of the diversification in livelihoods in peri-urban villages can be termed as distress diversification. This observation is further examined later in Table 10.6.

Income sources (livelihoods) are least diversified among landless, very poor and very rich households. This is true for all the three scenarios (Appendix Tables 10.1A and 10.2A). The explanation for this restricted diversification in each case is as follows: rich households do not resort to multiple occupations, as they have one or two stable sources of income with higher marginal productivity. On the other hand, though poor/landless households may resort to multiple occupations, they derive their maximum income from just one or two occupations. At the same time, many among the poor households are unable to undertake multiple occupations due to their poor resource endowments, particularly land. This finding negates a very common observation by studies on rural diversification (Ellis 2000; Sharma *et al.* 2001), namely that poor and landless households have comparatively more diversified sources of livelihood as compared to others, and this is reflected in the incidence of multiple occupations. The marginal and small land holding households have more diversified sources of livelihoods as the value of the Entropy Index ranges between 40 and 49. It can be seen in Appendix Table 10.1A that the value of the Entropy Index tends to increase as the land class of a household improves. This is true under all three types of scenarios. This also means that households tend to diversify their livelihood sources towards attaining more remunerative sources of livelihoods so as to avoid insecurity of income associated with the prevailing traditional low yielding practices of farming, irrespective of the land size that they own.

A look at Appendix Table 10.2A again shows the higher extent of diversification in livelihoods particularly among the lower- as well as middle-income group households (lower income group range: Rs. 2,500–7,500; middle-income group range: Rs. 7,500–22,500). There are about 21 per cent sample households whose sources of livelihoods are highly diversified, and they belong to the lowest three income groups. Though such diversification definitely adds to their overall income, yet its contribution towards meeting their basic minimum needs is very low as most of the occupations are not remunerative. In the case of the middle-income group households, who account for 30 per cent of the sample households, not only are livelihood sources more diversified but they are also more remunerative, due to the higher educational level of their members as also their relatively large possession of assets including land. In the case of rich households (income group Rs. 22,500 and above), the value of the Entropy Index is lowest at 0.20, and their mean occupation being 2.8 (Appendix Table 10.2A). Such households have already entered into the stabilization phase of livelihood diversification as postulated by Grown and Sebstad (1989), where they can invest in riskier enterprises.

In brief, a close examination of data given in Table 10.5 and Appendix Tables 10.1A and 10.2A bring forth the following four distinct types of scenarios emerging in the context of diversification in livelihoods among rural households in the hill areas of Uttarakhand:

(1) higher incidence of assetlessness, lesser number of occupations, low diversification in livelihoods and thus, lower per capita income;
(2) low value of assets, larger number of occupations, highly diversified livelihoods leading to moderate per capita income;
(3) moderate value of assets, more number of occupations, moderately diversified livelihoods and high level of per capita income; and
(4) high value of assets, least number of occupations, least diversified livelihoods yet highest per capita income.

To sum up, livelihoods among the rural households in the mountain region of Uttarakhand are highly diversified. However, this kind of diversification has been mainly in low yielding activities thus serving merely as a coping mechanism for nearly 60 per cent households. There is another one-fourth of households which have improved their income level significantly through diversifying into comparatively high-income yielding activities, which has been possible due to their relatively better resource endowments. This clearly implies that the livelihoods of high-income group households are least diversified.

Per capita income

The outcome of a strategy for diversifying livelihood sources is reflected in the per capita income levels of a household. It has been observed that despite the fact that an overwhelming majority of rural households in the mountain region of Uttarakhand are engaged in multiple activities, the per capita annual income of a majority of them is low. It is the lowest at Rs. 2,436 (at 1999–2000 prices) for the bottom 20 per cent households, which, therefore, may be called 'very poor'. Another one-third of the sample households are moderately poor as their per capita annual income is Rs. 3,842 or less than Rs. 320 per month (Appendix Table 10.2A). Thus, based on the income criterion, more than 45 per cent of the sample households in the mountain region of Uttarakhand are poor.

Income inequality

There exists an acute income disparity among rural households in the state as is seen in Table 10.7. The per capita income in the lowest three quintile groups of households (representing 60 per cent households) is much less than the average household income. This can also be seen in the relative income difference index in Table 10.7. It is abundantly clear that income inequality among the households tends to increase with the increase in per capita income. This is also reflected in the values of standard deviation. The per capita income in peri-urban areas is more than double than interior areas. The interior areas, in turn, have relatively least income inequality as reflected in the Gini coefficient, as compared to peri-urban areas (Table 10.6). Overall, the Gini coefficient for income distribution is high at 0.45 for the sample households. The values of

Table 10.6 Gini coefficients of income inequality

Location of household	Per capita annual income (Rs.) (At 1999–2000 prices)			Standard deviation	Relative income difference index
	Mean	Minimum	Maximum		
Peri-urban	12,853	480	59,730	13,564.61	0.50
Semi-interior	8,504	710	45,498	7,053.71	0.39
Interior	5,909	1,245	35,577	4,545.37	0.35
All	8,890	480	5,9730	13,564.61	0.45

Source: Mamgain (2004)

Table 10.7 Income inequality among sample households

Households' quintile*	Per capita income (Rs.) (At 1999–2000 prices)			Standard deviation	Relative income difference index
	Mean	Minimum	Maximum		
I (lowest)	2,436	480	3,760	776.53	27.40
2	4,257	2,981	5,855	687.97	47.89
3	6,299	4,180	10,457	1,587.68	70.85
4	9,573	5,242	19,274	3,093.64	107.68
5 (highest)	21,805	7,835	59,730	13,626.02	245.28
All	8,890	480	59,730	13,564.61	100.00

Source: Mamgain (2004)

Note: *Each representing 20% sample households

Gini coefficients for income distribution show that development perpetuates income inequalities at a larger degree unless accompanied by the measures of promoting income opportunities at a higher rate for those at bottom quintiles.

Determinants of per capita income

It is equally important to understand the effect of livelihood diversification on levels of per capita income in the mountain areas of Uttarakhand. It is generally argued that households with poor resource endowment (such as land holding, productive assets and education) resort to multiple activities. Though their livelihood sources are more diversified, they bring low incomes for the household, which typifies a distress phenomenon. Accordingly, we have fitted the following multiple linear regression model with the per capita income as dependent variable and livelihood diversification with other variables as independent variables:

$$pci = b_0 + b_1 X_1 + b_2 X_2 + b_3 X_3 + b_4 X_4 + b_5 X_5 + b_6 X_6 + b_7 X_7 + u$$

Where:

pci = Per capita income (Rs. '000)
X_1 = Entropy Index of livelihood diversification
X_2 = Per capita land (in acres)

X_3 = Value of productive assets per household (Rs. '000)
X_4 = Percentage of educated workers in all workers
X_5 = Number of principal status workers per household
X_6 = Percentage share of area under commercial crops in gross cropped area
X_7 = Percentage share of workers in rural non-farm employment
u = Unknown parameter

The model is fitted separately for three broad scenarios based on the distance of households from the district headquarters. These are peri-urban (Scenario I), semi-interior (Scenario II) and interior (Scenario III). As mentioned earlier, households in Scenario I have better access to infrastructure facilities like road, electricity, market, education, etc., whereas their counterparts in Scenario III lack such access. In Scenario I, nearly half the gross cultivated area is under commercial crops as compared to less than one-tenth in Scenario III. Similarly, percentage of non-farm workers is highest in Scenario I. The results of the model are given in Table 10.8.

Table 10.8 Impact of livelihood diversification on per capita income: results of regression analysis. Dependent variable: per capita income (Rs. '000)

Variable	Scenario I		Scenario II		Scenario III		Overall	
	Coefficient	*'t' value*	*Co-efficient*	*'t' value*	*Co-efficient*	*'t' value*	*Coefficient*	*'t' value*
Constant	7.87	1.62	0.73	0.32	2.75	1.67	5.27	3.28
X_1	−25.76***	−3.45	−2.54	−0.57	1.84	0.57	−11.55***	−3.85
X_2	10.75*	1.75	7.58***	2.62	3.56	1.40	7.08***	3.29
X_3	0.04***	4.44	0.08*	1.83	−0.01	−0.94	0.04***	8.39
X_4	−0.02	−0.64	0.07***	4.12	0.04***	2.72	0.02*	1.71
X_5	2.12**	2.37	0.36	0.94	0.23	0.79	0.99***	3.50
X_6	0.08**	2.31	0.10***	4.15	0.01	0.16	0.08***	6.14
X_7	0.05	1.29	0.08***	3.95	0.01	1.04	0.04***	3.26
R Square	0.46		0.34		0.10		0.39	
N	119		140		140		399	

Source: Mamgain (2004)

Note: (1) ***Significant at 1% level; **Significant at 5% level; *Significant at 10% level.
(2) Figures in parentheses are t' values.

First, we will discuss the results of the model for the overall scenario as can be seen in the last column of Table 10.8. It emerges clearly that a higher degree of diversification in livelihoods (as reflected in the higher value of the Entropy Index) does not significantly result in the increase in per capita income of rural households in the mountain region of Uttarakhand. Rather concentration in one or two livelihood options leads to increase in income. It is seen earlier in Table 10.2 that more than 40 per cent sample households are engaged in more than three occupations, and 60 per cent among them belong to the lowest three income strata. Thus, the significant negative sign of the Entropy Index typifies a case of a distress diversification of livelihoods wherein households struggle hard to retain their threshold income through resorting to multiple occupations (Table 10.8). The highly diversified livelihoods also show the critical importance of each source in the household's income as failure of any of these leads to rapid decline in the household income.

The positive sign of variable X_5 (i.e. number of principal workers in a household) with the per capita income suggests that the per capita income of a household tends to improve significantly with the addition of a principal status worker in its labour force. However, this kind of impact is significant only in a situation when households have access to infrastructure facilities like roads and markets (Scenario I), which in turn facilitates their resource allocation in favour of increased market orientation.

The other factors that have a significant positive impact on per capita income include availability of assets, both physical and human and their allocation. As is seen in Table 10.8, both per capita availability of cultivated land and percentage of educated among the workforce of a household significantly improve its per capita income. Bringing a larger area under commercial crops, such as fruits and vegetable production, significantly improves income levels of a household. Also, a shift in workforce (non-migrant workers) from farm to rural non-farm sector improves their income level significantly.

After analysing the determinants of per capita income in an overall scenario, these are analysed under the three different scenarios. In Scenario I, concentration in one or two livelihood options contributes a significant amount of income to household. Those households resorting to multiple livelihoods do so due to distress phenomenon as it does not increase income levels to any significant extent. This is reflected in the significant inverse sign of the Entropy Index. All the variables except 'percentage of educated workers' and 'percentage of non-farm workers' have significant impact on per capita income in this scenario. In fact, in

Scenario I there is an insignificant difference between the income levels of educated workers and other workers with very high farm income. Moreover, the percentage of educated workers is very high and widely spread across the households in this scenario, which underscores its significance. A shift towards rural non-farm activities tends to improve per capita income, but this relationship has not been found significant in Scenario I. This also implies insignificant differences in farm and non-farm income in this scenario.

Contrary to Scenario I, Scenario III is a typical case of backward household economy where no variable except 'education' has any significant impact on improving per capita income (Table 10.8). As mentioned earlier, per capita income in this scenario is lower by about three times than Scenario I. Lack of infrastructure like motor roads and markets and general apathy of government development agencies could hardly provide any incentive to rural households in this scenario to put their resources in commercial uses, which could otherwise have significantly added to their income. In fact, those households which have put some part of their land under commercial crops are unable to get any return due to lack of infrastructure. Thus, the education of the workforce is the single factor which has a significant impact on improving the income of households.

In fact, due to low-income levels in the farm sector and lack of employment opportunities outside the farm sector, incidence of migration is highest in Scenario III as more than 55 per cent households have at least one migrant worker.[1] Thus, education is the only asset which helps households to improve their income levels significantly. The positive yet insignificant relationship of the Entropy Index with per capita income in Scenario III is only indicative of the importance of multiple sources of livelihoods in supporting household income levels precariously in a low-income economy.

Scenario II of semi-interior villages supports a case where infrastructure facilities such as road networks have provided scope for commercialization of agriculture and rural non-farm employment, though on a limited scale, thereby resulting in a significant increase in per capita income. It is true for land and productive assets. The household's ability to allocate a higher proportion of its labour in non-farm activities, particularly in the rural non-farm sector has also resulted in a significant increase in per capita income in Scenario II. Improvement in the educational level of workers also significantly adds to the per capita income of a household. Here again in this scenario, diversification in livelihoods (Entropy Index), though predominated by distress conditions, has no significant impact on determining the household income. Unlike in Scenario I, additions to the number of principal workers in a household both in Scenario II and III do not contribute significantly to per capita income.

Thus, the important policy implications which clearly emerge from our results are providing infrastructure facilities (like motor roads, technical know-how, credit and market) in the rural areas of Uttarakhand, improving the educational levels of workers, particularly technical skills and promoting diversification of cereal dominated agriculture in favour of commercial crops. This will not only generate employment opportunities in large numbers but also improve the overall per capita income of the rural household economy in Uttarakhand.

Concluding remarks

Dependence on multiple livelihoods is a common feature among the rural households in Uttarakhand. Nearly 70 per cent households are engaged in three to four activities/occupations for maintaining their livelihoods. Apart from high workforce participation, nearly half of the main workers are engaged in multiple occupations. This, however, does not result in low levels of per capita income for the majority of the sample households. Our analysis shows more than 40 per cent sample households living below the poverty line. These are predominantly dependent on cultivation and casual wage labour. The income inequality is also quite evident as the lowest 40 per cent population has less than 15 per cent share in income.

That livelihoods are highly diversified in the mountain region of Uttarakhand is also seen in the index of livelihood diversification, which shows the critical importance of at least two livelihood options in contributing a major share in household income. In other words, a single livelihood source is not adequate for providing sustainable livelihoods to an overwhelming majority of the rural workforce in the mountain areas. There are nearly 60 per cent rural households whose livelihoods, though highly diversified, fetch very low incomes for the households. They merely do so as a coping strategy to meet their threshold income levels. Also, there is another one-fourth of households with highly diversified livelihoods, which bring for them high income. Such diversification is facilitated by better resource endowments of these households. It has also been observed that livelihoods are comparatively less diverse both in very poor and very rich households. The poor are constrained to diversify their livelihoods owing to their poor asset base as labour is their only major asset and that too is highly unskilled with very low educational attainment. At the same time, livelihood diversification is also associated with the increase in the vulnerability of poor households when one of the sources of livelihood fails to generate income.

In brief, our empirical analysis clearly shows that highly diversified livelihoods do not result in any marked impact on improving income levels for rural households, and, thus, much of the diversification in rural livelihoods is a coping mechanism. The factors that significantly contribute to income generation are availability of land, productive assets, number of principal workers and educational attainment. Diversification of traditional cereal-based agriculture into commercial crops, such as fruits and vegetable production has significant potential in improving income levels provided it is supported by infrastructure. Thus, a viable and effective development strategy for the mountain areas of Uttarakhand should focus on bringing more land area under cultivation, providing infrastructure facilities like technology, transport, markets and input supply towards promoting large-scale commercial farming. This would also entail providing reasonable food security at subsidized rates to marginal farmers, so that they are encouraged to switch over to commercial farming. Also equally important would be to promote the growth of rural off-farm and non-farm enterprises, and at the same time these are to be supported by infrastructure and various tax incentives. Improving the education and skill levels of the labour force, particularly of women who dominate the mountain agriculture, would be of utmost importance for enhancing their existing low levels of productivity and income levels. Particularly, training in adopting improved farm practices, post-harvest techniques, packaging and marketing will be very useful to promote the development of enterprises in the rural areas of Uttarakhand.

Appendix

Table 10.1A Diversification in livelihoods by land class size (income at 1999–2000 prices)

Household group	Entropy Index	Herfindahl Index	Per household value of productive assets other than land (Rs. '000)	Per capita mean income (Rs.)	Mean occupations (No.)
Peri-urban					
Landless	0.22	0.69	2.39	7,083	2.41
Up to 0.5	0.31	0.59	16.19	10,777	2.98
0.5 to 1.5	0.31	0.58	31.78	15,683	2.83
1.5 to 2.5	0.27	0.65	266.98	28,907	2.80
2.5 to 5.0	0.52	0.36	21.67	20,964	3.67
Total	0.29	0.61	37.84	12,853	2.81
Semi interior					
Landless	0.38	0.51	2.86	8,730	3.75
Up to 0.5	0.43	0.44	9.17	6,446	3.53
0.5 to 1.5	0.42	0.45	11.46	10,115	3.52
1.5 to 2.5	0.44	0.45	18.34	9,100	3.87
2.5 to 5.0	0.53	0.34	28.02	8,567	4.06
>5.0	0.49	0.37	28.85	7,102	4.00
Total	0.44	0.44	14.17	8,504	3.68
Interior					
Landless	0.39	0.50	5.97	4,701	3.60
Up to 0.5	0.41	0.47	10.22	4,706	3.39
0.5 to 1.5	0.44	0.42	19.11	7,056	3.47
1.5 to 2.5	0.41	0.44	10.74	5,424	3.20
2.5 to 5.0	0.44	0.43	13.56	7,045	3.46
>5.0	0.23	0.65	20.50	6,315	2.00
Total	0.42	0.45	13.98	5,909	3.41

Household group	Entropy Index	Herfindahl Index	Per household value of productive assets other than land (Rs. '000)	Per capita mean income (Rs.)	Mean occupations (No.)
All					
Landless	0.26	0.65	2.91	6,943	2.71
Up to 0.5	0.38	0.50	11.86	7,197	3.30
0.5 to 1.5	0.41	0.46	19.35	10,062	3.34
1.5 to 2.5	0.40	0.49	65.61	12,263	3.53
2.5 to 5.0	0.49	0.38	21.55	9,111	3.78
>5.0	0.41	0.46	26.07	6,840	3.33
Total	0.39	0.49	21.16	8,890	3.33

Source: Mamgain (2004)

Table 10.2A Diversification in livelihoods by per capita income class (income at 1999–2000 prices)

	Entropy Index	Herfindahl Index	Per household value of productive assets other capita mean income (Rs.)	Per capita mean income (Rs.)	Mean occupations
Peri-urban					
Less than 2,500	0.23	0.66	2.73	2,013	2.13
2,500–5,000	0.27	0.62	4.20	3,876	2.40
5,000–7,500	0.40	0.47	9.69	6,475	3.44
7,500–12,500	0.35	0.55	10.49	10,206	3.19
12,500–22,500	0.31	0.60	40.38	16,838	3.00
22,500 and above	0.16	0.80	184.22	41,769	2.59
Total	0.29	0.61	37.84	12,853	2.81

(Continued)

Table 10.2A (Continued)

Semi interior					
Less than 2,500	0.34	0.53	5.41	1,605	2.92
2,500–5,000	0.44	0.43	13.28	3,779	3.50
5,000–7,500	0.47	0.41	14.93	6,277	3.78
7,500–12,500	0.46	0.41	13.11	9,876	3.83
12,500–22,500	0.47	0.43	23.74	15,898	4.06
22,500 and above	0.31	0.64	11.33	33,482	3.67
Total	0.44	0.44	14.17	8,504	3.68
Interior					
Less than 2,500	0.34	0.52	28.14	1,850	2.74
2,500–5,000	0.43	0.44	9.59	3,857	3.46
5,000–7,500	0.44	0.43	12.75	6,305	3.57
7,500–12,500	0.47	0.39	16.10	9,751	3.62
12,500–22,500	0.45	0.43	16.66	15,334	3.86
22,500 and above	0.20	0.74	3.36	30,244	2.50
Total	0.42	0.45	13.98	5,909	3.41
All					
Less than 2,500	0.32	0.56	15.93	1,808	2.67
2,500–5,000	0.39	0.49	9.11	3,842	3.19
5,000–7,500	0.44	0.43	13.04	6,330	3.63
7,500–12,500	0.43	0.44	13.21	9,932	3.60
12,500–22,500	0.40	0.51	30.17	16,235	3.55
22,500 and above	0.20	0.75	128.26	38,858	2.84
Total	0.39	0.49	21.16	8,890	3.33

Source: Mamgain (2004)

Note

1 Mamgain (2004, see Chapter VI, Table 6.3).

References

Agarwal, Bina. 1991. 'Social Security and the Family: Coping with Seasonality and Calamity in Rural India', *Journal of Peasant Studies*, 17(3), pp. 341–412.
Bhalla, Sheila. 1990. 'A Theoretical Framework for a Study of Rural Labour Markets', *The Indian Journal of Labour Economics*, 33(2): 103–118.
Bora, R. S. 1996. *Himalayan Out-migration*. Sage Publication: New Delhi.
Chadha, G. K. 1994. *Employment, Earnings and Poverty: A Study of Rural India and Indonesia*. New Delhi: Sage Publications.
Dev, Uttam Kumar, G. D. Nageshwara Rao, Mohany Rao and Rachel Slater. 2002. 'Diversification and Livelihood Options: A Study of Two Villages in Andhra Pradesh, India, 1975–2001', Working Paper 178, Overseas Development Institute, London, UK.
Ellis, Frank. 1998. 'Household Strategies and Rural Livelihood Diversification', *The Journal of Development Studies*, 35(1): 1–38.
Ellis, Frank. 2000. *Rural Livelihoods and Diversity in Developing Countries*. Oxford: Oxford University Press.
Grown, Caren A. and J. Sebstad. 1989. 'Introduction: Towards a Wider Perspective on Women's Employment', *World Development*, 17(7): 937–52.
Harris, J. R. 1991. 'Agriculture-Non-agriculture Linkages and the Diversification of Rural Economic Activities: A South Indian Case Study', in J. Breman and S. Mundle (eds), *Rural Transformation in Asia*, pp. 429–57. Oxford University Press: Delhi.
Jodha, N. S., M. Ashokan, and J. G. Ryan. 1977. 'Village Study Methodology and Resource Endowments of the Selected Villages in ICRISAT's Village Level Studies', Economics Programme Occasional Paper 16 (Village Level Studies Series 1.2).
Kackbark, Merlin and D. A. Anderson. 1975. 'On Measuring Economic Diversification', *Land Economics*, 51(4): 110–12.
Mamgain, Rajendra P. 2004. 'Employment, Migration and Livelihoods in the Hill Economy of Uttaranchal', Unpublished Ph.D. Dissertation, Centre for the Study of Regional Development, Jawaharlal Nehru University, New Delhi.
Sharma, H. R., R. K. Sharma and Virender Kumar. 2001. 'Diversification of Rural Economy: Effect on Income, Consumption and Poverty', *Asian Economic Review*, 43(1): 107–14.
Singh, R. P. and M. Asokan. 1981. 'Concepts and Methods for Estimating Rural Income in ICRISAT Village Level Studies', ICRISAT Economics Programme Progress Report 28, Hyderabad.

Theil, H. 1967. *Economics and Information Theory*. Amsterdam: North Holland.

Vaidyanathan, A. 1986. 'Labour Use in Rural India: A Study of Spatial and Temporal Variations', *Economic and Political Weekly*, 21(52): A130–A146.

Walker, T.S. and J.G. Rayon. 1990. *Village and Household Economies in India in Semi-arid Tropics*. Baltimore: Johns Hopkins University Press.

Chapter 11

Agrarian distress and rural non-farm sector employment in India

Vinoj Abraham

The agricultural sector has been suffering from a crisis of low growth and low productivity since the 1990s, which have accentuated in the early 2000s. The compound annual growth rate of agriculture and the allied sector during 2000–1 to 2004–5 was 2.02 per cent, the lowest annual growth recorded in the sector since 1980–1 (Mathur *et al.* 2006). Chand *et al.* (2007) also show this decline in agriculture, putting the dates slightly earlier, starting from 1997 to 1998. They also show the widespread decline in the sector, covering all sub-sectors. This crisis in the agrarian sector has many deleterious consequences such as farmer indebtedness and farmer suicides. However, it is evident that the effect of the crisis will not be restricted to the households who depend on farm outputs alone. The effect, depending on the interlinkages of the farm sector with various other sectors and markets can be wider and have a cascading effect on the economy. This chapter focuses on one such example catalysed by the agrarian crisis in the rural labour market.

The rural labour market in India is still dominated by agriculture-related workers. Cultivators and hired workers together in agriculture consisted of more than 70 per cent of the rural workforce during the year 2004–5. However, since 1993–94 there have been signs of a shift from farm to non-farm occupation and to industry and service sectors at a magnitude relatively higher than has been experienced during the past three decades. This has brought a lot of optimism among economists and policymakers about the fact that there is at last a visible structural shift in employment, which was stubbornly slow for the past three decades, in comparison to the corresponding gross domestic product (GDP) share. Yet it needs to be recognized that this shift has occurred in a period when the economy was reeling under the effects of a severe agrarian crisis. What kind of a structural shift has this been? How did it occur during a crisis? These are the questions that this chapter seeks to answer.

The chapter is structured as follows: the first section deals with the theoretical context. The second section draws a profile of employment in the rural areas of India. The third section delves on the concepts and data on rural non-farm sector (RNFS) followed by the fourth section which characterizes the differences in employment between regions that are suffering with agrarian distress and normal regions. The fifth section provides a comparative analysis of the determinants of this structural shift in rural employment followed by conclusions in the final section.

Theoretical context

Structural change in India, which varies widely from the traditional Kuznets–Clark structural transformation hypothesis has come to be accepted as an empirical reality (Bhattacharya and Mitra 1990; Papola 2005). However, the service-oriented structural transformation in the composition of GDP is not accompanied by a similar transformation in the industrial structure of the workforce (Sharma and Abraham 2005). This is more true in the case of the rural sector than in the urban sector. Data shows that a substantial share of the rural workforce is still associated with the primary sector, though there have been some changes in the recent past. This has, in effect, disqualified the theoretical predictions of the Lewis-type dual sector models (Lewis 1979) wherein workforce mobility to the urban-industrial sector from the rural-agrarian sector leads to productivity in the rise and growth of both the sectors. The missing link is in the Lewisian predictions and structural change hypothesis arguably is the (RNFS) (Hazell and Haggblade 1991). The RNFS lies as the bridge between the rural-agrarian sector and the urban-industrial sector. The workforce and structural change in income in a rural economy depends crucially on the dynamism of the RNFS, which in turn provides effective backward and forward linkages between the rural and urban economy, thus establishing a rural-urban continuum, a bridge that facilitates the above-mentioned structural transformation.[1]

However, this professed role of the RNFS, crucially depends on the 'dynamic' relation that it has with the farm sector and the structure and performance of the farm sector. The RNFS, through a chain of backward and forward linkages functions closely with the farm sector (Mellor 1976). The performance of the RNFS depends on the growth of the agrarian sector and employment and wage conditions within the agrarian sector. If the agrarian sector is a laggard, surviving on subsistence forms of agriculture, the RNFS may act as a residual sector trying to provide a cushion for the excess labour in the sector to be accommodated in various non-productive low-end RNFS employment, which are most often traditional non-farm activities. Such rise in the RNFS is essentially distress driven. On the other hand, a productive and growing agrarian sector generates a lot of demand for a dynamic and modern RNFS, which is growth driven.

However, these broad changes in the rural economy may be observable only in case of output and input markets that are highly integrated both vertically and horizontally. When markets are not integrated but are segmented, often such shifts may occur in isolation, and within the same economy both distress-driven and growth-driven structural shifts may be visible. Given the fact that rural markets are highly segmented, both in the output market and input market, and segmented both vertically and horizontally, it can be expected that such phenomenon co-exist. The agrarian crisis provides for such a setting in the economy. While the overall effects of the agrarian crisis is very large, its incidence did not have a pan-India coverage. It was specific to some regions. The agrarian crisis in these regions had affected the employment opportunities in the agricultural sector adversely promoting distress driven mobility to RNFS. On the other hand, some regions were not affected by the crisis, and hence the emergence of RNFS employment was driven by conventional growth factors. To understand the effect of the agrarian crisis on RNFS employment we make a comparative study between affected regions and non-affected regions[2] in terms of characteristics of structural shifts and their determinants. But before we look into the regions that are affected by distress, it may be proper to present the description of the rural labour market in the context of the agrarian crisis. The next section presents analysis of trends and patterns of rural employment.

Trends and patterns of employment in rural areas

An analysis of the rural labour market done by Abraham (2009) showed that the agrarian crisis had a significant effect on the rural labour market. Drawing from the above-mentioned chapter the following observations can be made:

- First, both the Labour Force Participation Rates (LFPR) and work participation rate (WPR) trends suggest that a larger share of the population are job seekers compared to the previous period, and also employment in the economy has picked up momentum during the period 1999–2000 to 2004–5 compared to the previous jobless growth phase 1993–4 to 1999–2000.

• Second, the female LFPR, after declining continuously since the peak of 25.4 per cent in 1987–8, rose for the first time in 2004–5 to 24.9 per cent. Moreover, this rise is the largest between any two National Sample Survey (NSS) thick rounds, from 23.5 per cent to 24.9 per cent. It could be argued that this rise in female LFPR is a component of the distress participation in labour market that has come up due to the agrarian crisis that is gripping the rural economy. The highest LFPR for rural females recorded since 1983 was in the year 1987–8. It is common knowledge by now, that the Forty-Third round of NSS, in 1987–8, was conducted during a period of severe drought, which had struck the rural sector adversely. The Forty-Third NSS was also marked by a decline in rural male LFPR. The Sixty-First round of the NSS also exhibits patterns similar to that of the 1987–8 NSS round, wherein there is a spurt in the female LFPR due to agrarian crisis.

• Third, another probable indicator of distress employment is the rise in WPR and LFPR among the elderly, in the age group greater than 60. The LFPR among aged men had reached 684 per 1,000 in 1993–4 and declined to 622 in 1999–2000. But it increased to 631 in the sixty-first survey. More interesting is the trends among aged women workers. The LFPR had gradually increased from 156 to 174 per 1,000 between 1983 and 1999–2000. The increase in aged women LFPR during the five-year period 1999–2000 to 2004–5 from 174 to 199 is much higher than the increase that was experienced during the 17-year period of 1983 to 1999–2000. This rise in work participation of the aged population in the rural economy is indicative of distress employment seeking in the wake of poor earnings and fewer days of employment for the younger workers in the household.

• Fourth, trends in underemployment also reflect the trends in distress driven employment. Even when the open unemployment Usual Principal Status (UPS) for males is stable at 2.1 per cent, and PS + SS unemployment rates even decreased by a fraction from 1.7 in the Fifty-Fifth round to 1.6 per cent in the Sixty-First round, the measure of underemployment Current Daily Status (CDS) had increased from 7.2 per cent in the Fifty-Fifth round to 8 per cent in 2004–5, the highest rate of underemployment recorded since 1983. For females, both open unemployment and underemployment recorded an increase. Unemployment had increased from 1.5 per cent to 3.1 per cent, and the underemployment rate had increased from 7 per cent to 8.7 per cent during the same time period.

- Fifth, casualization of the workforce, which continued throughout the late 1980s and 1990s, seems to have been arrested as reflected in the latest round of the NSS. The rise in self-employment in the latest round, both among male and female workers from 544 to 576 and from 500 to 564, respectively, may need to be seen as distress mobility from wage employment to self-employment. It is generally argued that self-employment is a superior option for the workers compared to casual wage employment due to lesser vulnerabilities. However, it can be argued that the rise of self-employment, in the current context, is a sort of residual last resort employment option.
- Sixth, there has been wage stagnation in the rural areas, especially in the agricultural sector. Table 11.1 shows the level (at 1983 prices) and growth of wages during the period 1983 to 2004–5. The growth rate of wages for casual workers declined from 3.51 per cent to 3.14 per cent and further to 2.8 per cent during the periods 1983 to 1993–4, 1993–4 to 1999–2000, and 1999–2000 to 2004–5, respectively. This decline is more pronounced among females than males. While the casual male workers experienced a marginal rise in the growth rate during 1983 to 1993–4, the decline was across the board in the period 1999–2000 to 2004–5. If we

Table 11.1 Real wages in rupees per day in the rural sector – levels and growth rates (1983 prices)

Period	Regular			Casual		
	Male	Female	Persons	Male	Female	Persons
1983	15.33	10.44	14.63	7.79	4.89	6.77
1993	28.33	18.9	26.94	10.69	7.31	9.56
1999	36.98	24.88	34.99	13.02	8.39	11.51
2004	41.72	25.7	38.73	15.23	9.04	13.23
Compound Annual Growth Rate						
1983–93	6.33	6.11	6.3	3.22	4.10	3.51
1993–9	4.54	4.69	4.45	3.34	2.32	3.14
1999–2004	2.44	0.65	2.05	3.19	1.50	2.82
1993–2004	3.58	2.83	3.36	3.27	1.95	3.00

Source: Abraham (2007)

take the case of regular workers, the decline is severe, both for males and females during the entire period from 1983 to 2004–5. This slowdown in growth of wages, both for regular and casual workers, probably is a pointer towards the rise of distress employment in the form of self-employment.

* Seventh, the inertia among the rural male workers against intersectoral mobility seems to be gradually reducing. The total share of employment in the agricultural sector had declined from 77 per cent of the workforce in 1983 to 66 per cent in 2004–5 (Table 11.2). The largest decline was in the period 1999–2000 to 2004–5, where a reduction of 5 per cent point was recorded. Correspondingly the non-farm rural employment share among males increased from 23 per cent in 1983 to 34 per cent in the latest period. This increase in RNFS employment was spread within the manufacturing, construction, trade, hotel and restaurant, transport, storage and communication sectors.

However, among women intersectoral mobility is still very limited. The female dependence on the agricultural sector declined by just 5 per

Table 11.2 Industrial composition of rural workers (UPS) (in percentages)

		(0)	(1)	(2&3)	(4)	(5)	(6)	(7)	(8)	RNFS
Rural male	1983	77.2	0.6	7.1	0.2	2.3	4.4	1.7	6.2	22.8
	87–88	73.9	0.7	7.6	0.3	3.7	5.2	2.1	6.4	26.1
	93–94	73.7	0.7	7	0.3	3.3	5.5	2.2	7.1	26.3
	99–00	71.2	0.6	7.3	0.2	4.5	6.8	3.2	6.1	28.8
	04–.05	66.2	0.6	8	0.2	6.9	8.3	3.9	5.9	33.8
Rural female	1983	86.2	0.4	6.5	0	0.9	2.2	0.1	3.4	13.8
	87–88	82.5	0.5	7.5	0	3.2	2.4	0.1	3.7	17.5
	93–94	84.7	0.5	7.5	0	1.1	2.2	0.1	4	15.3
	99–00	84.1	0.4	7.7	0	1.2	2.3	0.1	4.3	15.9
	04–.05	81.4	0.4	8.7	0	1.7	2.8	0.2	4.6	18.6

Source: NSS REPORT NO 515 *Employment and Unemployment Situation in India*

Note: Agriculture (0), Mining and Quarrying (1), Manufacturing (2&3), Electricity and Water (4), Construction (5), Trade, hotel and restaurant (6), Transport, storage and communication (7), Other Services (8), RNFS = Rural Non-Farm Sector.

cent points during the entire period, from 1983 to 2004–5. An over-whelming share of more than 81 per cent still depended on agriculture as the main source of employment, while only 19 per cent depended on RNFS employment. Whatever little shift in share had occurred, the mobility was mainly into the manufacturing sector and other services.

- Eighth, industrial classification of workers by worker status shows that in the primary sector an overwhelmingly large share of work-ers, more than 60 per cent are self-employed, followed by casual workers consisting of nearly 40 per cent, while·the regular workers consisted of only about one per cent (Table 11.3). The share of casual male workers in the primary sector increased from 33 per

Table 11.3 Industrial distribution of workers by status (UPS) (per cent)

		Rural male				Rural female			
		Self-employed	Regular	Casual		Self-employed	Regular	Casual	
Primary	38	63.2	4.3	32.6	100	54.7	1.2	44.1	100
	43	61.4	4.2	34.4	100	56.7	2.5	40.9	100
	50	60.4	1.8	37.9	100	50.8	0.5	48.7	100
	55	58.1	1.9	40.1	100	48.5	1.0	50.5	100
	61	63.1	1.4	35.5	100	56.6	0.5	42.9	100
Secondary	38	50.4	30.4	19.3	100	52.6	18.4	28.9	100
	43	48.1	29.0	22.9	100	51.3	17.9	30.8	100
	50	36.7	18.3	45.0	100	52.4	9.5	38.1	100
	55	36.4	18.2	45.5	100	63.6	9.1	27.3	100
	61	34.5	15.5	50.0	100	61.5	7.7	30.8	100
Tertiary	38	NA	NA	NA	NA	NA	NA	NA	NA
	43	NA	NA	NA	NA	NA	NA	NA	NA
	50	54.9	34.1	11.0	100	56.3	31.3	12.5	100
	55	52.4	34.5	13.1	100	50.0	37.5	12.5	100
	61	57.7	32.0	10.3	100	50.0	44.4	5.6	100

Source: NSS REPORT NO 515 *Employment and Unemployment Situation in India*

Note: For the Thirty-Eighth and Forty-Third round the figures in the secondary sector includes the tertiary sector as well.

cent in 1983 to 40 per cent in 1999–2000, which declined to 36 per cent in 2004–5. The compensating rise was fully in the self-employed workers in the latest period, even with a slight decline in the regular workers. However, it may be interesting to note that even though casualization had been declining in general, within the manufacturing sector it had been increasing unabated since 1993–4 till 2004–5 from 45 per cent to 50 per cent. Correspondingly the share of self-employed and regular workers declined by varying levels. This rise in casual workers in the manufacturing sector meant that of all male casual workers in rural India, nearly 24 per cent were in the manufacturing sector (See Appendix Table 11.1A). Another important aspect to note is that decline in casual employment among rural males in the tertiary sector, is the decline in the share of regular employment, in place of which, the share of self-employment had increased from 55 per cent to 58 per cent. Similar to the male workers, female workers also experienced a rise in self-employment in the primary sector, during the last period while the share of casual workers in the manufacturing sector increased in the last period. The share of regular workers among female workers increased to 44 per cent in the tertiary sector. The rise of self-employment in the primary and tertiary sector and casualization in the manufacturing sector in the rural economy are points of concern. They point to the distressed nature of employment that is generated in the absence of farm employment.

RNFS: concepts, definitions and data

Given the above backdrop of the rural economy of India, we proceed to study RNFS employment in India. Rural non-farm sector employment is defined as any form of employment other than farm employment in the type of wage, self or unpaid family labour. Farm employment is taken to be those agricultural activities such as growing of crops; market gardening; horticulture (NIC 011); farming of animals (NIC 012); mixed farming, that is both crops and animal farming (013); agricultural and animal husbandry service activities (NIC 014); hunting and related services (NIC 015).

For the analysis, the household level data collected for the Sixty-First round of the NSS, on employment-unemployment was utilized. The data has been used without any multiplier. The total number of observations for rural employment in India is 1,45,443 individuals in 62.056

households. After cleaning we get 145,359 observations in 62,016 households. All tables generated and the analysis done are based on this dataset.

To compare and contrast between characteristics of employment an analytical exercise is conducted for two sets of regions, namely regions suffering from agricultural distress and non-distressed regions. The classification of regions into distressed and non- distressed regions was done at the district level. The 'Expert Group on Agricultural Indebtedness' formed under the behest of the Ministry of Finance, Government of India and headed by Prof. R. Radhakrishna had identified 100 distress-affected districts in the country.[3] Using this list the distressed districts were identified and the residual was taken to be not affected by agricultural distress.

Distress in farm sector and employment patterns

The rural sector is predominantly agriculture based. More than 60 per cent of the total employment in this sample of the rural area is still employed in the farm sector, while non-farm employment consists of nearly 40 per cent.[4] Rural employment is malecentric. However, compared to farm employment the relative shares are higher for males in non-farm employment. Of the total rural sample an overwhelming 69 per cent workers were male while only 31 per cent were female.

Once we divide the regions into agriculturally distressed and non-distressed then the patterns of employment tend to change substantially from the overall picture. In the non-distressed region, the share of male workers in the farm sector was 64 per cent, but in the distressed regions

Table 11.4 Distribution of workers according to sex (per cent)

	Non- distress region			Distress region		
	Farm	Non-farm	Total	Farm	Non-farm	Total
Male	64	78.31	69.74	55.5	75.77	63.06
Female	36	21.69	30.26	44.5	24.23	36.94
Total	100	100	100	100	100	100

Source: Sixty-First round of the NSSO (*Employment* and *Unemployment. Unit Level Data*)

the share declined drastically to 56 per cent (Table 11.4). Correspondingly, the share of women workers increased from 36 per cent to 45 per cent. Even in the non-farm sector the share of males declined slightly from 78 per cent to 76 per cent, while that of females increased from 22 per cent to 24 per cent. In total employment, the share of males declined from 70 per cent to 63 per cent, while the share of females increased from 30 per cent to 37 per cent, when one moves from non-distressed regions to distress regions.

This essentially suggests feminization of work in farms in regions experiencing agricultural distress. The incidence of this feminization seems to be much higher in the farm sector rather than in the non-farm sector. One probable reason is the distress-related male migration to other regions.

A look into the time dimension of employment of who reported 'being employed' as their Usual Principal Status shows that unemployment in their 'minor time' (less than six months) was higher among the workers in the distressed regions. While 79 per cent of the workers in non-distressed regions were not seeking or available for employment, in distressed regions, the corresponding figure was 74 per cent (Table 11.5). However, this underemployment is much more severe in the farm sector, in general and especially drastic in distressed regions. In the non-distressed regions nearly 24 per cent of the farm workers suffered unemployment in their minor time period, while 32 per cent

Table 11.5 Level of unemployment among UPS main workers (per cent)

	Non-distressed region			Distressed region		
	Farm	Non-farm	Total	Farm	Non-farm	Total
Unemployed less than 1 month	1	1.24	1.09	1.17	0.77	1.02
Unemployed 1 to 2 months	6.93	5.69	6.43	9.55	5.91	8.2
Unemployed 3 to 6 months	16.17	8.76	13.2	20.89	9.04	16.48
Did not seek/ not available	75.9	84.31	79.27	68.38	84.28	74.29
Total	100	100	100	100	100	100

Source: Sixty-First round of the NSSO (*Employment* and *Unemployment. Unit Level Data*)

of the farm workers in distressed regions faced unemployment in their minor period. In the non-distressed regions nearly 16 per cent of the workers were unemployed for three to six months, while in distressed regions it was much higher at 21 per cent.

The share of workers according to their status shows that nearly 39 per cent of the total workers are self-employed in non-distressed regions, while the share declines substantially to 33 per cent in distressed regions (Table 11.6). Correspondingly, the segment that shows the maximum increase is unpaid family workers. The share of unpaid family workers in distressed regions increased from 23 per cent in non-distressed regions by 4.5 per cent points to 27.47 per cent. Casual employment also is higher in the distressed regions at 28 per cent compared to 24 per cent in non-distressed regions. In contrast, the share of regular wage employees is higher in the non-distressed regions compared to the distressed regions. During distress, labourers shift from self-employed status to being unpaid family workers and casual workers. However, the distress in the agricultural sector seems to be keeping the non-farm sector insulated in terms of status of employment, except that regular employees share declined in distressed regions, while unpaid family workers share increased.

Table 11.6 Share of workers by status (per cent)

	Non-Distressed region			Distressed Region		
	Farm	Non-farm	Total	Farm	Non-farm	Total
Self-employed	38.45	39.35	38.81	29.55	39.29	33.18
Employer	1.91	0.94	1.52	1.72	0.83	1.39
Unpaid family worker	**30.9**	**11.03**	**22.94**	**34.96**	**14.88**	**27.47**
Regular salaried/ wage employee,	1.59	27.79	12.09	0.79	24.02	9.45
Casual labour: in public works	0.04	0.59	0.26	0.1	0.84	0.38
Casual labour on other works	**27.11**	**20.31**	**24.39**	**32.88**	**20.15**	**28.13**
Total	100	100	100	100	100	100

Source: Sixty-First round of the NSSO (*Employment* and *Unemployment. Unit Level Data*)

The determinants of RNFS: method of analysis

Now, we turn to analyse the factors that affect RNFS employment. As stated earlier, the objective is to identify the differential effects of these factors on RNFS in regions that are affected by agrarian distress vis-à-vis normal regions. To fulfil the objective we begin with a logit model to analyse the choice of individuals between farm and non-farm employment. The following model is set for analysis.

$$Emp_i = a + \beta X_i + u_i \qquad (1)$$

Wherein the dependent variable is $Emp = 1$ if the current status of the ith worker is employed in the RNFS and $Emp = 0$ if the current status of the worker is employed in the farm sector. The independent variables X are defined later; u is the error term.

Separate Logit estimations were done for regions affected by agrarian distress and normal regions. Further, comparative results are provided for different types of farm and non-farm employment such as casual wage employed, regular wage employed, self-employed and unpaid family workers, along with the total workers. The results are discussed in Table 11.7 and the odds ratios of logit are provided in Table 11.8.

While the logit model estimates give us a detailed scenario of the employment prospects in these regions, the model has an essential flaw that it considers each binary choice as independent of other options in the labour market. To overcome this flaw we turn towards a multinomial logit estimation of the same.[5] Here we assume that the workers have four choices.

1   To be employed in the farm sector in a distressed region
2   To be employed in the farm sector in a non-distressed region
3   To be employed in the farm sector in a non-distressed region
4   To be employed in the non-farm sector in a non-distressed region

We assume that the rational individual maximizes utility by choosing one among the four mutually exclusive employment alternatives. Extending the above logit equation into a generalized form, for the ith individual with j choices the utility choice may be assumed as follows (Greene 2003).

$$Emp_{ij} = a + \beta X_{ij} + u_{ij} \qquad (2)$$

For a particular revealed choice j, it may be assumed that Emp_{ij} generates the maximum utility. So, the statistical model is derived by the probability that choice j is preferred over all other choices k, which is

Table 11.7 Logit model results of employment in the non-farm sector in agriculturally distressed and non-distressed regions

	Total		Casual wage employment		Regular wage employment		Self-employed		Unpaid family labour	
	Non-distressed	Distressed	Non-distressed	Distressed	Non-distressed	Distressed	Non-distressed	Distressed	Non-distressed	Distressed
Male	0.53354 (35.35)**	0.74261 (23.20)**	0.91079 (29.13)**	1.54736 (23.05)**	-0.12242 (1.59)	-1.53367 (5.00)**	0.42008 (15.29)**	0.22733 (3.33)**	0.25795 (6.69)**	0.23465 (2.84)**
Age	-0.00270 (1.56)	0.03762 (7.36)**	0.01120 (2.95)**	0.02166 (1.91)*	-0.05494 (6.37)**	0.07408 (2.12)*	-0.00840 (3.13)**	-0.03786 (4.10)**	-0.01728 (3.60)**	-0.00405 (0.32)
Age 2	-0.00006 (2.65)**	-0.00053 (8.31)**	-0.00026 (4.93)**	-0.00056 (3.55)**	0.00079 (6.33)**	-0.00075 (1.65)*	-0.00017 (4.91)**	0.00010 (0.92)	0.00013 (1.98)*	-0.00004 (0.22)
Edu_lit	0.28713 (13.90)**	0.39238 (8.51)**	0.30404 (8.02)**	-0.01044 (0.12)	0.40180 (4.27)**	0.91565 (3.00)**	0.13982 (4.28)**	0.47164 (6.17)**	0.09064 (1.57)	0.22974 (1.91)*
Edu_prim	0.41184 (20.53)**	0.53247 (11.57)**	0.48302 (12.75)**	0.06705 (0.75)	0.92659 (9.64)**	1.87439 (5.62)**	0.22962 (7.14)**	0.45275 (5.82)**	0.18836 (3.52)**	0.25376 (2.18)*
Edu_mid	0.64387 (32.10)**	0.63784 (14.16)**	0.70100 (17.56)**	0.26168 (2.99)**	2.10353 (17.76)**	1.75464 (6.29)**	0.37909 (11.65)**	0.49975 (6.33)**	0.18210 (3.38)**	0.07065 (0.62)
Edu_sec	0.97223 (39.60)**	1.10364 (19.61)**	0.76188 (12.38)**	0.29980 (2.09)*	2.79485 (18.28)**	2.88228 (6.85)**	0.52700 (13.23)**	0.73381 (7.67)**	0.28031 (4.19)**	0.49192 (3.56)**
Edu_high	1.78004 (70.17)**	1.87117 (32.49)**	0.61736 (7.63)**	0.23201 (1.25)	3.24738 (24.80)**	4.09980 (8.59)**	0.98078 (23.23)**	1.22010 (11.66)**	0.58489 (8.13)**	0.31066 (1.99)*

(Continued)

Table 11.7 (Continued)

	Total		Casual wage employment		Regular wage employment		Self-employed		Unpaid family labour	
	Non-distressed	Distressed	Non-distressed	Distressed	Non-distressed	Distressed	Non-distressed	Distressed	Non-distressed	Distressed
Percap_landown	0.00001 (0.58)	-0.00019 (2.25)*	0.00037 (3.09)**	-0.00001 (0.05)	0.00085 (3.70)**	0.00145 (1.95)*	-0.00012 (1.89)*	-0.00005 (0.33)	-0.00035 (2.57)**	-0.00069 (2.95)**
Percap_landcult	-0.00338 (78.66)**	-0.00269 (24.73)**	-0.00040 (2.61)**	-0.00032 (1.03)	-0.00119 (5.31)**	-0.00189 (2.61)**	-0.00444 (44.23)**	-0.00373 (18.64)**	-0.00761 (36.14)**	-0.00680 (19.86)**
HH_size	-0.04765 (21.22)**	-0.07663 (14.70)**	0.00636 (1.27)	0.04013 (3.42)**	-0.02178 (2.05)*	0.02158 (0.58)	-0.02778 (7.47)**	-0.08088 (8.60)**	-0.09964 (16.54)**	-0.15483 (12.27)**
Soc_OBC	0.09007 (5.57)**	0.11545 (3.19)**	-0.17068 (4.71)**	-0.11382 (1.29)	-0.04730 (0.57)	-0.27497 (1.08)	0.21201 (8.35)**	0.45827 (7.77)**	0.36905 (8.82)**	0.36471 (4.40)**
Soc_SC/ST	-0.17602 (10.36)**	-0.26511 (6.69)**	-0.25679 (7.16)**	-0.15771 (1.80)*	0.13700 (1.58)	-0.13331 (0.48)	-0.30773 (11.21)**	-0.08970 (1.29)	-0.14130 (3.04)**	-0.44107 (4.46)**
Constant	-0.31410 (8.13)**	-1.05632 (9.81)**	-1.52796 (18.41)**	-2.18686 (9.71)**	2.05105 (11.28)**	1.02135 (1.40)	0.50548 (8.04)**	1.62308 (7.66)**	0.41751 (4.30)**	0.98316 (4.05)**
Observations	118727	26572	28950	7476	14358	2512	46062	8814	27248	7301
LR chi2	20702.80	5710.11	2178.60	882.59	1371.63	246.91	9555.69	2431.14	5709.78	2149.94
Pseudo R2	0.1295	0.1627	0.0591	0.1017	0.1731	0.2386	0.1536	0.2010	0.2137	0.2927

Source: Sixty-First round of the NSSO (Employment and Unemployment. Unit Level Data)

Absolute value of z-statistics in parentheses, *significant at 5% level; **significant at 1% level

Table 11.8 Odds ratio calculated from the logit model

	Total		Casual wage employment		Regular wage employment		Self-employed		Unpaid family labour	
	Non-distressed	Distressed	Non-distressed	Distressed	Non-distressed	Distressed	Non-distressed	Distressed	Non-distressed	Distressed
Male	1.705	2.101	2.486	4.699	0.885	0.216	1.522	1.255	1.294	1.264
Age	0.997	1.038	1.011	1.022	0.947	1.077	0.992	0.963	0.983	0.996
Age 2	1.000	0.999	1.000	0.999	1.001	0.999	1.000	1.000	1.000	1.000
Edu_lit	1.333	1.481	1.355	0.990	1.495	2.498	1.150	1.603	1.095	1.258
Edu_prim	1.510	1.703	1.621	1.069	2.526	6.517	1.258	1.573	1.207	1.289
Edu_mid	1.904	1.892	2.016	1.299	8.195	5.781	1.461	1.648	1.200	1.073
Edu_sec	2.644	3.015	2.142	1.350	16.360	17.855	1.694	2.083	1.324	1.635
Edu_high	5.930	6.496	1.854	1.261	25.723	60.328	2.667	3.388	1.795	1.364
Percap_landown	1.000	1.000	1.000	1.000	1.001	1.001	1.000	1.000	1.000	0.999
Percap_landcult	0.997	0.997	1.000	1.000	0.999	0.998	0.996	0.996	0.992	0.993
HH_size	0.953	0.926	1.006	1.041	0.978	1.022	0.973	0.922	0.905	0.857
Soc_OBC	1.094	1.122	0.843	0.892	0.954	0.760	1.236	1.581	1.446	1.440
Soc_SC/ST	0.839	0.767	0.774	0.854	1.147	0.875	0.735	0.914	0.868	0.643

Source: Sixty-First round of the NSSO (*Employment and Unemployment. Unit Level Data*)

Prob $(Emp_{ij} > Emp_{ik})$ for all other K ≠ j $\qquad$ (3)

The multinomial logit model allows us to estimate a set of coefficients ß corresponding to each occupational category as follows

$$Prob\ (Emp = j \mid X) = \frac{e^{\beta_j x_i}}{\sum_{j=1}^{j=4} e^{\beta_k x_i}}, j = 1, 2, 3, 4 \qquad (4)$$

Normalizing the model, we take the parameter vector associated with non-farm employment in non-distressed regions as zero ($\beta_1 = 0$) and the remaining coefficients b_j measure the change relative to this base group.

$$Prob\ (Emp = j \mid X) = \frac{e^{\beta_j x_i}}{1 + \sum_{j=2}^{j=4} e^{\beta_k x_i}} \qquad (5)$$

$$Prob\ (Emp = 1) = \frac{1}{1 + \sum_{j=2}^{j=4} e^{\beta_k x_i}} \qquad (6)$$

Though further classifications of choices are theoretically possible, such as self-employed, casual employed and regular employed, this is not attempted to avoid the classic problem multinomial logit regressions of irrelevance of independent variables. The results of the multinomial logit model are shown in Table 11.9. We also derive the marginal effects on change in the probabilities as we assume one unit change in continuous variables and a shift from one type to another in discrete variables.[6] This would help us to assign relative positioning of the choices with regard to each independent variable. The marginal effects are presented in Table 11.10.

Table 11.9 Multinomial Logit estimates of employment in distressed regions

	Farm employment in distressed regions	Farm employment in non-distressed regions	Non-farm employment in distressed regions
	Coef. (Std. Err.)	Coef. (Std. Err.)	Coef. (Std. Err.)
Sex (female = 0)	−.5310* (.0277)	.1026* (.0353)	−.38135* (.0146)
Age	.0348* (.0036)	.0923* (.0049)	−.0114* (.0017)

	Farm employment in distressed regions	Farm employment in non-distressed regions	Non-farm employment in distressed regions
Age 2	−.0002* (.00004)	−.0009* (.00006)	.0002* (.00002)
Education_only literate (illiterate = 0)	−.4180* (.0382)	.1621* (.0403)	−.2826* (.0185)
Education_primary	−.1260* (.0399)	.0150 (.0467)	−.0395* (.0197)
Education_Middle	−.6511* (.0429)	.0193 (.0430)	−.5546* (.0189)
Education_Secondary	.2880* (.0461)	−.1193* (.0610)	−.5747* (.0255)
Education_grad. above	−.8392* (.0560)	.4298* (.0468)	−1.545* (.0262)
Land cultivated per capita	.0017* (.00003)	.0001* (.00006)	.0016* (.00002)
HH monthly consumption exp.	−.00038* (.00001)	−.0003* (.00001)	−.00002* (.000003)
Household size	.2405* (.0056)	.1830* (.006)	.0671* (.0027)
Social group_SC (ST = 0)	−1.5144* (.0420)	−.6734* (.0523)	−.8737* (.0229)
Social group_OBC	−1.1297* (.0330)	.0340 (.0437)	−.7844* (.0204)
Social group_general	−1.2085* (.0383)	−.5205* (.0503)	−.6525* (.0218)
Constant	−1.7575* (.0797)	−3.876* (.1063)	1.0328* (.0386)

Number of obs = 142716

LR chi2(42) = 25201.50

Prob > chi2 = 0.0000

Log likelihood = −131461.73

Pseudo R2 = 0.0875

Source: Sixty-First round of the NSSO (*Employment* and *Unemployment. Unit Level Data*)

Base category is non-farm employment in non-distressed regions
*coefficients are significant at least at 5% level

Table 11.10 Marginal effects – changes in probabilities

Variable	Average change	Farm employment in distressed regions	Farm employment in non-distressed region	Non-farm employment in distressed region	Non-farm employment in non-distressed region
Sex (female = 0)	0.0460	−0.0156	0.0118	−0.0763	0.0802
Age	0.0028	0.0019	0.0033	−0.0057	0.0004
Age 2	0.00004	−0.00001	−0.00003	0.0001	−0.00003
Education_only literate (illiterate = 0)	0.0370	−0.0120	0.0133	−0.0620	0.0607
Education_ primary	0.0056	−0.0049	0.0015	−0.0063	0.0097
Education_ Middle	0.0689	−0.0154	0.0139	−0.1211	0.1226
Education_ Secondary	0.0750	0.0386	0.0060	−0.1501	0.1054
Education_ grad. above	0.1804	−0.0081	0.0640	−0.3526	0.2967
Land cultivated per capita	0.0001	0.00003	−0.00003	0.0003	−0.00035
HH monthly consumption exp.	0.00001	−0.00001	−0.00001	0.00001	0.00001
Household size	0.0097	0.0096	0.0044	0.0053	−0.0194
Social group_ SC (ST = 0)	0.1073	−0.0385	−0.0046	−0.1716	0.2147
Social group_ OBC	0.0957	−0.0318	0.0196	−0.1597	0.1719
Social Group_ general	0.0793	−0.0349	−0.0031	−0.1206	0.1587

Source: Sixty-First round of the NSSO (*Employment* and *Unemployment. Unit Level Data*)

Hypotheses

The factors that influence an individual joining the farm or non-farm sector work force, in a region characterized by a productive agricultural sector, may differ widely from a region suffering from agricultural distress. The former is related to an eclectic set of 'pull factors' while the latter to a set of 'push factors'. For the purpose of analysis we identify the factors that are argued to affect RNFS employment in theoretical and empirical literature both as push and pull factors.

Further, the factors that influence rural employment decisions may conceptually be identified as belonging to two different realms. One set of factors is related to the characteristics of the individual, and the other set to that of the household he belongs. The individual factors considered are gender, age of the individual and level of education. At the household level the factors considered are land ownership and cultivation, monthly consumption expenditure at household level, size of the household and social group to which the household belongs. The choice of variables is based on prior literature on the RNFS.

Gender: Previous studies argue that gender is an important determinant of RNFS employment, and it is also indicative of the character of RNFS employment in terms of growth versus distress driven patterns. If the RNFS employment experienced is growth oriented with a greater growth dynamism in the modern RNFS sectors then males and females may find new employment opportunities in the growing sector, though with a marginally higher level for males based on the prevailing level of the gender institutional structures of the region. However, males have a greater propensity to diversify into other forms of income generating activities, while females are more prone to continue in the farm sector in regions that experience poor farm sector growth and RNFS growth (Ellis 1998; Newman and Canagarajah 2001). In regions with poor pull factors, with distress-related RNFS growth of traditional sectors, males seem to 'push' females into the farm sector while males mopped up RNFS employment (Jha 2006). Thus, while it can be expected that in general females have a greater propensity to be working in the farm sector than males, in regions with poor opportunities in RNFS, the female propensity to work in the farm sector would be higher.

Age: Similarly, the age of the worker has been postulated as an important individual factor that influences the decision to join the RNFS. Non-farm work requires certain attributes such as skills, mobility and training (Bhaumik 2007). Also employment opportunities in the RNFS require greater information flow which, in the rural setting is acquired through informal social networks. The network externalities would increase as age increases and build greater social networks. Lanjouw and Shariff (2004) found that the probability of workers being engaged in the agricultural sector at a younger age was higher, but beyond a threshold age the probability of the RNFS would become higher than farm sector employment.

Level of education: The level of education of the individual also would influence one's decision to join the RNFS. Education acts as an asset that enables seeking opportunities outside of the farm sector. Studies show that education increases the probability of seeking wage and self-employment that is more remunerative in the non-farm sector (Escobal 2001; Lanjouw and Shariff 2004). However, education would play an important role in regions which experience the growth of the modern RNFS sector, where education and skills are demanded, while in traditional RNFS sector growth, which is related to distress-driven growth, education may not be a determining factor in obtaining employment in the RNFS.

Ownership and cultivation of land: Landlessness is an important push factor that drives the rural poor to search for RNFS employment. However, the effect of ownership is different from cultivation. Land is an asset, whose ownership is an insurance against a multitude of risks and uncertainties of rural life. Whether it is cultivated, left fallow or leased out, the land owned is a fallback for the rural household. Hence, it can be expected that rural households who own land may opt for the RNFS only if the RNFS is sufficiently remunerative. In contrast, the ability of those who don't own land, as an asset, to avail credit is severely restricted. This would imply that they are rendered more vulnerable and therefore may be ready to take up any employment in the RNFS in case the farm sector fails. Households that cultivate land have lesser propensity to join the RNFS if the farm sector is sufficiently remunerative. However, if the farm sector is experiencing poor growth and productivity then some members of cultivating households may choose to work in the RNFS to compensate for poor farm performance. Here again we should note that this is a risk aversion strategy in a distressed situation.

Size of the household: Households with a large number of members may tend to diversify into the non-farm sector if the size of the land holding is small, or alternatively, members would be able to find wage employment in the RNFS.

Social group: The social position in the rural areas plays an important role in land ownership and cultivation, which in turn determines the occupational choice that households have. Households belonging to lower castes, especially Scheduled Castes are traditionally landless agricultural workers. Hence there is a greater probability of their joining the RNFS than the higher caste workers. However, with the poor performance of the agricultural sector these caste differences may get mellowed down.

Empirical results

Logit model estimates

Gender: In general the results suggest that males, in comparison to females, have a greater probability of joining the non-farm sector. Across varying status of employment this trend seems to stand, except that of regular salaried employees, where it is not significant in the normal group. Lanjouw and Shariff (2004) made a similar observation that in rural India females tend to prefer agricultural wage labour than non-farm employment or cultivation. However, interestingly, the odds of male workers joining non-farm against farm employment are highest among casual workers even in normal regions. Moreover, these odds almost double to 4.79 in distressed regions from 2.5 in non-distressed regions. This is a very suggestive pointer towards the push factors that force male workers to be mobile across regions and sectors in the wake of their stagnation in their agrarian economy. If the pull factors were more important then the odds would have been higher in the non-distressed region, where non-farm employment would have been a complement to the farm sector rather than a substitute. This above mentioned trend could be due to two reasons: male selective migration for alternate employment in the wake of distress. The other reason is male shifting to more productive employment in the non-farm sector compared to the stagnant agricultural sector.

Age: On the one hand, age in the model for the non-distressed region does not turn out to be a significant determinant for the decision to join the non-farm sector, though the sign of the coefficient suggests a negative relation between age and probability of employment in the non-farm sector. But on the other hand, age is a highly significant variable in explaining the probability of an individual working in the distressed regions to join the non-farm sector. As age increases the odds favour more the non-farm sector rather than the farm sector in a distressed region. Within various categories, the wage employment sector, namely casual and regular wage employment groups is different from the non-wage sector, with respect to how age affects their probability of being employed in the non-farm sector. Within non-wage groups, as age increases, the probability of being in the non-farm sector declines (both for self-employed and unpaid family groups), whether they belong to a distressed region or non-distressed region. In contrast, in the distressed regions, in both wage employed sectors (casual and regular), age is positively related with the probability of joining non-farm employment. But in non-distressed regions the probability of regular wage employment in the non-farm sector tends to decline as age increases, while that of casual wage employment tends to increase.

The variable 'square of age' suggests that whatever be the sector of work, after a threshold age the probability of employment in the non-farm sector declines and that of farm sector employment increases.

Education: The general trend suggests that as the level of education increases, the probability of non-farm employment increases. In both distressed and non-distressed regions this trend does stand. Among the categories of employment, the probability of joining the non-farm sector is highest among regular wage employment. But there is one glaring exception. Again among casual workers, while non-distressed regions seem to fit into the conventional knowledge of increasing probability of non-farm sector employment with increasing levels of education, the case is different in distressed regions. Except for middle and secondary school education levels none of the education dummy variables are significant. In other words the relation between level of education and non-farm employment is not statistically significant in the case of casual wage employment in distressed regions. The lack of a clear relation between level of education and non-farm sector casual employment is suggestive of the low skilled less productive casual wage employment that is being generated within the non-farm sector in the distressed regions. However, casual employment in non-distressed regions continues to show the typical 'education-non-farm' relationship. These trends point towards push factors associated with farm distress in determining non-farm employment.

Per capita land ownership: While per capita land owned does not have any significant effect on the probability of non-farm employment in non-distressed regions, it does have a negative and significant effect in distressed regions, that is as the per capita ownership increases there is a greater probability of joining the farm sector in distressed regions. Casual workers have a greater probability of being employed in the non-farm sector in non-distressed regions, while for distressed regions it is not significant. Regular workers tend to get employed in the non-farm sector the more they own land. Land ownership being also a sign of their asset holdings, and hence their income levels, greater land holding also is having a positive effect on obtaining regular non-farm employment, be it in the distressed region or non-distressed region. The probability of being a farm unpaid family labourer is high as the per capita land owned keeps increasing.

Land cultivation: Land cultivation per capita is different from land owned per capita. Land cultivation includes the actual amount of land that is cultivated. For this we exclude land not cultivated and land leased-out. Further, we include land leased-in for cultivation. The common trend across most categories show that as the land cultivated per capita increases the probability of being employed in the farm sector increases, which is obvious. However, in the case of casual workers in distressed regions this relation does not show any statistical significance.

Household size: The household coefficients show that size of the household, in general, has a negative impact on the probability of the non-farm sector, be it in distressed sectors or non-farm sectors. However, the disaggregated analysis shows that among casual workers, as the size of household increases their probability of joining the non-farm sector increases. Another interesting observation is that the probability of being employed in the non-farm sector for both types of wage employment in distressed regions is much higher compared to non-distressed regions. In contrast, for self-employed and unpaid family workers, as the size of household increased their probability of joining the non-farm sector further declined. Thus there seems to be a dichotomous relation between household size and the probability of joining non-farm sector employment, wherein large family size seems to encourage wage employees to be employed in the non-farm sector, especially during times of distress, while self-employed and family workers seem to be employed in the farm sector with the increasing size of families.

Social groups (reference group is general category): Compared to the general category, the socially deprived castes and tribes (SC/ST) seem to have less probability of being employed in the non-farm sector, be it in the non-distressed region or distressed region.

Multinomial logit and marginal effects

Given the four choices of work, the probability of employment in the distressed region, whether it is farm or non-farm is negative for *males,* while it is positive for farm employment in the non-distressed region. Yet the constant for farm employment in the non-distressed region is −3.87, implying that after controlling for the effects of the various factors in the model, non-farm employment in non-distressed regions is preferred to farm employment in non-distressed regions. So in effect, though farm employment is a preferred choice for males in non-distressed regions, their preference would be greater for non-farm employment in non-distressed regions between the two. The reverse of this also implies that females have a greater probability of getting employed in farms, either in distressed or non-distressed regions. On the one hand, the marginal effect of a change from female to male shows that the probability for non-farm employment in non-distressed regions is the highest, implying the greatest preference for this type of employment, which is followed by farm employment in non-distressed regions (Table 11.10). On the other hand, the marginal effect is negative for all employment in distressed regions, and the size of the change is largest for non-farm followed by farm, implying the increase in probability of women employment in distressed regions, both in the farm and non-farm sectors

As *age* increases the probability of taking up farm employment, either in distressed regions or non-distressed regions is higher compared to non-farm employment in non-distressed regions, while non-farm employment in distressed regions is not a preferred choice with increase in age. However, age beyond a threshold level reduces the probability of doing farm employment in non-distressed regions as well. Comparison of marginal effects for age shows that for a unit change in age the probability of farm employment in non-distressed regions had the highest increase, followed by farm employment in distressed regions. Non-farm employment in the non-distressed region has the least positive effect, while non-farm employment in distressed regions has a negative sign implying that in distressed regions younger people preferred to do non-farm employment than farm employment. Thus there seems to be an age-based differentiation in employment choices in the distressed regions, with the younger members preferring non-farm employment while the older members choose farm employment.

Education has a systematic effect on employment choices. As can be seen from Table 11.10, as the level of education increases, the probability of farm employment in distressed regions reduces consistently, in comparison to non-farm employment in non-distressed regions, as shown with a negative sign and reducing size of the coefficient. The only aberration is secondary level education of workers, which shows a positive sign. In non-distressed regions only literates have a positive effect on farm employment compared to illiterates. However, higher levels of education have ambiguous effects on the employment choice of farm employment in non-distressed regions. Again, non-farm employment in distressed regions is having a negative relation to education. Education, thus, seems to act as risk averting strategy. The marginal effects also show that education is a clear marker for employment choice between distressed and non-distressed regions. Probability of employment increases in non-distressed regions with higher levels of education, with a greater preference for non-farm employment, while in the distressed regions the employment probability decreases with higher levels of education.

Size of land under cultivation per capita seems to favour farm or non-farm employment in distressed regions, or farm employment in non-distressed regions in comparison to non-farm employment in non-distressed regions. As the *monthly consumption expenditure per household* increased there is a visible preference towards non-farm employment in non-distressed region than any other type of employment. The probability of being employed in this sector is higher as the levels of income per household increase.

As the *household size* increased it decreased one's probability of joining non-farm employment in non-distressed regions compared to other types of employment. Marginal effects show that for a unit increase in the size of the household the probability of doing farm employment in distressed regions increases the highest among all choices. This is followed by non-farm employment in distressed regions, while there is a decrease in the probability of being employed in the non-farm sector in non-distressed regions.

One's social status also played an important role in determining one's employment choice. Keeping the Scheduled Tribes as the reference category, Scheduled Castes, Other Backward Castes and General Castes in general show higher probability to be employed in non-farm employment in non-distressed regions than farm employment or non-farm employment in distressed regions. Thus Scheduled Tribes as a social group seem to be the worst affected in terms of having inferior employment options compared to other social groups.

Conclusion

The chapter makes an attempt to study the employment effect of the agrarian crisis in the rural economy. In specific terms, it elicits the question of diversification into RNFS employment under conditions of crisis. Analysis showed that the rural labour market has shown signs of a deepening crisis, with underemployment increasing, participation rates of secondary workers rising, wage stagnation and rising self-employment. Further, owing to the crisis, there has been a structural shift in employment towards non-farm employment. We find that in crisis-affected regions, the push factors are largely at operation, while in normal regions, the pull factors are relatively more dynamic in generating RNFS employment. Some factors such as social group had significant effect in both distressed regions and normal regions. It is also interesting to note that the effects of pull factors such as education, land ownership, etc., that play an important role in RNFS employment in normal regions, get vastly muted in the distressed regions, while the push factors gain greater weight. Also the effects are most pronounced in the case of casual workers and unpaid family workers when compared to self-employed and regular workers. The multinomial logit model and marginal effects derived from the model also seem to support the argument that the RNFS in the distressed region is driven by push factors, while in the non-distressed regions the conventional results of pull factors are visible. The analysis points to the fact that the effect of the agrarian crisis is not limited to the agricultural sector, rather it would spread to the input market. Moreover, given the muted effects of pull factors to the RNFS in distress-affected regions regular policy interventions may not generate the desired result. Rather, the specificities of the RNFS in-crisis affected regions need to be understood within this context to stimulate productive employment both in the farm and non-farm sectors.

Appendix

Appendix 11.1A Districts experiencing severe agricultural distress in India

No	State	District Names
1	Andhra Pradesh	Adilabad, Nizamabad, Karimnagar, Medak, Ranga Reddy, Mehabubnagar, Nalgonda, Warangal, Khammam, Guntur, Prakasam, Nellur, Cuddappah, Kurnool, Anantapur, Chitoor
2	Bihar	Banka, Bhagalpur, Darbhanga, Jamui, Lakhisarai, Madhubani, Saran
3	Chattisgarh	Bilaspur, Janjgir, Jashpur, Kanker
4	Gujarat	Dahod, Patan
5	Jammu and Kashmir	Baramulla, Doda, Kargil, Kupwara, Udhampur
6	Jharkhand	Deoghar, Gumla, Hazaribag, Lohardaga, Pakaur, Sahibganj, Seraikela, Simdega
7	Karnataka	Belgaum, Chikmangalur, Chitradurga, Hassan, Kodagu, Shimoga
8	Kerala	Kasargod, Palakkad, Wyanad
9	Madhya Pradesh	Anuppur, Ashoknagar, Balaghat, Barwani, Betul, Burhanpur, Chhatarpur, Chhindwara, Dindori, Jhabua, Katni, Mandla, Panna, Rewa, Seoni, Shahdol, Sidhi, Umaria
10	Maharashtra	Akola, Amravati, Buldhana, Gadchiroli, Gondia, Nanded, Nandurbar, Osmanabad, Wardha, Wasim, Yavatmal
11	Orissa	Boudh, Koraput, Malkangiri, Nawapara
12	Rajasthan	Churu, Dungarpur, Jaisalmer, Nagaur, Pali, Rajsamand, Sikar, Udaipur
13	Tamil Nadu	Sivaganga
14	Uttar Pradesh	Banda, Chitrakoot, Hamirpur
15	Uttaranchal	Almora, Pauri, Garhwal, Rudraprayag, Tehri Garhwal

Appendix 11.2A Variable definitions

	Variable Name	Variable definition
Gender (Ref: Female)	**Sex**	Male = 1, female = 0
Age	**Age**	Age of the workers
	age2	Square of age
Education (Ref: Illiterate)	Edu_lit	Not illiterate, but has not attended a formal school
	Edu_prim	Primary education
	Edu_mid	Middle education
	Edu_sec	Secondary education
	Edu_high	Higher education
Land ownership	Percap_landown	Average land owned by a household/no. of persons in the household
Land Cultivation	Percap_landcult	Average Land cultivated by a household/ no. of persons in the household
Consumption Expenditure	HH_mpce	Household monthly per capita consumption expenditure
Size of HH	HH_size	Size of the household
Caste (Ref: SC/ST)	Soc_OBC	OBC
	Soc_gen	General

Notes

1 Papola (1992) argues the formation of this continuity through the emergence and dynamic growth of semi-urban areas and small towns that act as centres of non-farm activity that links them with the rural farm sector.
2 For details of classification of regions into distress-affected and normal regions please see the section on RNFS, Concepts, Definitions and Data.
3 Following GoI (2007), the criteria for identifying the distressed and less-developed regions were as follows: The list includes 31 distressed districts identified by the Government where the Prime Minister's special rehabilitation package is being implemented. The remaining 69 districts have been included on the following criteria: (1) the district ranks low on the three-year average land productivity for 2001–2 to 2003–4, (2) the credit-deposit ratio of the district is less than 60 per cent for 2006, (3) the proportion of urban population in the district is less than 30 per cent in 2001. Districts in Goa, North-Eastern states other than Assam, and union territories are not considered due to lack of data on land productivity. The list of crisis-affected districts are presented in Appendix 11.1A.

4 All data expressed in this section is estimated from the unit level data of the Sixty-First round of NSS as mentioned earlier.
5 For a similar application of multinomial logit model see Khan (2007).
6 For a continuous variable x_i Marginal Effect of x_i = limit [$\Pr(Emp = 1|X, x_i + \Delta) - \Pr(Emp = 1|X, x_i)] / \Delta]$, $\Delta \to 0$. For a categorical variable x_i the marginal effects are derived as follows: Marginal Effect $x_i = \Pr(Emp = 1|X, x_i = 1) - \Pr(Emp = 1|X, x_i = 0)$

References

Abraham, Vinoj. 2007. 'Growth and Inequality of Wages in India: Recent Trends and Patterns', *Indian Journal of Labour Economics*, December 50(4): 927–41.

Abraham, Vinoj. 2009. 'Employment Growth in Rural India: Distress-Driven?' *Economic and Political Weekly*, April 18 XLIV(16): 97–104.

Bhattacharya, B. B. and Mitra, A. 1990. 'Excess Growth of Tertiary Sector in Indian Economy: Issues and Implications', *Economic and Political Weekly*, November 3: 2445–50.

Bhaumik, S. K. 2007. 'Diversification of Employment and Earnings by Rural Households in West Bengal', *Indian Journal of Agricultural Economics*, October–December 62(4): 585–606.

Chand, Ramesh, Raju, S. S. and Pandey, L. M. 2007. 'Growth Crisis in Agriculture: Severity and Options at National and State Levels', *Economic and Political Weekly*, June 30: 2528–33.

Ellis, F. 1998. 'Household Livelihood Strategies and Rural Livelihood Diversification', *Journal of Development Studies*, 35(1): 1–38.

Escobal, Javier. 2001. 'The Determinants of Non-farm Income Diversification in Rural Peru', *World Development*, 29(3): 497–508.

GoI. 2007. 'Report of the Expert Group on Agricultural Indebtedness', Department of Economic Affairs, Ministry of Finance, Government of India, July.

Greene, W. H. 2003. *Econometric Analysis*, 5th ed. Prentice Hall: USA.

Hazell, Peter B. R. and Haggblade, Steven. 1991. 'Rural Urban Growth Linkages in India', *Indian Journal of Agricultural Economics*, 46(4): 515–29.

Jha, Brajesh. 2006. 'Rural Non-Farm Employment in India: Macro-trends, Micro-evidences and Policy Options', IEG Working Paper Series No. E/272/2006

Khan, Mohammad Asif. 2007. 'Factors Affecting Employment Choices in Rural North-West Pakistan', Conference on International Agriculture Research for Development, University of Kassel-Witzenhausen and University of Göttingen, October 9–11, 2007.

Lanjouw, Peter and Shariff, Abusaleh. 2004. 'Rural Non-farm Employment in India: Access, Incomes and Poverty Impact', *Economic and Political Weekly*, October 2: 4429–46.

Lewis, W. Arthur. 1979. 'The Dual Economy Revisited', *The Manchester School of Economic & Social Studies, Wiley Blackwell*, September 47(3): 211–29.

Mathur, Archana, Das, Surajit and Sircar, Subhalakshmi. 2006. 'Status of Agriculture in India: Trends and Prospects', *Economic and Political Weekly*, December 30, pp. 5327–36.

Mecharla, Prasad Rao. 2002. 'The Determinants of Rural Non-Farm Employment in Two Villages of Andhra Pradesh' (India), PRUS Working Paper No. 12, Poverty Research Unit at Sussex, University of Sussex, September.

Mellor, John. 1976. *The New Economics of Growth: A Strategy for India and the Developing World*. Cornell University Press.

Newman, C. and S. Canagarajah. 2001. 'Gender, Poverty, and Nonfarm Employment in Uganda and Ghana', Policy Research Working Paper No. 2367, Development Research Group, World Bank, Washington, DC.

Papola, T. S. 1992. 'Rural Non-Farm Employment: An Assessment of Recent Trends', *Indian Journal of Labour Economics*, 35(3): 238–45.

Papola, T. S. 2005. 'Emerging Structure of Indian Economy: Implications of Growing Inter-Sectoral Imbalances', Presidential Address, 88th Annual Conference, The Indian Economic Association.

Sharma, R. K. and Abraham, Vinoj. 2005. 'The Growth of Service Sector Income and Employment in India a Regional Analysis', *Indian Economic Journal*, 53(3): 3–16.

Part III

Market, trade and institutions

Chapter 12

Nature and extent of yield gaps in principal crops in India

Mondira Bhattacharya[1]

During the past six decades, India's agricultural sector has shown an impressive long-term record of taking the country out of serious food shortages, despite rapid population increase. Foodgrain production increased from 82 million tonnes in 1950–1 to 250 million tonnes in 2011–12. The production of oilseeds, sugarcane and cotton also increased more than fourfold in the same period. The main source of this long run growth was technology-led yield improvement. In order to meet the increasing demands for food due to increasing population and income, food production in India needs to be increased further. However, in recent years there are indications of slowdown in the growth rate of cultivated area, production and yield of principal crops in the country (Table 12.1).

All crops have certain yield potentials. The potential yields of crops are the achievable or attainable yield that are derived through experiments conducted in research stations in various regions across the country by the Indian Council for Agricultural Research (ICAR) and its regional agencies. Crop potentials are derived based on improved technology and the recommended package of practices, which are supposed to be practical and functional in different farm locations. The Frontline Demonstration surveys conducted by the ICAR have found evidences of large gaps in crop yield at the farmers' fields where improved technology has been adopted and what is obtained with the existing practices followed by farmers. This yield gap is mainly caused due to improper extension services, resulting in insufficient know-how of farmers and hence is called 'extension gap'. A study by E. A. Siddiq in the year 2000 showed statewise/regionwise yield gaps for rice in irrigated, semi-irrigated and shallow water rain-fed ecologies. The study presented findings of all India coordinated trials conducted in all the major ecologies in the country, providing the potential yield in those ecological regions.

Table 12.1 Growth rates of area, production and yield (per cent) (2000–1 to 2008–9)

Crops	Area	Production	Yield
Paddy	−0.84	2.25	3.11
Wheat	0.48	1.48	0.99
Maize	2.70	5.94	3.15
Sorghum (Jowar)	−3.07	0.14	3.30
Pearl Millet (Bajra)	−0.25	4.19	4.45
Pigeon Pea (Arhar/Tur)	0.91	1.96	1.04
Red Lentil (Masur)	−0.55	−1.18	−0.64
Bengal Gram (Chana)	4.32	5.62	1.24
Black Gram (Urad)	−0.46	−1.26	−0.80
Green Gram (Moong)	2.25	1.80	−0.44
Sugarcane	1.28	1.28	0.00
Jute	0.62	0.14	−0.48
Cotton	1.23	14.78	13.38
Sunflower	7.22	9.01	1.67
Groundnut	−0.08	2.71	2.80
Rapeseed & Mustard	4.77	7.16	2.28
Soybean	5.74	9.79	3.83
Onion	8.09	11.96	3.59
Potato	4.31	2.64	−1.60
Coconut	0.25	3.75	3.49

Source: Calculated from the data of the Directorate of Economics and Statistics, Department of Agriculture and Cooperation, Ministry of Agriculture, Government of India

Under irrigated ecologies the highest yield gap in rice was seen in Rajasthan (75.6 per cent), followed by Eastern Uttar Pradesh (71.5 per cent) and Bihar (70.2 per cent). The lowest yield gap was seen for Punjab (22 per cent). In rain-fed ecologies, the highest yield gap in rice was seen in Uttar Pradesh and Bihar (around 65 per cent) and the least in West Bengal (32.7 per cent). Another study on crop yield gaps was carried out by the International Crops Research Institute for the Semi-Arid Tropics (ICRISAT) in 2008. The report analysed the yield gaps between actual and potential yields of rice, wheat, mustard and cotton in rain-fed conditions. A crop simulation model known as 'Infocrop' was used to calculate the potential yields of these crops. These models derived the potential yield of crops based on an integrated assessment of the effect of weather, variety, pests, soil and management practices on crop growth and yield. Further, Plant Breeder's Fields and Frontline Demonstrations had also been used as additional measures for obtaining potential yields.

The results showed that there was a considerable yield gap across all states in all the four crops. The yield gap was 1,670 kilograms/hectare for rice, 770 kilograms/hectare for cotton, 460 kilograms/hectare for mustard and 70 kilograms/hectare for wheat. However, these studies did not explain the causes of yield gaps. It is therefore necessary to carry out a comprehensive analysis of the causes of gaps between the potential (achievable) yields of major crops and existing (actual) yields. Bridging such yield gaps through appropriate extension, credit and other support mechanism may help break the present stagnation and put the agricultural sector again on a rapid growth path.

Objectives

The objectives of this study are twofold;

- To examine the yield gaps in 20 principal crops, namely, paddy, wheat, maize, sorghum, pearl millet, lentil, pigeon pea, bengal gram, green gram, black gram, groundnut, rapeseed and mustard, soybean, sunflower, sugarcane, jute, cotton, coconut, onion and potato.
- To identify the crop- and region-specific factors accounting for yield gap, including farm inputs and infrastructural factors, through a factor analysis.

Database

This study is dealt at the secondary and primary level. Secondary data was collected for the latest period for which data was available, that is 2000–1 to 2006–7. The national, state and district-level data on crop yield was collected from the Directorate of Economics and Statistics, Department of Agriculture and Cooperation, Ministry of Agriculture, Government of India. Several other farm and infrastructural variables were collected from the Fertilizer Statistics, Fertilizer Association of India, Indian Meteorological Department, Directorate of Marketing and Inspection, Ministry of Agriculture, National Institute of Agricultural

Extension Management (MANAGE), National Bank of Agriculture and Rural Development, Rural Electrification Corporation Limited and Primary Census Abstract of the Census of India 2001.

In the present study, information on the potential yield of principal crops was obtained from the All India Coordinated Research Projects (AICRPs) conducted by the ICAR that are available in the public domain as well as published reports of Frontline Demonstration projects. The AICRPs had started in the early 1970s, and their mandate was to develop technology for increasing farm productivity. The green revolution in India has been accredited to successful AICRPs. Frontline Demonstration projects started in the mid-1980s and focused on newly released technologies. Potential yields of crops have also been obtained from the 'info-crop simulation models' (Aggarwal *et al.* 2008) and relevant publications such as Mathur & Gupta 1985, Hansra *et al.* 2001, Narula, Reddy, Chougala & Chahal 2007, Ali & Kumar 2008 and Rao 2008. It was observed that information on potential yields was available in a very disaggregate and scattered manner, across certain agroclimatic regions, locations, seasons and crop varieties. These disaggregated potential yields were then aggregated by using appropriate measures of central tendency to arrive at aggregate potential yield figures for each crop at the national, state, district and farm levels.

For the purpose of carrying out this exercise at the primary level, a farm household survey was conducted in four geographical regions of the country, that is north, south, east and west for the agricultural year 2008–9. One representative state was selected from each region on the basis of the largest number of crops that devoted higher proportion of their area to the gross cropped area (GCA) of the state between the years 2000–1 and 2006–7 (Table 12.2). The same criterion was used for the selection of districts in each state. From each district a developed

Table 12.2 States, districts and blocks selected for primary field survey

States	Districts	Developed blocks	Underdeveloped blocks
Uttar Pradesh	Hardoi	Tadiyavan	Kothawan
West Bengal	Burdwan	Memari	Kanksa
Karnataka	Chitradurga	Chitradurga	Hriyur
Maharashtra	Nanded	Deglur	Mukhed

Source: Primary field survey

block and an underdeveloped block were identified through purposive random sampling procedure, based on consultation with agricultural departments in each district. From each selected block a cluster of representative villages was chosen. Further, 50 farmers were chosen from each block, making a total sample size of 400 farming households. The households in each block were divided into three categories based on their area of operation into marginal, small and medium and large farmers. The number of farmers chosen within each farm size category was based on proportional sampling procedure.

Methodology

The yield gap has been calculated as the difference between the potential yield and the actual yield of crops expressed as a percentage and has been interpreted as the opportunity that exists to increase a crop yield from its current level. It also refers to the potential increase in production, if yields within the region rise to the best within that region. The study period were averaged for the years 2000–1 to 2006–7. Three types of yield gaps were calculated, namely:

- Yield Gap I – Difference between Potential Yield (PY) and National Average Yield (NAY)
- Yield Gap II – Difference between Potential Yield (PY) and State Average Yield (SAY)
- Yield Gap III – Difference between Potential Yield (PY) and On-farm Yield (OFY)

To understand the economics of crop production, an analysis of cost of cultivation was undertaken at the farm level. Further, a factor analysis was carried out at the state, district and farm levels to explain the effect of different variables on yield gaps in principal crops in different regions. All variables were taken as triennium averages for the years 2004–5, 2005–6 and 2006–7. A productivity function was carried out for farm inputs on crop yields using secondary data. This was done for each crops at the state level taking all districts within states. Double log function was used in all equations to introduce linearity. It was estimated as follows;

$$CY = f(F, I, R, P) \tag{1}$$

Where

CY = Crop yields (kg/hec)
F = Fertilizer consumption in the crop (tonnes/hec)
I = Crop irrigated area as a percentage of gross irrigated area (%)
R = Average annual rainfall (mms)
P = Farm harvest price of the previous year (Rs/qtl)

A productivity function was carried out for infrastructural inputs on the value of output of total crops cultivated in a state using secondary data. This exercise was done taking all crops together and not separately for individual crops in a state as, generally, infrastructure has an effect on all crops in totality and not separately for different crops. This exercise was done at the state level taking all districts within a state. It was estimated as follows;

$$GVO = f(M, E, RL, C, E) \qquad (2)$$

Where

GVO = Gross value of output of all crops (Rs/hec)
M = Number of regulated markets per GCA
E = Number of electrified villages per GCA
RL = Rural literacy rate (%)
C = Credit supply (Rs/hec)
E = Trained extension workers per GCA

In the primary field survey the productivity functions were estimated for different crops in different study areas and estimated as follows;

$$GVO = f(HL, MLD, S, FER, M, INS, FYM, I) \qquad (3)$$

Where

GVO = Gross value of output (Rs/hec)
HL = Human labour cost (Rs/hec)
ML = Machine labour cost (Rs/hec)
S = Seed costs (Rs/hec)
FER = Fertilizer costs (Rs/hec)
M = Micronutrients costs (Rs/hec)
INS = Insecticide and pesticide costs (Rs/hec)
FYM = Farm yard manure costs (Rs/hec)
I = Irrigation costs (Rs/hec)

Yield gaps in crops at the national level

It is seen from Table 12.3 that yield gap exists for all the principal crops in the country. The potential yield was much higher than actual yield resulting in a high yield gap for all crops. Among cereals, the yield gap was highest for sorghum (212.04 per cent) and lowest for wheat (28.22 per cent). Among pulses, it was highest for green gram (225.41 per cent) and lowest for bengal gram (115.39 per cent). For sugarcane, the

Table 12.3 Yield gaps in principal crops at the national level (Yield Gap I)

Crops	National average yields (Kg/Hec)	Potential yields (Kg/Hec)	Yield gap I (%)
Paddy	2,036.91	4,891.16	140.13
Wheat	2,674.41	3,429.08	28.22
Maize	1,921.33	4,553.75	137.01
Sorghum	780.46	2,435.38	212.04
Pearl Millet	844.05	1,928.24	128.45
Pigeon Pea	641.75	1,469.5	128.98
Red Lentil	653.3	1,448.63	121.74
Bengal Gram	797.25	1,717.2	115.39
Black Gram	430.8	1,375	219.17
Green Gram	353.78	1,151.22	225.41
Sugarcane	64.55 (Tons/Hec)	84.99 (Tons/Hec)	31.66
Jute	2,215.46	2,677.96	20.88
Cotton	395.62 (Kg Lint/ Hec)	989.42 (Kg Lint/ Hec)	150.09
Sunflower	524.11	1,471.92	180.84
Groundnut	1,036.43	1,689.88	63.05
Rapeseed and Mustard	1,043.06	1,297.7	24.41
Soybean	976.23	1,592.28	63.11
Onion	11,829.77	32,286.09	172.92
Potato	17,453.76	27,500	57.56
Coconut	7,032 (Nuts/Hec)	27,000 (Nuts/Hec)	283.97

Source: Calculated from data of the Department of Agriculture and Cooperation, Ministry of Agriculture, Government of India, AICRP and Frontline Demonstration Reports

yield gap was 31.66 per cent. Among fibre crops, it was high for cotton (150.09 per cent) and low for jute (20.88 per cent). Among oilseeds, it was highest for sunflower (180.84 per cent) and lowest for rapeseed and mustard (24.41 per cent). Among vegetables, the yield gap was highest for onion (172.92 per cent) and lower for potato (57.56 per cent). The yield gap for coconut was also quite high at 283.97 per cent.

Cropwise analysis of yield and yield gaps at the state level

Exploratory data analysis showed that in the seven years between 2000–1 and 2006–7, states showing the highest yield gap for different crops were the ones that had the relatively highest proportion of a particular crop area but the lowest yield level. These states and crops have been identified in Table 12.4. It is also observed that most of the crops with high yield gaps were in the states of Uttar Pradesh, West Bengal, Maharashtra and Karnataka. These four states have also been taken up for field surveys. Predominant crops in each of these states have been selected on the basis of area. Thereby, this study shall further focus, on the analysis of yield gaps in principal crops, at the district level within these four states only.

Table 12.5 shows the economic yield gap, that is the difference between the actual net returns and potential net returns, if crop yields were to reach their true potentials. It was seen that the economic yield gap expressed in percentage terms was positive and high for all the crops and highest for sorghum and black gram in Maharashtra, onion and sunflower in Karnataka, and jute in West Bengal. The actual net returns are negative for several crops, but by reaching high potential yields farmers would be in a better position to cover their cost of cultivation and realize profits.

Economics of crop cultivation

The analysis of crop yield gaps at the farm level through primary field surveys showed that in all the four states surveyed, the relatively developed blocks of Tadiyawan in Uttar Pradesh, Memari in West Bengal, Chitradurga in Karnataka and Nanded in Maharashtra showed higher yield levels, higher costs of cultivation and higher net returns per hectare of crops cultivated compared to the underdeveloped blocks. Further most crop yields, costs and net returns per hectare were found to be relatively higher in large size farms compared to small size farms in all the states. From Table 12.6 it is observed that overall the underdeveloped

Table 12.4 States with high area, low yields and high yield gaps

Crops	States with high area and low yield	Proportion of state area to total (%)	Average yield (Kg/Hec) (2000–6)	Potential yield (Kg/Hec)	Yield gap II (%)
Paddy	West Bengal	13.41	2,493.66	4,889.82	96.09
Wheat	Uttar Pradesh	34.69	2,674.92	4,199.89	57.01
Maize	Uttar Pradesh	12.10	1,450.85	4,880.33	236.38
Sorghum	Maharashtra	52.07	772.88	2,345.00	203.41
Pearl Millet	Maharashtra	15.88	684.44	1,910.2	179.01
Pigeon Pea	Maharashtra	29.39	686.34	1,565.76	128.13
Red Lentil	Uttar Pradesh	41.82	758.16	1,781.52	134.98
Bengal Gram	Uttar Pradesh	12.19	939.68	1,847.5	96.61
Green Gram	Maharashtra	21.21	426.99	900.14	110.81
Black Gram	Maharashtra	17.86	472.50	1,375.02	191.01
Sugarcane	Uttar Pradesh	42.62	57.61 (Tons/ Hec)	71.58 (Tons/ Hec)	24.25
Jute	West Bengal	74.00	2,442.74	3,420.08	40.01
Cotton	Maharashtra	34.84	207.74 (Kg Lint/Hec)	1,050.58 (Kg Lint/Hec)	405.73
Sunflower	Karnataka	55.75	391.30	1449.61	270.46
Groundnut	Karnataka	16.23	697.72	1,654	137.06
Rapeseed & Mustard	Uttar Pradesh	14.34	1,010.82	1,297.77	28.39
Soybean	Maharashtra	24.58	1,140.64	1,614.73	41.56
Onion	Karnataka	25.26	5,391.20	4,2370.00	685.91
Potato	Uttar Pradesh	32.39	22,312.24	27,499.84	23.25
Coconut	Karnataka	19.51	4,076 (Nuts/ Hec)	14,550 (Nuts/ Hec)	256.97

Source: Calculated from the data of the Department of Agriculture and Cooperation, Ministry of Agriculture, Government of India, AICRP and Frontline Demonstration Reports

Table 12.5 Economic yield gap

(i) Crops	(ii) States with high area and low yield	(iii) Average yield (Kg/Hec) (TE-2006)	(iv) Potential yield (Kg/Hec)	(v) Cost of cultivation (Rs/Hec) (TE-2006)	(vi) Gross returns (Rs/Hec) (TE-2006)	(vii) Actual net returns (Rs/Hec) (vi–v)	(viii) Gross returns with potential yields (Rs/Hec)*	(ix) Potential net returns (Rs/Hec) (viii–v)	(x) Economic yield gap (%) ((ix–vii)/vii)*100
Paddy	West Bengal	3,663.67	4,889.82	25,508.48	23,684.24	–1,824.24	31,610.82	6,102.34	435
Wheat	Uttar Pradesh	2,993.33	4,199.89	23,054.70	26,919.89	3,865.19	37,770.85	14,716.15	281
Maize	Uttar Pradesh	1,759.00	4,880.37	13,242.81	10,703.28	–2,539.53	29,696.39	16,453.58	748
Sorghum	Maharashtra	1,296.33	2,345.00	13,267.77	13,026.68	–241.09	23,564.60	10,296.83	4,371
Pearl Millet	Maharashtra	1,510.67	1,909.66	12,862.09	11,630.43	–1,231.66	14,702.17	1,840.08	249
Pigeon Pea	Maharashtra	1,057.67	1,565.76	17,530.01	19,737.03	2,207.02	29,218.37	11,688.36	430
Red Lentil	Uttar Pradesh	804.67	1,781.52	13,219.42	15,592.24	2,372.82	34,520.93	21,301.51	798
Bengal Gram	Uttar Pradesh	1,076.67	1,847.50	14,310.85	20,779.71	6,468.86	35,656.81	21,345.96	230
Green Gram	Maharashtra	376.00	900.14	11,258.70	8,699.70	–2,559.00	2,0826.91	9,568.21	474

Black Gram	Maharashtra	401.00	1,375.02	11,403.62	9,837.54	−1,566.08	33,732.76	22,329.14	1,526
Sugarcane	Uttar Pradesh	555.21	715.80	39,646.15	66,191.39	26,545.24	85,337.22	45,691.07	72
Jute	West Bengal	2,424.00	3,420.08	28,122.28	29,165.81	1,043.53	41,150.75	13,028.47	1,148
Cotton	Maharashtra	976.33	1,050.60	21,361.82	21,000.00	−361.82	22,597.56	1,235.74	442
Sunflower	Karnataka	455.00	1,449.61	8,874.42	8,032.92	−841.50	25,592.53	16,718.11	2,087
Groundnut	Karnataka	592.33	1,654.02	13,362.30	11,282.12	−2,080.18	31,504.05	18,141.75	972
Rapeseed & Mustard	Uttar Pradesh	1,281.67	1,297.79	16,314.96	21,295.93	4,980.97	21,563.81	5,248.85	5
Soybean	Maharashtra	1,271.67	1,614.69	16,251.63	15,670.38	−581.25	19,897.30	3,645.67	727
Onion	Karnataka	8,886.00	42,370.00	19,505.93	23,102.88	3,596.95	110,158.57	90,652.64	2,420
Potato	Uttar Pradesh	19,962.00	27,499.84	50,396.20	76,699.21	26,303.01	105,661.56	55,265.36	110
Coconut	Karnataka	4,076.00	14,550.10	30,000.00	57,000.00	27,000.00	203,472.90	173,472.90	542

Source: Calculated from the data of the Department of Agriculture and Cooperation, Ministry of Agriculture, Government of India, AICRP and Frontline Demonstration Reports

*Gross Returns with Potential Yields = Potential Yields * Farm Harvest Price

Table 12.6 Crop yield gaps at farm level (per cent)

Uttar Pradesh – Hardoi District

Blocks	Farm size	Crops													
		Pigeon Pea	Pearl Millet	Black Gram	Bengal Gram	Ground-nut	Sorghum	Red Lentil	Maize	Mustard	Onion	Potato	Sugar-cane	Wheat	Paddy
Tadiyavan (Developed)	Marginal	15.24	−1.89	153.4	15.5	69.93	154.61	120.7	153.41	−1.14	92.08	30.5	8.31	2.47	−14.35
	Small	10.22	−11.52	132.57	10.68	67.52	117.49	113.15	139.98	−5.94	89.47	35.84	2.51	−2.54	−19.13
	Medium and Large	20.43	−12.2	74.91	7.59	45.02	78.93	53.51	115.34	−10.95	80.79	27.18	−0.83	−1.84	−29.73
	Total	**16.38**	**−11.06**	**99.66**	**8.91**	**55.82**	**100.28**	**75.07**	**129.3**	**−7.92**	**86.09**	**30.01**	**0.56**	**−1.25**	**−24.56**
Kothavan (Under developed)	Marginal	45.88	14.61	209.02	84.8	211.17	275.94	202.6	184.87	25.19	100.5	53.51	13.65	11.06	3.73
	Small	50.62	7.89	195.18	73.68	181.99	230.06	185.94	161.84	10.65	93.55	68.88	11.36	3.44	−11.13
	Medium and Large	53.91	1.94	135.82	48.25	133.03	195.54	152.49	147.72	−0.58	89.47	62.72	3.62	0.42	−16.85
	Total	**50.62**	**3.61**	**159.52**	**54.67**	**164.27**	**222.43**	**171.61**	**162**	**10**	**96.39**	**61.67**	**6.65**	**3.48**	**−11.3**
Grand Total		**29.43**	**−3.84**	**130**	**31.64**	**95.88**	**149.08**	**110.02**	**144.34**	**1.78**	**90.76**	**43.5**	**2.81**	**0.98**	**−19.06**

Table 12.6 — (Cont'd) Crop yield gaps at farm level (per cent) West Bengal – Burdwan District

Blocks	Farm size	Crops								
		Groundnut	Mustard	Potato	Jute	Wheat	Paddy Aman	Paddy Boro	Paddy Kharif	Paddy Rabi
Memari	Marginal		29.4	11.18			23.83		31.11	
(Developed)	Small		17.3	10.69			2.47		3.49	
	Medium & Large		8.77	5.14	2.14		–11.86		–9.7	
	Total		**12.92**	**7.48**	**2.14**		**–0.92**		**–4.39**	
Kanksa	Marginal	273.9	76.45	60.16			45.8	50.84	51.04	
(Under	Small		61.75	44.6		130	33.02	19.22	21.98	25.38
developed)	Medium and Large	191.33	42.08	63.04		53.33	7.47	8.81	9.4	
	Total	**221.91**	**57**	**52.6**		**79.32**	**23.55**	**13.55**	**15.29**	**25.38**
Grand Total		**221.91**	**24.32**	**15.69**	**2.14**	**79.32**	**10.24**	**13.55**	**3.7**	**25.38**

(Continued)

Table 12.6 — (Cont'd) Crop yield gaps at farm level (per cent) Karnataka – Chitradurga District

Blocks	Farm size	Crops								
		Coconut	Cotton	Bengal Gram	Groundnut	Sorghum	Maize	Onion	Sunflower	Wheat
Chitradurga (Developed)	Small		2.12					344.75		228.36
	Medium and Large		3.47	60		212.51	54.51	308.12	37.43	183.8
	Total		**1.82**	**60**		**212.51**	**54.51**	**309.65**	**37.43**	**188.5**
Hriyur (Under developed)	Small		25.33		230.8	383.85		391.17	132.44	502
	Medium and Large	482			170.04	312.46		373.17	97.52	
	Total	**482**	**25.33**		**170.72**	**322.86**		**374.43**	**98.89**	**502**
Grand Total		**482**	**0.16**	**60**	**170.72**	**259.86**	**54.51**	**336.01**	**76.77**	**200.07**

Table 12.6 — (Cont'd) Crop yield gaps at farm level (per cent) Maharashtra – Nanded District

Blocks	Farm size	Crops										
		Pigeon Pea	Pearl Millet	Black Gram	Cotton	Green Gram	Groundnut	Sorghum	Soybean	Sugarcane	Sunflower	Wheat
Deglur (Developed)	Marginal	75.56						109.79			77	
	Small	63.61			48.83			87.16	17.23			
	Medium and Large	58.09	27.33	129.17	35.24	20.93	30.15	63.99	2.67	96.43	45.86	200.88
	Total	**61.23**	**27.33**	**129.17**	**35.95**	**20.93**	**30.15**	**79.74**	**4.57**	**96.43**	**49.34**	**200.88**
Mukhed (Under-developed)	Marginal	136.02		189.47		104		181.59	169			
	Small	134.1		218.74	123.25	79.41		160.24	36.05		141.67	
	Medium and Large	87.21		164.21	64.88	52.3	50.74	111.66	21.9	120	104.23	261.75
	Total	**99.39**		**182.59**	**67.24**	**65.95**	**50.74**	**128.72**	**25.87**	**120**	**109.17**	**261.75**
Grand Total		**78**	**27.33**	**170.62**	**43.97**	**48.06**	**39.59**	**103.3**	**13.31**	**102.63**	**67.33**	**230.42**

Source: Calculations based on primary field survey

blocks of Kothawan in Uttar Pradesh, Kanksa in West Bengal, Hriyur in Karnataka and Mukhed in Maharashtra showed higher yield gap for most crops compared to developed blocks and the crop yield gap of marginal and small farmers was also found to be higher than that of medium and large farmers. This means that resource constraints restrain realization of higher yield in underdeveloped regions and lower farm size groups. Further, for some crops like pearl, millet and paddy, specifically in the selected survey district of Uttar Pradesh, the yield gaps show a negative sign which means that farmers' actual crop yields for these crops were greater than potential yields.

From Table 12.7, it is seen that Yield Gap III (difference between potential yield and on-farm yield) for principal crops in the selected

Table 12.7 Yield Gaps II and III – difference between potential yields and state average yields and potential yields and farm yields (per cent)

States	Crops	Yield Gap II (potential yield – state average yield %)	Yield Gap III (potential yield – on farm yield %)
West Bengal	**Jute**	40.01	2.14
	Paddy	96.09	13.21
Uttar Pradesh	**Sugarcane**	24.25	2.81
	Potato	23.25	43.5
	Red Lentil	134.98	110.02
	Wheat	57.01	0.98
	Rapeseed and Mustard	28.39	1.78
	Bengal Gram	96.61	31.64
	Maize	236.38	144.34
Maharashtra	**Sorghum**	203.41	103.3
	Cotton	405.73	43.9
	Pigeon Pea	128.13	78
	Soybean	41.56	13.31
	Black Gram	191.01	170.62
	Green Gram	110.81	48.06
	Pearl Millet	179.01	27.33

States	Crops	Yield Gap II (potential yield – state average yield %)	Yield Gap III (potential yield – on farm yield %)
Karnataka	**Sunflower**	270.46	76.77
	Onion	685.91	336.01
	Coconut	256.97	482
	Groundnut	137.06	170.72

Source: As in Table 12.4 and Table 12.6

states is much lesser than Yield Gap II (difference between potential yield and state average yield). Exceptions are in the case of potato in Uttar Pradesh and coconut and groundnut in Karnataka. Yield Gap III is found to be generally lesser because Yield Gap II was calculated on the basis of the triennium ending 2006–7, while Yield Gap III was calculated on the basis of survey data pertaining to the agricultural year 2008–9. Hence, over two years, the crops yields seem to have increased, thereby reducing the yield gaps for most crops.

Factors constraining crop yields and yield gaps and recommendations to bridge yield gaps

The factors that are significantly constraining crop yields, thereby increasing yield gaps in principal crops in the various states were arrived at by comparing regression exercises based on secondary data across districts as well as primary field survey analysis in the four selected states. The identified yield constraining, crop- and region-specific factors warrant a serious effort to find appropriate technical and developmental remedies.

At the very outset it is important to note that the R squares in the regressions based on secondary data are much lower than those based on primary data (Table 12.8). This is because variables taken in the regressions based on secondary data are subject to lot of modifications, and there is also lack of availability of data for certain variables. For example fertilizer consumption data is not provided cropwise in every region. It has to be derived as follows *(Crop Area/Gross Cropped Area * Fertilizer Consumption of the Region)*. Such modifications are necessary wherever data is not available, but they also tend to dilute the robustness

Table 12.8 Farm factors influencing and constraining crop yields (elasticity coefficients)

States	Crops	Fertilizer consumption (tons/hec)	Crop irrigated area as a % of Gross Irrigated Area (GIA)	Average annual rainfall (mms)	Farm harvest price of the previous year (Rs/Qtl)	R square	Expenditure on human labour (Rs/hec)	Expenditure on machine labour (Rs/hec)	Expenditure on Fertilizer (Rs/Hec)	Expenditure on irrigation (Rs/hec)	Expenditure on seed (Rs/hec)	Expenditure on micronutrients (Rs/hec)	Expenditure on insecticides and pesticides (Rs/hec)	Expenditure on farm yard manure (Rs/hec)	R square
		District level regressions (secondary data)					Farm level regressions (primary data)								
West Bengal	Paddy	0.2	0.11	−0.56***	0.16	0.83	0.65***	0.94***	0.64***	0.11***	0.40***	0.0001	−0.75***	1.12***	0.99
	Jute	−0.05	0.06	−0.45***	0.15	0.56									
Uttar Pradesh	Wheat	0.225	0.06	−0.29*	0.02	0.56	0.15***	0.33***	0.29***	0.06**	−0.05	0.0001	−0.02	0.02***	0.99
	Maize	−0.08	0.3	−0.1	0.35	0.4	0.56***	1.01***	0.19***	0.19***	−0.33*	0.001	−0.11***	0.08**	0.996
	Red Lentil	−0.09	0.06	−0.21*	0.05	0.3	−0.52***	0.13***	0.14***	−0.23***	1.09***			0.05***	0.998
	Bengal Gram	−0.08	−0.003	−0.19*	0.33	0.25	−0.28	−1.53	−0.08	0.02	2.37***		−1.72***	0.97*	0.998
	Sugarcane	0.16	0.24	−0.03	0.04	0.64	0.21***	0.43***	0.06***	0.06***	0.002	0.0001	−0.005	0.01**	0.998
	Rapeseed & Mustard	−0.17	0.4	−0.16	0.26	0.33	0.43***	0.53***	0.19***	0.33***	−0.46***	0.001	0.24***	−0.09***	0.996
	Potato	0.3	−0.21	−0.09	0.102	0.32	−0.13***	2.37***	0.60***	0.04***	2.83***	0.001	−0.94	0.51	0.994
Maharashtra	Sorghum	−0.49**	−0.03	−0.39	0.88*	0.5	0.56***	2.45***	−0.03	0.17***	0.65***	0.001		0.07**	0.996
	Pearl Millet	0.28		−0.15	0.04	0.37									
	Pigeon Pea	0.22*	0.04	0.07	1.36**	0.57		8.85***	0.03		−0.13		0.30**	0.75***	0.994
	Black Gram	0.03	0.002	0.54***		0.55	1.004	0.19	0.95	−0.14	1.2		0.58	−1.18	0.964

	Green Gram / Crop												
	Green Gram	-0.23	-0.03	0.19		0.4	-3.68**	1.86	5.08*	0.003	-3.54	-0.08	-0.13	0.985
	Cotton	-0.02	0.03	0.04	-0.16	0.08	0.83***	3.17***	0.58***	-0.003	-0.15	0.94***	-0.16***	0.99
	Soybean	-0.15		0.114		0.35	0.58***	2.27***	0.36***	-0.09	0.48	-0.13***	1.95***	0.997
Karnataka	**Sunflower**	-0.29	-0.02	0.32	0.14	0.52	-0.005	0.60***	0.48***	0.05**	0.06	0.18		0.99
	Groundnut	-0.13	-0.02	0.59***	0.006	0.79	-4.23	2.4	0.9	0.75**	0.14***	-1.82		0.97
	Onion	-0.32**		-0.05		0.41	0.53***	0.16***	0.13	0.01	0.04	0.19***	-3.21***	0.99
	Coconut	-0.21*	-0.17	-0.1		0.44								

***Statistically significant at 1% level, **statistically significant at 5% level, *statistically significant at 10% level

of the model. Further data is not available for all variables that explain crop yields. Such problems are not encountered in the primary data, and hence the model tends to be stronger in the latter case.

Table 12.8 shows the farm factors affecting crop yields. It was found that fertilizer consumption and expenditure on fertilizer showed a significant negative relationship with crop yields in the case of onion and coconut in Karnataka and sorghum in Maharashtra. This shows that unbalanced use of fertilizer is constraining crop yields, and hence balanced use of fertilizers is required for these particular crops in both the states.

Rainfall showed significant negative relationship with crop yields of paddy and jute in West Bengal and wheat, red lentil and bengal gram in Uttar Pradesh. This shows the erratic and insufficient nature of rainfall received by these particular crops in these regions. Hence, there is a need to propagate both flood- as well as drought-resistant varieties of these crops in these states. It is recommended that one single department must be designated to maintain sufficient and systematic hydraulic data. This data would enable demarcation of the chronically drought-/flood-affected areas and the nature and the change in such areas over time. Further, rainwater harvesting technologies should also be exploited, which could be of help during periods of drought. Similarly, improper water management in terms of inadequate number of irrigations significantly affected yields of red lentils in Uttar Pradesh.

Ineffectiveness of pesticides and insecticides emerged as a major hindrance to crop yields of paddy in West Bengal, maize and bengal gram in Uttar Pradesh and soybean in Maharashtra. Hence, appropriate and effective pest management is required for these crops.

Unavailability of high-yielding quality seeds significantly affected yield of wheat, rapeseed and mustard and maize in Uttar Pradesh. Hence, there is an imperative need for provision of high-yielding variety of seeds for these crops in these regions.

Improper application of farmyard manure significantly affected yields of rapeseed and mustard in Uttar Pradesh, cotton in Maharashtra and onion in Karnataka. Hence, balanced application of farmyard manure is required for these crops in these regions.

Further, micronutrients such as iron, manganese, boron, zinc, copper, molybdenum and chlorine are essential nutrients that have an influence on crop yield. During the field survey in all four states, it was found that only 39 per cent farmers had used micronutrients in crop cultivation. However, in Uttar Pradesh all farmers and in West Bengal 55 per cent farmers had used micronutrients. None of the farmers in Karnataka and

Maharashtra reported use of any micronutrient. Micronutrients showed a positive though statistically non-significant relationship with crop yield of wheat, maize, rapeseed and mustard, potato and sugarcane in Uttar Pradesh and only paddy in West Bengal.

To see the effect of infrastructural and non-farm factors on crop yields, indicators such as regulated markets, electrified villages, extension services, rural credit and rural literacy rates were regressed on the total value of output per hectare of principal crops, at the district level in each of the selected states (Table 12.9). These indicators were based on secondary data. It was found that rural literacy rate significantly constrained the principal crop yields in the states of Uttar Pradesh. Rural literacy constrains crop productivity, presumably due to lack of interest on the part of literate youth in farming because agriculture is becoming a non-profitable occupation now. Thus, there is an imperative need for agriculture to be made intellectually stimulating and an economically viable option for young people.

Inaccessibility to regulated markets acted as impediments, though statistically non-significant, towards yields of principal crops of West Bengal and Maharashtra. Hence, associated infrastructural facilities like road connectivity and transportation should be improved in these states.

Inaccessibility to electrified sources of irrigation like pumpsets hindered yields of principal crops in West Bengal and Uttar Pradesh, though here too the relationship was statistically non-significant. Hence, appropriate water management through adequate number of irrigations is required. Further, better accessibility to electrified irrigation sources

Table 12.9 Elasticity coefficients of infrastructural factors affecting crop yields

States	Credit supply (Rs/Hec)	Regulated markets/ GCA	Electrified villages/ GCA	Extension workers/ GCA	Literacy rate (%)	R square
West Bengal	0.38	−0.11	−0.12	0.003	−0.58	0.41
Uttar Pradesh	0.36***	0.02	−0.02	0.08	−0.41***	0.56
Maharashtra	0.034	−0.12	0.001	−0.25***	0.8*	0.46
Karnataka	0.35***	0.28	0.28***	−0.39	0.018	0.91

Source: Calculations based on primary field survey

***Statistically significant at 1% level, **statistically significant at 5% level, *statistically significant at 10% level

like electric pumpsets is required for increasing these crop yields. Access to electricity for irrigation is important as it reduces the cost of irrigation as compared to diesel-operated pumpsets.

Extension services significantly constrained yields of principal crops in Maharashtra. The relationship between trained extension workers and crop yields in these particular states showed a significant negative relationship, which indicates inefficiency of trained extension workers. They seem to be diverted more towards other activities than their own work of imparting knowledge of new technology, inputs, etc. to farmers. Usually these workers are made to work on Census/Election operations and the like or show farmlands to important delegates when they come to pay a visit. Hence, these people seem to be diverted from their actual work of providing extension services which impacts crop yields. Hence, the system of providing extension services needs to be revamped and made efficient on an immediate basis.

Conclusions

From the study, it is seen that yield gaps in physical terms exist for all principal crops in the country, mainly because potential yields are much higher than actual yields, resulting in high yield gap for all crops. Second, yield gaps in value terms, that is the economic yield gap is positive and high for all crops in all the states meaning that the actual net returns that farmers receive from crop cultivation are much lower than the potential net returns that they could receive if crop yields realized their true potential. Third, from the field survey it was seen that underdeveloped regions showed higher yield gap for all crops compared to developed regions, and the crop yield gap of marginal and small farmers was found to be higher than medium and large farmers. This means that resource constraints restrain realization of higher yield in underdeveloped regions and lower farm size groups. Further, a factor analysis identified, several location-specific factors that had kept the crop yields and productivity low in several places, thereby increasing the yield gaps. However, many of these factors were common everywhere. Significant among these were the unbalanced use of fertilizers, lack of use of high-yielding quality seeds, inadequate use of manures and micronutrients, inefficient and poor water management, lack of proper marketing arrangements in the neighbourhood, lower access to electrified irrigation sources, inefficient extension services and less interest in agriculture. All these factors resulted in improper crop management and farming practices, which have to be addressed. Many of these lacunae could automatically get removed if extension services were revamped and supportive infrastructure services were strengthened and rendered more efficient. Research should incorporate properly farmers' constraints to high crop yields and productivity and provide farmers with appropriate technological packages for specific locations to bridge the yield gaps. Moreover, institutional and policy support to farmers is crucial for ensuring agricultural input supplies, farm credit, price incentives and adequate marketing systems in a holistic manner for increased crop productivity on a sustainable basis.

Note

1 The author acknowledges the funding support from National Bank for Agriculture and Rural Development (NABARD) to Council for Social Development (CSD), New Delhi for taking up this work under the project titled 'An Economic Analysis of Yield Gaps in Principal Crops in Various Regions of India' (Unpublished Project Report) in 2011. Sincerest thanks are due to Dr. T. Haque (Director, CSD) for his erudite guidance. The author also thanks CSD staff for their help.

References

Aggarwal, P. K., Hebbar, K. B., Venugopalan, M. V., Rani, S., Bala, A., Biswal, A. and Wani, S. P. 2008. 'Quantification of Yield Gaps in Rain-fed Rice, Wheat, Cotton and Mustard in India', Global Theme on Agro-ecosystems, Report No. 43, ICRISAT, Patancheru, Andhra Pradesh, India. http://www.iwmi.cgiar.org/assessment/files_new/publications/ICRI-SATReport43.pdf (accessed on 12 June 2014)

Ali, Masood and Kumar, Shiv. 2008. 'Wide Array of Important Varieties', in N. Ram (ed), *The Hindu Survey of Indian Agriculture*, Section 2 Pulses, Kasturi & Sons Ltd: Chennai.

Hansra, B. S, Das, S. K., Sudhakar, N. and Rajender Reddy, G. 2001. 'Performance of Frontline Demonstrations on Pulses (1999–2000)', Division of Agricultural Extension, Indian Council of Agricultural Research, Krishi Anusandhan Bhawan, Pusa, New Delhi.

Haque, T. and Bhattacharya, Mondira. 2011. 'An Economic Analysis of Yield Gaps in Principal Crops in Various Regions of India', Unpublished Project Report, Council for Social Development, New Delhi.

Mathur, P. N. and Gupta, M. P. 1985. 'National Demonstrations Project – An Overview', Publications and Information Division, Indian Council of Agricultural Research, New Delhi.

Narula, A. M., Rajender Reddy, G., Chougala, Shashi Kumar, and Chahal, V. P. 2007. 'Frontline Demonstration on Cotton, Technology Mission on Cotton, Mini Mission II', Division of Agricultural Extension, Indian

Council of Agricultural Research, Krishi Anusandhan Bhawan, Pusa, New Delhi.

Rao, M. V. 2008. 'Several Constraints in Increasing Productivity', in N. Ram (ed), *The Hindu Survey of Indian Agriculture*, Section 2 Oilseeds, Kasturi & Sons Ltd: Chennai.

Siddiq, E. A. 2000. 'Bridging the Rice Yield Gap in India', Bridging the Rice Yield Gap in the Asia-Pacific Region, Bangkok, Thailand. http://www.fao.org/docrep/003/X6905e/x6905e09.htm (accessed on 12 June 2014)

Chapter 13

Performance of participatory irrigation management in Odisha

A study of Pani Panchayats in two irrigation projects

Bibhu Prasad Nayak and S. Manasi[1]

Participatory irrigation management (PIM) has emerged as a popular institutional approach worldwide for the efficient management of irrigation water and field structures of irrigation systems. These decentralized institutions emphasized the greater involvement of farmers and other stakeholders in the process of decision-making as well as management of irrigation water (Ostrom 1990; Vermillion 1997). Over the past few decades, the policy discourse in India too emphasized such decentralized management of water and promotion of PIM institutions. The National Water Policy 1987 for the first time advocated for the participation of users in the management of water resources. Subsequent policy changes in the centre as well as in the states have facilitated the emergence of water user associations (WUAs) as formal institutions for stakeholders involvement in addressing the problems related to operation and maintenance (O&M) of irrigation systems and low irrigation efficiency (Ghosh 2009; Marothia 2005; Parthasarathy 2000; Raju 2000). Several states have enacted legislations and as of 2008–9, there were 56,539 WUAs covering an area of 13.156 million hectares (GoI 2009). Under this participatory regime, a part of the management responsibilities such as water delivery, canal maintenance and fixing the water fee are delegated to the WUAs, while the authority of final approval of O&M plans and budgets lies with the government. The extent of delegation varies across the states depending upon the policy of the respective states.

Different studies have developed indicators and frameworks for the performance assessment of irrigation systems. Rao (1993), based on an extensive review of literature, advocates certain indicators for irrigation performance assessment in terms of three broad categories, that is water delivery system, irrigated agriculture system and agricultural economic system. Indicators such as adequacy, timeliness and equity in respect of water distribution are performance indicators of the water delivery system. Agricultural performance indicators include cropping intensity, ratio of area planned and area harvested, annual yield, productivity of land and water. Economic indicators like gross revenue from crop production, gross value added, net income for farmers and average labour productivity are used for performance assessment. Apart from these indicators, the review also highlighted sustainability indicators, systemic descriptors and process indicators, and social indicators.

Gorantiwar *et al.* (2005) developed a framework for performance assessment of irrigation water management across heterogeneous irrigation schemes. His framework takes into account seven indicators for assessing performance under two broad groups, that is allocative measures (productivity and equity) and scheduling measures (adequacy, reliability, flexibility, sustainability and efficiency). In another study, Bos *et al.* (1994) classified the performance indicators into water supply performance, agricultural performance, economic, social and environmental performance (Bos *et al.* 1994).

The socio-economic composition of the WUAs also reflects the democratic structure of the community institutions and influences the participation of the users in the collective action. Such community-based organizations are often vulnerable to elite capture (Iversen *et al.* 2006; Platteau and Gaspart 2004). Such dominance could be due to the fact that it's convenient for the government officials or officials of the donor agencies to interact with the wealthy and influential in the community, as they exercise greater control of others or may be due to the fact that these elites often take the lead in such activities. There are also several other factors like social capital, group size, homogeneity, leadership, etc. that explain the success or failure of any specific PIM institutions (Meizen-Dick *et al.* 1997).

The outcome of this decentralized management is mixed and varies across states and also across the regions within the state. Though several thousands of WUAs are formed to facilitate stakeholder participation, they have been very effective managing irrigation systems for different factors like inadequate understanding of institutional issues in PIM on the part of the irrigation administrators, top-down management approach, half-hearted implementation, lack of users' participation in decision-making, etc. (Marothia 2005; Pant 1999; Parthasarathy 2000; Reddy and Reddy 2005; Upadhay 2002). There have not been adequate institutional and operational innovations at the grass-roots level to promote efficient management of irrigation and sustainability of these participatory institutions though legislative measures were initiated at the state level (Ghosh 2009; Marothia 2005; Pant 2008; Paranjape and Joy 2003; Reddy and Reddy 2005; Saleth 1999; Selvarajan 2001).

This chapter makes an attempt to analyse the performance of the *Pani Panchayats* (PPs) based on some of the indicators like institutional dynamics of PPs, quality of O&M, financial performance, participation in collective action and institutional sustainability of these participatory institutions. The chapter is organized as follows – the second section of the chapter discusses the status of PIM institutions, known as PPs in the State of Odisha, the initiatives of the government and issues pertaining to their implementation in the state. The third section briefly discusses the study area and methodology of the study. The fourth section analyses the performance and functioning of PPs in the study area based on the finding from field surveys in two irrigation projects covering 64 PPs. The conclusion of the chapter is presented in the fifth section.

Pani Panchayat and irrigation management in Odisha

In consonance with the PIM guidelines of the central government, the state government also initiated required policy reforms to involve farmers and other stakeholders in the management of the irrigation water. Odisha's State Water Policy of 1994 paved the way for PIM implementation with the transfer of irrigation management to the farmers in all major, medium, minor and lift irrigation projects and drainage systems in the state. PIM evolved in the state with the enactment of the Odisha[2] Pani Panchayat Bill, 2002. The first initiative towards PIM was the Odisha Water Resources Consolidation Project (OWRCP) launched in 1996 with funding from the World Bank in which the Farmers' Organization and Turnover (FOT) programme was a major component (GoO 2009). FOT included the handing over of the management of the canal system, minors and sub-minors to WUAs with the responsibility of collecting water taxes, distribution of canal water and O&M. Based on the experience of the pilot projects under this programme, the state government extended PIM to all the irrigation and drainage projects following a government resolution under its Scheme for Pani Panchayat (GoO 2000). The WUAs formed under this Pani Panchayat scheme were institutionalized as legal entities after the enactment of The Odisha Pani Panchayat Act, 2002, by the Government of Odisha in 2002, and the existing WUAs were reregistered as *Pani Panchayat* under the new act.

The Odisha Pani Panchayat Act, 2002, contained legal provisions for the autonomous management of irrigation systems by farmer organizations called (PPs) with regard to the maintenance and distribution of irrigation water (Odisha Gazette 2002). This Act was complemented by the Odisha Pani Panchayat Rules, 2003, which specified the operational rules of PP formation and functioning (Odisha Gazette 2002). The PPs were formed by the farmers within a hydraulically delineated block of 300 hectares to 600 hectares with the assistance of the state irrigation department. The responsibility of O&M of the tertiary irrigation systems (below minor/sub-minor) was vested with the PPs, whereas the responsibilities for managing O&M of all other systems rested with the irrigation department. Further, the government decided to give a grant-in-aid of Rs. 35 per acre, which was later increased to Rs. 100 per acre to PPs for O&M of these tertiary irrigation systems in their respective command areas. The Odisha Pani Panchayat Act, 2002, was amended in 2008 to make it more inclusive by including other stakeholders like fishermen and extending the tenure of the elected body from three to six years (Odisha Gazette 2009).

The PP in Odisha consists of a three-tier structure with three statutory bodies (Pani Panchayat, Distributory Committee, Project/Apex Committee) at three different levels and one informal body (Chak Committee). The general body of the farmers from each *chak* (command area of each irrigation outlet) elects or nominates three members representing the head, middle and tail reach of the *chak*. So the number of *chak* committee members in a PP depends upon the number of authorized irrigation outlets in the territory of the PP. These chak committee members within the PP elect the president, secretary and treasurer, and the Executive Committee (EC) of the PP contains one member from each chak. Once the PPs are formed in the region, they can federate themselves to form Distributary Committees (DCs) at the distributary level and Apex/Project Committee (ACs/PCs) level. The president, secretary and treasurers of all the PPs in a distributary form the general body of the DC and elect the office bearers of the DC. The AC/PC is also formed on similar lines by the office bearers of the DCs within the irrigation project once all the DCs are formed with elected members. At all levels of these farmer organizations, the officials of departments concerned like water resources, agriculture and revenue also serve as members without voting rights. The organizational structure of PPs in Odisha is presented in Figure 13.1.

There has been a significant achievement in terms of the formation of PPs in the state. There were 18,622 PPs with a command area of 17,72,732 hectares in the state as on March 2010. All these PPs are formed and registered as per the provisions of the PP Act, 2002. The details of the progress are presented in Table 13.1. The number increased to 21,447, managing 18,32,393 hectares by the end of March 2013. However, the delineation of the PP area as well as the official handover

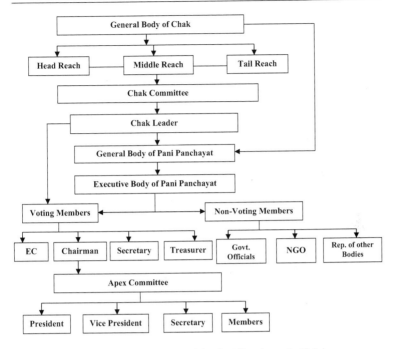

Figure 13.1 Organizational structure of the Pani Panchayat in Odisha

Source: Mahapatra (2006)

of irrigation systems to the PPs are yet to be completed with regard to all the PPs in the state. As per the sources of the Directorate of CAD-PIM, Government of Odisha, elections for the ECs of PP were held only for 16,500 PPs in the state during 2009.

The state government supports the PIM by providing grant-in-aid to PPs, organizing various training for capacity development of WUA leaders, undertaking awareness campaigns to popularize PIM among farmers and few other incentives. A grant-in-aid of Rs. 100 per hectare for O&M to PPs which have registered 75 per cent or more farmers in the PP command area as members of PPs was initiated. This grant continues up to five years upon successful increase in the membership of PPs. After five years, the policy suggests a grant proportional to the water fees collected by the PPs in the previous financial year. Although the first part of this provision is partially working, the government does not have an action plan for implementing the second provision of proportional grant

Table 13.1 Status of PPs in Odisha (as on 30 March 2010)

Sl No	Projects	Total programmed		Handed over to PPs		Delineation completed		PP formed as per PP Act and rules	
		Nos	Area (ha)	Nos	Area (ha)	Nos	Area (ha)	Nos	Area (ha)
1	Major and Medium	2,565	1,124,158	1,569	6,79,136	2,565	11,24,158	2,565	1,128,600
2	Minor (Flow)	1,883	328,293	1,883	325,833	1,883	328,293	1,883	328,293
3	Minor (Lift) OLIC	15,103	335,788	14,567	325,005	14,046	314,631	14,174	315,839
	Grand Total	19,551	1,788,239	18,019	1,329,974	18,494	1,767,082	18,622	1,772,732

Source: Directorate of CAD-PIM, Government of Odisha, Bhubaneswar

for PPs. As it is evident from Table 13.2, only a few PPs in the state are receiving grants-in-aid from the government for O&M.

The Government of Odisha also formulated various guidelines to incentivize PPs. For instance, each of the registered PPs can take up works up to a maximum limit of Rs. 3 lakhs under Mahatma Gandhi National Rural Employment Guarantee Act (MGNREGA) for taking up repairs and maintenance of minor and sub-minor canals through PPs (GoO 2008). Similarly, schemes like *Biju Krushak Vikask Yojana* (BKVY) emphasize user involvement in the minor irrigation sector (flow as well as lift) in backward regions of the state from inception and provide subsidies on capital costs of irrigation systems managed by PPs (GoO 2009).

The government has also made provisions for the construction of Pani Panchayat buildings for each PP by the MP and MLA local area development (LAD) funds if a PP satisfies some criteria like carrying out regular O&M activities, enrolment of more than 80 per cent of the farmers as members of PPs and also if the collection of water fees in the past three years accounts for more than 75 per cent of the demand. However, there are no statistics available of PPs availing of this provision for constructing buildings. The government has also made provisions by assigning the PPs with the responsibility of procuring paddy from farmers at government prices (Minimum Support Price) after the harvest so as to prevent distress selling; the PPs can also sell the procured paddy to the Food Corporation of India (FCI) at government prices (GoO 2009).

The implementation of PIM in Odisha is still in its infancy with differential outcomes across irrigation projects in the state. There is a huge gap between the PIM policy and its implementation. The 2008 amendment to the PP Act extended the tenure of PP Executive Committees from three to six years. But this provision is yet to be implemented even after three years of the amendment. The amendment had also made a provision for an inclusive framework in terms of involving fishermen and other stakeholders as members of PPs. This also is yet to be translated into action. The PIM initiative seems euphoric in the absence of adequate follow-up programmes. Although PPs are independent bodies, the irrigation department still has significant control over the functioning of PPs from releasing grants to facilitating different activities. There are many instances of PP office bearers and irrigation department officials manipulating the membership figure to qualify for grants. In the absence of any coherent strategic plan, the government is following an ad hoc approach for the release of grants and also issuing of permits to

Table 13.2 Grants in aid to PPs in Odisha

Year	Major and medium		Minor (flow)		Minor (lift)		Total	
	Nos.	Amount (Rs. lakh)	Nos.	Amount (Rs. lakh)	Nos.	Amount (Rs. lakh)	Nos.	Amount (Rs. lakh)
2001–2	58	8.37	–	–	–	–	58	8.37
2002–3	–	–	–	–	–	–	–	–
2003–4	110	43.79	–	–	–	–	110	43.79
2004–5	389	159.08	–	–	–	–	389	159.08
2005–6	221	85.63	187	30.00	–	–	408	115.63
2006–7	442	168.75	203	28.11	180	204.37	825	401.23
2007–8	1,086	446.10	164	29.96	47	153.90	1,297	629.96
2008–9	751	308.12	474	86.35	–	–	1,225	394.47
2009–10	1,023	441.81	323	49.91	–	–	1,410	491.76

Source: Office of the Engineer-in-Chief, Department of Water Resources, Government of Odisha

procure paddy from farmers to PPs. The formation of PPs took place without the explicit knowledge of the majority of farmer members in many instances. The agencies prepared a list of farmers on the basis of land records available with the revenue department, while PPs were formed by involving a few elite and influential farmers or former landlords in the villages. The elections were also conducted without adequate publicity and involvement of users. Though PIM has been initiated to reduce the huge gap between the water fee demand and the actual collection among other objectives, the government lacks an action plan towards cost recovery. The revenue department collects water tax and has an independent reporting format without any coordination. There is no database for WUA level water fee collection. Although capacity-building efforts are being made by Water and Land Management Institute (WALMI), the training seems to be half-hearted and not targeted at the appropriate groups. The village elites are generally selected for training, and they often treat the training programmes more as an outing trip to the capital city rather than for any training.[3] The training components are theoretical and lack ground realities.

The study area and methodology

The study was conducted in two major irrigation projects namely Upper Indrāvati and Upper Kolab in the State of Odisha. Agriculture contributes around 20 per cent of the state gross domestic product in Odisha employing 65 per cent of the population (GoO 2010). The state has cultivable land of 6,165 thousand hectares of which 4,990 thousand hectares can be brought under irrigation through major, medium and minor (flow and lift) irrigation projects (GoO 2009). However, only 45 per cent of the total cultivable area is irrigated in the state. The irrigation potential created during 2009–10 for both Kharif and Rabi amounts to 4,224.277 thousand hectares out of which 44.31 per cent accounts for major and medium irrigation, 14.56 per cent for minor irrigation (flow), 17.59 per cent for minor irrigation (lift), and the remaining 23.53 per cent accounts for other sources like private tanks, ponds, dug wells, water harvesting structures, etc.

The Upper Indrāvati Irrigation Project (UIIP) is located in Nawarangpur District having its command area in Kalahandi District. The UIIP has an irrigation network comprising three main canals – right main canal, left main canal and lift canal, with a potential to irrigate 1,28,000 hectares. This project has brought about a significant economic transformation in Kalahandi virtually turning the district into a major rice-producing area in the state. The left main canal started operating from 1987–8 with a command area of 3,840 hectares which increased to 47,605 hectares in 2008–9. There are 155 PPs in the left main canal, and elections for all the PPs in upper and middle reaches and some in tail reaches were held during 2008. Similarly, DCs were formed in upper and middle reaches. The AC/PC will be formed after the DC formation process across all the PPs is completed.[4]

The Upper Kolab Irrigation Project is part of the Upper Kolab Multipurpose Project initiated by the state government in 1976 in Koraput District. This multipurpose project has three components: (1) Dams and Reservoirs; (2) Irrigation Canals; and (3) Hydroelectric Power Generation. The dam across River Kolab was constructed in Jeypore with 59 kilometres of left main canal (Jeypore canal) and 13 kilometres of right main canal (Padmapur Supply Waterway). The left main canal commenced functioning from 1998 onwards, and the command area of the left canal constitutes 28,771 hectares in 2009. This study covered the PPs located in the middle reach of the left main canal (from the 14-kilometre point to the 41.78-kilometre point). Of the 97 PPs in the left main canal, 38 PPs are located in this middle stretch. Although all these PPs were formed since 2003, the major activities like preparing of delineation maps and conducting elections were carried out in 2008. The DCs and AC/PC have also been formed.

Paddy is the major irrigated crop grown during both Kharif and Rabi in the Upper Indrāvati. Few farmers also reported cultivating pulses, groundnut and vegetables. In the Upper Kolab, the major crops grown in the irrigated lands include paddy, sugarcane, vegetables and spices like turmeric during both Kharif and Rabi. Canal is the major source of irrigation in both the project areas. With very limited number of farmers reported to have private dug wells or bore wells in the command area, the other sources of irrigation in the region are community ponds/tanks and *nalas*.[5] The farmers have pointed out several difficulties concerning irrigation. In the Upper Indrāvati, the major problems are undue delays in the release of water, which further delay the sowing/cropping season; unequal distribution of water due to the presence of unauthorized outlets and poor maintenance of canals. However, the farmers in Upper Kolab face problems like delayed release of water during the Rabi season, water logging and soil erosion due to lack of adequate field channels and drainage systems and poor maintenance of the canals. Warabandi is the usual practice followed for sharing of water in both the study areas. In Upper Kolab command area, the Command Area Development Authority (CADA) commenced the construction of field channels with PPs playing an active role in completing the construction work of field channels. However, field channels are yet to be constructed in the Upper Indrāvati command area, and water courses constructed in the beginning have disappeared and have even been encroached upon in many cases.

The study has used the 'before-after' approach for evaluating the impact of PIM with the help of data collected from farmer members and the officer bearers (president/secretary and EC members) of PPs. The study is based on extensive field survey that includes questionnaire survey, focused group discussion, informal discussions at different levels, that is (1) farmer-members, (2) office bearers of PPs (president/ secretary and EC member) and (3) irrigation department officials. The questionnaire designed for farmer members focused on the impact of PIM on crop productivity, water requirement and availability, extent of canal maintenance, water fees, participation in collective activities, conflicts arising in operationalizing PP activities and the awareness level of the farmers. The questionnaire relating to the president/secretary and EC members focused on irrigation management practices, PP activities, impact of PIM on water availability, agricultural productivity, O&M of irrigation systems, conflict resolution mechanisms, financial support and other similar aspects. The questionnaire for irrigation department officials included a checklist and open-ended questions, focusing on issues of water management by PPs and practical difficulties involved in the implementation of PIM.

The field survey was conducted during April-June 2010. The data was collected from one-third of the total PPs in both the projects through the stratified random sampling method representing PPs across all the reaches of the canal/sub-canal. Out of the 193 PPs in the study region, a total of 64 PPs (52 PPs out of 155) in Upper Indrāvati and 14 PPs (out of 38 in Upper Kolab) are covered in the survey. In Upper Indrāvati, a total of 154 farmers and 104 presidents/secretaries/EC members spread across 52 PPs were interviewed, whereas in Upper Kolab, 42 farmers and 28 presidents/secretaries/EC members from 14 PPs were interviewed. Three farmers were selected randomly (preferably representing head, middle and tail reach) for each of the sample PPs. The EC questionnaire was administered to the president/secretary of PPs and EC members of the PPs. The data from Irrigation Department officials were collected using a questionnaire as well as informal discussion[6] that covered junior engineers and sub-divisional officers at the field level, executive engineers at the project level and senior officials at the state level.

Findings of the study

As discussed earlier, the study aimed at analysing the performance of PPs with respect to some of the indicators like institutional dynamics, the impact on quality of O&M, financial performance, participation of user members in collective action and sustainability of these participatory institutions. The findings are discussed below.

Institutional dynamics of PPs

The institutional dynamics of the participatory institutions like PPs in terms of socio-economic composition often reflects the existing power structures in the society. The PPs are also subject to elite capture like other community-based resource management institutions and such trends hinder democratic and inclusive decision-making. The composition of the ECs of the PPs in the study area reflects a similar trend with the village elites (land rich households or households from the dominating caste) representing the ECs (see Tables 13.3 and 13.4). The

Table 13.3 Social categories of the respondents

Sl. No	Social category	% of PP member farmers		% of PP President/ Secretary/EC members	
		Upper Indrāvati	Upper Kolab	Upper Indrāvati	Upper Kolab
1	Scheduled Caste (SC)	18	14	6	4
2	Scheduled Tribe (ST)	13	38	8	15
3	Other Backward classes (OBC)	48	31	26	36
4	General	21	17	60	45

Source: Field Survey 2010

Table 13.4 Distribution of respondents by land ownership categories

Sl. No	Land ownership categories (in acres)	% of PP member farmers		% of PP President/ Secretary/EC members	
		Upper Indrāvati	Upper Kolab	Upper Indrāvati	Upper Kolab
1	< 1	8	5	2	7
2	1.0 to 2.5	21	10	11	11
3	2.5 to 5.0	30	36	18	21
4	5.0 to 10	27	28	29	25
5	>10	14	21	40	36

Source: Field Survey 2010

majority of the PPs in Upper Indrāvati are headed by the members of *gauntia*[7] families, and in some cases both the president and secretary belong to the same family. However, in Upper Kolab study villages the EC members are mostly from the dominating caste as the institution of *gauntia* is not so prevalent. In Upper Indrāvati the holding size works out to 5.03 acres for farmer members of PPs on an average, while for the president/secretary/EC members 11.62 acres. Around 60 per cent of the presidents/secretaries/EC members belong to the general caste categories followed by other backward classes (OBC),[8] who belong to farming community and in some villages form the dominant caste group. Similarly in Upper Kolab, among farmers 17 per cent belonged to general category, 31 per cent to OBCs, 14 per cent to Scheduled Castes and 38 per cent to Scheduled Tribes. However, 45 per cent of the presidents/secretaries/EC members belong to general category.

Where the land ownership is concerned, marginal and small farmers hold around 58 per cent of the total land, and the remaining 42 per cent is held by others in Upper Indrāvati. However, among the office bearers of the PPs, the marginal and small farmer office bearers hold 30 per cent of the land, while others hold 70 per cent of the land. This reflects the relatively skewed distribution of land holdings among the office bearers of PPs as compared to members. Similarly, in Upper Kolab also the majority of the farmers belong to marginal and small categories, but large farmers enjoy a higher representation in the ECs of PPs.

Impact on quality of O&M

The quality of maintenance work of canals has declined markedly with all PPs complaining about poor quality of structures like falls and culverts in both the irrigation projects though the quality of O&M is reported to be much worse in Upper Indrāvati. The PPs have a limited role in the O&M of canals with the irrigation department carrying out all major works. The PPs are assigned with desiltation and weeding activities in the minor and sub-minor canals, utilizing grants-in-aid they receive from government. Around 65 per cent of the PPs in Upper Indrāvati and 45 per cent of PPs in Upper Kolab have received grant-in-aid. Many of the respondents have stated that the grant-in-aid is too meagre to carry out even desiltation and weeding activities. In some cases the grants are not even utilized as the PPs got the money during the peak agricultural season. It has been found during discussions that in some cases the office bearers misappropriate these grant-in-aid funds.

As far as the perception of farmers and EC members about the impact of PIM on maintenance of canals is concerned, in Upper Indrāvati around 16.3 per cent of the farmers opined that the quality of canal lining work is good while the remaining farmers didn't respond. However, only 10 per cent of the presidents/secretaries/EC members observe that the lining of canals has been good (see Table 13.5). However, as indicated in the table below, maintenance activities like desiltation and removal of weeds from the canal bed has improved after the formation of PPs. These are the two activities entrusted to the PPs by the irrigation department.

In Upper Kolab, about 24 per cent of farmer members find the quality of work on the lining of the canals average to poor, while 38 per cent

Table 13.5 Extent and quality of maintenance in Upper Indrāvati (in per cent to total respondents)

Maintenance activities	Respondents	Before PP			After PP		
		Good	Average	Poor	Good	Average	Poor
Lining of canal	President/ EC members	10.1	24.24	19.19			
	Farmers	16.23	26.63	16.88			
Desiltation	President/EC members	15.15	11.11	9.09	53.54	12.12	0
	Farmers	15.58	19.48	14.29	24.03	13.64	12.99
Removal of weeds	President/EC members	15.15	11.11	9.09	37.37	12.12	6.06
	Farmer	15.58	16.88	12.99	21.43	10.39	10.39

Source: Field Survey 2010

Table 13.6 Extent and quality of maintenance in Upper Kolab (in per cent to total respondents)

Activities	Respondents	Before PP			After PP		
		Good	Average	Poor	Good	Average	Poor
Lining of canal	President/ EC members	35.5	17.86	17.86			
	Farmers	38.1	19.05	4.76			
Desiltation	President/ EC members	13.57	25	27.14	42.86	10.71	10.71
	Farmers	29.95	26.05	28.38	52.38	19.05	11.9
Removal of weeds	President/ EC members	12.65	17.86	17.14	25	10.71	10.71
	Farmers	30.95	20.29	14.76	38.1	19.05	9.52

Source: Field Survey 2010

find it good. As far as the response of presidents/EC members of PPs is concerned, about 35.5 per cent find the canal lining as good, whereas around 34 per cent viewed it as average to poor (see Table 13.6).

There have been instances of canal repair in middle of the cropping season affecting the water supply for standing crops. Some PP members and office bearers point out that the quality of work can be improved if the irrigation department executes the civil works through PPs. One president of a Pani Panchayat (PP) says, 'As leaders of PP, we are accountable to the farmer members, but we neither have any power to supervise the works of contractors ensuring quality structures nor have any say in the release of funds for canal maintenance.' Though the farmers often mobilize resources for repairs and desiltation work, it's limited to minor maintenance work. The irrigation department officials also feel that lack of adequate funding is the major hindrance for carrying out maintenance works. For instance the irrigation department gets Rs. 400[9] for every hectare of command area from the government for O&M, which is grossly inadequate.

The major operational issues in canal irrigation constitute the timeliness and adequacy of water supply. However, PPs have little control over this, and there has not been much change in the situation after the formation of PPs (Table 13.7). Lack of timeliness in release of water results in delays in crop calendar and has adverse impact on the crop productivity. The summer paddy gets most affected as the delay often results in more crop loss during the harvesting period. This problem is more acute for the tail-end farmers, and sometimes they get water towards the end of the cropping season. A majority of farmers opine that though duration of water supply is adequate, the volume of water flow in the canal is inadequate for the standing crops while tail-end farmers say they do not get water for their crops even in the Kharif season. The farmers don't get any information about the possible non-availability of water well in advance to plan their crops.

Table 13.7 Timeliness and adequacy of water supply (in per cent to total respondents)

Responses of the farmers	Upper Indrāvati				Upper Kolab			
	Before PP		After PP		Before PP		After PP	
	Yes	No	Yes	No	Yes	No	Yes	No
1. Whether water supply received at your field is timely?	22	78	22	78	12	88	14	86
2. Is the duration of water supply adequate?	80	20	80	20	73	27	69	31
3. Is the volume adequate for crops?	15	85	15	85	34	66	28	72

Source: Field Survey 2010

As the equity in water distribution is concerned, the response of the farmers varies significantly across these two irrigation projects. The discussions with farmers and PP EC members suggest that inequity in the distribution of water is a major issue in Upper Indrāvati. It is disheartening to note that the number of unauthorized outlets is four to five times higher than the authorized outlets. Thus, WUA farmers in the middle and tail end in all reaches face difficulties in getting water. Many farmers in the tail and middle observe that during the cropping season they work through the night in regulating the outlets to get water to their fields. And the farmers in the head reach reopen their unauthorized outlets in the morning again making the tail enders toil for water all through the season. Such incidents have resulted in conflicts among farmers in the same village and across villages over water sharing in a crop season. However, in the Upper Kolab, a majority of the farmers view that water distribution has been more equitable after the formation of PPs. Besides, farmers claim that they co-operate with each other in terms of sharing water as long as there is adequate water in the canal.

Financial performance

Financial performance as an indicator is crucial in terms of assessing the performance of PPs as it affects the regular functioning of PPs and also the very sustainability of these participatory institutions. In fact, one of the major rationales for initiating PIM is the reduction of O&M expenditure of the government by transferring the O&M responsibilities to the users. Involvement of the farmers in the financial management of the irrigation systems is also expected to improve the financial health of the systems in terms of increased collection of water charges. However, the government expenditure on O& M of the irrigation systems in the state increased from Rs. 210.224 million in 1994–5 to Rs. 1490.980 million in 2008–9. Hence, introduction of PIM since 2002 does not seem to have had any impact on the expenditure burden of the state. Interestingly, the PPs are not assigned with that task of collection of water charges. Hence, grants-in-aid from the government are the only source of funds for the PPs. The water tax is collected by the irrigation department annually and the irrigation department fixes water charges for each season. In Upper Indrāvati, the water rate for Kharif is Rs. 100 per acre and Rs. 180 per acre for the Rabi season. The water charges have not been revised since the inception of the project. The farmers report that the government did not collect any water charges for the first two years of the canal irrigation. Out of 156 farmers surveyed 124 (79.49 per cent)

Table 13.8 Water charges collected and the rates

Irrigation project	Water charges/taxes (Rs. per acre)				% of farmers paying water taxes regularly	
	Before PP		After PP		Before PP	After PP
	Kharif	Rabi	Kharif	Rabi		
Upper Indrāvati	100	180	100	180	82.05	79.49
Upper Kolab	100	180	100	180	83.33	88.09

Source: Field Survey 2010

view that they pay water fees regularly now and 128 (82.05 per cent) of them report that they were paying water taxes regularly even before PPs. The water taxes in Upper Kolab are also the same as in Upper Indrāvati. Out of 42 farmers surveyed 37 farmers (88.09 per cent) have reported paying water taxes regularly now, whereas 34 (83.33) reported paying water fees regularly even before PPs (see Table 13.8). The PP leaders in Upper Kolab also observe that very few farmers are defaulters with respect to water fee payment as the revenue department is very strict.

As per the PP Rules 2003, the respective PPs are supposed to get a proportionate share of the water tax collected in their jurisdiction after five years of fixed grants from the government. Although many of the PPs have been in existence for more than five years, they are yet to receive even the first grants-in-aid, and there is no mechanism in place to transfer the proportion of water tax collected to PPs. So PPs have no incentive to involve themselves in water fee collection. This defeats the very objective of PIM towards designing a better cost recovery mechanism.

User participation in collective action

Participation of user farmers in the collective activities of water management is a crucial indicator of the performance of PPs. The study found that each farmer spends at least 5 person days on an average in a year for such collective activities in Upper Kolab whereas in Upper Indrāvati, it is 11 person days. PP members readily come forward in contributing labour for repairing or constructing of civil structures for better irrigation for lands. The level of collective action is observed higher among the tail-end farmers across reaches as they need to put in more effort to get water to their fields. The tail-end farmers often get together for putting up closures to many of the unauthorized outlets in the head reach of the sub-canals and also for clearing cross-bundings to let the water flow to the tail end of the canal. This happens sometimes with discussions and in consensus with farmers in the head reach after few days of irrigations, or they do it during night times without informing the head-reach farmers. As a few farmers have pointed out, 'We work like thieves at night to get water to our fields even though we pay the same water fee as farmers in the head reach of the canal.' The farmers in the tail end face more difficulties both in case of deficient water and surplus water in the canal and hence need to contribute more labour. So the participation of farmers in collective activities is often not for the PIM institutions but also to deal with such situations.

The rules of PPs mandate that there should be at least two meetings with farmers in a year before the onset of the agricultural season. However, very few of the PPs conduct regular meetings. Only 21 per cent PPs in Upper Indrāvati and 38 per cent of PPs in Upper Kolab have conducted meetings as per the stipulated norm. Around 71 per cent of PPs in Upper Indrāvati and 45 per cent PPs in Upper Kolab report that they had no meetings in the whole year (see Table 13.9)

The qualitative aspects of the participation like individual members participation in meetings and in the decision-making process are crucial and hold significance for the functioning of the PPs. However, more than 70 per cent of the farmers in Upper Indrāvati and 55 per cent of the farmers in Upper Kolab never participated in any meetings (Table 13.10). Though the situation is better in Upper Kolab when compared to Upper Indrāvati, such lower level of participation reflects the poor state of democratization of decision-making. Among those who reportedly attend the meetings, a significant percentage don't participate in the proceedings of the meetings; only 8 per cent of these

Table 13.9 Number of meetings held in last year (in per cent to total)

Number of Meetings	Upper Indrāvati	Upper Kolab
No meetings	71	45
1–3	21	38
3–8	8	17

Source: Field Survey 2010

Table 13.10 Meeting Attendance and participation in proceedings (in per cent to total respondents)

Attendance/ participation	% Farmers attending PP meeting		% Farmers participating in the proceedings of PP meetings	
	Upper Indrāvati	Upper Kolab	Upper Indrāvati	Upper Kolab
Always	11	35	8	19
Sometimes	19	10	16	5
Never	70	55	76	76

Source: Field Survey 2010

farmers in Upper Indrāvati and 19 per cent of the farmers in Upper Kolab participate in proceedings always. Interestingly 76 per cent of them don't participate in proceedings even though they attend the meetings in both the areas

Institutional sustainability

The issue of institutional sustainability is important from the perspective of the long-term viability of these participatory institutions. The aspects such as conflict situations in PPs and their resolution mechanism, maintenance of documents and awareness of member farmers about PP and its activities has implications on the sustainability of these community-based collective action institutions.

With regard to conflicts in PPs, in Upper Indrāvati about 69 per cent of PP leaders have acknowledged conflicts in water sharing, whereas 96 per cent of farmers have reported the same (Table 13.11). Similarly in Upper Kolab, 76 per cent of farmers have observed that there exist conflicts over water sharing, whereas only 57 per cent of the PP leaders admit to having water sharing-related conflicts in PPs.

However, a majority of the farmers and PP leaders view that most of the conflicts concerning water sharing get resolved quickly after PPs were formed. Many a time conflicts concerning water distribution get resolved at farmers' levels. The other major conflicts reported by farmers relate to the reluctance of members to participate in the collective activities. Around 19.05 per cent of the farmers and 10.71 per cent of PP leaders in Upper Kolab have reported some financial irregularities happening in PPs. In Upper Indrāvati too, similar trends has been observed (though marginally higher than Upper Kolab). Although this

Table 13.11 Instances of conflicts and reasons for these conflicts

Conflict particulars	Upper Indrāvati		Upper Kolab	
	Perception of the president/ secretary/EC members (%)	Perception of the farmers (%)	Perception of the president/ secretary/EC members (%)	Perception of the farmers (%)
Water sharing	69.23	96.10	57.14	76.19
Reluctance in doing collective work	67.31	87.66	67.86	53.85
Financial management	11.54	38.96	10.71	19.05
Award of work / Contract	7.69	31.17	17.86	21.43

Source: Field Survey 2010

percentage is less, given the fact that very few of the PPs have availed the grants-in-aid, this seems to be a major issue concerning the functioning of PPs. Conflicts over financial management or award of work/job contracts are reported by a small percentage of respondents. Interestingly, the percentage of farmers reporting conflicts turns out to be relatively high compared to PP leaders.

The maintenance of documents and access to these documents show the degree of transparency and accountability prevailing in the PPs. This maintenance of documents like maps of PP area and membership details also develops a sense of belongingness among members. In Upper Indrāvati, about 29 PPs (55.77 per cent) out of a total of 52 PPs surveyed have reported possessing maps with boundary details. Only 35 per cent of the PPs are found to be maintaining property register records and none of the PPs maintain water flow registers. About 85 per cent of PPs keep cash registers, whereas 79 per cent of PPs maintain detailed registers containing details of the proceedings of the meetings and resolutions. The PPs in Upper Kolab perform better in respect to record keeping. More than 70 per cent of the PPs surveyed have maps with boundary details of their PP. Only 57.14 per cent of the PPs are found to have maintained property register records, while none of the PPs maintain water flow registers and 42 per cent of PPs have maintained training modules with them (see Table 13.12).

Table 13.12 Availability and maintenance of documents (per cent to total)

Sl. No	Particulars	Upper Indrāvati	Upper Kolab
1	Map with boundary	55.77	71.43
2	Map with notified localized area	0.00	42.9
3	Map showing irrigated area under notified localized area	34.62	0.00
4	Property register records	0.00	57.14
5	Water flow register	84.62	0.00
6	Cash register	78.85	71.43
7	Minutes register	59.62	71.43
8	Training modules	55.77	42.86

Source: Field Survey 2010

The poor level of awareness about various activities of PPs reflects the inherent weaknesses of PPs in terms of their non-democratic structure. One of the prime reasons for this is that not much effort was put in to involve all stakeholders in the formation process of PPs. In Upper Indrāvati, less than 50 per cent of the members are found to be aware of the objectives of PPs, 54 per cent about election of EC members, 43 per cent about grants/aid to PPs, while only 17 per cent are found to be aware of grants from the government for O&M (Table 13.13). Similarly in Upper Kolab, about 47 per cent of the farmers have been found to be aware of the objectives of PPs; however, the level of awareness as regards other functions and activities were found to be lower. More than 70 per cent of the members of PPs have no idea about the functions and responsibilities of PPs and elections. All these are pointers to the kind of information asymmetry prevailing across the members of PPs.

Conclusions and the way forward

Though the state has initiated PIM by enacting legislations to facilitate the participation of farmers in irrigation management and launched several programmes to incentivize it, the implementation has not been very effective in terms of involvement of farmers in the management of irrigation structures and water. The constraining factors concerning this could be lack of adequate measures to engage the farmers in decision-making, focus on formation of PPs rather than strengthening these

Table 13.13 Awareness among farmer members about different aspects of PPs (per cent to total)

Sl. No	Aspects	Upper Indrāvati	Upper Kolab
1	Objective of PP formation	49.01	47.6
2	Functions and Responsibilities of PPs	39.06	28.6
3	Functions and Responsibilities of DCs/PCs	27.43	9.5
4	Benefits of management transfer	12.82	11.9
5	Election of EC members	53.77	19
6	Records of PPs	12.72	11.9
7	Grant-in-aid for PPs	43.07	11.9
8	Utilization of grants in aid	17.23	4.8

Source: Field Survey 2010

institutions and the responsibility shifting attitude of government officials with very little sharing of funds and power with the PP, etc. PIM implementation does not seem to have invoked much interest among the farmers to take up the responsibility of managing their own systems. Inadequate and non-effective training didn't add to the capacity building of the PP leaders as well. So the PPs have emerged as mere paper institutions rather than having any effective impact on irrigation management at ground level.

The assessment of the performance of the PPs for some of the indicators discussed also shows a grim picture. Most of the PPs are subject to elite capture with the wealthy farmers and the farmers from dominant social groups as their leaders. PPs have very limited role in the O&M of the irrigation structures and hence very little impact on this front. However, some of the PPs took up some of the activities with whatever little money they got, and there seems to be some improvement in activities like desiltation and weed removal. Lack of timeliness and inadequate water supply are reported to be faced by farmers, though at different degrees across the canal reaches, and PPs have almost no role to play in these issues. Inequitable water supply has been a major problem in one of the irrigation projects with a huge number of unauthorized outlets. The PPs still depend on government grants as they neither have power to levy any fees nor get any share from the water fee paid by the farmers. There is yet to have any system in place for cost recovery. Though the farmer members participate in several activities concerning repair and maintenance, there is little participation in decision-making processes as few meetings are held, and many farmers though they attend the meetings, don't participate in the proceedings of meetings. The PPs have quick resolution mechanisms for conflicts related to water sharing, but the conflicts concerning irregularities in managing funds and participation in collective activities are reported to remain unresolved. Many of the PPs have been found to have inadequate documentation and have not maintained the documents they are supposed to. There is little awareness among the farmer members and even among EC members about various issues concerning PPs reflecting the information asymmetry.

In the wake of several such shortcomings, the government needs to adopt a series of initiatives to do away with the inertia associated with implementation of PIM in the state. Participatory institutions should not be promoted with the hidden objective of reducing expenditure and escaping from the responsibility of providing irrigation infrastructure. A special drive should be initiated by the irrigation department for closure of unauthorized outlets and handover of the irrigation systems to the farmers in good condition. The principle 'water should reach the tail end first' being followed with regard to main canals should be extended to branch canals and sub-canals also. The irrigation department needs to a develop mechanism to involve PP members in planning and executing the regular O&M work of canals. If works were to be carried out by contractors, then work quality should be supervised by the EC members of PP along with department engineers. There are instances where farmers have complained about the poor quality of structures besides lamenting that these works are repeatedly carried out almost every year with a repair life of just one year. The present system of command area acreage allocation for canal maintenance needs to be revisited. The PPs need to have greater financial authority to determine water charges, collection mechanism and retain revenue for O&M expenses. The government should prepare a time-bound and practical action plan for cost recovery. The irrigation department also should be made accountable for irregular supply of water. The irrigation department should respond to the grievances of PPs within a limited time frame in whatever capacity it could. PPs must get adequate support from government agencies like the irrigation department, district administration and police for resolving conflicts whenever required. There is a need to establish a proper monitoring and evaluation mechanism to assess the progress and identify the bottlenecks hampering the performance of PPs. A date base with both real-time and time-series data on PP membership, elections, receipt and utilization of O&M grants and other aspects of PPs should be maintained at the project level as well as the state level.

Notes

1 Acknowledgement: this chapter is based on a larger study titled 'Towards Improving Participatory Irrigation Management and Performance of Water Users Association under JICA Assisted Irrigation Projects in India: Understanding the Institutional Dynamics, Performance and Benefits' sponsored by Japan International Cooperation Agency (JICA), New Delhi. The authors duly acknowledge the comments and suggestions of Prof. R. S. Deshpande, other consultants and anonymous referees for this study. The authors also benefited from the inputs by Mr. Ranjan Panda for this chapter. However, the usual disclaimer applies.

2 The change to 'Odisha' from its anglicized version 'Orissa' became effective since 1 November 2011. The authors have used 'Odisha' throughout the text though many of the bills and acts referred in the study were initiated earlier.

3 It has been pointed out by some respondents during field survey that in some cases the children of these farmers who study in colleges in Cuttack and Bhubaneswar proxy their fathers in the training programme and claim the travel expenses.

4 During the survey DCs were not formed in the tail end of the canal. The reason for delays as explained by the official of the irrigation department is that a large part of the tail end was in the erstwhile Dharmagarh division which got merged later with Kusumikhuti division (Division 1) of the UIIP. So in the tail end of the canal, many of the PPs surveyed have the same presidents/secretaries who had been nominated during the formation of PPs in 2003.

5 *Nalas* are the natural waterways for rainwater drainage and have existed before canal irrigation. *Nalas* run full in the region during cropping season after canal irrigation started. As indicated by farmers, this is because farmers in the head reach allow water to flow to their fields all the time and hence there is a regular flow of surplus water to the *nalas*. Nalas are not connected to canals, but are connected to rivers.

6 Government officials at the field level are more comfortable with informal discussion, whereas the senior officials in the state capital insisted on sending them the questionnaire in advance.

7 *Gauntias* are former landlords in the village and are land rich individuals.

8 OBCs in study villages mostly belong to the farming community, and in some villages they constitute the dominant caste group.

9 This is same for all the canals in the state though the nature of canal maintenance and its cost varies depending upon the geographical characteristics of the command area as well as the canal structure.

References

Bos, M. G., Murray-Rust, D. H., Merrey, D. J., Johnson, H. G., and Snellen, W. B. 1994. 'Methodologies for Assessing Performance of Irrigation and Drainage Management', *Irrigation and Drainage Systems*, 7: 231–61.

Ghosh, S. 2009. 'Linkage Mechanism between Different Institutional Nodes of Irrigation Management in Odisha', *Indian Research Journal of Extension Education*, 9(2): 28–34.

Gorantiwar, S. D., and Smout, Ian K. 2005. 'Performance Assessment of Irrigation Water Management of Heterogenous Irrigation Schemes: A Framework for Evaluation', *Irrigation and Drainage Systems*, 19(1): 1–36.

Government of India, Ministry of Water Resources. 2009. 'Status of Participatory Irrigation Management (PIM) in India, Policy Initiatives Taken and Emerging Issues', http://mowr.gov.in/writereaddata/mainlinkFile/File421.pdf (accessed on 10th July 2011).

Government of Odisha. 2009. 'Department of Water Resources, Annual Report 2008–09'.

Government of Odisha. 2010a. 'Economic Survey 2009–10, Directorate of Economics and Statistics', Government of Odisha, Bhubaneswar.

Government of Odisha. 2010b. 'Participatory Irrigation Management', http://www.Odishapanipanchayat.gov.in/projects1.php (accessed on 26th July 2011).

Government of Odisha, Department of Water Resources. 'Resolution No. Irrr.-I-WB (FOT) 38/2000 38711 dated 26.09.2000, Scheme for Pani Panchayat', 2000.

Government of Odisha, Department of Water Resources. 'Resolution No. Irr.I-WB (Fot)-24/08 18645 dated 16.05.2008, Guidelines for Execution of Works by Water Resources Department through Pani Panchayats under National Rural Employment Guarantee Scheme (NREGS)', 2008.

Iversen, V., Chhetry, B., Francis, P., Gurung, M., Kafle, G., Pain, A., and Seeley, J. 2006. 'High Value Forests, Hidden Economies and Elite Capture: Evidence from Forest User Groups in Nepal's Terai', *Ecological Economics*, 58: 93–107.

Jairath, J. 1999. 'Participatory Irrigation Management: Experiments in Andhra Pradesh', *Economic and Political Weekly*, 34(40): 2834–7.

Mahapatra, S. K. 2006. 'Functioning of Water Users Associations or Pani Panchayat in Odisha: Principle, Procedure, Performance and Prospects'. Paper Presented at in the workshop on 'Water, Law and the Commons' New Delhi, 8–10 December 2006. Organized by the International Environmental Law Research Centre (IELRC).

Marothia, D. K. 2005. 'Institutional Reforms in Canal Irrigation System: Lesson from Chhattisgarh', *Economic and Political Weekly*, 40(28): 3074–84.

Meinzen-Dick, R., Mendoza, M., Sadoulet, L., Adiad-Shields, G., and Subramanian, A. 1997. 'Sustainable Water User Associations: Lessons from a Literature Review', in A. Subramanian, N. V. Jaganathan and R. Meinzen-Dick (eds), *User Organizations for Sustainable Water Services*. World Bank Technical Paper No. 354, Washington, DC: World Bank.

The Odisha Gazette. 2002. 'The Odisha Pani Panchayat Act, 2002, No. 1053', July 8, Government of Odisha Press, Cuttack.

The Odisha Gazette. 2009. 'The Odisha Pani Panchayat Amendment Act, 2008, No. 83 (Extraordinary)', January 20, Government of Odisha Press, Cuttack.

Ostrom, E. 1990. *Governing the Commons: The Evolution of Institutions for Collective Action*. Cambridge: Cambridge University Press.

Pant, N. 1999. 'Impact of Irrigation Management Transfer in Maharashtra: An Assessment', *Economic and Political Weekly*, 34(13): A17–26.

Pant, N. 2008. 'Some Issues in Participatory Irrigation Management', *Economic and Political Weekly*, 43(1): 30–6.

Paranjape, S. and Joy, K. J. 2003. 'The Ozar Water User Societies: Impact of Society Formation and Co-management of Surface Water and Groundwater', Study Report, Society for Promoting Participative Ecosystem Management, Pune.

Parthasarathy, R. 2000. 'PIM Programme in Gujarat: Institutional and Financial Issues', *Economic and Political Weekly*, 35(35/36): 3147–54.

Platteau, J.-P. and Gaspart, F. 2004. 'Disciplining Local Leaders in Community-Based Development', http://siteresources.worldbank.org/INTPUBSERV/Resources/platteau.pdf [accessed on 3rd August 2011].

Raju, K. V. 2000. 'Participatory Irrigation Management in Andhra Pradesh: Promise, Practice and A Way Forward'. ISEC Working Paper 65, ISEC, Bangalore.

Rao, P. S. 1993. 'Review of Selected Literature on Indicators of Irrigation Performance'. IWMI, Colombo.

Reddy, V. R. and Reddy, P. R. 2005. 'How Participatory is Participatory Irrigation Management? Water Users Associations in Andhra Pradesh', *Economic and Political Weekly*, 40(53): 5587–95.

Selvarajan, S. 2001. 'Sustaining India's Irrigation Infrastructure', NCAP Policy Brief 15, NCAP: New Delhi.

Swain, M. 2000. *Turning over Irrigation Management to Farmers-Issues for Concern in Farmer and Local Participation in Irrigation Management*. New Delhi: Commonwealth Publishers.

Upadhaya, V. 2002. 'Water Management and Village Groups: Role of Law', *Economic and Political Weekly*, 37(49): 4907–12.

Vermillion, D. L. 1997. 'Impacts of Irrigation Management Transfer: A Review of the Evidence', IWMI, Colombo.

Chapter 14

Impact of organized retail channels on revenue of farmers

Models of direct procurement of vegetables in Haryana

Jitender Singh

The widening gap between demand and production of vegetables has been evident in rising prices of vegetables in recent past. The average increase in the prices of vegetables at wholesale markets was 9.5 per cent during 2006–10. The contributory factors for this increase have been an increase in demand and sticky supplies. On the demand side, the per capita income of the country is rising, and the consumption pattern is getting diversified towards vegetables. On the supply side the production of vegetables is not keeping the pace with demand. The low growth of vegetable production during 2008–9 and 2009–10 has been both because of low yield as well as low area put under vegetables. This indicates that the incentives for crop diversification perhaps were not sufficient enough to induce allocation of area to vegetables. Why is the farmer not diversifying area towards vegetables when prices of vegetables have been very high? The main reason for slow crop diversification towards vegetables is the high risk-high return pattern of the vegetables (Pingali and Rosegrant 1995; Rao, Birthal and Joshi 2006). The high risk is due to fluctuating prices in the local market and low share of the producer in the price paid by the consumer. The farmer may not necessarily be risk averse but may have a low risk appetite. Lack of credible institutional mechanism which could result in an increase in his share in each rupee a consumer spends on vegetables is further reinforcing this risk aversion.

The small size of the local market and its disintegration have made the prices supply sensitive. But while farmers are not able to benefit from the increase in prices, a fall hits them immediately. Demand for vegetables from farmers is a derived demand that comes through intermediaries. The existence of perfect competition among the farmers as sellers of vegetables and a few oligopolistic buyers or middlemen, therefore, results in distortion of the incentive structure (Brester and Goodwin

Table 14.1 Production and inflation in vegetable crops in India

Year	Production ('000' Tone)	Production growth (%)	Yield (tonne/ hec.)	Area ('000 hec.)	Area growth (%)	Yield growth	Inflation in vegetable (%)
2006–7	114.99	3.0	15.2	7581	5.0	–2.0	0.5
2007–8	128.45	11.7	16.4	7848	3.5	7.9	19.9
2008–9	129.08	0.5	16.2	7981	1.7	–1.2	3.5
2009–10	133.74	3.6	16.7	7985	0.1	3.6	14.0

Source: National Horticulture Board and the Office of the Economic Adviser

1993; Rogers and Sexton 1994). Fluctuating prices of vegetables, that are kept low by the intermediaries, do not provide enough incentives to the farmers to produce more. Prevalence of high prices/inflation is also due to the high transaction cost of vegetables and high margins of the middlemen (Suzuki and Sexton 2005). Besides, the perishable nature of the vegetables together with inadequate storage facility, improper demand management and inefficiency in supply chains creates huge waste in transit. In this situation, while increased supply results in a price crash for farmers, lower supply does not provide them any economic rent (Richard, Marsh and Atwood 2009). This also explains why low growth of area under vegetables and high rate of inflation and perhaps potential profitability in vegetables coexist (Table 14.1). This may be because the price advantages do not accrue to the farmers or because producing vegetables is a risky business that further reinforces the risk aversion of the farmers. One feasible option for increasing efficiency in the supply chains is setting up organized retail chains (Birthal, Joshi and Gulati 2005) that is discussed in the following paragraphs.

Rise of organized retail chains

The evolution and patterns of the diffusion process of the modern food retail industry has varied worldwide, but its entry and consistent increase in market penetration have had significant implications across all countries, including the United States, the European Union and the developing countries of Latin America and East Asia including China. For India, the size of food retail in 2008–9 was estimated at about Rs. 10,700 billion, which is 61 per cent of the total retail industry. While 95 per cent retail is in the unorganized sector, the organized retail which constitutes only 5 per cent is likely to grow at an annual rate of around 11 per cent and is projected to touch business levels of Rs. 53,000 billion by 2020. Agrifood retailing accounts for 18 per cent of the organized retail today and is likely to have a lower share (12 per cent) by 2020 (NAB-ARD 2011). According to the Indian Council for Research on International Economic Relations (ICREAR) report, the annual growth rate of organized retail in food and grocery is estimated at 16 per cent during 2004–7 (ICREAR 2009). Other estimates put the growth rate of organized food and grocery at a higher level of 42 per cent in 2006 over 2005 (Government of India 2007).

The share of expenditure towards food and beverages in total consumption expenditure of the households is expected to decline. Such a decline, as per Engel's Law, is a normal happening as part of the process of development. The organized retail may also, therefore, experience a decline in ratio of their business turnover derived from the sale of food-related products. There would, however, be two positive factors. The rising incomes and standards of living are expected to push up the demand for high-value foods. The changes in consumer behaviour and preferences in favour of processed foods as a result of an increasing participation of women in the labour force could help in sustaining the organized retail's share in food and related products. Moreover, increasing urbanization is also associated with a change in the shopping behaviour of the middle class due to higher incomes and increasing opportunity cost of time for the consumers (buyers), particularly women. Improvement in processing technology, progress on account of road connectivity, investment in storage facilities, fast and safe transport and the information technology revolution are likely to solve many of the problems of the marketing system and provide opportunities to private traders.[1]

Increased investment in organized retail by domestic and foreign players brings about upstream changes in supply chain and an increased centralized procurement of agriproducts from farmers as the experience of East Asian countries suggests. The rapid rise of supermarkets in different countries has transformed their agrifood system, though the speed of transformation has been different. In the case of India, the transformation as of now has been slow both upstream as well as downstream. In the downstream changes, the retail sector is now open for the corporates to develop supermarket infrastructure while foreign investment is likely to flow in, in the near future.

Direct procurement in fresh fruits and vegetables may offer better price, provide knowledge of market demand, technological inputs and access to credit on account of assured market to the farmers. While it is estimated that direct procurement of fresh fruits and vegetables could reduce wastage by about 7 per cent and can improve the chain efficiency by as much as 17 per cent, there is no consensus whether the upstream operation of the supply chain would be inclusive and cover farmers of all sizes of land holdings. The traditional channel where huge wastage of commodities, lack of infrastructure, missing institutions, lack of standardization, lack of incentives to invest in storage facilities, standardization, packaging etc. are very much evident.

Experiences of other institutional innovations in agrimarketing

The experiences of contract farming, particularly regarding the inclusion of small farmers under contract farming, the distribution of profits between farmers and contractors, sharing risk by agribusiness firms and minimization of the adverse impacts on environment and society have led to mixed results. There are various price and non-price effects on agriculture. Some positive impacts of contract farming include crop diversification, increase in productivity, improvement in the profitability of farmers, improved decision-making, increase in wages and employment of agricultural labour and technology transmission. The issue of inclusion is more important because of emerging trends of large numbers of small farmers in India and decreasing size of land holdings. A small farmer operating predominantly with family labour has many advantages which reduce the cost of labour supervision, cost of monitoring, screening of hired labour, cost of contract enforcement and cost of negotiation (Key, Nigel and Runsten 1999). On the one hand, collectively, it is easier to deal with small farmers through contracting firms, which reduce the possibility of getting involved in conflicts. On the other hand, there are disadvantages due to high dependency on farm income, which reduces the small farmer's bargaining power, low capacity to invest, which restricts implementation of new technology as well as experiment with new farming practices and crops, etc.

The small farmer is interested in taking up contract farming because it facilitates availability of modern inputs, which are either unavailable or will have to be obtained through other sources at a very high cost (Porter and Phillip 1997). Contract farming also reduces his price risk and eventually stabilizes income. The firms, however, prefer large growers to avoid dealing with a large number of small farmers. It is not only easy to bargain with a small number of large farmers, it is also advantageous to the firms to reduce the input supply cost and cost of supplying extension services. Large farms have a higher risk taking ability and can put in larger investments in land. They have relatively better quality land, which is more uniform and consolidated. Many studies (Kumar 2006) reveal that the system of contract farming is skewed towards medium and large farmers, though there were no significant differences in productivity between small, medium and large farms. There was no discrimination in procurement by agribusiness firms as well as price obtained by small and large farmers.

The exclusion of the small farmer evident in contract farming may have severe consequences for the rural economy. If a firm chose to contract primarily with large commercial farms, then small farmers may fail to benefit directly from contract arrangements. In the context of liberalized markets, contract farming that excludes the small farmer can lead to more concentrated land ownership and displacement of the rural poor (Key, Nigel and Runsten 1999). The way contracts and the income earned from contracting is distributed within a rural community can have important implications for economic and social differentiations within that community (Korovkin 1992). These issues are particularly important in the context of India where 85 per cent of land holdings are small and marginal and more than 40 per cent of the rural population is landless. Additionally, there is social stratification with high-income inequalities in rural areas.

Even if small farmers are incorporated in contract farming, there is no guarantee that the contracting firm would not exploit or at least provide some benefits to the small farmer. In the absence of representative farmer's organizations, the contract-farming scheme may have a limited regional/local impact (Porter and Howard 1997). Large numbers of small farmers are more prone to remain unorganized due to missing networking, lack of information and limited awareness of organizational benefits. In the long run, however, if the contracting firm becomes pervasive, farmers may not have any option but to sell their produce through these channels, but if these channels become non-operational, farmers may need to terminate their contract and switch over to other firms. There are other possibilities as well; the firm can maximize its short run profits without being concerned about the sustainability of the farm and the farmer and by exhausting the potential of the region, it may switch over to other relatively non-exhausted regions.

This easy switch over by firms to other regions, to contracts or to procure the produce and any limits on the exit of the farmer from the contract may distort the bargaining power equation in the long run in favour of the firm. Some alternatives, however, have emerged. The schemes to promote direct marketing channels are Apni Mandi, Rythu Bazars, Hadspar, Uzhavar Sandhais, etc. in various states. The promotion of investment in supermarkets and retail chains also is a step in that direction.

Studies of marketing efficiency

There are many studies on the estimation of the operational marketing efficiency of traditional marketing chains, mostly using the farmer's share in the consumer price. Thakur *et al.* (1994) has observed that in the case of tomato, cauliflower, capsicum and peas in Himachal Pradesh during 1991–2, market efficiency was 46–52 per cent. Another study of Karnataka State during 1985–6 by Kiresur *et al.* (1989) revealed low marketing efficiency (36 to 51 per cent) in perishable commodities like tomato and brinjal, while in the case of potato and onion, which are relatively durable vegetables with a longer shelf life, marketing efficiency was 60 to 67 per cent. In a study of wholesale markets in Bangalore by Chengappa and Nagaraj (2005) it was found that retail chains had enhanced farmers' profitability by 10–15· per cent as compared to traditional channels and reduced the marketing cost by about 4.25 to 8 per cent.

Despite the claims that organized retail chains would impact farmers in a better way in terms of enhancement of income, farm efficiency and updating farmers with market-related information, these positive impacts on farmers are dependent on the terms and conditions of the procurement contracts. These terms and conditions define the legality and enforceability of the contract. The design of the procurement contract also provides for some obligations on the company and the farmer, which once institutionalized could serve as a model contract, beneficial to both the contracting firm and the farmer.

The direct procurement contracts, with binding or flexible supply options, need to design an incentive mechanism which benefits farmers. The focus of this chapter is, therefore, also on the analysis of alternative models of direct procurement of fresh vegetables. There are many contracts with different terms and conditions operating simultaneously based on the varying bargaining powers of the contracting parties. However, not all these contracts are sustainable in the future. It may, therefore, be necessary to study the nature of contracts closely to assess their efficiency and sustainability and their impact on parties. This study examines the relative efficiency of vegetable procurement contracts of Mother Dairy and Reliance Fresh and the traditional channels of marketing of these products and validates the impact through field observations.

Objectives of the study

(I) Examination of the design of the alternate models of direct procurement.

(II) Comparing the price instability of alternate channels.

(III) Estimation of revenue effect of the alternative marketing channels on the farmers.

Database and methodology

The study is based on primary data on prices and quantity collected from growers' payment sheets supplied by Mother Dairy (MD) centres from 2005–7. Procurement centres selected for the study included Puthi, Moi, Rabhra, Balyana and Khandrai in Sonepat District in Haryana. The whole-sale prices for respective vegetables were collected from the records of the marketing committee of the nearest mandi. The data on marketing cost was collected from farmers during the primary survey. A set of randomly selected farmers were interviewed. The vegetables covered under the study were selected on the basis of data availability from the MD centres, which also indicate the largest grown vegetables in the sample villages. The vegetables, for example, bottle gourd, carrot, onion, green chillies, tomato, lady's finger, cauliflower, and musk melon are included in this study.

Comparison of the alternative models of direct procurement of vegetables

Model: Mother Dairy

MD under the National Dairy Development Board (NDDB) was started in 1985 as an organized retail chain of fruits and vegetables in India. The popular brand under which MD is doing business is 'Safal'. It procures 40–5 seasonal items of fruits and vegetable from over 17 states in India. Around 22,000 small and big farmers are supplying their produce to MD, which are directly linked to it upstream of the chain. Downstream, there are around 350 outlets spread across the National Capital Region (NCR), Delhi, selling the procured fruits and vegetables. The distribution centres at Pallabakhtavarpur and Mangolpuri in Delhi link the farmers and the consumers. At distribution centres huge storage and logistic facilities have been put in place.

Upstream, MD procures fresh and quality vegetables from growers through procurement centres spread across the country. It procures locally produced top quality fruits and vegetables at remunerative prices from the farmers. Farmers' Associations (FA) responsible for coordinating procurement operations at the village level are constituted by member farmers who also elect one president among themselves. The secretary, who is also responsible for the entire arrangement of procurement and record maintenance, is appointed by MD in consultation with the FA. The secretary is entitled to get salary for the services rendered at procurement centres. Major costs incurred during procurement such as payment of salaries to secretary, helper, *safai karamchari* (employees for cleaning) and rent payment for the land and shed of the centre are paid from the associations' funds. These funds are generated from the contribution of 1.75 per cent of the total value of procured quantity from centres. All these costs including transportation, handling charges and the market fee are deducted from the growers' price. The price paid to the farmer is net of all the charges and costs incurred until the produce reaches the distribution centre.

Farmers bring their vegetables to the procurement centres on a daily basis, and after packaging and weighing, these are transported to the distribution centres of MD every evening. During procurement special care is taken by the staff at the procurement centres to ensure that the procurement meets the quality norms of MD. The rest of the product is returned to the farmers to be disposed of by them at the nearest *mandi*. *Mandis*, therefore, face an adverse selection as the produce arriving is residual produce after what is supplied to MD. Besides a loss in terms of the prices, farmers are required to incur expenditure on transportation and marketing. It also involves spending a minimum of three to four hours which has an opportunity cost. MD does not lift the entire quantity produced. The secretary at the procurement centre, as the key agent of the MD, coordinates the procurement. MD informs the secretary of its requirements on a daily basis and these are communicated to the farmers. The total quantity procured by MD on a daily basis, particularly during the peak time of the season in terms of the produce, is less than the total produce of the day. Consequently, only a part of the farmers produce is procured and not the whole produce, irrespective of its quality. Being in the nature of perishables, vegetables cannot be held; the excess produce, therefore, after supplying to MD, is sold in the local *mandi*.

MD does not provide the farmers any credit or input support. Vegetable growers, who do not have market surplus of foodgrains, depend on commission agents for meeting their credit and input needs. Since these farmers bring relatively poor quality of vegetables (as the first grade has already been offered to MD), it affects their credit rating. Farmers visited during the survey were requested to give their opinion on the issue of difficulties faced by them in getting credit. It was observed that the small farmers who mostly grow vegetables have a relatively greater dependency on commission agents for credit and inputs and they are the worst affected. The famers also mentioned that the quoted price of the supply is not known at the time of supply. It is only on the next day that the tentative prices are informed. The actual price is delivered to the farmers after ten days when their payment sheet is received by the secretary from MD. The actual weights and quantity that has finally been accepted is indicated only in the grower's payment sheet, though tentative quantity and percentage of rejection is informed to the farmer on the next day of the supply. The payments are made after ten days of the supply through a bearer cheque.

The prices are a little more uncertain in MD than in the *mandi*, in the sense that in the *mandi* the prices are known to the farmer on the spot. While in MD, first the products are supplied and on the next day prices are told to farmers. Compared with contract farming, in MD there is no price or quantity contract formalized with the farmer. Neither is MD is bound to procure from the farmers, nor are farmers bound to sell only to MD. Compared to formal contract farming, the flexibility which MD offers to farmers is often risky, particularly to a small farmer, because the prices and quantities procured are determined on a daily basis.

Many of the farmers during the survey mentioned that if they were informed of the prices at the time of supply of their produce, their decision to sell to MD or in a *mandi* would be based on better information. The quality control of MD was also reported to be of a higher grade and stringent, which leaves a sizable portion of the produce to be marketed through the *mandi*. Some of the farmers also informed that the price told at the time of procurement was higher than the actual prices finally realized. There was also a general observation that MD's procurement was related to the prevailing prices, declining during the periods when prices were depressed and that accentuated the risk of the farmers.

Model: Reliance Fresh

Reliance Fresh (RF) operates through a procurement centre at each selected village. There is no formal written contract between the farmers and RF, and farmers are free to sell to MD or any other channel. However, the RF centre is more sophisticated and uses better technology including a computer to consolidate procurement information. The manpower at RF is better trained and qualified unlike MD, where the secretary may not have any technical qualification. The procurement terms and conditions of RF are simple, and they give the price information and accept or reject the quality and quantity on the spot. Both, MD and RF procure only best quality products from the farmers, and the rest is left with the farmers to be sold by them. There is no farmers association like in the case of MD. The mode of payment in RF is both cash and cheque. In the context of the procurement contracts of MD and RF, it seems that the contract of the latter (RF) is relatively better than the former (MD) in terms of price information, quality monitoring, mode of payments, etc. Despite the complexity of the contract of MD, it provides a relatively better deal to the farmer as compared to the traditional marketing channels.

Variation of prices

The standard deviation (SD) and Coefficient of Variation (CV) are used as measure of price variations (Table 14.2). The net revenue [2] of the farmers in MD is observed to be more volatile for all the vegetables except bhindi (lady's finger) and tomato, whereas the CV is

Table 14.2 Variability of prices

Vegetables	TM		MD	
	SD	CV (%)	SD	CV (%)
Carrot	114	62	143	63
Lauki	24	111	44	120
Green Chilli	18	76	35	104
Onion	197	50	375	62
Bhindi	38	129	53	125
Tomato	76	0.86	80	0.71
Musk Melon	43	0.67	90	0.81
Cauliflower	47	94	51	146

Source: Author's calculations from data compiled from records of marketing committee and farmers' association
*SD is standard deviation, CV is coefficient of variation.

estimated to be less in MD than in the traditional market (TM). This is quite opposite to the notion that organized retail chains will reduce the volatility of prices for the farmers and consequently stabilize the returns (Table 14.4); however, the net revenue may still be higher in MD because of mean differences between two channels. The instability reflected in linear measures such as SD and CV can be partly because of the non-linear upward rise in MD prices which may not necessarily be harmful for creating instability as reflected in SD and CV. Moreover, instability of the returns measured by SD and CV, counts deviation in the prices from either side of the mean by assigning equal weights, while price deviation above the mean would be beneficial for the farmer compared to a downward fluctuation from mean.

Impact on revenue: theoretical relation between elasticity of demand and total revenue

There are some studies on the relation between demand elasticity and revenue, such as Fisher (1981), Gardner (1975), Helmberger, Peter G. and Jean-Paul Chaves (1996) etc., including the standard micro-economics text books. This relation is based on assumptions such as homogeneous goods, large numbers of small sellers and buyers and the objective of a seller or firm is maximization of profit. With an auctioning system to determine the prices in the market through competitive bidding, the market equilibrium is determined by equality of demand and supply, and prices are determined at the level of market clearance. The demand curve is assumed to be negatively sloped and the supply fixed in a day. In the dynamic equilibrium, if there are changes in the demand and supply in the market, this would impact on the farmer through respective changes in the total revenue. The relation between demand elasticity and revenue for a profit-maximizing farmer can be defined as in equation (1), where change in total revenue would be either because of change in the price or due to change in the quantity or both.

$$dR = q(1+\eta d)dp + p(1+\frac{1}{\eta d})dq \tag{1}$$

Where

p = is net price (excluding marketing cost) received by the farmer
q = quantity sold in the market by the farmer
R = revenue of a farmer
ηd = Elasticity of demand

Table 14.3 The hypothetical values of changes in revenue due to changes in price or quantity at a given elasticity of demand

Elasticity of demand	100% increase in price	100% increase in quantity
0.5	66	33
1	50	50
2	33	66

Source: Author's calculations from data compiled from records of marketing committee and farmers' association

Table 14.3 is derived based on equation (1), which explains the relationship between the changes in the revenue of the farmer with respect to the changes in price and quantity. The changes in total revenue consequent upon the changes in price and quantity are in opposite direction for a given elasticity of demand. The higher the elasticity of demand, the lower would be the increase in the revenue with an increase in the price. There is, therefore, a negative relation between price changes and revenue changes at high elasticity of demand and vice versa. At high elasticity of demand, a decline in price is more effective to increase revenue, and at low elasticity of demand, price increase would be a good strategy to increase total revenue. For the quantity changes, there is a positive relation between increase in revenue and the elasticity of demand. The increase in quantity in the market at high elasticity of demand would also increase the revenue of the farmer, while at lower elasticity of demand, any increase in quantity would also decrease the revenue of the farmer. This explains the paradox of agriculture where good crop season may not be remunerative for the farmer because of low elasticity of demand of the products. In the event of a bumper crop, the increase in the revenue would be less not only due to the depression in the prices but also due to the low elasticity of demand in the market.

The revenue impact on the farmer generally gets aggravated in the case of vegetables because of the nature of the commodity and its yield pattern. Vegetables being perishable in nature require storage facilities to reduce the extent of a fall in price. The season also plays an important role in the yield pattern of vegetables. Besides, the small size of the market and disintegration in the local market lead to overreaction of the supply changes on the revenue would be through price depression. Given this inverse relation between quantity increase and the low increase in revenue at low elasticity of demand, there are moral hazards for the producers. There is no incentive for the farmers to increase production when the market demand curve is inelastic, because increase in the quantity will add less to their revenue. This is all the more true in vegetables where the demand is very inelastic. The low elasticity of demand in the local market is the general phenomenon in India. This may be due to the small size of the markets, low integration with other markets or phenomenon of isolated markets.

Empirical estimation of revenue effect

The net prices of MD are estimated in the following way. P_{ij} is price of ith vegetable for j^{th} marketing channel and Q_{ij} is unit of quantity supplied of ith vegetable to j^{th} marketing channel. MC_{ij} is per unit marketing cost of the ith vegetable for j^{th} marketing channel and R_{ij} is the rate of rejection for i^{th} vegetable under j^{th} marketing channel.

$$NP_{ij} = P_{ij} * (Q_{ij}, R_{ij}) - MC_{ij}$$

i = vegetable, j = marketing channel

The rejection rate is calculated from the farmer/grower's sheets, and the marketing cost is calculated from the primary data of field survey. Applying rejection rate, R_{ij}, to the quantity supplied we can get the actual quantity for which the price, P_{ij}, is received by the farmer. Table 14.4 shows that if a farmer sells a quantity of vegetables to either of the marketing channels how much will be the average net revenue. For example, in November 2005, if a farmer could have sold a quintal of carrot to TM, he would have got on an average Rs. 192 as net revenue as compared to Rs. 221 in MD, which is 16 per cent more compared to TM. The net revenue of the farmers for selected vegetables is found,

Table 14.4 Average net revenue of the TM and MD channel (Rs. per qtl)

Vegetables	Year	Month	Average net revenue MD (Rs.)	Average net revenue TM Price (Rs.)	MD Premium (%)
Carrot	2005	Nov	221.2	192.4	16.4
		Dec	312.0	263.4	15.3
	2006	Nov	251.3	161.7	54.1
		Dec	135.5	113.2	10.6
	2007	Jan	77.9	85.8	−10.7

Vegetables	Year	Month	Average net revenue MD (Rs.)	Average net revenue TM Price (Rs.)	MD Premium (%)
Lauki	2005	Jun	15.8	6.5	189.4
		Jul	87.4	43.8	179.0
		Aug	19.4	6.2	223.0
		Sep	28.3	26.7	47.1
		Oct	13.5	11.1	33.8
Green Chilli	2005	May	8.0	7.7	14.5
		Jun	22.4	17.6	17.3
		Jul	65.5	42.9	43.9
		Aug	29.3	31.7	−7.6
Onion	2005	Jun	581.7	372.7	50.7
		Aug	611.3	390.0	70.0
	2006	Jun	510.7	435.6	16.1
Bhindi	2005	May	65.2	47.1	46.4
		Jun	45.0	29.1	75.1
		Jul	22.9	16.1	42.5
		Aug	23.9	19.1	21.7
		Sept	55.4	33.7	66.8
		Oct	26.9	22.8	14.1
	2006	May	26.1	19.8	33.1
		Jun	20.1	10.4	103.4
Tomato	2005	May	7.8	24.7	7.8
Musk Melon	2005	May	83.8	41.3	104.4
		Jun	114.4	72.1	59.6
		Jul	51.6	40.2	7.1
Cauliflower	2005	Nov	16.3	34.6	−51.7
		Dec	53.4	47.7	−5.3
	2006	Jan	42.8	88.6	−47.2

Difference between Prices

Source: Author's calculations from data compiled from records of marketing committee and farmers' association

on an average, to be 134 per cent for lauki, 17 per cent for green chilli, 45 per cent for onion, 50 per cent for bhindi and 57 per cent for musk melon. Out of the three years for which data is available, except 2007, in the other two years, that is 2005 and 2006, MD had been a more remunerative channel for carrot as compared to TM, which is also true for all other crops except a few.

A regression equation is used to check whether the difference between MD and TM prices is significant or not. First the difference between the prices $D_{in} = P_{i1} - P_{i2}$ of alternative marketing channels is calculated and then to test the significance of the difference between prices the following equation is specified:

$$D_{in} = a_{in} + b_{in}t + u_{in}$$

n = number of observations.

Hypothesis tested are

H: $a_{in} = 0$

Ha: $a_{in} \neq 0$

The intercept term (a_{ij}) in the function will give the difference in net marketing prices. If the prices are significantly different then the intercept would be significant. The results given in Table 14.5 show that

Table 14.5 Results on the difference of prices

Vegetables	a_{in}	$b_{in}t$
Carrot	93.7*	0.09
Lauki	270*	−2.7*
Chilli	111*	−0.15
Onion	131*	−0.47
Bhindi	222*	−0.01
Tomato	86*	1.77*
Musk Melon	198*	0.26
Cauliflower	−83*	4.02*

Source: Author's calculations from data compiled from records of marketing committee and farmers' association

MD prices are significantly higher than the TM prices for the vegetables except cauliflower.

Supply chain efficiency and inefficiency impacts the whole agriculture system. Traditional marketing chains are characterized by the high margins of the middlemen, low prices to the farmer, low elasticity of derived demand, huge wastage of agricultural produce, etc. The new marketing arrangements such as farmers market, for example Apani Mandi, contract farming and emergence of direct procurement by organized retail chains are hopes for the emergence of efficient agriculture markets. However, there could be problems of exclusion of small farmers, a short-term view being taken by the contracting company. Institutional reforms need to reduce the multiple layers of intermediation. Direct procurement is still geographically restricted to the hot spots of the vegetable producing regions, and not for all, and its impact on farmers depends on the terms and conditions of the procurement contract. The procurement system adopted by the two agencies, MD and RF, suggests that the approach adopted by RF is more informative in terms of price information, quality monitoring, mode of payments, etc.

This simplicity of the contract of RF could be considered to provide an edge to it, but multiple agencies and a variety of contracting arrangements could co-exist. Despite the complexity of the contract, MD still provides a relatively better deal to the farmer as compared to the traditional marketing chains. This may be the reason that it has been sustained for such a long time in many areas. On the practical side of the impact of MD, it is observed that the net revenue of the farmers for selected vegetables is found, on an average, to be 16 per cent higher for carrot, 134 per cent for lauki, 17 per cent for green chilli, 45 per cent for onion, 50 per cent for bhindi and 57 per cent for musk melon.

Appendix

Note on revenue and elasticity relation

Suppose

    p = is net price (excluding marketing cost) of a channel
    q = quantity sold in the market by the farmer
    R = revenue of a farmer
    So, a profit maximizing farmer will calculate its R as

$$R = p.\,q$$

Taking first derivative of R w.r.t. p

$$R'(p) = q + p\frac{dq}{dp} \quad \text{or} \tag{1}$$

$$q.\eta d + q = 0$$

where ηd = elasticity of demand

$$R''(p) = f''\left\{p\frac{dq}{dp}\right\} < 0 \tag{2}$$

Taking the first derivative of R w.r.t. q

$$R'(q) = p + q\frac{dp}{dq} \tag{3}$$

$$p.\frac{1}{\eta d} + p = 0$$

$$R''(p) = f''\left\{q\frac{dp}{dq}\right\} < 0$$

In the situation of profit maximizing the change in total revenue of the farmer would be either contributed by change in the price or by change in the quantity or both. Therefore the total change in the revenue of the farmer is:

$$dR = R'(p).dp + R'(q)dq \tag{4}$$

$$dR = q(1 + \eta d)\,dp + p(1 + \frac{1}{\eta d})dq \tag{6}$$

Notes

1 FAO, 'Conceptual issues of Market Structure in Agriculture Commodity Value Chains'.
2 Revenue is defined as 'net price' multiplied by 'quantity supplied' by the farmer, where the net price excludes marketing costs such as transportation, loading and unloading, etc.

References

Birthal, P. S., Joshi, P. K., and Gulati, A. 2005. 'Vertical Coordination in High Value Food Commodities: Implications for smallholders', IFPRI, Discussion Paper, No. 85.

Brester, W. and Goodwin, B. 1993. 'Vertical and Horizontal Price Linkages and Market Concentration in the US Wheat Milling industry', *Review of Agriculture Economics*, 15, 507–20.

Chengappa and Nagaraj. 2005. 'Marketing of Major Fruits and Vegetables in and around Bangalore', Report, Department of Agricultural Economics, University of Agricultural Sciences Bangalore.

Fisher, B. S. 1981. 'The Impact of Changing Marketing Margins on Farm Prices', *American Journal of Agricultural Economics*, 63(2): 261–3.

Gardner, Bruce L. 1975. 'The Farm-Retail Price Spread in a Competitive Food Industry', *American Journal of Agricultural Economics*, 57(3): 399–409.

Government of India. 2007. 'The India Retail Report', Ministry of Commerce and Industry.

Helmberger, Peter G. and Chaves, Jean-Paul. 1996. *The Economics of Agricultural Prices*. Prentice Hall Publisher: USA.

ICREAR. 2009. 'Impact of Organized Retail Chains on Income and Employment', ICREAR Mimeo, New Delhi.

Kerisur, V. R., Hiremath, K. C., and Kiresur, S. 1989. 'Economics of Production and Marketing of Vegetables in Karnataka a Comparison of Organized and Unorganized Sector of Marketing', *Indian Journal of Agriculture Marketing*, 3(3): 98, Conference Special.

Key, N. and Runsten, D. 1999. 'Contract Farming, Smallholders, and Rural Development in Latin America: The Organization of Agroprocessing Firms and the Scale of Outgrower Production', *World Development*, 27(2): 381–401.

Korovkin. 1992. 'Peasants, Grapes and Corporations: The Growth of Contract Farming in a Chilean Community', *Journal of Peasant Studies*, 19(2): 228–254.

Kumar, Parmod. (2006). 'Contract Farming Through Agribusiness Firms and State Corporation: A Case Study in Punjab', *Economic and Political Weekly*, December, 30: 5367–75.

NABARD. 2011. 'Organized Agri-Food Retailing in India', National Bank for Agriculture and Rural Development, Government of India.

Pingali, P. L. and Rosegrant, M. W. 1995. 'Agriculture Commercialization and Diversification: Processes and Policies', *Food Policy*, 20(3): 171–85.

Porter, G. and Howard, K. P. 1997. 'Comparing Contracts: An Evaluation of Contract Farming Schemes in Africa', *World Development*, 25(2): 227–38.

Rao, P. P., Birthal, P. S., and Joshi, P. K. 2006. 'Diversification Towards High Value Agriculture: Role of Urbanization and Infrastructure', *Economic and Political Weekly*, 41(26): 2747–53.

Richard T. Rogers, Marsh, J. M., and Atwood, J. A. 2009. 'Evaluating the Framer's Share of the Retail-Dollar Statistics', *Journal of Agriculture and Resource Economics*, 34(2).

Rogers, Richard T. and Sexton, Richard J. 1994. 'Assessing the Importance of Oligopsony Power in Agriculture Markets', *American Journal of Agriculture Economics*, 76: 1143–50.

Suzuki, A., and Sexton, Richard J. 2005. 'Transaction Cost and Market Power of Middleman: A Spatial Analysis of Agricultural Commodity Markets in Developing Countries', presented at American Agricultural Economics Association Annual Meeting.

Thakur, D. S., Sanjay, D. R. Thakur and Sharma, K. D. 1994. 'Economics of Off-Season Vegetable Production and Marketing in Hills', *Indian Journal of Agricultural Marketing*, January, 8(1): 77–8.

Index